'Toronto' in Perspective

Papers on the New Charismatic Wave of the mid-1990s

Edited by David Hilborn

Sponsored by ACUTE (the Evangelical Alliance
Commission on Unity and Truth among Evangelicals)

acute

First Published in 2001 by Acute

07   06   05   04   03   02   01   7   6   5   4   3   2   1

Acute is an imprint of Paternoster Publishing,
PO Box 300, Carlisle, Cumbria, CA3 0QS, UK
And PO Box 1047, Waynesboro, GA 30830-2047, USA
www.paternoster-publishing.com

The right of David Hilborn to be
identified as the Author of this Work has been
asserted by him in accordance with
Copyright, Designs and Patents Act 1988

British Library Cataloguing in Publication Data

A catalogue record for this book is available from
the British Library

ISBN 1-84227-099-0

Cover design by Campsie
Printed in Great Britain by
Bell and Bain, Glasgow

'Toronto' in Perspective

Contents

Part III: Key Statements on the Toronto Blessing

Acknowledgements

Thanks are due to the six contributors whose papers form Part I of this volume, and to Joel Edwards for his Foreword. I should also like to thank my ever-efficient PA, Carolyn Skinner, for her administrative help. Mark Finnie, Peter Little, Jill Morris and the staff at Paternoster Press have shown their characteristically high level of support, encouragement and care. Finally, I should like to thank my wife, Mia, for her staunch support over the course of this project, and my children, Matthew and Alice, for their patience when I was in the study rather than with them.

David Hilborn
West London, Epiphany 2001

About the Authors

David Hilborn (Editor) is Theological Adviser to the Evangelical Alliance UK and Co-ordinator of the Alliance Commission on Unity and Truth among Evangelicals (ACUTE). He edited the ACUTE reports *Faith, Hope and Homosexuality* (1998) and *The Nature of Hell* (2000), and authored *Picking Up the Pieces: Can Evangelicals Adapt to Contemporary Culture?* (1997). Since gaining a doctorate on the subject of religious language and communication in 1994, he has also published several papers in this field. He is a graduate of Nottingham and Oxford Universities, an Associate Research Fellow of the London Bible College and an ordained minister of the United Reformed Church. He is married with two children.

Martin Davie is Theological Adviser to the Church of England's House of Bishops. Previously he was Tutor in Doctrine at Oak Hill College and Librarian of Latimer House, Oxford. A graduate of Mansfield College, Oxford, his publications include *British Quaker Theology Since 1895* (Lewiston Lampeter Mellen, 1997). He is married with one child.

Stephen Sizer is the Vicar of Christ Church, Virginia Water. Prior to ordination he worked as an evangelist with Agape, among university students. For many years he has travelled extensively to Russia, Eastern Europe and the Middle East to assist with Bible teaching conferences, pilgrimages, evangelistic initiatives and ecumenical projects. He is a trustee of the International Bible Society (UK), a director and trustee of Highway Journeys and a trustee of Amos Trust. He is also a member of Reform. In 1997 he gained a doctorate in the ethical management of pilgrimages to the Holy Land from International Management Centres. He is now undertaking further doctoral studies into Christian Zionism through

Oak Hill Theological College and Middlesex University. His first book, *Panorama of the Holy Land*, was published by Eagle in November 1998. The sequel, *Panorama of the Bible Lands*, was published in 2000. He is married with four children.

Mark Cartledge is Chaplain and Tutor to St. John's College in the University of Durham. An ordained Anglican priest, he has worked previously in the dioceses of Liverpool and Akure, Nigeria (Church Mission Society). He has recently completed a doctorate on the phenomenon of glossolalia, published as *Charismatic Glossolalia: An Empirical-Theological Study*, Ashgate 2001. He is involved in the editorial group of the new Grove *Renewal* booklet series and is a Co-convenor of the Anglican Charismatic Theological Seminar (ACTS). He is married with one child.

David Pawson has an itinerant ministry, mainly to church leaders, in the UK and overseas. A graduate of Cambridge University, he served for twelve years as a Methodist minister, working as an evangelist in British coalfields and as a chaplain in the RAF. He then served two Baptist pastorates, including the Millmead Centre in Guildford, Surrey. He has written several books, including *When Jesus Returns, The Road to Hell, Word and Spirit Together* and *Is the Blessing Biblical?* (Hodder) – a study of the Toronto phenomenon which was published in 1995. He is married with three children (one now in heaven), and five grandchildren.

Patrick Dixon is a medical doctor who has written and broadcast extensively on healthcare and social ethics. His publications include *The Truth about AIDS, The Genetic Revolution, The Rising Price of Love* and *The Truth about Westminster* (all Kingsway). A member of the Pioneer People church network, he leads a congregation in South West London. In 1994, he published one of the first in-depth analyses of the Toronto Blessing, *Signs of Revival*. He is married with four children.

Margaret Poloma taught Sociology of Religion for 25 years at the University of Akron in Ohio, USA, prior to her retirement in 1995. She is the author of some eight books and 75 articles and serves on the boards of five professional journals. A specialist in

Pentecostal and charismatic Christianity, she has published a number of studies on the Toronto Blessing, including *The Toronto Report* (Terra Nova, 1996) and 'The 'Toronto Blessing' in Postmodern Society', in Murray Dempster et al, *The Globalization of Pentecostalism* (Regnum, 1999).

About ACUTE

ACUTE is the Evangelical Alliance Commission on Unity and Truth among Evangelicals. It was established by the Alliance in 1994, at the time of the Toronto Blessing, to work for consensus on issues that test evangelical unity, and to provide, on behalf of evangelicals, a co-ordinated response to matters of wider public debate. As well as Evangelical Alliance members, ACUTE's Steering Group includes representatives of the British Evangelical Council and the Evangelical Movement of Wales.

ACUTE is committed to an ongoing programme of research and publication on theological issues that are of concern to evangelicals. As well as this collection of essays and papers, it has published two formal reports with Paternoster Press: *Faith, Hope and Homosexuality* (1998) and *The Nature of Hell* (2000). It has also produced a discussion paper: *What Is an Evangelical?* Forthcoming books will focus on the prosperity gospel, Evangelical-Eastern Orthodox relationships, generational issues, and the history of the Alliance.

For further details, information and queries, contact ACUTE, Evangelical Alliance, 186 Kennington Park Road, London SE11 4BT. E-mail: acute@eauk.org. Tel: 020 7207 2114. Fax: 020 7207 2150. Web: www.eauk.org

Foreword

Between mid-1994 and early 1996, the phrase 'Toronto Blessing' was never far from my ears, eyes and mind. At that time, I was UK Director of the Evangelical Alliance, and had special responsibility for dealing with one of the most potentially divisive issues faced by British evangelicalism since the Second World War. I drafted the first Alliance statement on the new movement in June 1994, and shortly afterwards co-hosted a London Leaders' meeting at which many key church figures experienced 'Toronto' for the time. Subsequently, I worked with my colleagues and, in particular, with the then-Co-ordinator of ACUTE, Dave Cave, on three Alliance-organised consultations. These consultations helped to foster debate and, as it turned out, to maintain a degree of unity and mutual respect which might not otherwise have prevailed. All the while, my in-tray was filled with letters on 'Toronto' – some passionately in favour, some deeply opposed, and many others somewhere in between.

After two decades or so of growth and relative success, it was perhaps inevitable that evangelicals would sooner or later face stern tests of their relationships, identity and theology. As it happened, the Toronto Blessing provided all three. Looking back seven years on from the dawn of the movement, it seems to me that at the time, the Alliance handled the relationship and identity issues relatively well. On theology, however, there was always room for more detailed work. Those who attended the consultations certainly shared in helpful theological discourse, but the form of that discourse did not readily lend itself to book publication. Various Alliance team members, myself included, wrote on Toronto for the Christian press and spoke about it from public platforms. But we were aware that a fuller, more reflective study of the issue would also be helpful. I am therefore delighted that Dave Cave's successor, David Hilborn, has now edited such a study. It must be admitted that it has taken longer to produce than we originally envisaged. Then again, as David points out in his Introduction, theology cannot be confined to a journalistic time scale. It was important to examine the immediate effect of the Toronto Blessing and its longer-term implications. I believe that this book fulfils this task admirably.

There are important lessons here, many of which have only become apparent with hindsight. David's essay spells these lessons out clearly in relation to evangelicalism and the Alliance, but all the other contributors to this volume have shed valuable light on the events of 1994-96, and on their longer-term implications. If their papers at times diverge in opinion or focus, the book also offers more objective content in the extensively researched Chronicle, which makes up Part II, and in the collection of key statements on the Blessing assembled in Part III. Both serve as valuable resources – resources that are richer and more definitive for having been compiled now, rather than in the 'heat of the moment'.

All in all, I am glad to be able to commend this book within and beyond the Alliance's constituency. It deserves to become a standard text on an extraordinary period of recent church history – one with which I was closely involved at the time, but which I now understand much better, having read what follows in these pages.

Joel Edwards, General Director of the Evangelical Alliance (UK)
Kennington, January 2001

PART I

ESSAYS ON THE TORONTO BLESSING

1

Introduction

Evangelicalism, the Evangelical Alliance and the Toronto Blessing

David Hilborn

The Toronto Blessing Then and Now

The movement that became known as 'The Toronto Blessing' (TTB) represented a crisis for modern-day evangelicalism. I believe that this book bears out such an assessment, and shall here seek to explain why. I shall also seek to explain why the Blessing more particularly represented a crisis for the Evangelical Alliance, and why its theological commission, ACUTE, has now sponsored this volume of papers on that crisis.

I should stress from the outset that I am using the word 'crisis' in a particular way. It is a preacher's staple that despite the largely negative connotations it now carries, the term actually 'means' both judgement and opportunity. This double sense attached to the Greek noun from which our English word is formed – particularly in its Septuagint and New Testament usage.[1] So, the logic goes, times of what we call 'crisis' can in fact teach salutary lessons, suggest fresh possibilities, and be turned to constructive ends. In a general sense, this is the understanding of 'crisis' that I would apply to the Blessing. More specifically, of course, one should beware here of what John Lyons calls the 'etymological fallacy'[2]. Language changes over time, and the 'original meaning' of a root word from an ancient tongue may be far from reliable as a clue to the meaning of its derivative. On these grounds, our current, almost wholly pejorative notion of 'crisis' is no less 'real' or 'actual' than its apparently more paradoxical Greek denotation. As long as we bear such provisos in mind, however, the older reference can still shed important light on issues faced by the church today. And no doubt, TTB was a significant issue. As we shall see, it was significant not merely, nor even so much, for what it was *in and of itself*, but for what it revealed about the state of evangelical and charismatic Christianity at the turn of the millennium.

The background, genesis and development of TTB are detailed exhaustively in Part II of this book. For now it is worth noting that the phrase 'Toronto Blessing' first appeared in the public domain courtesy of the London *Times* journalist Ruth Gledhill. In an article printed on Saturday 18 June 1994, Gledhill reported that it was becoming popular as a nickname for a 'religious craze' of 'mass fainting' that had 'crossed the Atlantic to cause concern in the Church of England'.[3] As it was, the 'craze' to which Gledhill alluded had several antecedents, involved rather more than 'mass fainting', and prompted debate and discussion well beyond the Church of England.

Gledhill's geographical reference was to the Toronto Airport Vineyard (TAV) – a church led by John and Carol Arnott, and overseen by the influential evangelist and teacher John Wimber. Wimber's Association of Vineyard Churches (AVC) had grown remarkably through the 1980s to become a major force within North American evangelicalism. TAV had started as an independent congregation, but contact with Wimber in the late 1980s led the Arnotts to place it within the Vineyard network. During the same period a number of Vineyard churches were planted overseas, and Wimber made a significant impact on historic denominations beyond the USA and Canada – not least among Anglicans and Baptists in Great Britain.[4]

Peter Wagner, Wimber's friend and former Fuller Seminary colleague, described the distinctive approach of Wimber and the Vineyard as 'Third Wave' renewal. According to Wagner, it represented a development from the 'first wave' of classical Pentecostalism, which had emerged at the beginning of the twentieth-century through Charles Fox Parham's Topeka Bible College and the Azusa Street revival of 1906-9, and from the 'second wave' of charismatic renewal, which had assimilated Pentecostal emphases into the mainline churches while upholding the distinctive traditions and disciplines of those churches (hence its alternative designation as 'neo-Pentecostalism'). 'Third Wave' renewal borrows extensively from these two movements but, as Wagner defines it, differs from one or both of them on certain key points. In contrast to classical Pentecostalism, it disavows the notion that the baptism of the Holy Spirit is a second work of grace subsequent to conversion. Rather, it expects multiple fillings of the Holy Spirit consequent upon new birth, some of which may be akin to what others would call 'baptism in the Spirit'. Also in distinction from Classical Pentecostalism, 'Third Wave' understanding views the gift of speaking in tongues (1 Cor. 14:2-40) not as 'initial evidence' of Spirit baptism, but as one of many gifts given by God to the church, which may be granted to some and not to others. In comparison with both First and Second Wave renewal, the model of ministry developed by Wimber and the Vineyard places particular emphasis on the *power* and *demonstration* of the Holy Spirit's work in 'signs and wonders' such as healing and deliverance. In addition, it is more overtly committed to 'body ministry' – that is, to a corporate expression of spiritual gifts and a team ethos in leadership, as distinct from either the 'anointed man'/'faith healer' focus of much classical Pentecostalism, or the clergy-driven ecclesiology of many historic denominations.[5]

As well as these defining features, Vineyard-style meetings through the 1980s exhibited other marked elements. From at least 1986, significant instances of 'holy laughter' were recorded, along with already-established phenomena like slumping or falling to the floor, trembling and weeping.[6]

Despite the growth and rising profile of the Third Wave/Vineyard movement, by the early 1990s a number of its pastors and leaders appear to have been seeking fresh impetus and 'anointing'. John Arnott had periodically pursued new sources of blessing and inspiration through his life and career, having previously drawn much from the healing evangelist Kathryn Kuhlman and the Israeli-born preacher Benny Hinn.[7] In late 1993, he and various colleagues visited key figures in the 'Argentinian Revival'

– a significant wave of evangelical church growth centred on Buenos Aires.[8] While they were looking towards South America, another Vineyard leader, Randy Clark of the St Louis Vineyard in Missouri, was undergoing a radical personal transformation under the ministry of Rodney Howard-Browne.

Rodney Howard-Browne had come to the USA from his native South Africa in 1987, convinced that God was about to visit a 'mighty revival' on the nation. A child of devoutly Pentecostal parents, he testified to having been converted at the age of five, and to having been filled with the Holy Spirit at eight.[9] After an unremarkable beginning, Howard-Browne's American ministry gained considerable momentum in 1989, when laughter and 'slaying' or falling down in the Spirit became more prominent in his evangelistic meetings.[10] While such things were hardly unknown in Vineyard circles, Randy Clark found them occurring around Howard-Browne at a level of intensity that deeply impressed him. Clark had been virtually burned-out by a demanding pastorate; this condition appears to have prompted him to overlook doubts about Howard-Browne's style and theological background. Very much a classic 'front man' Pentecostal, Howard-Browne had also trained and ministered in the 'Rhema' and 'Word of Faith' constituencies, which were key engines of the so-called 'prosperity gospel' movement. Indeed, it was in Tulsa, Oklahoma – a major Word of Faith centre – that Clark first encountered Howard-Browne in August 1993, and duly ended up on the floor laughing.[11]

Subsequently, as Arnott and other Vineyard leaders returned from Argentina, Clark informed them of what had happened to him, and of the effect it had begun to have on his congregation, some 95% of whom had 'fallen under the power' on his return from Tulsa. At this same meeting, Arnott invited Clark to visit TAV in the New Year.[12] Clark accepted, and on Thursday 20 January 1994 he led a 'family night' at the airport church. As he called people forward for prayer, large numbers manifested a range of dramatic physical phenomena, from falling and then 'resting' in the Spirit, to laughing, shaking, prostration and healing. Such was the impact of this meeting that Clark extended his time in Toronto through until mid-March, leading meetings on a regular basis. By the time of his return to St Louis, word had spread, visitors to TAV were increasing, and some had begun to fly in from overseas to investigate.[13]

Back in St Louis, during April and May Rodney Howard-Browne led a series of equally spectacular meetings, some of which were attended by Terry Virgo, leader of the British-based charismatic network New Frontiers International. Along with other Britons who had attended TAV during this period, Virgo reported what had been happening to his colleagues in the UK, and various outbreaks of 'Toronto-style' manifestations began to occur here.[14] Queen's Road Baptist Church and the Ichthus Fellowship in South London had already started to experience such manifestations when Eleanor Mumford, of the Vineyard's own Putney congregation, met with leaders of the high-profile Anglican charismatic church Holy Trinity, Brompton, on Tuesday 24 May[15]. After reporting a recent visit to TAV, Mumford saw key members of 'HTB's' leadership team rendered virtually immobile as they, too, fell, shook, rested and laughed.[16] The next Sunday, she preached at HTB with similar effect,[17] and news that hundreds of largely upper middle-class Knightsbridge churchgoers were rolling around as if 'drunk' and 'helpless' at services soon caught the attention of the press; hence the interest of *The Times*, and Ruth Gledhill's coinage of the term 'Toronto Blessing'.

Within weeks, the 'Blessing' had spread to hundreds of churches across the British Isles, and by the end of 1994, estimates were suggesting that between 2000 and 4000 congregations had embraced it.[18] It became one of the biggest stories covered by the British Christian media in recent times, and remained so through 1995 and into early 1996. It also appeared frequently as a subject of debate and discussion in the secular press – not only in the religious pages, but in the news sections, too. The Evangelical Alliance press archive on the Blessing, on which my Chronicle in Part II of this book is partly based, is six inches thick. Between late 1994 and 1998 the Blessing prompted the publication of at least 30 books in the UK, not to mention a slew of papers, conferences, tapes, videos, web sites, radio features and TV programmes.[19] The Methodist Conference, the Church of Scotland, the House of Bishops of the Church of England, the Presbyterian Church in Ireland, and numerous smaller bodies in Britain and elsewhere all commissioned major studies of TTB (see Part III). I have read, heard and viewed most of this material, and at certain points it has been overwhelming. As will become clear, TTB engaged the time, attention and pastoral capacity of the Evangelical Alliance more than any unprogrammed issue since Martyn Lloyd-Jones and John Stott famously clashed over evangelical church allegiance in 1966.[20]

This remarkable level of comment and interest came about not least because the Blessing was so controversial. While 'first wave' Pentecostalism had seemed striking and disturbing to many in the mainline churches and media, until the 1960s they were able to treat it largely as an exotic, sectarian religion with its own dedicated networks and institutions.[21] The 'second wave' of the charismatic/neo-Pentecostal renewal brought things more centre-stage, and certainly led to higher-profile tensions and splits. But it was gradually absorbed and, in some cases, actively welcomed into the mainstream as a positive force for growth, partly because so many of its leaders remained loyal, their existing denominations, liturgies and spiritual traditions, and partly because no one episode or incident served to concentrate those tensions sufficiently to threaten really cataclysmic division.[22] By contrast, TTB seemed to many – including some established charismatics, as well as liberals, traditionalists and conservatives – to represent a dangerously potent and fast-breeding strain of fanaticism that could seriously destabilise the church. Even those who rejected this view, and who instead championed the Blessing, sometimes did so with a zeal that only provoked further polarisation.

Not surprisingly, arguments about the Blessing were most numerous and most heated among evangelicals. More often than not, crisis is born of contention, and for better or worse, evangelicalism is a naturally contentious movement. Once the Protestant Reformers determined to promote the authority of 'Scripture alone' over the magisterium of the church, the resultant prerogative of interpretation led, almost inevitably, to divergence, tension and fissure. However much they hold the Bible itself to be supremely trustworthy, those who expound it are fallible, and are thus liable at some point to disagree. Inasmuch as evangelicalism is rooted in the Protestant tradition, it can be seen to have reflected this tendency to an especially marked degree. Of the 25,000 or so Christian denominations in the world today, evangelicals have contributed proportionally more to the division that figure represents than any other Christian group. Indeed, uncomfortable though it is to accept, Kenneth Hylson-Smith's analysis does seem to have history on its side:

> The whole ethos of Protestantism – its theological basis, the behavioural patterns it inculcates, its attitudinal emphasis and its authority structure – make it inherently liable to schism and fragmentation. It has a built-in tendency to be centrifugal rather than centripetal ... By its very nature it encourages individuality, stresses personal faith and promotes distinctive individual or group expressions of faith and practice. Such characteristics ensure a large measure of personal and corporate creativity; but they almost guarantee divisiveness ... And what is true of Protestantism as a whole is especially so for those archetypal Protestants, the evangelicals.[23]

Over the years, the majority of Pentecostals and charismatics had readily identified with evangelicalism's typically high view of Christ and Scripture, its commitment to conversion, its activism and its objective view of atonement. Not every evangelical – and especially not those in more classically Reformed circles – had been happy to confirm this identity, and a good deal of familiarly heated evangelical debate arose as a result. Even so, in all but the most separatist and fundamentalist quarters, a degree of tolerance and mutual co-operation developed in the British context during the 1970s and 1980s. This was particularly evident in the diverse and growing membership of the Evangelical Alliance, the common organisation of Billy Graham missions, and the resurgence of that broad-based evangelical social concern which was both epitomised and boosted by the 1974 Lausanne Covenant.[24] With the rise of Toronto, however, old fault-lines were once again exposed, and concerns, which had either been sublimated or suppressed for the greater cause of unity, were reiterated. Many of those who welcomed the emergence of 'Toronto' (mostly charismatic evangelicals) were confirmed in their view that those who opposed it (mostly non-charismatic conservative evangelicals) had an insufficiently dynamic understanding of the Holy Spirit. Similarly, opponents tended to present the Blessing as evidence of a long-held conviction that despite its protestations to the contrary, the charismatic movement in fact relied too much on experience, and not enough on Scripture.

If it initially recalled familiar conservative-charismatic divides, however, the disputatious potential of the Blessing was most tellingly realised by a cleavage within the very ground from which it had sprung. To widespread surprise, in December 1995 John Wimber's Association of Vineyard Churches formally expelled TAV from its membership. While Wimber's own ministry had long featured most of the eye-catching manifestations associated with the Blessing, the AVC Board judged that the Toronto church's focus on them had become excessive in comparison with established Vineyard priorities of evangelism, teaching and discipleship.[25] Although personal hurts were later addressed, and although the Toronto church continues to this day as an independent proponent of the Blessing, this very public and somewhat messy divorce effectively put paid to it as a major international movement. If the Blessing has continued as a force within global renewal at all, it has done so inasmuch as it has transmuted into other initiatives – not least Holy Trinity Brompton's *Alpha* Course, which appears to have gained considerable impetus from the Toronto outpouring.[26]

The fact that TTB per se is no longer headline news should not, however, detract from its ongoing *theological* and *ecclesiological* significance. For at least a year and a half, it posed a genuine threat to evangelical unity, even while presaging, in many evangelicals' eyes, a full-scale, longed-for revival. With hindsight, and given the circumstances of its demise, it might be tempting now to brush the Blessing under the carpet, and to move on. This would, however, be to perpetuate the short-termism and pragmatism which, as Os Guinness and David Wells have pointed out, all too often blight the integrity of the evangelical movement.[27] At its height, the Blessing was, indeed, a crisis, and crises such as this deserve to be assessed on more than a purely journalistic time scale. Crises in the life of the church – whether the crises of true revival or the crises of heresy – are studied by historical and systematic theologians centuries after they have occurred, and can still prompt new and valuable insights. There is no reason why this book, at just seven years' distance from the rise of the Blessing, should not at least aspire to the same purpose.

Taken together, the essays and records collected here more specifically highlight three main areas of crisis that were opened up for evangelicalism by TTB. In doing so, they also suggest key lessons to be learnt. As I perceive them, the three areas are: a crisis of definition, a crisis of discernment, and a crisis of unity. These all in their own way impinged on the particular role and work of the Evangelical Alliance vis-à-vis the Blessing. I shall therefore deal with each in turn while reflecting more specifically on the Alliance's position.

A Crisis of Definition

As we have seen, the phrase 'Toronto Blessing' was first popularised by a London journalist. It does not appear to have been used by TAV in the six months between Randy Clark's historic visit on 20 January 1994 and *The Times'* circulation of it in mid-June. From an early stage, TAV in fact preferred more explicitly biblical descriptions, most notably the phrase 'times of refreshing', which was borrowed from Acts 3:19 and endorsed in a formative 'guideline' paper distributed through the Vineyard network by the Illinois pastor Bill Jackson.[28] In due course, however, 'Toronto' became an affectionate shorthand, especially among British supporters of the movement, and appeared on the cover of several books published in the UK, including Marshall Pickering's edition of TAV pastor Guy Chevreau's early study, *Catch the Fire*.[29] Despite all this, the Airport church and AVC leadership remained uneasy about its use as a definition of what was taking place. Indeed, by February 1996, John Arnott was insisting, 'It isn't the Toronto Blessing; it's the Father's Blessing', and was encouraging people to read a book he had just written under the preferred title.[30]

This tension between ad hoc, media-driven phraseology and more self-consciously scriptural language was indicative of a broader tension. While the ministry model emerging from Toronto was proving phenomenally popular, those most responsible for promulgating it realised that they must demonstrate its theological validity, lest they be accused of mere manipulation, superficial emotionalism and plain hype. Allowing the movement to be associated with its city of origin rather than with a New Testament text might fuel such accusations, since it could suggest something vaguely religious and spiritual, rather than anything specifically Christian or orthodox. As it was, the accusations came anyway, and despite the best efforts of Arnott and others, the 'Toronto Blessing' moniker not only stuck, it flourished. Today, at a distance of years, it looks to have established itself as the standard term by which the movement is known, and by which it will be referenced in textbooks on the late twentieth-century church.

In and of itself, this is not a major issue. Language has a habit of wriggling free from the attempts of those who would seek to control or 'correct' it,[31] and in any event, some of the keenest users of the phrase 'Toronto Blessing' were the firmest advocates of what it stood for (a marked contrast, for instance, with the word 'Protestant', which started out as a term of abuse used mainly by opponents, rather than supporters, of the Reformation).[32] More profoundly, however, the struggle between journalistic and theological discourse was symptomatic of the struggle for a frame of reference that would locate the Blessing in the context of church history, i.e. within a recognisable Christian 'tradition'. As we have hinted, the specific 'tradition' at stake in this case was the characteristically evangelical tradition of 'revival'.

At various points during the rise of the Blessing, its proponents publicly cast it as a 'sign of revival'. Patrick Dixon went so far as to adopt this very phrase as the title of his influential book on the movement.[33] In the early phase of the Blessing, a few journalists defined it as revival *per se*.[34] Those directly involved in it, however, tended to be somewhat more cautious. The 'signs' which Dixon highlighted would, he hoped, point the way to a much fuller in-breaking of God's power, but did not confirm that revival itself had yet arrived. Others wrote in similar terms of the Blessing bearing the 'hallmarks' of revival,[35] and of being a 'preparation' for, or 'initiation' of, revival.[36] Indeed, in a key pronouncement on the Blessing, the 'Euston Statement' of December 1994 (reproduced here in Part III, 18), an Evangelical Alliance-sponsored consultation concluded:

We do not believe that the Church in the United Kingdom is presently experiencing revival. However, many have testified to an increased sense of the manifest presence of God in recent months, and to empowered preaching and conversions. This enrichment has been observed in some measure across the evangelical spectrum. This encourages us to hope that we may be in a period of preparation for revival.

Now 'revival' is a disputed term among church historians and theologians. Most especially, there is considerable debate about its relation to what is often called 'awakening'.[37] Some see the two terms as synonym-ous, while others reserve the former to the revitalisation and expansion of the church, and the latter to wider social transformation. Beyond these nuances, however, most define 'revival' in relation to the archetypal evangelical movements of the 1730s and 1740s led by the Britons John Wesley and George Whitefield, and by the American Jonathan Edwards.[38] It is then typically applied to such resurgences of spiritual life as occurred in Ulster in 1859, South Wales in 1904 and the Outer Hebrides in 1949.[39] As Earle Cairns describes it, revival may be summarised in this respect as 'the work of the Holy Spirit in restoring the people of God to a more vital spiritual life, witness, and work by prayer and the Word after repentance in crisis for their spiritual decline.'[40] While acknowledging that such elements might distinguish relatively small gatherings and movements, Timothy Beougher follows the majority of commentators in relating revival more specifically to outpourings whose effect is felt on significant numbers of people and churches beyond a single congregation, village or town.[41]

Against this background, it is hardly surprising that so many advocates of 'Toronto' were keen to *associate* the movement with revival, even while recognising that it had some way to progress before it could actually bear comparison with the established 'canon' of revivals. On reflection, however, it must be said that this 'anticipatory' use of the term probably did more harm than good.

In a world of rapid communications, instant analysis and 'spin', sincerely-expressed hopes that the Blessing might become full-blown revival sometimes risked appearing to 'talk it up' *into* revival. In this sense, the criticism of Tim Thornborough, Gethin Russell-Jones and Andrew Walker, that it at times came closer to reviva*lism* than true revival, must be taken seriously[42]. As defined by Beougher and Iain Murray, the distinction between revival and

revival*ism* in this sense is the distinction between an unambigu-
ously sovereign work of God and a more questionable application
of what Charles Finney, the nineteenth-century American evangelist, called 'new measures', i.e. 'man made' techniques of persuasion and emotional direction designed to stir up response to the
gospel.[43] The following comments about the Blessing, for instance,
though couched as aspirations rather than *faits accomplis*, would
surely have heightened expectations, as well as simply reflecting
them:

> We are on the edge of what could be the greatest thing to hit our
> nation this century.[44]

> What if, as I believe, we are on the brink of a great revival this cen-
> tury – and God sovereignly chose [Rodney Howard Browne's] min-
> istry as the embryonic phase of it? [45]

> It has to go to revival. [We are] daring to believe that this could be
> the last move of God before revival.[46]

> We praise God for the times of refreshing we have been enjoying,
> but our plea must be that they are no more than a prelude. We long
> to see the glory and power of the living God sweeping across the
> face of the earth as never before. A global revival to prepare the
> world for the return of Christ. Send revival, Lord, and send it in our
> day![47]

By 'raising the stakes' like this, proponents of the Blessing were
always liable to incur greater disappointment if and when the
movement lost momentum. Indeed, Rob Warner, who authored
the last of the above comments, has recently articulated this disappointment in strikingly blunt terms:

> Toronto came in with a bang but, frankly, seems to have ended with
> a whimper. For me, it was a time of deep spiritual enrichment and
> rekindled hope for revival. Yet it was also a time of being turned off
> by the threefold ministries of unreality – exaggeration, manipulation
> and hysteria … Perhaps Toronto is best seen as a parable of the mixed
> brew that is renewal.[48]

No doubt some will argue that it is better to aim high and miss than not to aim at all – that, as John Wimber himself was fond of saying, faith implies risk; there will consequently be failures and embarrassments along the way. Even so, it is noticeable that with hindsight, Warner prefers to confine Toronto within the more modest parameters of 'renewal'. This in fact echoes the line taken at the time by many of those who were seeking to steer a 'middle way' through debate on the Blessing. Not least, it reflects the guidance of the Evangelical Alliance's Director General, Clive Calver, given at a conference organised by Holy Trinity, Brompton in early August 1994:

> Just after this move of God started I was in a set of churches and they said, 'Is this an awakening?' And I said, 'No. An awakening is what God does in the world when he turns society around as he did in the 18th century.' They said, 'Is this revival?' I said, 'I don't think so. Revival is what God does when he brings the world into the church.' They said, 'Is this renewal?' I said, 'Yes, definitely. It's as important as this: you have never had an awakening in history that hasn't started in renewal and revival.' Now I want to see an awakening. I want to see God touch our nation and to see God turn our society upside down and inside out. But he won't start in society. He'll start with the people of God.[49]

In the model proposed by Calver, 'renewal' constitutes an internal reinvigoration of existing believers, and indeed, even sharp critics of Toronto, like Steven Sizer in his essay for this volume, have tended to accept that Toronto prompted some into a deepened relationship with God. Most, in fact, would now concur with Rob Warner's conclusion – which itself reflects that put forward by another of our contributors, David Pawson – that Toronto was a 'mixed blessing'. Some, however, have rejected even this description, and have maintained that the movement was an overwhelmingly harmful, and even demonic, distraction from the true purpose of the church. Among those who propounded this view at the time were Christian Research Ministries, Tricia Tillin, and Steve and Cheryl Thompson.[50] It was also prominent in the many severe attacks on the Blessing made by the Derbyshire Baptist minister Alan Morrison, whose Diakrisis organisation launched a range of broadsides against the Blessing from July 1994 onwards:

> ...when any phenomena occurred in the revivals of earlier eras – such as the Evangelical Awakenings in the UK and the US in the eighteenth and nineteenth centuries – they always took place as a result of powerful preaching of the cross from the Bible, an overwhelming sense of one's foulness in the face of an infinitely holy God, the shocking realisation of the impending reality of eternal punishment in hell, and a desperate desire to be free from the scorching blaze of God's wrath. In genuine revivals, any 'falling down' which occurred was the result of a sense of horror at one's sin and grief at the offence caused to an omnipotent God – certainly not an experience one would want to be repeated. In complete contrast to this, the current phenomena that we are seeing in churches today are completely unconnected to any of these contexts and are, at best, the outworkings of a childish and hysterical mimicry; at worst, they are the result of something far more sinister.[51]

It must be said that detractors like Morrison were handed an easy chance to draw odious, rather than flattering, comparisons once the Blessing's apologists had eagerly invoked giants like Wesley, Whitefield and Edwards. The result was a sometimes helpful, but often frustrating debate – a debate that centred most intensely on the legacy of Edwards. It says much about the character of evangelical rhetoric that spokespeople on both sides claimed Edwards for their own position. To opponents of the Blessing he was the model Calvinistic cessationist, who would have been unmoved by physical manifestations and horrified at the lack of genuine gospel preaching, true repentance and sound conversion in the Toronto movement.[52] To supporters, he was the anointed evangelist who took exotic emotional responses to the Spirit in his stride, and would have seen considerable affinity between what happened in his own Northampton revivals of 1735 and 1740-42, and what was emerging from Toronto.[53] Both versions caught aspects of the truth. Yet ultimately, they offered partial assessments that were unduly skewed by the presuppositions with which their advocates had started, and by the conclusions that they had all too obviously determined to draw. The charges of institutional demonization cited above, for example, conveniently underplayed the many and varied reasons given in Edwards' seminal work, *The Distinguishing Marks of a Work of the Spirit of God*, for *discounting* any such accusation in respect of a spiritual movement[54] – not to mention the plain warning of Jesus about blaspheming the Holy Spirit (Mk. 3:29; Mt. 12:32). By the same token, those who rushed most enthusiastically to declare 'this is that' in respect of Toronto and Edwards often failed adequately to take account of the deeper pneumatological differences between Vineyard-style teaching and that of the Northampton Congregationalist.

By contrast with all this, Roy Clements, in one of the best-informed and most fairly balanced articles published at the height of the Blessing, managed simultaneously to pinpoint the true relevance of Edwards for what was taking place, and to shift the debate about him onto more fertile ground:

> Jonathan Edwards remains the classic source of Christian reflection on the kinds of phenomena associated with religious revival. His three works, *Distinguishing Marks, Thoughts on Revival* and *A Treatise on the Religious Affections*, are absolutely essential reading for anyone who wants to make sense of the Toronto Blessing (or indeed, of the modern charismatic movement in general). Guy Chevreau, whose chronicle of the Toronto experience, *Catch the Fire*, has been widely influential in promoting the movement, makes uses of Edwards' work in his fourth chapter, drawing many sympathetic comparisons with the Great Awakening. It is perhaps worth noting that Chevreau draws almost exclusively from *Distinguishing Marks*, which is only the earliest of Edwards' books. In many respects, his *Treatise on the Religious Affections*, published a couple of years later, represents his maturer reflection on these matters, following the excesses associated with less-cautious revival preachers like James Davenport. In particular, it is important to note how Edwards distinguishes 'religious affections' from mere 'passions'. Affections are not just emotions, but include the delight of the mind and engagement of the will. Edwards is scathing about mere emotional froth. Nevertheless, Edwards refused to denounce the emotional and physical manifestations which accompanied the revival. He insisted that they proved nothing either positive or negative regarding the authenticity of the experience. The only reliable test of the Spirit's work is the behavioural changes in a person's life which attend it.[55]

Clements' implication here is that both positive and negative assessments of the Blessing were prone to the same error so carefully avoided by Edwards – namely a fixation on physical phenomena. Indeed, it is ironic that the very outrage voiced by some at the others' indulgence in the manifestations ensured that those manifestations remained in the foreground of the debate, when more attention ought to have been given to the impact of the Blessing on people's lives and churches. No doubt such analysis did occur, but hindsight raises serious questions as to how it was conducted and presented. This leads us to the second crisis we have identified in respect of Toronto: the crisis of discernment.

A Crisis of Discernment

The New Testament word translated 'discernment' is itself bound up with the notion of 'crisis' which we have outlined. The compound *diakrisis* can convey both negative denunciation and constructive assessment. Hence while in Romans 14:1 it denotes a quarrel, in 1 Corinthians 12:10 it suggests a positive facility for distinguishing the spiritually good from the spiritually evil (cf. 1 Cor. 2:14; 11:29; Heb. 4:12).[56] As Ernest Larkin defines it, the object of discernment as understood in this more positive biblical context is 'to identify the presence or absence of God in given human activity'. As such, it is concerned with 'affective movements within the person', which are to be 'evaluated in their orientation or direction according to the gospel principle, "You shall know them by their fruits"' (Mt. 7:16)[57].

As we shall see, this emphasis on fruits was widely observed in relation to the Blessing, even if the specific application of it was often hotly disputed. Before we examine the discernment of such fruits, however, it should be noted that some commentators on the Toronto movement were at least as much concerned with its *roots*, i.e. with its historical provenance. This focus on the aetiology of the Blessing – on its origination and causation – featured especially in the work of those who were minded to discern it as a force for harm. Hence both Alan Morrison and Eric Wright made much of John Arnott's avowed debt to Kathryn Kuhlman and

Benny Hinn, both of whom had attracted high-profile repudiations of their doctrine and methods, while W.J. Oropeza painstakingly traced the connection which led from the much-maligned Latter Rain movement and the sectarian 'Oneness' Pentecostalism of William Branham, through Branham's protegé Paul Cain, to the subsequently scandalised 'Kansas City Prophets', and on into the Vineyard network and the Blessing itself.[58] In these instances, there is little doubt that links existed – links which are examined and detailed in Part II of this book. However, it must be emphasised that merely establishing some sort of connection between two people or groups does not mean that the one is necessarily or exclusively in thrall to the influence of the other. More orthodox role models can offset the deleterious effects of a dubious mentor; a follower may imbibe teaching of questionable source and content, but may later manage to filter it under more benign guidance. Besides, even those who work closely together under the same banner (like Cain and Branham or, indeed, Wimber and Arnott) may in due course develop markedly divergent views. No doubt, the process of discernment can usefully take account of such historical investigation, but in biblical terms, it must also recognise the dangers of guilt by association. It was the Pharisees, after all, who carped in relation to Jesus' own background in John 1:46: 'Nazareth? Can anything good come from there?'

Where roots are concerned, there is another strategy which is more problematic than condemning people by the company they might once have kept. This is indulgence in what rhetoricians call the 'fallacy of the undistributed middle'.[59] Essentially, it involves undue ascription of the terms of a major premise to a minor inference. Where the discernment of Toronto has been concerned, this has most clearly manifested itself as a confusion of *resemblances* with *causes*. Hence, certain opponents of the Blessing have sought to 'prove' that it is erroneous by drawing parallels between various practices associated with it, and apparently similar practices associated with mesmerism, the occult and eastern polytheistic religion.[60] The difficulty here is that while, say, charismatic 'laying on of hands' and repetitive chorus-singing, or Toronto-style trembling and 'resting in the Spirit' may look like phenomena which occurred in the meetings of the occultist Franz Anton Mesmer (1734-1815), they are not therefore, *ipso facto*, 'mesmeric'. Those who make this leap of logic are effectively suggesting that such practices must *always* be occultic and heretical because they occur in some recognisable form in mesmerism, and mesmerism is occultic and heretical. But this is a falsely absolutist presupposition – a defective syllogism. Repetitive song singing may be a feature of both mesmerist meetings and Toronto-style worship, but it can also be witnessed on innocent display in folk clubs and nursery schools. The laying on of hands may feature in the Hindu *shakti-pat*, but it is involved in a good deal else besides, not least biblical, apostolic ministry (Mk. 16:18; Acts 6:6, 13:3, 19:6; 28:8; 1 Tim. 4:14; 2 Tim. 1:6). A similar methodological point is made with respect to so-called 'altered states of consciousness' in the papers contributed here by Patrick Dixon and Mark Cartledge: while such states *may* be induced by dubious acts of suggestion, manipulation or drug-taking, this does not in itself mean that they cannot or should not be considered as a legitimate part of Christian spiritual experience. From a Christian perspective, the errors of mesmerism or eastern polytheism lie more crucially in their philosophical and theological assumptions, than in the physical techniques that they might deploy, or the external manifestations by which they might be identified.

All this confirms that while responsible study of the background and development of new movements within the church can aid discernment, it cannot in itself determine such discernment. For this, we must indeed turn to the question of fruits.

Scrutiny of fruits was, as we have already noted, the chief means by which Jonathan Edwards sought to identify the work of the Holy Spirit. In *Distinguishing Marks*, he famously advances five 'tests' to determine whether a spiritual experience is genuine and godly. All are related to the longer-term effects of that experience in terms of devotion and discipleship. First, he writes, it must 'raise the esteem' of Christ in the life and witness of the believer. Secondly, it must work 'against the interests of Satan's kingdom, which lies in encouraging and establishing sin, and cherishing men's worldly lusts'. Thirdly, it must cause 'a greater regard to the Holy Scriptures' and should establish people more deeply in 'truth' and 'divinity'. Fourthly, it should lead *others* into truth, as it overflows into evangelism. Fifthly, it should issue in love of both God and fellow human beings.[61]

These tests were widely cited by commentators on the Blessing, and were strongly commended in the Alliance's own Euston Statement.[62] The problem, however, is that they are not entirely self-evident, and must be interpreted and applied in each situation. And not surprisingly, they were applied quite differently, and with quite different results, by different 'camps'. While it was harder to deny personal claims to enhanced devotion, Bible-study and relationships, more sceptical observers moved to condemn the lack of scriptural and doctrinal substance in Toronto-style meetings, the dearth of that corporate contrition and repentance which Edwards had viewed as so characteristic of revival, and the relatively low number of new converts made through the movement. In response, the pro-Toronto lobby presented accounts of impassioned, cross-centred preaching, radically enhanced communal discipleship, and influxes of new Christians. The problem in each case was that the evidence given was so often parochial or anecdotal and, sometimes, decidedly 'second-hand'. As such, it could have only limited value for an objective, thoroughgoing discernment of the fruit being produced by the Blessing as a whole. So typically, just as critics like Alan Morrison, Chris Hand and the Centre for Christian Ministry would make broad-brush accusations about pro-Toronto churches lacking in repentance, evangelistic impact and holiness,[63] Sandy Millar would counter-claim that Holy Trinity, Brompton had seen the Blessing bring 'many hundreds of people to renewed faith in Jesus Christ, a greater depth of repentance, and a fresh desire to pray and read the Bible',[64] or Ken Gott would describe Sunderland Christian Centre as an exemplar of reverent lamentation and conversion-growth.[65] For every 'scare story' about casualties of the Blessing published by arch anti-Torontoites like Mark Haville,[66] Gerald Coates or Terry Virgo would be ready with edifying stories of how the new movement had transformed lives for the better.[67] For all the 'hard-soft' stereotypes of conservative v. charismatic, Toronto showed that where these exchanges were concerned, each party could give as good as it got. So for the prosecution, Chris Hand could generalise from personal experience at Queen's Road Baptist Church, Wimbledon to tar the Blessing with homiletic neglect, church decline, doctrinal error and hype,[68] while Rob Warner, who joined the same congregation shortly

after Hand left it, could address those who levelled such accusations in the following terms:

> Such is not the blessing I preach and encounter week after week. A
> movement of God cannot be properly evaluated by caricature. A
> work of God cannot be undone by such caricature. Smears, distortion
> and guilt by association are not devices of good evangelical theology.
> Are you opposed to emotionalism and manipulation? So am I. Are
> you equally opposed to what Paul described as 'holding to the form
> of religion while denying its power'? So am I.[69]

Nowhere was such fevered argumentation more potently illustrated, however, than in the matter of 'animal noises'. Interestingly,
these are not listed as a distinctive manifestation of the Blessing
in Bill Jackson's early, landmark Vineyard paper 'What in the World
is Happening to Us?', and do not seem to have featured significantly in debate about the movement until Clifford Hill reported
in the magazine *Prophecy Today* that an anonymous Pentecostal
pastor had told him that they had occurred at 'a meeting in
Brighton'[70]. A few days later, the *Observer* journalist Martin Wroe
wrote of Christians 'barking, crowing like cockerels, mooing like
cows, pawing the ground like bulls and, more commonly, roaring
like lions' – although he notably admitted that such things had not
been on display at the actual meeting on which his piece was
based.[71] The gap between what Hill and Wroe heard from others
and what they saw for themselves is significant. Certainly, animal
noises did play some part in the Blessing. It remains unclear,
however, exactly how prominent they were. It is known that
Bishop David Pytches did 'roar like a lion' on a visit to TAV in the
summer of 1994. It is also well documented that he then publicly
expounded this experience in relation to Hosea 11:10-11.[72]
Beyond this, however, the true picture becomes warped by the
same sort of rhetorical heat-haze we have observed with regard to
other aspects of the Blessing. So as debate develops, we see Tony
Higton, Stanley Porter, John Stott, Brian Edwards and others
expressing grave reservations about such noises on the grounds
that they lack biblical backing and debase the image of God in
humanity,[73] while John Arnott, Gerald Coates, Rob Warner and
John Noble defend them as legitimate 'acted signs' of a kingdom

which Scripture often symbolically depicts in terms of lions, lambs, doves and other fauna.[74]

Although this exegetical and theological debate was no doubt intriguing, it often appeared to take on a life of its own quite apart from any consideration of whether the actual incidence of such noises was in any way sufficient to warrant the energy and time spent scrutinising them. Indeed, it seemed at times that the sceptics in particular were more concerned with the *idea* of animal noises, and with their with negative emblematic potential in respect of Toronto, than with such animal noises as were in fact being made 'in the field'. By the same token, Toronto apologists seem to have defended animal behaviour on principle – out of allegiance to an assumed 'right' of freedom in worship – whilst at the same time seeking to play down its actual importance for the Blessing *per se*. At the end of all this, however, the neutral or non-aligned observer is still left relatively unclear about the *de facto* role of animal noises in the Toronto movement, even if they can be seen to have served incidentally as a catalyst for more general evangelical arguments about epistemology, cultural assimilation and hermeneutics. These arguments are obviously vital, and are considered more thoroughly in Martin Davie's and David Pawson's papers for this volume. However, it is doubtful that the debate on animal noises proved either appropriate or particularly illuminating as a 'way in' to such issues.

If nothing else, the animal noises dispute pointed up the need for more sober, distanced, empirical evaluation of the Blessing. The febrile tone of the immediate, media-fuelled controversy hardly facilitated this, but over time, a more scientific evaluation of the 'fruit' of the movement has begun to emerge. The work of Margaret Poloma has been highly significant in this regard, and the paper she has contributed here stands as a welcome antidote to the more impressionistic approach that characterised so many earlier assessments of the movement. Beyond her sociological, case-study based analysis of how the Blessing has 'transmuted' into various other modes of renewal, however, it is also worth noting the statistical findings of the Christian Research Association, whose most recent English Church Census (1998) offers a helpful tool for discernment of Toronto's fruit – albeit within England alone.

In his account of the census, CRE Director Peter Brierley high-lights the fact that between 1989 and 1998, i.e. the period which included the rise and fall of the Toronto Blessing, regular church attendance in England dropped from 10% to 7.5%.[75] In blunt terms, this would appear to confirm that the Blessing cannot now seriously be defined as a revival, let alone an awakening. For all the great claims and hopes attached to it at its inception, its medium-to long-term impact on both church and wider society in England appears to have been negligible. Some might even say that it contributed to the decline charted by the census, although any direct causation here would be hard to demonstrate.

Viewed against these stark figures, the so-called 'Gamaliel Principle', which was invoked by a number of commentators in defence of the Blessing,[76] would seem now to have found it wanting (cf. Acts 5:34-9). If the main test of a movement's godliness and fruitfulness is its ability to 'thrive', then Toronto would appear to have withered on the vine. Having said this, Tom Smail and John Lyons are surely right to question whether longevity alone should be the decisive criterion in discernment.[77] As Smail points out, such a test would, after all, work very well for Buddhism. And even full-blown revivals have rarely lasted more than three years. There is, as we have recognised, a case for arguing that Toronto lives on in other more obviously durable and successful initiatives – and it is a case that Margaret Poloma makes skilfully in this volume. Yet the problem with TTB lies not so much in how long it lasted, or in what other renewal paradigms it might have spawned, but in its effect on relationships within the church, and most particularly, within the evangelical wing of the church.

Brierley himself makes an intriguing observation about the possible effect of Toronto on evangelical identity and self-understanding. Despite stressing that evangelicals as a whole have declined less rapidly than other streams within the English church, Brierley points out that the proportion who would now define themselves as 'charismatic' has seen a comparatively dramatic, 16% fall since 1989. In particular, he notes that this fall owes much to the fact that around a quarter of mainly white-majority Pentecostal congregations switched from describing themselves as 'charismatic evangelical' to 'mainstream evangelical'. As Brierley presumes it, this change has occurred because such churches 'wish to disassociate themselves from the churches who have experienced the Toronto Blessing, probably all of whom would describe themselves as charismatic'.[78]

While somewhat speculative, the inference drawn by Brierley here suggests that at least on one level, the Blessing has left a legacy of embarrassment and retrenchment among those who might have been among its most obvious allies. Neither, it seems, is this mood confined to classical Pentecostals. We have already cited Rob Warner's disappointment with the fruit produced by Toronto, but the recent reflections of HTB's own Nicky Gumbel are also salient: 'I don't talk about it now', he told *The Guardian* in October 2000, 'It divides people. It splits churches. It is very controversial'.[79]

This retrospective assessment by a sometime leading proponent of the Blessing suggests that whatever else might have accrued from it (and Gumbel went on to describe it otherwise as 'a wonderful, wonderful thing'), the movement generated a major crisis of evangelical unity. This indeed, was the crisis which most immediately drew the Evangelical Alliance into the Toronto debate, and it merits some re-examination in the context of this book.

A Crisis of Unity

The December 1995 split between the Toronto Airport Vineyard and the Association of Vineyard Churches was symptomatic of the growing divisions that the Blessing had provoked within the evangelical world as a whole. As Part II of this book confirms, almost from the moment of its arrival in Britain, the movement seemed to draw out tensions which had existed under the surface of evangelicalism for some time. In particular, as we have noted, it re-catalysed long-standing mutual suspicions between non-charismatic and charismatic evangelicals. Also, however, as Peter Brierley's findings suggest, it prompted significant debate between those who were generally at ease with the presence of supernatural charismata, emotional responses and physical phenomena, but who differed on the relative profile which should be accorded to these things in worship and mission, and who questioned their specific status vis-à-vis Scripture, preaching, evangelism and personal holiness. Hence, while the Blessing predictably incurred the scorn of many traditional Reformed evangelicals, it was also vigorously challenged by the self-professed charismatics of the Centre for Christian Ministry, and of the Sheffield University group that produced the stinging 1998 critique *Mark of the Spirit?* In addition, it was viewed with concern rather than enthusiasm at the 17th World Pentecostal Conference which met in Jerusalem in October 1995.[80]

Against this rather fraught backdrop, the role and work of the Evangelical Alliance became crucial. No doubt the Blessing spurred many conferences, consultations, studies and statements, but the truth is that these tended to reflect the views of one 'side' or another in the debate, and thus tended to reinforce, rather than ameliorate, existing differences. Of course, some of those who took it upon themselves to attack the movement saw themselves in a 'prophetic' role – warning the church against a perilous deception. As such, they presented any attempt at dialogue or co-operation with proponents of Toronto as a compromise to be avoided.[81] On the other hand, there were those in the forefront of the movement who, when it was at its height, saw little point in having to justify something so self-evidently 'of God' to those whose theological presuppositions ensured that they would always be set against it. As the largest pan-evangelical body in the UK, the Alliance was probably the only organisation which could seriously hope to work through and beyond these polarities, and thereby reiterate a unity which could be neither cheap nor monolithic, but which would be grounded in genuine biblical collegiality.

To this end, the Alliance organised three major forums on the Blessing in 1994-95, which could together claim to have gathered the most widely representative body of evangelical leadership and opinion at the time.[82] Contrary to the jibes of some on the separatist hard right,[83] these forums were not fronts for an Alliance overrun by charismatics, but significantly engaged leaders from that 42% of our membership that does *not* define itself as charismatic.[84] The 'Euston Statement' issued by the first of these forums, and signed by the overwhelming majority of those present, may have been less sharp-edged and detailed than many other statements produced from more partisan quarters, but it remains one

of the few documents published on the Blessing which can claim
a genuinely 'conciliar' and 'ecumenical' evangelical authority.[85] It is
often forgotten by evangelicals that the early church worked out
its theology in characteristically *ecclesial* fashion – whether through
the biblical Council of Jerusalem (Acts 15), or in later meetings
such as those at held at Nicea and Constantinople. As the record
shows, the discussions that took place in such settings were
hardly superficial or uniform; indeed, they were very often highly
charged.[86] Yet by God's grace, positions were defined, and texts
produced, which could realistically claim to have articulated the
mind of the church. Granted, they might have looked like 'compromise' to some, and granted, in the case of post-apostolic councils like Chalcedon, they often marked out boundaries rather than
presenting exact definitions on every point. But it is doubtful that
anything better, or more representative, could have been produced
at the time. While it only claims to act for one stream of the wider
church, and while it clearly does not carry the authority of such
ancient councils, the Alliance does seek to operate on the same
basic, ecclesial model when it engages in theology and lends guidance on movements such as Toronto. This approach is embodied
in its theological commission, ACUTE, which was in fact formed
just prior to the rise of the Blessing, and which has since produced
major reports on the equally controversial questions of homosexuality and hell.[87]

This book operates very much on the model I have just outlined. It gathers together diverse essays and sources on the
Blessing, the better to inform understanding of what the Toronto
movement meant for evangelicals when it emerged, and what it
means now. It also seeks, in Part II, to offer the fullest documen-
tary record yet published in the UK of the events, personalities,
texts and discussions which together constituted 'The Toronto
Blessing'. In Part III, it offers a unique compendium of statements
on the Blessing from churches and Christian organisations around
the world. Unlike ACUTE's studies on homosexuality and hell, it
does not purport to speak 'with one voice' on behalf of the
Alliance as a whole. This is partly due to the prior existence of the
Euston Statement, which does come with such a pedigree. It is
also due, however, to the recognition that discernment on this
matter is still going on, and that a presentation of different

perspectives therefore probably still offers the most helpful way ahead. What I myself have written here obviously reflects my own view from within the heart of the Alliance, and benefits from access to the Alliance's archive and resources. Even so, it should not be treated as 'the official version'. Rather, the format adopted for this book might be more closely compared to that of the IVP series, *When Christians Disagree*, which so many found helpful when it was published during the 1980s, and which is still widely consulted today.

Admittedly, some have questioned why it has taken so long to issue this volume, and as Part II confirms, the Alliance did commit itself to publishing more detailed material within a year of the Euston text. I myself did not join the Theology Department of the Alliance until 1997, but on its behalf, I should apologise for the fact that the wait has been so extended. Having said this, I am sure that the delay has afforded certain benefits – not least the benefits of hindsight and enhanced perspective.

It may be seven years since the birth of the Blessing; it may well take another seven years, or longer, before its full implications are realised. As things stand, it is to be hoped that in addition to offering judgements on Toronto, this book provides opportunities for the further reflection, study and response that are still needed.

Notes to Introduction

[1] K. Schneider, 'Judgment', in Colin Brown (ed.), *Dictionary of New Testament Theology* (Vol. 2), pp.362-7.

[2] J. Lyons, *Semantics* Vol. 1, p.244. Cf. J. Barr, *The Semantics of Biblical Language*, pp.76-291.

[3] R. Gledhill, 'Spread of Hysteria Fad Worries Church', *The Times*, 18th June 1994, p.12.

[4] For a helpful account of Wimber's ministry and its impact on the UK, see N. Scotland, *Charismatics and the New Millennium: The Impact of Charismatic Christianity from 1960 into the New Millennium*, pp.199-250.

[5] C.P. Wagner, 'Third Wave', in Stanley M. Burgess et al (eds.), *Dictionary of Pentecostal and Charismatic Movements*, pp.843-4.

[6] M. Robertson, 'A Power Encounter Worth Laughing About', in K. Springer (ed.), *Power Encounters Among Christians in the Western World*, pp.149-57; W.J. Oropeza, *A Time To Laugh: The Holy Laughter Phenomenon Examined – Guidelines for Distinguishing Genuine Renewal from Human-Induced Phenomena*, p.17.

[7] G. Chevreau, *Catch the Fire: The Toronto Blessing – An Experience of Renewal and Revival*, p.21.

[8] Ibid., p.23; Oropeza, *A Time to Laugh*, p.22; D. Roberts, *The 'Toronto' Blessing*, p.31.

[9] R. Howard-Browne, *Manifesting the Holy Ghost*, p.5.

[10] Roberts, *'Toronto'*, p.85.

[11] 'Rumours of Revival', *Alpha*, July 1994, p.46; Oropeza, *A Time to Laugh*, p.22, citing R. Riss, 'History of the Revival, 1993-1995', unpublished paper (7th ed., January 17th, 1995).

[12] Chevreau, *Catch the Fire*, p.23-4.

[13] Roberts, *'Toronto'*, pp.20-1.

[14] T. Virgo, *A People Prepared*, pp.13-4.

[15] R. Warner, *Prepare for Revival*, pp.2-3; P. Dixon, *Signs of Revival: Detailed Historical Research Throws Light on Today's Move of God's Spirit*, pp.19-21.

[16] Roberts, *'Toronto'*, p.25; 'A Day By Day Diary of What We Have Seen', *HTB in Focus*, 12th June, 1994, p.3; M. Fearon, *A Breath of Fresh Air: A Balanced and Informed Perspective on the Unusual Phenomena Sweeping the Worldwide Church*, pp.115-6.

[17] E. Mumford, 'Spreading Like Wildfire', in W. Boulton (ed.), *The Impact of Toronto*, pp.17-9. For a fuller transcript, see 'A Mighty Wind from Toronto', *HTB in Focus*, 12th June , 1994, pp.4-5.

[18] M. Fearon, 'Principal of Laughter', *Church of England Newspaper*, November 11th 1994, p.8; C. Price, 'Surfing the Toronto Wave', *Alpha*, May 1995, pp.6-9; G. Coates in *Rumours of Revival* (Video)

[18] C. Gardner, 'Catching a Glimpse of God's Glory', *Joy*, March 1995, pp.17-8.

[19] See Part II and Bibliography for further details.

[20] The debate in question was over the relationship of evangelicals to mainline, 'mixed' denominations. For fuller accounts of it, see D. Bebbington, *Evangelicalism in Modern Britain*, pp.267-70; I.D. Murray, *D. Martyn Lloyd-Jones: The Fight of Faith, 1939-1981*, pp.513-67.

[21] Bebbington, *Evangelicalism*, p.198; W.K. Kay, *Pentecostals in Britain*, pp.1-36.

[22] P. Hocken, *Streams of Renewal: The Origins and Early Development of the Charismatic Movement in Great Britain*; Bebbington, ibid., pp.247ff.; Scotland, *Charismatics*, pp.9-35.

[23] K. Hylson-Smith, 'Roots of Pan-Evangelicalism 1735-1835', in S. Brady & H. Rowdon (eds.), *For Such a Time as This: Perspectives on Evangelicalism, Past, Present and Future*, p.137.

[24] P. Lewis, 'Renewal, Recovery and Growth: 1966 Onwards', in Brady & Rowdon (eds.), *For Such a Time as This*, pp.178-94; Bebbington, *Evangelicalism*, pp.249-70.

[25] J.A. Beverley, 'Vineyard Severs Ties with 'Toronto Blessing' Church', *Christianity Today*, 8th January 1996, p.66; E.E. Wright, *Strange Fire? Assessing the Vineyard Movement and the Toronto Blessing*, p.29.

[26] D. Roberts, 'The Toronto Divide', *Alpha* February 1996, pp.4-6; G. Russell-Jones, 'Whatever Happened to the Promised Revival?', *Christianity*, December 1997, p.30; J. Ronson, 'Catch Me if You Can', *Guardian Weekend*, 21st October 2000, pp.10-21.

[27] O. Guinness, *Fit Bodies, Fat Minds: Why Evangelicals Don't Think and What to Do About It*, pp.57-61; M.A. Noll, *The Scandal of the Evangelical Mind*; D.F. Wells, *God in the Wasteland*, pp.68-71.

[28] B. Jackson, 'What in the World is Happening to Us?: A Biblical Perspective', in P. Dixon, *Signs of Revival: Detailed Historical Research Throws Light on Today's Move of God's Spirit*, pp.303-26.

[29] Chevreau, *Catch the Fire*.

[30] A. Boyd, 'Toronto: Calm After the Storm?', *New Christian Herald*, 17th February 1996; J. Arnott, *The Father's Blessing*.

[31] For studies of this phenomenon, see J. Aitchison, *Language Change: Progress or Decay?*; R. Wardhaugh, *Sociolinguistics*, pp.192-216.

[32] A. McGrath, *Evangelicalism and the Future of Christianity*, p.13.

[33] Dixon, *Signs of Revival*.

[34] For example, J. Lindsay, 'Revival Breaks Out in London Churches', *Church of England Newspaper*, 17th June 1994, p.1; F. Langan & P. Goodman, 'Faithful Fall for Power of the Spirit', *Sunday Telegraph*, 19th June 1994, p.5.

[35] R.T. Kendall, Address to London Leaders' Meeting, 6th July 1994, cit. Warner, *Prepare for Revival*, pp.17-8.

[36] D. Roberts, 'From the Editor: When the Holy Spirit Comes', *Alpha*, August 1994, pp.10-11; J. Wimber, quoted by P. Goodman, 'The Evangelist Who Is Refreshing Religion', *Sunday Telegraph*, 2nd October 1994, p.22; Warner, ibid.

[37] For a helpful analysis of these terms and their application see T.K. Beougher, 'Revival, Revivals' in S. Moreau, H. Netland & C. van Engen (eds.), *Evangelical Dictionary of World Missions*, pp.830-33.

[38] Beougher, ibid.

[39] For a historical overview of these and other such revivals around the world, see W. Duewel, *Revival Fire*.

[40] E.E.Cairns, *An Endless Line of Splendor: Revivals and their Leaders from the Great Awakening to the Present*, p.22.

[41] For example, Beougher, 'Revival, Revivals'; S.J. Brown, 'Revivals (British Isles)', in D.K. McKim & D.F. Wright (eds.), *Encyclopedia of the Reformed Faith*, pp.325-7; I.H. Murray, *Revival and Revivalism: The Making and Marring of American Evangelicalism, 1750-1858*.

[42] T. Thornborough, 'An Evening at the Airport', *Evangelicals Now*, February 1995, pp.6-7; G. Russell-Jones, 'Whatever Happened to the Promised Revival?', *Christianity*, December 1997, p.30. Walker is cited in Russell-Jones' article.

[43] Murray, *Revival and Revivalism*; Beougher, 'Revival, Revivals'.

[44] G. Coates, 'A Mighty Convulsion', *Christian Herald*, 30th July 1994, p.9

[45] R.T. Kendall, 'R.T. Responds', *Evangelicals Now*, January 1996, p.24.

[46] K. Gott, interview for *Rumours of Revival* (Video).

[47] Warner, *Prepare for Revival*, p.175.

[48] Rob Warner, '21st Century Renewal: Only Just Begun', *Renewal*, January 2001, p.54.

[49] Quoted in *HTB in Focus*, 14th August 1994, p.10.

[50] Christian Research Ministries report, cit. Steve Dube, 'Holy Spirit "Blessing" Dismissed as Demonic', *Western Mail*, September 5th 1994; T. Tillin, *Looking Beyond Toronto: The Source and Goal of Pentecost*; S. and C. Thompson quoted in J.A. Beverley, 'Toronto's Mixed Blessing', *Christianity Today*, 11th September, 1995, pp.23-6.

[51] A. Morrison, *We All Fall Down*.

[52] For the quintessential expression of this view, and kindred references, see Wright, *Strange Fire?* pp.121ff.

[53] For example, Chevreau, *Catch the Fire*, pp. 70-144.

[54] J. Edwards, *The Distinguishing Marks of a Work of the Spirit of God*, pp.112ff.

[55] R. Clements, 'Toronto: A Personal Appraisal', *Evangelicals Now*, June 1995, p.16.

[56] W. Arndt, and F.W. Gingrich, *A Greek-English Lexicon of the New Testament and Other Early Christian Literature*, p.185.

[57] E.E. Larkin, 'Discernment of Spirits', in G.S. Wakefield (ed.), *A Dictionary of Christian Spirituality*, p.115.

[58] A. Morrison, *A Different Gospel: The Origin and Purpose of the Toronto Blessing* (Video); Wright, *Strange Fire?*, pp.202-16; Oropeza, *A Time to Laugh*, pp.15-81.

[59] R. Cockroft & S.M. Cockroft, *Persuading People: An Introduction to Rhetoric*, p.92.

[60] For example, Morrison, *We All Fall Down*; M. Haville, 'An Illusion of Power', in P. Glover (ed.), *The Signs and Wonders Movement: Exposed*, pp.34-7 cf. Dixon, *Signs of Revival*, pp.227-32; D. Middlemiss, *Interpreting Charismatic Experience*, pp.242-52; R. Clements, 'Toronto: A Personal Appraisal', *Evangelicals Now*, June 1995, pp.16-7.

[61] Edwards, *Distinguishing Marks*, pp.109-20.

[62] D. Roberts, 'The Finger of God', *Alpha*, August 1994, pp.32-4; R. Davies, 'Physical Manifestations in Revival', *Renewal*, January 1995, pp.28-30; D. Atkinson, 'Why my Middle Name is Certainly Not Gamaliel', *Church of England Newspaper*, 3rd February 1995, p.17; T. Sargent, 'Physical Phenomena and Revival', *Evangelism Today*, March 1995.

[63] A. Morrison, *Falling for the Lie*; and *We All Fall Down*; C. Hand, 'Tasting the Fruit of the Toronto Blessing', in P. Glover (ed.), *The Signs and Wonders Movement – Exposed*, pp.38-60; Centre for Christian Ministry, *Charismatic Crossroads: The Report of a Leadership Consultation on the Current Situation in the Charismatic Churches*.

[64] Quoted in A. Brown, 'Church at Odds Over "Waves of Faith"', *Independent*, 28th January 1995, p.2.

[65] K. Gott and L. Gott, *The Sunderland Refreshing: How the Holy Spirit Invaded One British Town*.

[66] M. Haville, 'Giving Their Lives for "The Faith"', *Evangelicals Now*, June 1997, p.10.

[67] G. Coates, 'A Mighty Convulsion', *Christian Herald*, 30th July 1994, p.9; G. Coates, 'On the Crest of the Spirit's Wave', *Renewal*, February 1995, pp.18-20; Virgo, *A People Prepared*.

[68] Hand, 'Tasting the Fruit'.

[69] R. Warner, Address to third Evangelical Alliance Consultation on the Toronto Blessing. For more details see entry for 21st December 1995 in the Chronicle in Part II/Ch. 10 of this book.

[70] C. Hill, 'Toronto Blessing – True or False?', *Prophecy Today* Vol. 10 No. 5 (September-October 1994), p.10-11.

[71] M. Wroe, 'A Drop of the Holy Spirit Has Them Rolling in the Aisles', *The Observer*, 4th September 1994.

[72] P. Nodding, 'The Holy Spirit in Our Midst', in W. Boulton (ed.), *The Impact of Toronto*, p.32; Fearon, *Fresh Air*, pp.98-9.

[73] Higton, quoted in C. Price, 'Surfing the Toronto Wave', *Alpha*, May 1995, pp.6-9; S.E. Porter, 'Shaking the Biblical Foundations?: The Biblical Basis for the Toronto Blessing', in S.E. Porter & P.J. Richter (eds), *The Toronto Blessing – Or Is It?*, pp.58-60; R. McCloughry, 'High Profile: Interview with John Stott', *Third Way*, October 1995, pp.21-3; B. Edwards, Address to Third Evangelical Alliance Consultation on the Toronto Blessing, see entry for 21st December 1995 in Part II/Ch. 10 of this book.

[74] C. Price, 'Taste for the Exotic', *Alpha*, p.29; R. Warner, 'The Stott Debate: Truth and Toronto', *Alpha*, October 1996, pp.4-7; J. Noble, 'A Very English Blessing?', *Renewal*, November 2000, pp.34-5.

[75] P. Brierley, *The Tide is Running Out: What the English Church Census Reveals*, Eltham: Christian Research, p.27.

[76] See, for example, Evangelical Alliance (UK) 'Preliminary Statement on the Toronto Blessing', reprinted here at Part III.9; Showers are 'Strong Meat', *Salvationist*, 29th October 1994; A. Bateman, 'Whatever Happened to the Toronto Blessing?', *Salvationist*, 1st August 1998, pp.12-3.

[77] T. Smail, 'Why my Middle Name is Certainly Not Gamaliel', *Church of England Newspaper*, 3rd February 1995, p.8; J. Lyons, 'The Gamaliel Principle', in L. Pietersen (ed.), *The Mark of the Spirit? A Charismatic Critique of the Toronto Blessing*, pp.92-121.

[78] Brierley, *Tide is Running Out*, pp.147. See also p.54.

[79] J. Ronson, 'Catch Me if You Can', *Guardian Weekend*, 21st October 2000, p.19.

[80] Centre for Contemporary Ministry, *Charismatic Crossroads*; Pietersen, *Mark of the Spirit*; J.L. Grady, 'Classical Pentecostals Wary of the 'Toronto Blessing', *Charisma*, November 1995, pp.41-2.

[81] See, for example, A. Morrison, 'No Great Surprise', *Evangelical Times* (Letters), September 1995, p.18.

[82] For summaries of these consultations, see entries for 19th-20th December 1994, 2nd June 1995 and 21st December 1995 in Part II/10 of this book.

[83] A. Morrison, 'No Great Surprise', *Evangelical Times* (Letters), September 1995, p.18; 'Comment', *Evangelical Times*, September 1995, p.2.

[84] This figure is derived from a 1998 survey of 848 Alliance member churches, the results of which were published in the Spring 1999 edition of *Ear*, p.1.

[85] I realise that the term 'ecumenical' has negative connotations for some evangelicals, but I am using it here in its general, biblical sense of Christian co-operation, rather than in any necessary relation to the so-called 'Ecumenical Movement' characterised by the World Council of Churches. M. Lloyd-Jones, who was deeply suspicious of this movement, nonetheless regularly spoke of 'evangelical ecumenicity', and this comes close to what I am implying here.

[86] For an accessible evangelical account of these councils, see G. Bray, *Creeds, Councils and Christ*.

[87] ACUTE, *Faith, Hope and Homosexuality*; ACUTE, *The Nature of Hell*.

2

A Real but Limited Renewal

Martin Davie

The Questions that Remain

Back in 1994 the Toronto Blessing was, quite literally, headline news. As the Chronicle presented in Part II of this book makes clear, it was reported not only by Christian newspapers such as the *Church of England Newspaper* and the *Church Times*, but also by secular newspapers like the *Sunday Telegraph* and *The Sunday Times*. The BBC also covered it in some detail. Today it is no longer news, and although the Toronto Airport Christian Fellowship, where the Blessing first came to prominence, continues its ministry, it goes almost completely unreported, even in the Christian media. However, although the publicity may have died away, key questions remain:

- What exactly was the 'Toronto Blessing'?
- Was it an act of God?
- What have been the results of the Blessing over the past five years?
- Why wasn't it the precursor to a more widespread revival?

It is these questions that I shall attempt to answer here.

What exactly was the 'Toronto Blessing'?

This question is by far the easiest question to answer, since there is little dispute about the phenomena that the term 'Toronto Blessing' has been used to describe. As the Church of England's Board of Mission report *The Toronto Experience* explains:

> The 'Toronto Experience' is a label which has become attached to the incidence of particular phenomena in congregations, and has been more popularly known as the 'Toronto Blessing'. These phenomena, which might also be called 'manifestations' or 'reactions', are typically expressed during a worship session, when members of the congregation exhibit not only common manifestations of charismatic worship, including praying in tongues, ecstatic ululation etc., but also shaking, falling down ('being slain in the Spirit'), an imperative need to laugh or to cry, or to make unusual noises, especially sounds analogous to animal noises such as 'roaring' or 'barking'.[1]

As the report further states, these phenomena did not actually start in Toronto itself, but the title 'Toronto Blessing' was coined because '…these phenomena came to new prominence at the Airport Vineyard Church in Toronto in January 1994 and appear to have 'spread' from there.'[2]

What we are dealing with in the case of TTB is, then, a particular development of the 'Pentecostal-charismatic' tradition within worldwide Christianity. The Blessing is related to this tradition by the manifestation of ecstatic spiritual phenomena, but differs from it in that the phenomena in question are more extreme and, to the outside observer, more bizarre than those normally seen in this tradition.

Was it an act of God?

This second question is more difficult to answer because the issue of whether the Blessing was a result of divine activity is one that has been hotly disputed. Those involved with it have maintained that it was indeed the result of the work of God, while critics have asked whether it was not simply a human phenomenon, or even the work of the Devil.

In considering which of these explanations of the Toronto phenomena is the correct one, the first point we need to tackle is whether God does actually intervene in visible ways in the lives of human beings. If, for example, God is in fact the God depicted in the Greek philosophical tradition or in eighteenth-century Deism – ultimately responsible for the creation and continued existence of the world but never actually acting within it – then clearly these phenomena cannot be God's work. Equally, if we were to follow Maurice Wiles' argument in his book *The Remaking of Christian Doctrine*[3], that God is at work in the world, sustaining it and guiding it to a good end, but that we cannot identify any events in the world as examples of special divine action, then we could not talk about the phenomena associated with TTB as specific acts of God. We would have to look for an alternative explanation.

For someone who takes the biblical witness as their starting point, however, none of the views of God and his relation to the world that I have just described are defensible. The God depicted in the Bible is the God who does indeed create and sustain the world. As Paul puts it, quoting the Greek poets, 'In him we live and move and have our being' (Acts 17:28). However, he is also the living triune God, the Father who from Genesis to Revelation acts in the world in specific and identifiable ways too numerous to mention, in and through his Son, in the power of the Holy Spirit. Moreover, there is no evidence in the Bible to suggest that God has ceased to act in this way. There is no suggestion in the Bible that the close of the apostolic age, for instance, marked the end of the period of specific divine action in the world. Evangelicals critical of charismatic activity have often advanced this so-called 'cessationist' view[4] but even those who remain sceptical of such activity now tend to base their critique on grounds other than sheer dogmatic cessationism.[5]

All this being the case, there is no *a priori* reason why we should not consider the possibility that the Toronto phenomena are the result of the specific and direct action of God through the work of the Holy Spirit. We are still left with the question, however, about whether these phenomena are not only possibly, but actually the work of God.

At this point we need to reject as red herrings the simple sociological or psychological explanations that have been put forward to explain these phenomena. It has been argued that the Blessing is an example of group hysteria or psychological manipulation, which has brought comfort to Christians feeling increasingly beleaguered in an increasingly secular world, and has been promoted by church leaders whose power and prestige has depended on their ability to offer their followers new forms of spiritual experience.[6]

Such reductionist interpretations are red herrings for two reasons. First, the extremely varied way in which the Blessing spread, and the fact that it often affected people who were neither seeking nor expecting it, makes it hard to subscribe to the view that it was all the result of emotionalism or auto-suggestion, or that it was it was all engineered by charismatic leaders to bolster their own ministries. As Patrick Dixon wrote at the time, 'simplistic explanations just will not do. What we are seeing are highly complex phenomena of varying kinds, caused by a variety of factors, often mixed together, in people of different backgrounds, different expectations, different histories and different personalities.'[7]

Secondly, even if such psychological and sociological factors *were* involved to some degree, this would not rule out the activity of God. Christian theology has long been familiar with the fact that God can work through what the Westminster Confession calls 'secondary causes', that is to say, factors that are part of the created order – in this case any psychological or sociological issues affecting the people concerned.[8]

The question as to whether the Blessing was actually a work of God remains, however, and in order to answer it we need to go back to theological basics and ask how we can establish whether any putative divine action is or is not a work of God. One approach which evangelicals in particular tend to favour, is to ask whether the phenomenon in question is 'biblical'. The difficulty with this approach is trying to pin down what we mean by 'biblical'. It could be argued, for example, that something is biblical only if it has specific precedent within Scripture. Thus preaching the good news of Jesus Christ crucified and risen would be biblical because that is what the earliest Christians are recorded as having done in the Acts of the Apostles. In the literature which has been produced as a response to the Toronto phenomena, there has been much discussion concerning whether the phenomena are biblical in this sense, with apologists for the Blessing such as Gerald Coates and Rob Warner arguing that there is biblical precedent for matters such as trembling (Ps. 2:11), laughing (Lk. 6:21) and appearing drunk (Acts 2:13-15),[9] and others such as Stanley Porter and Vivian Culver arguing that the references in question are not relevant to the specific phenomena encountered in the context of TTB. Thus, for example, Porter and Culver agree that there are biblical references to laughter, but suggest that there is no biblical evidence for believers engaging in the sort of helpless laughter encountered as part of the Toronto experience.[10]

If the argument is conducted purely on this basis, writers like Porter and Culver would appear to have the better case. The specific phenomena encountered in TTB do not seem to be referred to in Scripture. However, this does not close the issue, since it is clear throughout the Bible that God does things in the history of his people that he has not done before. For instance, God appears to Moses out of the burning bush (Ex. 3:1-6), flattens the walls of Jericho (Josh. 6), turns water into wine (Jn. 2:1-11), and sends the Holy Spirit in tongues of fire at Pentecost (Acts 2:1-4). None of these were things he had ever done before or would ever do again. To put it simply, the God of the Bible is, as Karl Barth declares, the God 'who loves in freedom'[11] – the God who in his freedom acts in ways that are often unprecedented or unpredictable, and in ways he may never repeat.

This of course raises the issue of how we can then tell what gives consistency to God's activity. How can we judge if it is God who is at work if his actions are frequently unpredictable? The answer lies in the fact that because God's actions are *his* actions they have consistency in terms of the purpose for which they are done. To return to Barth's declaration, the God whose nature is love (1 Jn. 4:8) is the God who *loves* in freedom, and in all his works and ways, when properly understood, his actions manifest his love.

As the Orthodox theologian Kallistos Ware argues in his book *The Orthodox Way*, it is the trinitarian love of God that is the basis of creation itself:

God is not just one but one-in-three, because he is a communion of persons who share in love with one another. The circle of divine love, however, has not remained closed. God's love is, in the literal sense of the word 'ecstatic' – a love that causes God to go out from himself and to create things other than himself. By voluntary choice God created the world in 'ecstatic' love, so that there might be besides himself other beings to participate in the life and the love that are his.[12]

God's long term plan is therefore to bring the whole of creation into relationship with himself through Christ (Eph. 1:10), and in terms of his human creation this means entering consciously into that relationship in the power of the Holy Spirit (Rom. 8:14-16, Gal. 4:4-6). The key thing about TTB is that it led innumerable people to experience this relationship in a fresh and powerful way. To quote Michael Mitton in his Grove Booklet, *The Heart of Toronto*, 'This is the heart of the 'Toronto Blessing'. Thousands and thousands of Christian people, whose love for God had grown lukewarm, are being brought into a new experience of the intimacy of his presence.'[13]

Vast numbers of testimonies could be cited in support of Mitton's claim, but for reasons of space one will have to stand for the many – the testimony of 'Sarah' quoted in Guy Chevreau's book *Catch the Fire*:

> The Lord has taken me into a realm of grace that I've never before known: I'm actually just enjoying Jesus, and have the sense he's enjoying me. I'm not doing anything special at all for the kingdom, just loving him and enjoying him. Yet every day when I share with friends what God has done for me, and can do for them, the Holy Spirit comes; I feel his presence and others are touched simply out of the overflow of what he's done.[14]

It is these testimonies to the experience of renewed intimacy with God, received by so many through TTB, that answer the criticism of the phenomena associated with the Blessing by David Pawson among others – namely, that the phenomena constituted a public humiliation of people, and that God would not inflict such humiliation upon his children.[15] The majority of people supposedly humiliated do not seem to have seen it like that. Their response has not been one of anger and shame at being humiliated, but of awe and wonder at what God did in their lives.

Furthermore, the Blessing did not just manifest itself in terms of renewed feelings of intimacy with, and love for, God. It also led to the other signs of a genuine move of God specified by Jonathan Edwards in his classic *The Distinguishing Marks of the Work of the Spirit of God*: that is, a greater esteem for Christ and the Bible, a greater knowledge of the truth about both God and themselves, a greater detestation of sin, and a greater love for other people.[16]

This being the case, it is hard to see TTB as anything other than a work of God himself. Who but God, working through his Holy Spirit, could bring about these results?

Certainly they cannot be the work of the Devil. Doubtless there were failures and even sins committed by those involved with Toronto, and these can rightly be attributed to the Devil's pursuing his age-old strategy of seeking to destroy the work of God. However, to attribute all the good things that came out of Toronto to the Devil would be absurd, since it would involve the idea, rejected by Jesus in Luke 11:15-20, that the Devil is engaged in conflict against himself. Whatever else the Devil may do, he does not bring about the works of God.

One issue that remains is the connection between the phenomena associated with the Toronto experience and the spiritual blessings that flowed from it. At first sight, it is difficult to see a connection between the two. What has rolling about on the floor or being subject to fits of hysterical laughter to do with attaining a greater intimacy with God and leading a changed life thereafter?

What seems clear from the testimonies of those involved is that there *was* a connection; the most plausible explanation of its nature that I have come across is that put forward by Patrick Dixon in his book *Signs of Revival*, from which I quoted earlier. There, and in this book he argues that many of the physical phenomena observed at Toronto can be accounted for as the result of what he calls an 'Altered State of Consciousness' (ASC). This is a state in which a person becomes aware of things of which they are not normally conscious. ASCs can be triggered in various ways and can result in the kind of apparently bizarre manifestations observed at Toronto and elsewhere. In themselves, ASCs are spiritually neutral but because, as Dixon says, they 'confront us with the reality that there is more to life than we ordinarily see, feel, or touch', they can serve in a Christian context to open people up to the reality of God, and to what he wants to do in their lives. If Dixon is right, these ASCs would be an example of God using secondary causes to touch people's lives in the way mentioned above.

What have been the results of the 'Blessing'?

Apart from the ongoing sociological research of Margaret Poloma, a recent example of which is included later in this book, very little academic work seems to have been done on the long term impact of TTB in the seven years or so since it first emerged. In the absence of such research it is impossible to be more than tentative about what its deeper effect has been. However, anecdotal evidence suggests that the Toronto experience was an extremely significant turning point in the lives of many individuals and Christian communities around the world, resulting in a closer walk with God, greater evangelistic zeal and activity, and the foundation of new churches and church plants. What has not resulted, however, has been the wave of revival hoped for by many back in 1994 and 1995. Both the church at large and the world outside the church have been largely unaffected by the Blessing, and the decline of the Western Church continues as before.

Why was the 'Toronto Blessing' not the precursor to a more widespread revival?

A simple answer to this question would be to say that this was not the will of God. Taking divine sovereignty seriously, this answer would suggest that only God can send revival and that in this case he did not chose to do so. However, such an analysis overlooks the historical evidence that God wills to send revival when large numbers of people come together to ask him to do so; the revival of religion can be prematurely terminated through human opposition, indifference or folly.[17]

In the case of TTB, we need to ask whether revival might not have resulted had more people been inspired by the initial reports of what was happening, to seek seriously for themselves the kind of renewed intimacy with God experienced by those who had been touched at Toronto Airport Vineyard and elsewhere. Surely if those of us who were not involved with Toronto had seriously sought God's face in this way, he would not have withheld his blessing. It might not have come in the same manner as TTB, since God is the free God who blesses his people in a variety of different ways. But surely it would have come.

Dixon declares in *Signs of Revival*:

> History will record one of several things: either that we criticised and analysed the latest move of God until the rise of faith was all but crushed; or that the flame continued to burn, bringing limited revival to some groups, some churches, some areas, before fading away under apathy and neglect; or that the church reached out to God in fervent prayer, willing to pay the cost of change, repenting of personal sin, corporate sectarianism and lack of mutual love, embracing the mighty power of God, and bringing the whole nation a challenge of repentance and new life, with a national awakening, the like of which numerically we have never seen.[18]

Seven years on, these words remain a challenge to us all. It is still possible for us to respond to TTB in a positive way, and to see the widespread revival God longs to give. Let us do so.

> *...if my people, who are called by my name, will humble themselves, and pray and seek my face and turn from their wicked ways, then will I hear from heaven, and will forgive their sin and will heal their land.* (2 Chr. 7:14)

Notes to Chapter 2

[1] A. Richards, *The Toronto Experience: An Explanation of the Issues*, Board of Mission Occasional Paper No. 7, p.1.

[2] Ibid.

[3] M.F. Wiles, *The Remaking of Christian Doctrine*.

[4] For a contemporary cessationist critique of the Toronto Blessing, and a review of past anti-charismatic cessationist literature, see Wright, *Strange Fire?*.

[5] For non-cessationist critiques of the Blessing see C. Hill et al, *Blessing the Church?*; L. Pietersen, (ed.) *The Mark of the Spirit? A Charismatic Critique of the Toronto Blessing*.

[6] See, for example, P.J. Richter, '"God is not a Gentleman!" The Sociology of the Toronto Blessing', in S.E. Porter and P.J. Richter (eds.), *The Toronto Blessing – Or Is It?*, pp.5-37; and M. Percy, *The Toronto Blessing*.

[7] Dixon, *Signs of Revival*, p.247.

[8] *Westminster Confession* V:II.

[9] G. Coates, ' 'Toronto' and Scripture', in W. Boulton (ed.), *The Impact of Toronto*, pp.47-52; R. Warner, *Prepare for Revival*, pp. 21-36, 81-116.

[10] S.E. Porter, 'Shaking the Biblical Foundations?', in Porter & Richter (eds.), *Toronto Blessing*, pp. 54-6; V. Culver, 'Ecstatic Laughter' in Pietersen (ed.), *Mark of the Spirit?*, pp.63-91.

[11] K. Barth, *Church Dogmatics* II/I, pp.257-321.

[12] K. Ware, *The Orthodox Way*, p.56.

[13] M. Mitton, *The Heart of Toronto*, p.24.

[14] Chevreau, *Catch the Fire*, pp. 161-2.

[15] D. Pawson, *Is the Blessing Biblical? Thinking Through the Toronto Phenomenon*, pp. 78-81

[16] C.C. Gone (ed.), *The Works of Jonathan Edwards Vol. 4*. For evidence to support the claim that these fruit resulted from the impact of the Blessing see for example M. Stibbe, 'Putting it to the Test', in Boulton (ed.), *Impact*, pp.58-60, and the unpublished paper by M. Poloma, 'By Their Fruit …: A Sociological Assessment of the 'Toronto Blessing', accessible via the Toronto Airport Christian Fellowship Web Site at http://www.tacf.org.

[17] See R. Davies, *I Will Pour Out My Spirit: A History and Theology of Revivals and Evangelical Awakenings*.

[18] Dixon, *Signs of Revival*, p.279.

3

A Sub-Christian Movement[1]

Stephen Sizer

The Dubious Roots of the Blessing

The wave of interest in what came to be known as 'The Toronto Blessing' reflects a subtle but significant move away from sound doctrine. The writings of the Blessing's proponents show clearly that the Bible has been neglected, distorted and superseded by strange doctrines and novel teaching based on extra-biblical revelation. This has led to the uncritical acceptance of an existential theology compromised by worldly values. Under the guise of a supposed 'move of God' a major paradigm shift, away from the biblical faith traditionally recognised and embraced by evangelicals, and into the realm of the cultic and the heretical, has occurred. It is not hard to infer from the Chronicle which forms Part II of this book that the roots of TTB lie not in the Bible, but deep within the 'Health and Wealth', Prosperity or 'Word of Faith' movement associated with the South African Pentecostal evangelist Rodney Howard-Browne and the American charismatic preacher Benny Hinn.

As the Chronicle shows, John Arnott, Pastor of TAV church, was searching for 'a fresh spiritual anointing' in the early 1990s. This quest led he and his wife Carol to attend a meeting convened by Hinn in September 1992 at Toronto's Maple Leaf Gardens. Hinn by this point had become highly successful, but had also attracted controversy for claiming, among other things, that Adam could fly through space and that there are nine in the Trinity.[2] His distinctive emphasis was upon a powerful 'anointing', which he claimed to be able to bestow simply by blowing on people. According to TAV leader Guy Chevreau, Arnott and Hinn had in fact known each other since the mid-Seventies, and Arnott had for some time 'longed for a similar kind of empowerment' as Hinn had been displaying.[3] By June 1993, Arnott's spiritual search had also prompted him to attend a Rodney Howard-Browne meeting in Fort Worth, Texas, where he experienced first-hand the 'holy laughter' which had, over the preceding few years, become a hall-mark of the South African's ministry.[4]

In August 1993, Randy Clark, a Vineyard pastor from St Louis who would become another key figure in the Toronto movement, received his 'anointing' through Rodney Howard-Browne. Significantly, this took place when, in a period of some despair and dryness, Clark attended a meeting at leading Word of Faith teacher Kenneth Hagin's Rhema Bible Church in Tulsa, Oklahoma. Clark had had 'theological differences' with Hagin, and with the pros-perity movement in general. However, he believed that the Holy Spirit was now rebuking him and asking, 'How badly do you want to be touched afresh?'[5] Having brought Howard-Browne's emphases back to his own congregation in St Louis, and having seen spectacular growth as a result, Clark was soon contacted by Arnott and asked to lead meetings at TAV.[6] The meetings in ques-tion began on 20th January 1994. The manifestations broke out dramatically that night and the 'Toronto Blessing' was born.[7]

This background detail confirms that both Arnott and Clark, who would emerge as protagonists in the rise of the Blessing, sought spiritual empowerment from men whose teachings had been widely criticised as heretical and cultic. Nor is it surprising that the manifestations of hysterical laughter, growling, shaking, and falling which had previously been associated with Howard-Browne and Hinn were soon thereafter experienced not only at the Toronto Airport Vineyard and other Vineyard churches, but all over the world, as leaders and lay people flocked to Toronto to receive the 'anointing' and take it back to their home congregations.

If Randy Clark's renewal had its origin in the ministry of Rodney Howard-Browne at Kenneth Hagin's Word of Faith church, and if John Arnott received his empowerment at the hands of Benny Hinn, the origin of TTB must seriously be questioned.

The Debate about Terminology: 'Revival', 'Renewal' or Less?

Advocates of TTB implied or explicitly stated at the time that they believed this to be evidence of revival. A major report in Holy Trinity, Brompton's *Focus* newspaper on 12th June 1994 carried the sub-heading, 'The Word Revival is On Everyone's Lips'.[8] *Alpha* magazine editor Dave Roberts referred to the Toronto events a month later as 'rumours of revival',[9] and entitled subsequent articles on the Blessing 'Revival Call' and 'Revival Fire'.[10] Guy Chevreau took the same line when he subtitled his influential book on the blessing 'An Experience of Renewal and Revival'.[11] Speaking at a Wembley meeting alongside Rodney Howard-Browne on 13th December 1994, Pioneer People leader Gerald Coates was reported by *Evangelicals Now* as having described the Toronto Blessing as 'revival', and as having said 'This is perhaps the greatest outpouring of God in our land ever.'[12]

Despite these designations, it is important to note that the noun 'revival' does not actually appear in the Bible. The verbs 'revive' and 'reviving' are used in the Old Testament to describe the action of God following his punishment, and his people's repentance (Ps. 80:18, 85:6, Is. 57:15; Hos. 6:2). Psalm 19:7 describes the 'reviving' activity of God's Law, as do many verses in Psalm 119. It is worth noting, however, that there are no such references in the New Testament.

Beyond the use of 'revival' as a description of TTB, probably the most common word applied to it was 'renewal'. This term, however, is also not without its problems in contemporary application. 'Renewal' appears four times in the Bible, in each case in very specific ways. In Job 14:14 it relates to the day of resurrection; in Isaiah 57:10 it denotes gaining strength from pagan worship rather than trusting in God, and in Matthew 19:28 Jesus uses the word to describe what will happen when he returns to sit in judgement.

The term 'renewal' is used once to describe the Christian, in Titus 3:5, where the focus is very clearly on regeneration and 'rebirth', not a subsequent experience of the Spirit: 'He saved us, not because of righteous things we had done, but because of his mercy. He saved us through the washing of rebirth and renewal by the Holy Spirit.' The concept of 'being renewed' as a present, ongoing experience is found in Romans 12:2; it refers to our minds, not to our spirits or bodies. Similarly, 2 Corinthians 4:16 describes 'renewing' as a continual daily process by which we are becoming more like Christ. While our physical bodies are 'decaying', or wearing out, our inner nature is being 'renewed'. There is no sense, therefore, in which the word here could be taken to refer to physical healing. Some Christians equate 'renewal' with 'receiving' the Spirit subsequent to conversion, evidenced by unintelligible sounds, or 'tongues'. Mike Fearon, for instance, refers to churches holding 'receiving meetings', at which TTB was apparently bestowed.[13] To believe or teach that Christians need to pray to receive the Spirit is, however, quite fallacious. The Scriptures clearly teach that a person cannot be a Christian without the presence of the Holy Spirit (Rom. 8:9). The theological interpretation of Pentecost, as a unique historical event, is explained in 1 Corinthians 12:13: 'For we were all baptised by one Spirit into one body - whether Jews or Greeks, slave or free – and we were all given the one Spirit to drink.' Notice that Paul here describes a corporate, past-tense event, not something to be sought by Christians subsequently. There is no sense biblically, therefore, in which the Toronto Blessing can be associated with either the word 'revival' or 'renewal'.

Biblical Issues

The Toronto Blessing became particularly notorious, at least in the secular press, because of claims that people involved in it were 'drunk in the Spirit', and for its association with animal noises, roaring, shaking and other ecstatic phenomena. These things need to be assessed, first and foremost, from a biblical perspective.

Drunk in the Spirit?

It was repeatedly claimed by advocates of the Blessing that the 'drunken' behaviour linked with it parallell events witnessed on the Day of Pentecost and recorded in Acts 2. However, the second chapter of Luke's narrative in general, and verses 13ff. in particular, show that the only sign which could have given rise to this accusation was an eagerness and boldness on the part of the apostles to proclaim the message of Jesus Christ. This was preached in clearly understood languages. Those who ridiculed the apostles with the accusation that they were drunk were hearing the gospel, but presumably rejecting it. Their criticism was the excuse of a guilty conscience, and therefore quite unfounded. It is significant that no serious commentator interprets the text as teaching that the apostles *actually* displayed drunken behaviour. To suggest that they did, as some advocates of Toronto have done, is wishful eisegesis. Logically, on the same basis, such advocates must also presumably believe that the Lord Jesus spoke with slurred speech, staggered about, or rolled on the floor, since he too was criticised for drunkenness! (Mt. 11:18-19). Yet as Christ himself put it, 'Wisdom is proved right by her actions.'

Despite all this, the Blessing prompted numerous, well publicised reports of people supposedly being 'intoxicated' in the Spirit – unable to walk or drive. Mike Fearon, for example, quotes Toronto proponents describing themselves variously as 'legless' and 'merrily sozzled', as enjoying 'a skinful of the Holy Spirit' and as tasting the 'undiluted 100 percent proof Spirit'.[14] Yet it is surely grievous to hear the third person of the Trinity represented in these terms. Fearon attempts to mitigate such descriptions by remarking that the Spirit does not come simply to make people 'pissed as newts',[15] but it would have been better to question whether this could ever be even *part* of his purpose.

What remains widely unanswered is the question of how drunken behaviour can be compatible with self-control, which is a vital facet of the fruit of the Spirit (Gal. 5:23). Moreover, purporting to justify such experiences merely by labelling them 'altered states of consciousness', as Patrick Dixon does, will not suffice.[16] Without self-control, we have no defence against the Devil. The apostle Peter warns, 'Be self-controlled and alert. Your enemy the devil prowls around like a roaring lion looking for someone to devour' (1 Pet. 5:8). Indeed, Peter says that if we are not self-controlled and clear-headed we cannot be in communion with God: 'The end of all things is near. Therefore be clear minded and self-controlled so that you can pray' (1 Pet. 4:7).

'Holy Laughter'

Joy is as much the fruit of the Spirit as self-control, and there is no excuse for glum Christians. However, throughout the Bible, the great majority of references to laughter are associated with scorn, derision or evil. Of 40 references in Scripture, (34 in the Old Testament and 6 in the New), 22 refer to scornful laughter. Of the other 18, seven refer exclusively to Abraham and Sarah's initial disbelief and astonishment that God would give them a child in old age. Only three refer to authentic laughter in the New Testament, and two of these warn *against* it (Luke 6:25, and James 4:9-10, which is particularly severe in tone: 'Grieve, mourn and wail. Change your laughter to mourning and your joy to gloom. Humble yourselves before the Lord, and he will lift you up').

This overview suggests that there is little warrant for the so-called 'Holy Laughter' associated with TTB. As Warren Smith has observed:

> There is no biblical precedent for 'holy' laughter ... Substituting the word 'joy' for 'laughter' is a non sequitur. It is inaccurate and misleading. 'Holy' laughter advocates rarely, if ever, discuss the need to 'test the spirits' [1 John 4:1] ... or the dangers of demonic deception. Many laughter advocates condescendingly discourage and even openly intimidate sincere Christians who question the 'laughing revival' ... [Charles and Frances] Hunter's book, *Holy Laughter*, refers to sceptics as 'God's frozen chosen'. Mona Johnian writes, 'sceptics, hesitators and procrastinators do not get anointed.' She warns that 'any person or church that wavered could be eliminated.' ... 'Holy' laughter advocates blatantly disregard the biblical admonition that things be done 'decently and in order' (1 Corinthians 14:40).[17]

We might also do well to heed the response of Watchman Nee to an outbreak of laughter in the church in China: 'They could not contain themselves and kept on laughing. What is this? Can this possibly be the fullness of the Spirit? No, this is plainly one of the works of the soul.'[18]

Roaring

One of the most controversial phenomena associated with TTB was the expression of animal noises – particularly in the form of roaring like a lion. In a November 1994 article, Clifford Hill recounted that the Anglican bishop, David Pytches, had rolled on the floor at the Toronto Airport Vineyard while uttering such leonine sounds; he also described a meeting in Brighton at which a young man had at one point shouted 'The beast is dead! The beast is dead!' – and saw his words greeted with a growing crescendo of growls from the whole congregation.[19]

At the peak of the controversy surrounding TTB, Mark Dupont, one of the prophetic leaders of TAV, wrote specifically about the 'roaring' or growling phenomenon associated with the new movement. In a paper entitled '1994: The Year of the Lion',[20] Dupont insisted that Amos 3:8 applies to the present-day Church: 'The lion has roared - who will not fear? The Sovereign Lord has spoken - who can but prophesy?' Emphasising that it is God who inspires his people to express themselves after this pattern, Dupont comments, 'There have been many people who have been roaring as lions in the meetings as the Spirit of God has come on them.' Nevertheless, a cursory reading of the context (Amos 3:1-4) shows that here, as in just about every other reference to 'roaring' in the Scriptures, we are presented with a sign of God's judgement on Israel and her impending punishment. Any good Bible concordance shows conclusively that references to 'roar', 'roaring' and 'roared' in relation to lions have to do with the presence of evil and destruction, or, when applied to the Lord God, with his penalty for sin. They do not refer to blessing. Indeed, the bankruptcy of Dupont's exegesis is confirmed when he has to quote from C.S. Lewis's fictional story *The Lion, the Witch and the Wardrobe* to explain this apparently new mode of divine activity. Citing something the lion Aslan says in Lewis's narrative, Dupont asserts, 'This in essence is the revelation that the bride of Christ needs today...' I suspect, however, that Dupont and others caught up in the roaring phenomenon were influenced more by Walt Disney's film *The Lion King* than by the Holy Spirit of God. With a comparable disregard for Scripture, Mike Fearon asserted that 'roaring people are usually intercessors involved in promoting unity.'[21] As Clifford Hill points out, however, the prophet Jeremiah associates roaring like a lion with the occult spirit of Babylon and views their shouts of laughter as a sign of their imminent destruction:

> 'Babylon will be a heap of ruins... an object of horror and scorn, a place where no-one lives. Her people all roar like young lions, they growl like lion cubs. But while they are aroused, I will set out a feast for them and make them drunk, so that they shout with laughter – then sleep forever and not awake,' declares the Lord. 'I will bring them down like lambs to the slaughter' (Jer. 51:37-40).[22]

Ignoring this warning of judgement, Dupont equates TTB with what he describes as 'a party the Father is throwing' – an idea he infers from the Parable of the Prodigal Son (Lk. 15:25-27). Others have similarly compared it with the Great Banquet of Luke 14:16-24. But such interpretations follow a rather dubious form of 'realised eschatology' in which promises that relate to the future are applied to the present. The Scriptures teach that the 'marriage supper of the Lamb' will be in heaven in the future – not now, on earth (Is. 25:6-9). Certainly there is joy and celebration now, but essentially the Christian calling is one of battle and toil (Jn. 16:33; 2 Cor. 4:7-18; Rom. 8:19-25; Eph. 6:10-18; 1 Tim. 1:18; 2 Tim. 2:1-6; 1 Pet. 2:21). The Banquet is something to which we look forward with sure and certain hope (Rev. 19:7-9).

Most worrying of all, Dupont's paper is littered with biblical references to a divine judgement that he insists will fall on those who doubt or question that the Toronto movement is a work of God. It is very disturbing to find so-called Christians speaking in this way of other believers. Dupont refers to, or quotes from, an amazing array of passages to silence criticism. These include 1 Kings 13:4 (the unbelieving King receiving a withered arm); Judges 1:2; 20:18; Proverbs 6; Isaiah 58; 2 Corinthians 3:6; Malachi 3:16; 2 Kings 5:26 (Gehazi's disobedience leading to leprosy); 1 Kings 13:26 (the disobedient prophet killed by a lion); Ephesians 4:30; James 4:5; John 15:2 (the lopped off branch); Jeremiah 6:14;

8:14, and Isaiah 42:13,16. Dupont is at least honest when he says, with reference to the story of the prophet mauled by a lion, 'This may sound like a harsh Old Testament story for Christians today, but I believe this is really a picture of God's jealousy over those that he gives revelation of himself to.' Perhaps Dupont should have read John 10:27-30, in relation to our security, and Revelation 22:18, in relation to new, extra-biblical revelations.

The Importance of the Mind

As we have seen, scrutiny of the biblical witness on drunkenness, laughter and roaring clearly suggests that for all the glowing personal testimonies to their benefits, there is no biblical basis for the manifestations associated with TTB. Perhaps this is why proponents of the Blessing have so often attempted to avoid detailed theological evaluation of its distinctive features. For example, Rodney Howard-Browne is on record as having disparaged those who seek to apply such a test to his methods: 'You can't understand what God is doing in these meetings with an analytical mind,' he once told his audience; 'The only way you're going to understand what God is doing is with your heart.'[23]

While it is true that the genuine work of God affects our heart as well as our mind, it is worrying that like the 'Faith Teaching' cultists, some Christians appear to downgrade the mind as the prmary means of discerning truth from error. Yet the Scriptures repeatedly warn us to be on our guard, and to use our minds to understand God's will (Rom. 12:1,2; Eph. 4:17-24, 5:17,18; Col. 1:21,22, 3:10; 1 Tim. 6:3,4; 2 Tim. 2:15, 4:1-4; 2 Pet. 2:1-3).

Dave Roberts, in his book *The 'Toronto' Blessing*, disparages the example of the noble Bereans in Acts 17:11 who 'examined the Scriptures every day to see if what Paul said was true'. Under the title 'Explain, Explain, Explain', Roberts insists that 'It is vital we help our congregational Bereans and those simply shocked by the new and different and that we seek to remind people of appropriate scriptures.'[24] He is clearly criticising those who want to justify everything from Scripture. But the Berean Christians are praised rather than pitied by Luke. They are held up as the norm, as a universal model, and are not depicted as the weak, narrow biblicists of Roberts' imagination. At best, the hermeneutic used by advocates of Toronto is unconvincing; at worst, it is appalling. It is, frankly, an 'Alice in Wonderland' hermeneutic – one in which words can mean whatever their users want them to mean because those users have had an 'experience' which somehow validates that meaning. No doubt, spiritual experiences have a vital place in the Christian life; but they must always be weighed and tested according to Scripture.

Regrettably, Mike Fearon fails to apply such testing in his book *A Breath of Fresh Air*. He quotes extensively from my own criticisms of the Toronto Movement and apparently concedes the wisdom of caution when the church 'appears to be experiencing phenomena which go beyond the parameters set down in Scripture'. But he proceeds to ignore such parameters when he asks rhetorically, 'If it is the Spirit himself who is transcending these barriers, what can the church do?'[25] By so reasoning, Fearon assumes to be true (on the basis of experience or extra-biblical revelation), the very point in question. Surely such 'logic' sets in contradiction the work of the Holy Spirit and Scripture, which he inspired. It destroys any basis for rational discussion on the meaning and interpretation of God's Word, for at any point where the basis for unusual phenomena is questioned, appeal can be made to 'discernment' or 'experience' to justify it. This is in reality merely a modern and more insidious variation on the 'higher knowledge' of the third-century Gnostic heresy.

According to Eleanor Mumford, on the influential tape of the address she gave at Holy Trinity, Brompton on Sunday 29th May,[26] the Vineyard leaders at Toronto told her 'not to analyse or question this, but just receive it ... or you will lose it'. Precisely – because when subjected to proper scriptural analysis and questioning on the model of 1 John 4:1, the Blessing is exposed for the erroneous movement that it was.

The Blessing in Retrospect

With the benefit of hindsight, it is clear that TTB was a major distraction from the church's evangelistic mandate, and that it caused a great deal of confusion and division within evangelical and charismatic circles. It was neither 'a season of favour', nor does it have a future, other than to show the perils of basing our Christian faith on experience rather than the sure Word of God.

Some people would still say that they have a greater love for God as a consequence of the Blessing. My assessments here do not necessarily invalidate the personal experiences individuals may have had; they are, however, sufficient to warn us against uncritical acceptance of every wind of doctrine blowing across the Atlantic. It must also be said that many of the so-called 'testimonies' I have heard, either in person or on tape, have focused on manifestations; they have thus been highly subjective. They have often claimed a consequently 'greater love' or 'zeal' for God, but it is impossible to assess such feelings objectively. At the height of TTB, John Richardson offered a helpful assessment in this respect:

> We need to ask in conclusion not whether the Toronto Blessing might be something God is doing, nor whether it is changing peoples' lives, but whether it is consistent with the biblical theology of the blessing of God and the work of the Holy Spirit. The essence of the work of the Holy Spirit will be the holy life, and for this we do not have to pass through the Toronto Blessing. Rather, we need to immerse ourselves more and more in the whole counsel of the gospel which is sufficient for our relationship with God. This is the teaching of the rest of Galatians, and I would suggest it is the consistent teaching of the whole of Scripture. And if the preaching of the whole of Scripture on the basis that Christ gave himself for our sins to deliver us from the present evil age is not adequate to bring the Toronto Blessing to those who hear with faith, then whatever does bring the Toronto Blessing is another gospel and whatever it brings is not the blessing promised to Abraham, nor a result of receiving the Holy Spirit.[27]

It is usually quite easy to spot a 'Gospel minus' heresy, and evangelicals and charismatics alike rush to condemn bishops who deny fundamental Christian doctrines. Yet it is not often so easy, and I fear evangelicals and charismatics are not so willing, to contest teaching which in effect is a 'Gospel plus' heresy – especially when uttered by those who themselves claim an evangelical pedigree. That, however, is what we were offered in TTB. We were presented with more than God has actually promised. The gospel has been likened to a canoe perfectly capable of carrying us through life to heaven. If, however, we try to add baggage to the canoe we shall sink it just as quickly as by punching holes in it. The effect of adding to the gospel is the same as taking away from it. John Richardson continues:

> But could it not be claimed that the Toronto Blessing is a blessing beyond the simple blessings of the gospel? Could it not be, as Michael Green has also suggested, God's way of by-passing our rationalism and reaching the parts other approaches – such as gospel preaching – haven't reached? This is perhaps the hardest claim to answer in sup-port of the Toronto Blessing. To deny it seems to deny either the power or the sovereignty of God. And yet, as we said at the outset, one vital function of systematic theology is to insist that, whilst God can do anything he doesn't do everything. The blessing of which Paul speaks in Galatians 3, the blessing which may be summed up as the outpouring of the Holy Spirit even on the Gentiles, is the blessing God promised to Abraham and it is received through hearing the gospel with faith. So we must say that any blessing which goes beyond the blessing promised to Abraham, and any blessing which comes by some other means than hearing the gospel with faith, is a blessing too far because, as Paul points out in Galatians 1, it must come from 'a dif-ferent gospel'.[28]

It does seem most unfortunate, even embarrassing, that media reports of Toronto's self-styled 'Time of Refreshing' coincided with a period of almost apocalyptic suffering in places like Rwanda, Burundi, Sudan and Bosnia. The Scriptures give us no warrant for believing that the evangelistic mandate and call to compassionate service has been revoked in these 'last days', to be replaced by egocentric and introverted ecstatic displays of laughter, animal noises, shaking and falling to the floor.

In his book *Laid-Back Religion*, J.I. Packer presents a perceptive critique of what he dubs 'Hot Tub Religion'. He writes:

> Hot tub religion ... attempts to harness the power of God to the pri-orities of self-centredness. Feelings of pleasure and comfort, springing from pleasant circumstances and soothing experiences, are prime

goals these days, and much popular Christianity on both sides of the Atlantic tries to oblige us by manufacturing them for us ... Now we can see hot tub religion for what it is – Christianity corrupted by the passion for pleasure ... Symptoms of hot tub religion today include ... an overheated supernaturalism that seeks signs, wonders, visions, prophecies, and miracles; constant soothing syrup from electronic preachers and the liberal pulpit; anti-intellectual sentimentalism and emotional 'highs' deliberately cultivated, the Christian equivalent of cannabis and coca.[29]

The Toronto Blessing is representative of a sub-Christian movement in which the basis of faith has shifted from the historic Jesus of the cross to the present 'spirit' of personal experience. This is existential Gnostic heresy. Subjective experience must never take precedence over objective fact. Faith means 'I trust', not 'I feel'.

In this and in every generation, what is at stake is the truth of the gospel and the unity of the Body of Christ. This unity can only be maintained, not created. It is maintained as we remain faithful to the faith once received, according to Scripture.

Francis Schaeffer wrote an emotive book shortly before his death, entitled *The Great Evangelical Disaster*. In it, he speaks of a 'watershed' dividing evangelicals. On the one side are those who hold to 'a strong uncompromising view of Scripture'. On the other are those who adhere to what Schaeffer calls a 'neo-orthodox existential theology'. The heart of this neo-orthodox existential theology, he writes, is that 'the Bible gives us a quarry out of which to have religious experience'. The watershed, for Schaeffer, falls between a theology based on 'inner feeling' and one based on 'objective truth':

It is surprising to see how clearly the liberal, neo-orthodox way of thinking is reflected in the new weakened evangelical view ... By placing a radical emphasis on subjective human experience, existentialism undercuts the objective side of experience. For the existentialist it is an illusion to think that we can know anything truly ... all we have is subjective experience, with no final basis for right or wrong or truth or beauty.[30]

In an article published later the same year, Schaeffer went on to challenge evangelicals to take a stand on this watershed issue:

> You cannot wait for others to draw the line. You must draw the line. Will it be with tears? I hope it will be with tears. I remember as a young man in the 1930's when harshness and un-love reigned, but harshness and un-love do not need to reign when the line is drawn. It can be with tears and it can be with love. But unless those who have responsibility of leadership are willing to draw the line, they cut the ground from under the Church of our Lord Jesus Christ.[31]

In drawing the line identified by Schaeffer, there are three key prerogatives which we must recognise and apply. We need to re-emphasise Christian doctrine, separate from error and contend for the truth. Let us consider each of these prerogatives in turn.

The Need to Re-Emphasise Christian Doctrine

The chief reason for the success of the cults in general, and TTB in particular, is the spiritual naiveté and ignorance of the Word of God among Christians. Too many are content with a superficial knowledge of the Bible. This is made worse by the prevalence of an arrogant and overconfident reliance on spiritual discernment, which allegedly keeps one impervious to deception. More common still is the unspoken and naive belief that only other people are deceived by cults.

We must instead give ourselves to a life-long and detailed study of Scripture and the doctrines it contains. Theology is simply right thinking about God, something we should approach reverently and systematically.

We live at a time when doctrine is seen as a dirty word; it is downplayed in favour of ecstatic religious experiences of dubious origin. This is utter foolishness and plays into the hands of cultic wolves who prowl the edges of the flock.

The Need to Separate from Error

The apostle Paul was most emphatic when he warned Timothy and the Ephesians to have nothing to do with 'godless myths' (1 Tim. 4:7).

Advocates of TTB have said to me, 'You make it sound so black and white ... but many Christians seem to have been helped by this movement.' I agree that it is not all 'black and white'. My argument is that a little cancer is too much, a little adultery is still adultery, a little AIDS infection is enough to ruin the whole body. The apostle Paul knew the devastating influence of just a little error: a small amount yeast, he advised, works through the whole batch of dough (1 Cor. 5:6). Paul goes on to define the bread free from such yeast as the bread of 'sincerity and truth' (1 Cor. 5:8). Sincerity, indeed, is never enough on its own. This is surely why Jesus warned so strongly against the subtle but pervading influence of false teaching: 'Be on your guard against the yeast of the Pharisees and Sadducees' (Mt. 16:6-12). As Luther would reflect some fifteen centuries later, 'If I profess with the loudest voice and clearest exposition every portion of the truth except precisely that little point which the world and the Devil are at the moment attacking, I am not confessing Christ, however boldly I may be professing Christ.'[32]

Ultimately we may disagree as to the extent of error in the roots, teaching and manifestations associated with the Toronto Blessing, but error there clearly is, and that is sufficient reason for disassociating from it - no matter how tantalising its apparent rewards. Nor do we have to read everything offered by particular heretics before we speak critically of false doctrine. We need only become familiar with the truth of God's Word for error to become plain. The argument which says 'You cannot know it until you have tried it' is a satanic doctrine – the very one used to subvert Eve and bring the terrible cancer of sin into the world. We must watch out for heretical teaching not just outside the church (from well-defined sectarian organisations), but also within the church. God has forbidden contact with those who teach error. We cannot float through life on a permanent spiritual high, or on a wave of existential euphoria. Rather, we are commanded again and again to be careful, take heed, watch out and remember. We are to be wise and sober, and at all times to be 'self-controlled and alert.' Our enemy, the Devil, 'prowls around like a roaring lion looking for someone to devour' (1 Pet. 5:8).

The Need to Contend for the Truth

The Lord calls upon us earnestly to contend for the faith, in the face of satanic adversaries (Jude 3). Sometimes, as happened between Paul and Peter, this may even mean coming to a point of confrontation with friends and associates where the truth of the gospel is at stake (Gal. 2:11).

Indeed, Jesus had on one occasion to turn to his beloved friend and say 'Get behind me, Satan!' (Mt. 16:23). The true servant of Jesus Christ must be careful that his allegiance is absolute. By comparison, all human relationships are relative.

I believe the Lord is testing the Western church at this time, over its infatuation with 'health and wealth', and over its titillation by 'signs and wonders'. Against this background, we would do well to heed the following advice:

> If a prophet, or one who foretells by dreams, appears among you and announces to you a miraculous sign or wonder, and if the sign or wonder of which he has spoken takes place, and he says, 'Let us follow other gods' (gods you have not known) 'and let us worship them,' you must not listen to the words of that prophet or dreamer. The Lord your God is testing you to find out whether you love him with all your heart and with all your soul (Deut.13:1-3).

The first principle of the universe is truth; this must be defended even at the cost of our lives. We live in a relativist culture which values tolerance and mutual respect more highly than truth. Our spiritual sentiments – and this is probably the most sentimental age in the history of the church – might lead us many times to feel that to contend for the faith of the gospel is somehow eccentric, unspiritual or undignified. Yet nothing could be further from the truth. God warns a few verses later in Deuteronomy against being influenced even by friendship or personal loyalty when the truth is at stake: 'do not yield to him or listen to him. Show him no pity. Do not spare him or shield him' (Deut.13:8).

The apostle Paul was similarly very serious when he likened us to soldiers of the cross, describing in detail the armour we must wear in order to contend for the truth (Eph. 6:10-20). Here Paul equates the 'mighty power' of God with truth, righteousness, the Gospel and faith, not with signs and wonders. Above all, he stresses, we must bear 'the sword of the Spirit, which is the Word of God' (Eph. 6:10-19).

We are indeed soldiers of Christ. The world is a battleground. The struggle is between truth and error. Our only weapon is the sword of the Spirit, the Word of God. May God enable us to handle it more accurately, as those who need never be ashamed (2 Tim. 2:15).

Notes to Chapter 3

[1] This critique grew out of a series of papers produced for my own congregations on TTB. In these I concentrated on the theological roots of the movement, and the biblical hermeneutic used to justify the phenomena associated with it. In December 1994, I was asked to debate with Sandy Millar and Nicky Gumbel of Holy Trinity, Brompton before the Church of England Evangelical Council on the significance of Toronto. That same month, I participated in a 24 hour consultation on the subject under the auspices of the Evangelical Alliance. Rob Warner and I drafted the agreed statement signed by those participating; the full text of this statement is included in Part III of this book. In the Spring of 1995 I contributed to a video entitled *Rumours of Revival* produced by Nelson Word, and in October 1995 I addressed the Annual Rally of the Church Society at Westminster Central Hall on this subject. In 1997 I contributed to a video series produced by National Prayer Network exposing the errors of the Signs and Wonders Movement. A more detailed critique of TTB and related phenomena is available from my web site under 'articles and papers': www.virginiawater.co.uk/christchurch.

[2] Beny Hinn, *Praise the Lord* (TV Show), Trinity Broadcasting Network, 26th December 1991; Benny Hinn, *Benny Hinn* (TV Show), Trinity Broadcasting Network, 3rd/13th October 1990: 'Each one of them is a triune being by himself ... there's nine of them.' This was subsequently accepted by Hinn in an interview with *Christianity Today* magazine to have been 'a very dumb statement' (Randy Frame, 'Best-Selling Author Admits Mistakes, Vows Changes', *Christianity Today*, 28th October 1991, p.44). Despite this retraction, however, Hank Hanegraff and others still doubt the orthodoxy of Hinn's doctrine of God: H. Hanegraff, *Christianity in Crisis*, p.344.

[3] G. Chevreau, *Catch the Fire*, pp.22-3.

[4] Ibid., p.23; Roberts, '*Toronto*', p.64.

[5] D. Roberts, 'Rumours of Revival', *Alpha*, July 1994, p.46.

[6] Oropeza, *A Time To Laugh*, p.22; Roberts, '*Toronto*', p.31.

[7] Ibid., p.21.

[8] *HTB in Focus*, 'A Mighty Wind from Toronto', 12th June 1994, p.3.

[9] D. Roberts, 'Rumours of Revival', *Alpha*, July 1994, pp.25-8.

[10] D. Roberts, 'Revival Call', *Alpha*, August 1994, pp.32-4; 'Revival Fire', *Alpha*, August 1994, pp.14-7.

[11] G. Chevreau, *Catch the Fire*.

[12] *Evangelicals Now*, February 1995, p.9.

[13] M. Fearon, *Fresh Air*, p.248.

[14] Ibid., p.27.

[15] Ibid., p.28.

[16] P. Dixon, *Signs of Revival*, pp.233-80; *Church Times*, 2nd June 1995, p.7.

[17] W. Smith, 'Holy Laughter or Strong Delusion?', *SCP Newsletter* (Fall 1994, Volume 19:2) pp.1-13.

[18] W. Nee, *The Latent Power of the Soul*, p.71.

[19] C. Hill, 'Toronto Blessing – True or False?', *Prophecy Today* 10.5 (September-October 1994), pp.10-11.

[20] Published by Mantle of Praise Ministries Incorporated, Mississauga, Ontario, Canada.

[21] Fearon, *Fresh Air*, p.99.

[22] C. Hill, 'Toronto Blessing – True or False?', *Prophecy Today* 10.5 (September-October 1994), pp.10-11.

[23] Cit. J. Duin, *Charisma*, August 1994, p.26.

[24] Roberts, 'Toronto', p.138.

[25] Fearon, *Fresh Air*, p.157.

[26] For more detail, see entry for this date in Part II of this book.

[27] From an address given at the conference, 'Toronto Blessing? It's OK to ask Questions', held at St Andrew's Street Baptist Church, Cambridge, 16th September 1995.

[28] Ibid.

[29] J.I. Packer, *Hot Tub Religion*, pp.53, 58.

[30] F. Schaeffer, *The Great Evangelical Disaster* in *The Complete Works of Francis Schaeffer: Volume Four: A Christian View of the Church*, pp.334-5.

[31] F. Schaeffer *United Evangelical Action*, Fall 1976, p.4.

[32] Cit. Schaeffer, *Great Evangelical Disaster*, p.333

4

A Spur to Holistic Discipleship

Mark Cartledge

Introduction

I make this contribution as one involved in the UK charismatic movement, both at a personal and an academic level.[1] As I write, I am about to complete a doctoral thesis on charismatic glossolalia.[2] Ten years ago I submitted a master's thesis on the subject of charismatic prophecy.[3] I write from the standpoint of a 'critical participant'. I believe that a theologian is primarily one who prays – that is, one who talks *to* God and not just *about* God. As a charismatic, I want to add that a theologian is someone who also prays 'in the Spirit', which may or may not include glossolalia! It would be easy here to attempt a quasi-objective academic discourse, as if objectivity were actually possible in this matter, and as if my personal experiences were irrelevant. But theology is holistic. It concerns one's heart, mind, soul and strength. In hermeneutical terms, I am situated within a particular life setting, theological tradition and culture, and these affect my own approach to any theological concern. While I wish to give to Scripture its proper place as the supreme authority in matters of faith and practice, I also wish to engage with theological tradition and contemporary ecclesial experience as mapped by social science research methods. So I shall start from a personal perspective. In that way the reader can better evaluate my position.

I first heard about TTB when I came back to the UK from Nigeria, where I had been working as a missionary with the Church Mission Society. My wife and I had travelled home for the birth our child, Rebekah, but we were unable to return to Nigeria because of my wife's ill health. Shortly after starting a new job in Liverpool, my wife became very ill and was diagnosed as having multiple sclerosis. She has dual British-Canadian citizenship and has relatives living in Toronto. A year or so later (1995), we visited these relations at a time when the Toronto Airport Vineyard (later Toronto Airport Christian Fellowship (TACF)) was extremely busy with visitors. I paid two evening visits to the church and also attended a pastors' teaching seminar. When I first heard about the Toronto Blessing, I thought that it was really about bored middle-class charismatics who had nothing better to do but laugh, dance and fall over. I reckoned that it was trivial compared to the situation faced by the church in the Third World. However, one visit to the church changed my mind – even if I do retain some reservations about bored middle-class charismatics! The effects of some traumatic experiences in Nigeria for my wife and myself were healed at Toronto, and yet she still has multiple sclerosis. For my part, it proved to be a significant marker in my spiritual and theological journey. I went as a charismatic who was sceptical. I returned as someone who was not entirely sure of what was going on, but who was nevertheless considerably more open than closed.

As part of my theological research, I wanted to find out more. I duly attended a conference at Holy Trinity, Brompton, and visited St Andrew's, Chorleywood – two Anglican churches which, as the Chronicle which forms Part II of this book confirms, emerged as major centres of the Blessing in Britain. My reflections are informed by a variety of literature, as well as by TACF's own video teaching material.

Defining Terms

Before we proceed further, it is important to define what is meant by TTB. The 'Toronto Blessing' is an umbrella category which church and secular media used from mid-1994 onwards to classify certain behaviour within the charismatic movement. Typically, it refers to phenomena such as bodily weakness and falling to the ground, shaking, trembling, twitching and convulsive bodily movements, laughter, wailing or weeping, apparent drunkenness and intense physical activity such as running or bouncing.[4] The churches in which such phenomena are located narrate and give meaning to the phenomena in terms of an encounter with the Holy Spirit. There is a dual emphasis in the TACF material on love and power: the person, it is claimed, has encountered the power of God, which has so transformed the heart that s/he is now able to love God more as a result. The corollary is that the person is more able to love others also. This in turn leads to renewed discipleship. In the experience, people are often healed of emotional wounds as they encounter the power of love.

While the Toronto phenomena are odd and attract wide interest, proponents of TTB assert that it is the inner work of the Spirit that counts most. They argue that unless we are able to hear and understand the testimony of a person who claims to have been affected by the Holy Spirit, we cannot (perhaps dare not) pass judgement on what we see. The 'fruit', proponents argue, is what matters. Therefore, the transformation of people's lives must be the true and biblical benchmark of authenticity.[5]

Supernaturally Natural

God works both interactively and interventionally. He acts in and through the created order; after all, he sustains the whole cosmos. God can, on occasion, suspend what we might call the natural ordering of causation and intervene over and against nature. Such an action we would normally qualify as a miracle. I regard TTB largely as an example of God working in and through the created order – that is, in an interactivist manner, or to put it another way, in a 'supernaturally natural' fashion. God is working in and through social psychological mechanisms rather than suspending natural causation. However, there may have been occasions where God has intervened miraculously, and these may still occur today.

As with another contributor to this volume, Patrick Dixon, my experience and study leads me to consider TTB in terms of an altered state of consciousness (ASC). ASCs are complex states, but in basic terms they denote an intermediate condition between the conscious and the unconscious. Such states are common to all humanity and at a simple level they represent what we experience when we daydream, or drive the car through a red light because we are thinking about dinner. The mechanisms whereby ASCs are introduced can include hunger, social isolation and dislocation, repetitive noise or light, boredom, body immobilisation, intense mental absorption, music, liturgy, incense, biochemical alterations and hyperventilation.[6] On these grounds, I take TTB to have its basis in humanity, and would therefore view it as more properly associated with an interactivist position than an interventionist one.

Research into TTB has produced an interesting set of interpretations. By and large, with the exception of another writer featured in this volume, Margaret Poloma,[7] social science research has been conducted by interested but unsympathetic researchers.[8] Any rigorous attempt to compare what is happening today with the Bible is, therefore, problematic. It is difficult to categorise the manifestations in contemporary terms before we can then take them to Scripture for comparison and evaluation. As a consequence, the hermeneutical issue is complex. Despite this, I shall proceed on the basis of the definition given above.

On the whole, people come with a relatively fixed agenda: either to prove continuity with Scripture (charismatic evangelicals) or to prove discontinuity with it (conservative evangelicals). Charismatic evangelicals, it has to be said, have often handled Scripture so badly that they have been easily dismissed as naive. Most conservative evangelicals, on the other hand, seem to have been quite unprepared to consider the manifestations in any more than a superficial manner. My own position is that once we recognise that TTB is essentially concerned with ASC-type phenomena, we can begin to detect meaningful parallels within Scripture. Even if it is impossible that this approach will allow us *exactly* to match each Toronto-style phenomenon to a biblical precedent, it does work from the assumption that we are in experientially related territory. Indeed, a basic charismatic pre-supposition is that the Spirit of God operates in the same way now as in biblical times. This is one reason why the Bible is normative for charismatics.

Elsewhere, I have argued that there are points of contact between biblical experiences of the Spirit, which seem to indicate the presence of an ASC, and contemporary experiences.[9] One important biblical example is Peter's trance (Acts 10.9-23). In Luke's account, Peter is situated on the roof of a house at noon. He is praying and becomes hungry. While food is being prepared he falls into a trance (v.10, *ekstasis*),[10] and has a vision accompanied by a voice (vv.11-16). This, especially given its content, leaves Peter puzzled (v.17). Initially the experience is enigmatic and Peter needs further revelation by the Spirit for him to make sense of it.[11] It is my suggestion that he was having an ASC. This becomes rather more plausible when one realises that a typical physiological cause of ASCs is hunger.[12] Peter had a trance experience concerned with food while waiting for a meal. Nevertheless, for the early church it proved to be highly significant. If the hermeneutic key lies in comparing ASC states rather than proof texts, it means that there is perhaps rather more of a biblical link than has previously been established.[13] This does not mean, however, that all manifestations are *ipso facto* authentically Christian. It simply means that the experiential matrix from out of which such claims are made probably has a common basis. From an exegetical perspective, it becomes an important component in the contextual information that is required to interpret any ancient text correctly. Other biblical instances where ASCs may give additional contextual information include: Jacob (Gen. 32:22-32, solitude v.24), Elijah (1 Kgs. 19:9b-18, anxiety, v.10, solitude v.9), Isaiah (Is. 6:1-13, grief and consequent anxiety, since King Uzziah was a good king and Israel had enjoyed peace and security, v.1), Ezekiel (Ezek. 1:1, social and cultural dislocation, v.1), Daniel (Dan. 8:1-14, anxiety and concentration, 7.28), Zechariah (Lk. 1:8-20, incense, v.9), Jesus (Lk. 4:1-13, hunger, v.2), Paul (2 Cor. 12:2-4) and John (Rev. 1:9-11, social dislocation? solitude?, v.9).

The real test, of course, lies in the 'fruit' of the Spirit, not just in the stories of charismatics. For us to judge TTB in terms of

a 'work' of God, we need to ask about such fruit. If real transformation occurs in the lives of Christians, so that they confess
the Lordship of Jesus Christ (1 Cor. 12:3), increase in love for
God and their neighbour,[14] and become more trinitarian-
centred and mission oriented,[15] then ASCs within the Christian
context begin to make sense at the level of consequence (Mt.
7:16-18).

The Place of the 'Blessing' in the Church Today

Although it seems that the distinctive Toronto phenomena have
subsided, there are still examples of them continuing in certain
churches. Personal research using a congregation survey method
in the Merseyside area during 1997 indicated that TTB was still
being widely experienced.[16] There was a statistically significant
correlation between experience of the Blessing and other
charismatic activity, namely: 'prophecy', 'dancing in the Spirit',
'words of wisdom and knowledge', 'answered prayer', 'being led
to perform an action', 'being slain in the Spirit', 'hearing God
through dreams and visions', 'miracle testimony' and 'laughing
in the Spirit'. Further analysis (using a statistical method called
multiple regression) indicated that the key factors most likely to
influence the experience of TTB were: 'laughing in the Spirit',
'being slain in the Spirit' and 'prophecy'. These activities were
experienced with the Pentecostal and charismatic movements
well before TTB, which indicates that certain features most
associated with TTB have perhaps been highlighted as contrib-
utory factors. In frequency terms, 'prophecy' is most common,
followed by 'being slain in the Spirit' and 'laughing in the
Spirit'.

However, both 'laughing' and 'falling over' are understood to be
more significant causal factors for those having experienced the
Blessing. This means that in terms of definition, 'laughing' and
'falling over in the Spirit' are considered to be more closely associated with the umbrella category of TTB than other forms of
charismatic activity measured in the survey.

Outstanding Questions

Revival or Renewal?

The TACF initially preferred to talk in terms of renewal rather than revival, but latterly the language of revivalism has become more prominent.[17] The church was praying for revival when the phenomena 'hit'.[18] I have personally preferred to think of it as renewal. This is because it did/does not seem to (1) touch non-Christians in a massive way; and (2) to impinge upon social structures outside of the church in any significant way.[19] Most people living in Toronto did not seem to know anything about it. It was mostly known via Christian networks. This suggests to me that it is largely a Christian renewal movement.

For a Season?

The Blessing was not new, and the manifestations associated with it were around for most of the 1970s and 1980s. I regard these manifestations as possible human reactions to the presence of the Holy Spirit that could occur at any time and place, given the appropriate conditions. Because TTB was 'caught', i.e. socialised via popular evangelical media, it swept through British evangelicalism. The more recent manifestation of 'gold fillings' is, however, more bizarre.[20] Why does not God do a proper restoration job and renew the tooth? That would surely be more biblical. If certain leaders promote such examples as the best that God is doing at the moment, then charismatic churches are in dire straits. However, this is probably not the case. Despite the claims of TACF, only a small number of churches have made similar testimony in the UK.

The Toronto Blessing was probably for a season only. However, the TACF continue to receive visitors and host conferences for those seeking it. It is certainly the case that manifestations in the UK have subsided, even if they continue to some extent.

Lessons for the Future

The Holy Spirit blows where he wills. We, however, like to control God, either by a form of sacramentalism or a form of legalism. If charismatics think that they have God pocketed through the 'sacramental' action of laughing or falling over,[21] then they will be shocked because God certainly cannot be confined in that way. Likewise, if conservative evangelicals think (unconsciously) that they can make the Holy Spirit into a post-Enlightenment rationalist, they will also be disappointed. God works by means of reason, but he will not be constrained by it (especially fallen human rationalism), since we are called to love God with our hearts as well as our heads.

The main lesson to be gleaned from TTB, and from the debate it prompted, is that God is concerned with the whole person. He is just as much concerned with Western middle-class Christians who may or may not be bored, as with Third World Christians living in poverty. The challenge is for the comfortable to become uncomfortable for the sake of the gospel. The fact that Pentecostals/charismatics are a global ideological force,[22] not least in the Third World, restores my hope in the Lord of creation who is also Saviour and Healer of the whole person.

Notes to Chapter 4

[1] I am grateful to my colleague, Mark Bonnington, for reading and commenting on this paper.

[2] See M.J. Cartledge, 'Tongues of the Spirit: An Empirical-Theological Study of Charismatic Glossolalia'.

[3] M.J. Cartledge, 'Prophecy in the Contemporary Church: A Theological Examination'.

[4] Richter, '"God is not a Gentleman!"', pp. 7-9.

[5] J. Arnott expounds this view in two videos: *Decently and in Order* and *God's Love: Bottom Line*, both produced by TACF.

[6] Dixon, *Signs of Revival*, pp. 266-74. Dixon is a well-respected medical doctor and a charismatic Christian with first-hand experience of TTB. As such, he is well placed to comment on the physiological aspects of charismatic phenomena.

[7] M. Poloma's papers and publications on this issue include: *The Toronto Report: A Preliminary Sociological Assessment of the Toronto Blessing*; 'The Spirit and The Bride: The "Toronto Blessing" and the Church Structure', 26th Annual Meeting of the Society for Pentecostal Studies, Patten College, Oakland, CA, 1997; 'The "Toronto Blessing": Charisma, Insitutionalization and Revival', *Journal for the Scientific Study of Religion*, 36.2 (1997), pp. 257-271; 'Inspecting the Fruit of the "Toronto Blessing": A Sociological Perspective', *PNEUMA: The Journal of the Society for Pentecostal Studies*, 20.1 (1998), pp. 71-84; 'The Spirit Movement in North America at the Millennium: From Azusa Street to Toronto, Pensacola and Beyond', *Journal of Pentecostal Theology* 12 (1998), pp. 83-107.

[8] For example, M. Percy, 'Making Waves: a Perspective on Ministry and Revivalism', *Ministry Today* (RBIM) 8 (1996) pp. 27-37; *Toronto Blessing*, Oxford; 'Sweet Rapture: Subliminal Eroticism in Contemporary Charismatic Worship', *Theology and Sexuality* 6 (1997), pp. 71-106; *Power and the Church: Ecclesiology in an Age of Transition*, pp. 101-20. See also Richter, 'God is not a Gentleman!', pp.5-37; 'The Toronto Blessing: Charismatic Evangelical Global Warming', in S. Hunt et al (eds.), *Charismatic Christianity: Sociological Perspectives*, pp. 97-119. Note, too, S. Hunt, 'The "Toronto Blessing": A Rumour of Angels?', *Journal of Contemporary Religion* 10.3 (1995) pp.257-71.

[9] M.J. Cartledge, 'Interpreting Charismatic Experience: Hypnosis, Altered States of Consciousness and Holy Spirit?', *Journal of Pentecostal Theology* 13 (1998), pp.117-32. For an example of the use of ASC as a 'reading' strategy within the context of the Mediterranean world, see

J.J. Pilch, 'The Transfiguration of Jesus', in P.F. Esler (ed.), *Modelling Early Christianity: Social-Scientific Studies of the New Testament in its Context*, pp. 47-64; cf. D.E. Aune, *Prophecy in Early Christianity and the Ancient Mediterranean World*, pp. 19-20.

[10] Literally, the Greek text says: 'ecstasy came upon him'; so J.D.G. Dunn, *The Acts of the Apostles*, p.137. It is important to note, however, that our popular understanding of ecstasy as being out of control is not necessarily what the word meant in ancient times. In the Bible, the word *ekstasis* appears to have a broad semantic range which includes the notions of distraction, confusion, astonishment and terror, as well as trance: see W. Mundle, 'Ecstasy', in C. Brown (ed.), *Dictionary of New Testament Theology*, Vol. 1., p.527. None of the above connotations necessarily implies loss of control: such an understanding must be inferred from other contextual information. The use of 'ecstasy' by M. Stibbe in relation to contemporary culture is, though, highly problematic; see M. Stibbe, *Times of Refreshing: A Practical Theology of Revival Today*, ch.3, and the sharp retort of L. Pietersen in his edited essay collection, *Mark of the Spirit*, ch.1. I myself prefer to use the language of altered states of consciousness rather than ecstasy, by which I mean a perfectly normal social psychological state between consciousness and unconsciousness, even if the outward appearance of such a state seems strange to the western mind.

[11] M. Turner, *Power from on High: The Spirit in Israel's Restoration and Witness in Luke-Acts*, p.379.

[12] Dixon, *Signs of Revival*, pp. 266-7.

[13] S.E. Porter's critique of existing charismatic justification for the phenomena is, in my view, entirely justified. See 'Shaking the Biblical Foundations?', pp. 38-65.

[14] Poloma, 'By Their Fruit', pp.20-22.

[15] T. Smail et al, 'From "The Toronto Blessing" to Trinitarian Renewal: A Theological Conversation', in *Charismatic Renewal*, pp.152-66.

[16] The survey sampled 29 charismatic churches in the Merseyside area.

[17] A recent visit to their website (http//www.tacf.org) reveals the use of the word 'revival' as a main category label. P. Drnovscek, the assistant to J. Arnott at TACF, indicated that the church uses the terms 'renewal' and 'revival' interchangeably (e-mail correspondence dated 26.11.99).

[18] P. Hocken has argued that the TACF leadership has imbibed a revivalistic framework of understanding which reflects the Baptist and Pentecostal backgrounds of the leadership; see 'Theological Reflections on the "Toronto Blessing"'.

[19] However, Richard Riss constantly argued the case for a revivalist interpretation through his webpage, see: 'Letters in Defence of
Revival', 1994–1995. This webpage was linked to the former
TACF webpage (http://www.grmi.org/TAV, which has become
http://www.tacf.org).

[20] As David Hilborn's Chronicle of TTB in Part II of this book shows,
gold teeth fillings were claimed at TACF meetings from early-mid
March 1999. Their website from this time contained articles, an official statement and photographs of people's mouths with gold/metal
fillings.

[21] I have suggested elsewhere that 'falling over' or 'being slain' can appear
to function in a sacramental sense within a charismatic context. See
my 'Interpreting Charismatic Experience', p.132.

[22] See H. Cox, *Fire from Heaven: The Rise of Pentecostal Spirituality and the
Reshaping of Religion in the Twenty-First Century*; D. Petersen, *Not by
Might Nor by Power: A Pentecostal Theology of Social Concern in Latin
America*.

5

A Mixed Blessing

David Pawson

Introduction

'I don't like that woman, and from all I've said about her I never will.' That comment, overheard on a bus, reminds us that prejudice (literally, pre-judgement) is alive and kicking. It also underlines that presuppositions can direct the course and outcome of any debate. So I had better begin by declaring two of my own.

On the one hand, I believe that biblical theology must be experienced, especially in the realm of pneumatology. It is only too easy to be familiar with the doctrine of the Holy Spirit and remain a stranger to his dynamic.

On the other hand, I believe that all experiences claimed to be of the Holy Spirit need to be tested at the bar of biblical theology. I am a charismatic evangelical, not an evangelical charismatic (the noun is primary, the adjective secondary).

Let me add that I accept many, if not most, of the phenomena associated with TTB as genuine experiences. Some may have been feigned by eager participants or forced by enthusiastic proponents, but by no means all. However, the key issue is not whether they were 'real', but what was their source and significance.

Initially, I declined many requests for my analysis, since I was lacking in experience and limited in observance – although this handicap has not prevented me from speaking about other issues like heaven and hell, drugs and homosexuality. Even in these contexts, however, I have sought, as a Bible teacher, to focus first and foremost on the relevant biblical data. Eventually, I did resolve that it was right to produce a book on TTB, and my ongoing commitment to scriptural understanding was reflected in its title: *Is the Blessing Biblical?*. It is now out of print, interest having faded, though much of its content is relevant to many other situations. My motives for writing were as important as the message.

First, I found it increasingly difficult to turn down so many requests for help in discernment. As a known 'teacher' (some said a 'prophet'!), I was expected to have 'a word' from the Lord about it.

Second, most of the early publications were either all for or all against. I feared polarisation and division due to such contradictory opinions, neither of which I felt was adequate. My own diagnosis was already in terms of a 'mixed' blessing.

Third, I had a 'vision', rare for me but preferable to old men's dreams! I was pondering in my study whether to write the book when, unexpectedly and vividly, I 'saw' a preacher exhorting his congregation to cast off restraint and inhibitions, let themselves go and do whatever they felt like doing to express their release in Christ. Their behaviour became the very opposite of 'decency and order' (cf. 1 Cor. 14:40). Some began to strip off their clothes and dance naked. The preacher then justified this from Scripture. God was restoring the innocence of Adam and Eve, he said, and the 'tabernacle before which David danced naked' (although, in fact, David only stripped to his undergarment, divesting merely his royal robes). The preacher I saw even said that all this was a 'prophetic sign' to the nation, as had been Isaiah's 'streak' through Jerusalem.

I 'came to' in a cold sweat, unable to believe such things could happen. Yet within a short time I had received two reports of exactly such an event. I realised then how dangerous it could be to flout that self-control which is a fruit of the Spirit (Gal. 5: 23)

My deepest horror, however, was at the abuse of Scripture to justify such a situation. I recognised that the same kind of superficial exegesis as had been applied in the vision was already being used to justify the Toronto wave. This exegesis was based on what I would call 'precedents out of context'.

So I wrote *Is the Blessing Biblical?*, although I did not mention the decisive visionary encounter which had prompted it. The book sold well, even reaching the Toronto fellowship itself. Predictably, it was attacked from both sides, as either too critical or too concessionary. But correspondence indicates that it took some heat out of the debate and opened up dialogue, in which I became personally involved. Then again, a few seem to think I contributed to the decline of the 'Move'.

The heart of my thesis was that TTB was, indeed, a mixture of divine, human and demonic activity. I did not hazard a 'guestimate' of the ratio or proportions, but I probably attributed more to the flesh than those who saw it as either almost all divine or all demonic.

I urged caution and discretion. For me, the light was yellow, rather than red or green (though one critic said it was nearer orange!). We need to remember that fleshly substitute and satanic counterfeit appear in the context of the genuinely divine. The great need then is for discernment, springing from a balanced blend of scriptural ground and spiritual gift.

Of course, there were and are those who claim that the Spirit is not bound by Scripture, can do things without precedent in Scripture, and is 'moving us beyond Scripture' (a radical suggestion often now associated with 'postmodernism'). But this writer believes the Spirit who inspired Scripture acts in line and harmony with what he has already revealed of himself, and will not therefore contradict the written Word.

General Problems of Language and Interpretation

As I have indicated, the key issue which arose in regard to TTB was whether its supporters could claim biblical sanction for what they were experiencing and promoting. In calling the characteristic happenings associated with the Blessing 'manifestations', they were invoking a New Testament word linked to the Spirit's work (1 Cor. 12:7). At a stroke, apostolic approval was thereby often implied, discussion foreclosed, and criticism linked with the unforgivable sin of blasphemy against the Holy Ghost (Mk. 3:29; Mt. 12:32; Lk. 12:10). The Bible was ransacked for precedents of unusual behaviour – falling down, leaping about, etc. And yet three aspects of this 'evidence' were widely ignored.

First, the sole use of the word 'manifestations' in relation to the Spirit in 1 Corinthians 12:7 refers to the exercise of supernatural gifts in service to others. Second, physical behaviour in Scripture is typically seen as human reaction rather than divine action (Ezekiel, like Paul and John, fell to the ground when encountering the Lord; he was not pushed over, but was lifted to his feet again by the Spirit). Third, in all the New Testament records of the Spirit coming upon people, there is a noticeable absence of any reference to physical or emotional effects; the result every time is an overflow of the filling from the mouth in some form of 'prophesying', in accordance with Joel's own prophecy of the last days (Joel 2:28). As a footnote to all this, it is worth adding that 'animal' behaviour in the Bible is associated with unclean spirits rather than the Holy Spirit. It is the evidence of divine absence, not divine presence (as with Nebuchadnezzar's experience in Daniel 4).

The slender biblical basis on which TTB advocates rest their case explains two other features of their apologia. One is the development of non-biblical jargon to describe key features of the movement: 'going down under the power', 'resting in the Spirit' (even 'carpet time') and, worst of all, 'slain in the Spirit' (a phrase that ought to be confined to the fate of Ananias and Sapphira in Acts 5:1-11!). The other is the persistent appeal to tradition rather than Scripture – to post-apostolic church history, and to Jonathan Edwards in particular, rather than to the apostle Paul (I shall deal with the church-historical aspect of 'revival' in more detail below).

Mixed Motivations: Psychological, Socio-Cultural and Spiritual

TTB attracted worldwide attention, more perhaps in the UK than any other country. Vast sums were spent on pilgrimages to Canada; others were content to crowd into churches nearer home, where similar things were happening. Why did they go? What were they seeking?

Some wanted a boost for their jaded spirits, especially if they had suffered a 'burn-out' in Christian service. Others, yearning for revival in flagging churches, hoped that this would be its harbinger. Some came out of curiosity, with an open mind; a few came in hostility, with a closed mind. God alone knows what a variety of motives lay behind the pilgrimages.

But one basic quest was common. All but the most hardened cynics were looking for tangible evidence of God's presence, and were hoping to see this in others and feel it for themselves. They desired a 'real' and meaningful experience of the Lord.

Critics have dismissed this as a product of our age – as 'existentialist' and 'postmodern'. Certainly there is a contemporary obsession with new experiences, the more sensational the better – particularly in 'youth culture'. The embrace of romanticism in reaction to rationalism goes back two hundred years or so. But the reliance on 'feelings' as the touchstone of reality is relatively new. Physical sensations now play a major role in discovering the meaning and value of life. Yet these pall with repetition, leading to an obsession with novelty, and a susceptibility to passing fads or fashions. The 'drug culture' is not limited to chemical stimulants. TTB has been dismissed as yet another 'ecstatic' response to postmodernity, albeit in a Christian guise, and could well be said to reflect this both in the initial enthusiasm it provoked, and in its fairly rapid decline. But this is ultimately a superficial analysis which risks missing the key question: whether there is a genuine encounter with the eternal that is the reality we really need as creatures made in the image of God, and of which so many contemporary 'experiences' are substitutes or counterfeits.

Epistemological and Pneumatological Concerns

Consideration of the motives which people brought to TTB raises the related issue of epistemology, or how we gain knowledge – and in this case, knowledge of God's presence in particular. Since this presence is mediated through the Holy Spirit, epistemology must here also interact with pneumatology and spirituality.

Should we seek a meeting with God that is primarily evident to our *senses*, or should we rely principally on our reason and intellect? From here on I shall use the word 'sensate' (which the Oxford English Dictionary defines as 'perceived by the senses', and chiefly by sight and hearing). Is such a sensate encounter a normal or even a valid experience? Once we broach this question we find ourselves inevitably concerned with the Christian doctrine of assurance. There is a clear biblical basis for believing that the heavenly Father wants his children to *know* that they have been brought from death to life, that their sins are forgiven, that they are on 'the Way' of salvation and, above all, that he loves them and wants to bless them. He wants them to be sure of all this and more. Such confidence is not in dispute. What is debated is the nature of such 'knowledge'. How, exactly, are we to know these things?

The traditional evangelical answer is based on syllogisms – logical deductions from major and minor premises. Immediate assurance is based on the profession of *faith* ('The Bible says it; you believe it; that settles it'). Ultimate assurance is based on the production of *fruit* ('You are more loving; love is a fruit of the Spirit; you must have the Spirit'). Note that in neither case is the knowledge immediate or direct; it is, rather, the conclusion of a mental process which may or may not be convincing. Significantly, this kind of assurance is associated with appeals to 'receive Christ' – a notion alien to post-Pentecost apostolic preaching, which had urged hearers to repent toward God, believe in Christ, be baptised in water and 'receive the gift of the Holy Spirit'.

Some go further and offer an intense awareness as the privilege of believers. This intense awareness is often described as the 'inward witness' of the Spirit. Proponents of such a view characteristically appeal to Romans 8.16: 'The Spirit himself testifies with our spirit that we are God's children.' From this they infer that 'assurance' must be internal and 'spiritual', not external and sensate. To expect evidence of the latter kind, they say, borders on the sensual, suggesting, as it does, immature carnal and fleshly desires.

Actually, this 'inward witness' approach owes more to Greek philosophy than the predominantly Hebrew thought-forms of the Bible. Indeed, there is a greater emphasis on 'seeing and hearing' in Scripture than many would care to admit. The 'spiritual' view of assurance tends, for example, to ignore the fact that the Greek verb translated 'testify' in Romans 8:16, *krazein*, denotes an involuntary crying *out* (cf. Mk. 6:49). In fact, *every* reception of the Holy Spirit recorded in the New Testament is accompanied by audible and visible evidence, making the event clear and definite to recipient and observer alike.

By contrast to all this, many evangelical expositors have tried to portray these events as atypical, abnormal and unique. They present them as time-specific 'little Pentecosts' which marked once for all the incorporation of new ethnic groups into the covenant: Samaritans in Acts 8 and Gentiles in Acts 10. (John's disciples in Acts 19 are usually dismissed as an anachronism). Yet a more careful reading of these chapters reveals a different picture. What these three groups experienced was in fact normal to all other 'disciples' in the early church.

The Samaritan episode recounted in Acts 8 makes quite clear that it is perfectly possible:

- to repent, believe and be baptised without receiving the Spirit;
- to know that the Spirit has not been received;
- to observe when the Spirit is being received.

The key to these conclusions is found in verses 15 and 16 (the literal translation of the Greek is: 'who, going down, prayed concerning them so as they might receive Spirit Holy, for not yet was he not any one of them having fallen on ...'). In simple English: if the Spirit has not yet 'fallen on' someone, they have not yet received the Holy Spirit. This means that the Spirit had fallen on all other disciples up to this point, and that the Samaritans were an exception to the rule. Prayer with the laying-on of hands was the remedy for this deficiency. Once this had happened, the Spirit did fall on them and Simon saw it happening, person by person.

So what does 'fall on' mean here? It does not mean to repent, believe or be baptised. Is there another context in which it is described? Yes – it is used of Cornelius and his household when they 'spoke in tongues and praised God' (Acts 10:46; 11:15, which use the same verb: *pipto*). Three times Peter would justify his venture among Gentiles by pointing out that their experience of the Spirit was identical to that of all other disciples, including the brothers from Joppa (10:47), the circumcised believers (11:15) and the apostles and elders in Jerusalem, together with 'the whole church' (15:8,22). That it was a sensate event seems confirmed by the strong synonyms used to describe it: 'baptised in' (lit. plunged, drenched), 'filled with', 'poured out upon', 'come upon'. It is difficult to accept that all this could happen without a person being fully aware of it happening. Significantly, evangelicals who hold to a non-sensate reception of the Spirit avoid such language.

Such sensate events are the basic ground of assurance in the New Testament. 'We know ... because he has given us of his Spirit' (1 Jn. 4.13; 3.24, where the verbs indicate a past activity). This is the biblical syllogism which underlines true assurance: only God's children receive the Spirit ('the world cannot accept him', (Jn. 14.17)); he has given you the Spirit; you are a child of God. But that is where the logic stops. The apostles would have been astonished to be asked how anyone might know that they have been given the Spirit. Anyone asking this would have been presumed not to have received it. Paul's questions to the Ephesian disciples (Acts 19:2), and to his Galatian converts (Gal. 3:2), clearly assume that they knew perfectly well whether and when they had 'received Holy Spirit'. The event was taken to be self-evident. It was a bedrock of sensate experience on which other implications and applications could be based.

Here, then, was an authentic encounter with the living God, a sensate experience granted to penitent and baptised believers, a token of God's *presence* and a confirmation of disciples' sonship in him. At the same time, it gave them an anointing with his *power*, enabling them to be fully saved themselves, and to serve others effectively. Such was the event known as 'receiving' or 'being baptised in' the Holy Spirit in the New Testament.

Now what has all this got to do with Toronto? For one thing, it offers a biblical standard by which current experiences may be tested. Could TB exponents genuinely apply to the Blessing the 'This is that' designation applied by Peter to the phenomena of Pentecost in respect of the signs promised by God through his prophets? (Acts 2:16; cf. Joel 2:28-32). Such a link was strikingly absent from much Toronto advocacy, and such mention of Spirit baptism as arose in relation to the Blessing tended to be ambiguous. Why this anomaly? It was not an oversight. The answer lies in the history of the 'renewal' movement. TTB did not spring out of nothing. It had a genealogy. It had roots.

The Historical Context of Pentecostal and Charismatic Renewal

One of the roots of TTB went back to the beginning of the twentieth century. On 1st January 1901 (the true first day according to Dionysius' Anno Domini calendar), a group of students at Charles Fox Parham's Bible School in Topeka, Kansas rediscovered the authentic encounter with God described in Scripture as being 'baptised in Holy Spirit'. As part of this experience, they spoke in 'tongues' (the Greek word *glossolalia* means 'languages' with grammar and syntax, not meaningless babbling). From this small beginning sprang the 'Pentecostal' movement, which is now widely described as 'the third force in Christendom' alongside the 'catholic' and 'evangelical', and which is almost certain to be the main stream of Christianity in the twenty-first century. For its first fifty years the Pentecostal movement was largely rejected by existing churches and was expressed in new denominations. Then, in the 1960s, it found its way into mainline churches, both Protestant and Catholic. Experience of the Spirit and exercise of spiritual gifts became increasingly acceptable in these contexts, with advocates being dubbed 'neo-Pentecostals'. This development was only one among many other major changes within historic denominations, as they struggled to adapt to a rapidly changing world.

For all its influence upon them, classical Pentecostal teaching about Spirit baptism began to be questioned by a number of neo-Pentecostals as the movement spread within the mainline churches. Three elements in particular were challenged: the view that Spirit baptism occurred subsequent to conversion, as a 'second blessing' unrelated to initiation; the view that it had no connection with being saved, and was instead a means of power for service; and the view that the definitive and acceptable evidence of it was speaking in tongues. In the absence of a coherent alternative more firmly rooted in the biblical data, emphasis on Spirit baptism duly began to fade. The label 'neo-Pentecostal' gave way to 'charismatic', which only referred to spiritual gifts.

As a result of these developments, many 'renewal' leaders reverted to the traditional evangelical stance that all believers are 'baptised in the Spirit' (though the term is hardly ever used) at the moment of believing, whether this is accompanied by any inward experience and outward evidence or not. Indeed, this stance allows that Spirit baptism could happen without the recipient even being aware of it.

As the Chronicle presented in Part II of this book shows, this trend was brought to a climax by the ministry of John Wimber, backed by the writings of his friend and academic mentor Peter Wagner. Wimber was convinced that the evangelical world would welcome the gifts of the Spirit if they were separated from any 'baptism' in the Spirit (which he himself had never experienced). In this he had considerable success, and as a result of his ministry many evangelicals were happy to be called 'charismatic'. But it left a vacuum in spiritual experience. Denied baptism in the Holy Spirit, the valid hunger for sensate experience of the supernatural was now vulnerable to the offer of sub-biblical experiences, ranging from the banal to the bizarre. It cannot be mere coincidence that the Toronto Airport Fellowship was one of Wimber's congregations, and one of the first to embrace the unusual behaviour which made TTB so controversial. As the Chronicle goes on to show, Wimber had increasing problems with his offspring, leading to an eventual break. Whether he realised that his own deliberate neglect of Spirit baptism, and his preference for a model of 'power evangelism' based on the pre-Pentecostal healing and deliverance ministry of the disciples rather than on the broader pneumatic mission of the early church recorded in Acts 2, had prepared the way for what was happening, I do not know. But I believe that it was one of the major factors in the emergence of TTB. There were others.

The intense interest in, and rapid spread of, TTB can also be attributed to growing expectancy of an 'end-time revival' within charismatic evangelicalism. This arose on the fringes of the movement, but shifted steadily towards the centre in the period leading up to TTB. As the Chronicle confirms, the eccentric eschatology of 'Latter Rain' and 'Manifest Sons of God' teaching had some influence here, but the major cause of expectancy was, I believe, a series of disappointments within the renewal itself. The hope that the older denominations would be transformed was not realised: by the 1980s and 90s, it had become clear that charismatics would at best be tolerated, even if their music was being widely used! Many formed or joined new 'house' fellowships, hoping that these would constitute a 'restoration' of the church to its true apostolic state, but these came increasingly to resemble more established congregations. The hope lingered on that the church of the last days would be perfected in unity, power and holiness; it would come to rule the nations in peace and justice. It was obvious that the various 'waves' of renewal (firstly Pentecostalism, secondly, the charismatic movement and thirdly Wimber's 'signs and wonders' approach) had not achieved this. A sovereign intervention of God was the only way it could be brought about. Prayer for revival began in earnest.

Ardent longing is prone to seize on any sign of what is sought, and then to exaggerate its significance. I detect this in the eagerness with which any 'move of God' is talked about, often with the unspoken thought: 'Is this IT? The BIG ONE? The revival that we need and have been promised?' TTB fitted this syndrome, as the Pensacola outpouring would later. Both were hailed as harbingers of revival, the showers that heralded the downpour. But the downpour has not materialised and this has led to further disappointment, even disillusion.

The Status of 'Revival'

Bearing the historical context I have just outlined in mind, it is important to realise that the New Testament does not, in fact, contain a theology of revival. Nor was this because the churches were then 'in a state of revival'. Corinth was certainly not. Other letters of Paul, Peter, John and Jesus himself (in Rev. 2-3) were written to deal with the problems of belief and behaviour which accompany real life. The verse most often cited by Toronto advocates to link the Blessing to the end-time was Acts 3:19, with its report of Peter's phrase, 'times of refreshing'. If 'the Old Testament is the dictionary of the New', the times referred to here must mean periods of respite from God's wrath and judgement. Yet the phrase is now more usually applied to much later bursts of intense spiritual activity within church history, especially during the last three centuries.

Such 'revivals' are usually brief, though they leave lasting fruit. Whether they represent 'normal' church life is open to question. Whether a revival is the answer to our problems depends on who is responsible for the current state of church and nation. Has God withdrawn his resources from us, or is he waiting for us to make proper use of them? New Testament churches which had fallen into a parlous condition were not told to pray for revival, but to practise repentance.

Conclusion

Leaving aside arguments about whether it should be described as 'revival', 'renewal', 'refreshing' or something more pernicious, TTB clearly did not prove to be a new dawn. That does not mean that it is to be written off. Far from it. But it does mean a more sober analysis needs to be made – something which should perhaps be easier now that the excitement has abated. There are lessons to be learned, both positive and negative. I have not had reason to revise my earlier published assessment; I am still being attacked from both sides for taking the 'middle ground', or, as some say, 'nailing my colours to the fence'! I still see the Blessing as a mixture of divine, fleshly and demonic activity.

I meet those who have been genuinely blessed by God as a result of Toronto, the proof not to be found in what happened to them at the time, but in their walk with the Lord since. Nor does this demonstrate divine approval of the circumstances in which they found TTB. The Lord is so gracious and generous that he will bless those who sincerely seek him, even if they do so in questionable ways (I think here of the hem of Jesus' garment, Peter's shadow and Paul's sweatband, none of which should be developed into a technique for ministry). It would be a stony heart that could not rejoice with those who rejoice.

I also meet those for whom the experience was of the flesh, either because of external manipulation or auto-suggestion. Such things do neither good nor harm and they are prone to fade until lost without trace. They only do damage when persons feel the need to seek repeated 'topping up' experiences of the same kind and thereby become vulnerable to serious exploitation.

Further, I have met those whose spiritual progress has been halted by their involvement, and others who have needed 'deliverance' from the after-effects of what was a disturbing and debilitating experience. To have been led into ridiculous and demeaning behaviour can be traumatic. It can also be demonic.

Some years ago I expressed the hope that we would see Word and Spirit integrated, as they were in the New Testament. I set out this hope in a book called *Fourth Wave*, which has been now re-issued as *Word and Spirit Together* – mainly because the original title has been applied to TTB! Now I fear that Word and Spirit are drifting apart again, with some seeking the Spirit but less interested in Scripture; others are returning to the Bible but shying away from direct encounters with the Spirit. At least part of the blame for this sad situation must be laid at the door of the events associated with Toronto.

We must press on to that maturity which is not easily tossed about by every gust of teaching, and which resists seeking the latest 'word' from the Lord or the most exciting 'move' of his Spirit. There is a need for the solid foundation of the knowledge of God, based on knowledge of his Word and the dynamic experience of his Spirit.

6

An Altered Christian Consciousness

Dr Patrick Dixon

Introduction

Writing this has been a difficult task. It is hard to sit in judgement on a controversial movement which has resulted in tens of thousands declaring that their faith in Christ, passion for prayer and commitment to evangelism have been strengthened.

Even after seven years, it is not easy to understand the full impact of TTB. The measurement of that impact (both negative and positive) is still likely to be largely subjective. The ultimate test is the fruit in people's lives – but how does one assess such fruit in concrete terms? Beyond the sort of case study-based sociological work done by Margaret Poloma and presented elsewhere in this volume, rigorous scientific analysis is difficult. There are too many factors at work.

A cut-and-dried justification or damnation of every aspect of what occurred on the basis of Scripture is also likely to fail, for several reasons. First, as we shall see, it is very hard to generalise about what happened, not least because many second-hand observations were based on myths. Second, as a matter of integrity, the degree of rigour which we apply to Toronto ought also to apply to every other aspect of church life, e.g. to forms of worship, women speaking in church, church government or denominational structures.

Few churches today would dare claim that in every respect their day-to-day life exactly reflects the pattern of the early church. Indeed, the very idea of different 'churches' in the same town or city is impossible to support from Scripture. There is one church, one body, one bride, one great community of all who love God, who are called according to his purpose. On all these matters, we are faced with huge issues of interpretation and application.

We each see only in part; we understand only in part until we see God face to face. We are wise therefore to soften those of our statements on scriptural interpretation which are not central to salvation or personal morality, recognising that however certain we may be of our case, our attitude itself can be proud, arrogant and offensive to our Creator. Who are we to be so sure of the mind of God, when others find themselves forced to a different view, having carefully examined in context the same biblical texts and arguments?

Two Myths

For the sake of future historians, let us at least get today's facts right, and deal first with two of the greatest myths which surrounded the Toronto movement.

Loss of Control

Many who claim to have been touched by God have spoken of losing control, involuntary movements, falling and other phenomena. This has been deeply worrying to those who believe that being 'out of control' is contrary to Scripture and contrary to the will of God.

As a doctor, I have been particularly insistent on exploring this apparent psychomotor failure. I have never yet seen an instance of 'involuntary movement' or loss of muscle power in TTB that did not stop instantly on challenge. People have claimed that they have been unable to stand, or indeed to get up, or have described being fixed or rooted to the floor, almost as if paralysed, or being affected by 'uncontrollable' shaking. However, all I have questioned readily admit that they would have got up and left the building immediately if a fire had broken out, with no untoward effects whatever. People say that they could not help falling, that they could not physically stand. Yet invariably they have told me that they did make a voluntary decision about whether to 'let go'. Indeed, this is obvious from the very low number of injuries, as a proportion of the vast number of 'falls' that occurred. The 'loss of control' myth was sometimes promoted by those who had an experience, and who expressed themselves in language which was often emotionally charged and scientifically imprecise. Yet is it such an odd thing that someone totally overwhelmed with an intense understanding of the nearness, or the holiness, or the love and forgiveness of God should be affected not just in spirit and in mind, but also in emotion and in physical response? We are whole beings.

A more accurate account would perhaps run as follows: 'As I stood when prayed for, I felt an intense sense of the presence of God, which caused me to feel physically weak to the point where it would have been a great relief to have sat down, to have knelt or to have lain down on the floor. There came a point where I relaxed, knowing others were around and behind me, and allowed myself to fall.'

The Blessing also prompted a strange controversy about whether it is more holy to fall forwards or backwards in the presence of God. Both positions are valid places of worship, whether looking up to be reminded of the glory of God, or looking down in shame at our humanity. To suggest otherwise would imply that it is impossible or inappropriate ever to pray or worship while resting on one's bed, or lying on the ground. Such an implication would clearly be absurd.

Animal Noises

Press accounts of TTB often dwelt on reports of people making various animal noises. Once again, this led to concern that these things could be a sign either of soulish emotionalism or, worse still, of demonic activity.

Since TTB emerged, I have attended a great number of meetings where phenomena have been taking place, in groups ranging from ten to five thousand. Yet in none of these gatherings have I ever heard a human being imitate an animal. If this manifestation has happened at all, it must have been very rare. I have also questioned some who have been deeply involved in Toronto-style phenomena, and they have the same answer. So what has powered the 'animal noise' myth?

Many, in the heat of the moment, have cried out in various ways with inarticulate noises, but not with the barking of a dog, the baa-ing of a sheep, the cry of a cock crowing, the moo of a cow. Some have talked of the symbolic roaring of a lion – but then most loud groans sound like a roar of some kind. The image of a zoo or farmyard inside churches influenced by TTB was far from reality and was, perhaps, based more on distorted second-hand accounts than on direct observation.

Assessing Reality: The Nature of Christian Experience

The truth is that perhaps over three hundred thousand people in Britain alone would say today that in some way they were touched by what they believe to have been an intense experience of God's presence and power during 1994-1996. No doubt, this experience was often perceived as unusual. But for the vast majority there were no physical consequences whatsoever.

Most of those affected by the Blessing to whom I have talked would say that as an immediate result of it they felt closer to God. Their faith was strengthened, not least in the area of intercessory prayer. They felt strengthened and encouraged in their Christian discipleship. Many have also told me that the process was to some degree traumatic, because it highlighted areas of sin and disobedience that required repentance and immediate action. Other church leaders have described how TTB enabled intractable pastoral issues to be resolved rapidly, and of how it allowed difficult character issues to be dealt with effectively. In particular, they have described the release of emotion associated with the Blessing as a helpful catharsis, e.g. for the assuaging of unexpressed grief. Furthermore, many have testified to the strongly therapeutic effect of laughter, which has itself occurred in response to a relief of guilt, a recognition of forgiveness and new life, and a fresh sense of light-heartedness which has counterbalanced an over-ponderous, serious or even depressed mental state.

Of course, when such a large number of people, all of them subject to human failings, experience so intense an encounter with God, problems do inevitably ensue. The more dramatic the experience, the more likely it is that the person will want everyone else to share it. Where the Blessing was concerned, focus was all too easily centred on the outward effects experienced by some, rather than on the inward transformation which took place in many more. Visible effects on the body came to be seen as a hallmark of God's favour. This placed damaging pressures on those who, by dint of God's mysterious ways, or through difference in temperament, were profoundly blessed in the depths of their being, but who did not display any outward sign of that blessing.

As a consequence of all this, some began to seek a sign rather than an inner work of grace. Mature teaching and godly direction in many cases prevented excesses, but other church leaders created (usually unwittingly) expectations which were at best unfortunate, and at worst dangerous. It became clear that the spectrum of manifestations in any particular gathering could be hugely influenced by the testimonies or comments of those who had led or preached earlier in the same meeting. It also became clear that the collective atmosphere of Toronto-style meetings provoked some to purely soulish reactions. Disinhibition was widespread. In most cases it was mild and inoffensive, but occasionally it meant that someone would have to be removed from the meeting.

It is a fact that in any large gathering of, say, one thousand people, a significant number will be mentally ill, or will be suffering from various personality disorders. It only takes one person who is psychotic with severe delusions to create a difficult situation. Most ordinary church services are so ordered that those who are mentally unwell feel constrained. But where manifestations are prevalent, disruption will be far more likely. This also applies to those who wander in off the street drunk, or who are high on drugs. It applies, too, to those who react strongly to Christian faith and teaching, perhaps due to heavy involvement in occult practices. However, it is foolish to judge the impact on the spiritual lives of 995 people by the loud, disruptive and clearly soulish or satanic interruptions of just five others.

A more constructive approach to the experience of TTB would draw on the insights of medical science in general, and of psychology and psychiatry in particular. These disciplines help us to understand the state of mind in which a mystic sees a vision, or in which a charismatic Christian feels overwhelmed by the intensity of God's nearness, as in TTB.

The human brain is able to oscillate between two kinds of wakefulness, or states of consciousness. One of these states seems to be the place where the majority of people find the most profound experience of God. The first state is normal wakefulness, such as is experienced when driving or sitting an examination. The second is a so-called 'altered state of consciousness' (ASC). This occurs when, for example, a person allows classical music to 'communicate' images and emotions. An ASC can also occur, however, when someone finds himself or herself in a 'twilight zone' between waking and sleeping. Medical research shows that certain things encourage altered states of consciousness, and it is these commonly recognised 'prompts' which shed significant light on the phenomena associated with TTB. Altered states of consciousness can be characterised by some or all of the following to a greater or lesser degree. All, however, are dominated by a sense of the temporal dropping away, so that one becomes more aware of a spiritual dimension in life:

1. Alterations in thinking – disturbances in concentration, attention, memory and judgement.
2. An altered sense of time.
3. Feelings of weakness and dizziness.
4. Changes in emotional expression, e.g. rapid switching between ecstasy, tears and laughter.
5. Body image changes (e.g. 'My limbs felt so huge, they seemed rooted to the floor').
6. Perceptual changes – increased visual imagery, heightened sensory awareness.
7. Changes of meaning or significance, including feelings of profound insight and illumination.
8. A sense of the ineffable, making it finally impossible to express what has happened in words.

9. Feelings of rejuvenation – hope, renaissance and new birth.
10. Hypersuggestibility – a heightened susceptibility to the influence and opinions of other people.

One immediately recognises some of the above in the manifestations which came to distinguish TTB. Typical testimonies from those involved included the following sentiments: 'I was caught up in a different world'; 'It was as if time stood still'; 'I could hardly move or stand'; 'One moment I was laughing at the relief of God's amazing forgiveness; the next overwhelmed with tears at the suffering of the world'; 'Everything seemed so intense'; 'It was as if I could hear God speaking'; 'I felt I could see angelic beings in the room'; I saw my own destiny and calling'; 'Afterwards, I could not explain adequately what I had seen'; 'It was as if my faith was being completely restored'; 'I was caught up in what was happening to others around me'.

One also recognises parallels with some of the above in Scripture. Examples would be Paul's perception of a 'third heaven' (2 Cor. 12:2-4), Peter's odd comments about building shelters at the transfiguration (Mt. 17:1-3 and par.), and his subsequent trance and vision on the way to Joppa (Acts 10: 3-6, 9-16), as well as John's 'revelation' of heaven opened (Rev. 1:10ff.).

Some have ascribed various Toronto phenomena to group hypnosis or suggestibility. The group effect is undoubtedly important, but has been overstated. I have seen no medical evidence of individual or mass hysteria, but much of group influence. This is inevitable, unavoidable and often perfectly normal. There is a group dynamic in all social activity, from a family meal to a football match. All Christian gatherings exert crowd power: those who attend will often be influenced by others in the congregation or audience. We often realise this most starkly when we encounter church services in different countries or denominations.

We are clearly commanded in Scripture not to neglect meeting together, in recognition that group dynamics are an essential feature of normal Christian living (Heb 10:25). However, we do need to recognise that someone in an altered conscious state may well be unusually open to suggestion; this requires maturity and responsibility on the part of counsellors, as well as those leading meetings.

Of course, the primary trigger of an altered state of consciousness for a Christian can be the direct, overwhelming activity of the Holy Spirit, as seen in Acts 2. How can a frail, feeble human frame possibly contain this Pentecostal encounter with God without some alteration in thinking, some disturbance in normal concentration, some effect on the physical nervous system, some emotional reaction, some perceptual change, some sense of profound insight which is ultimately beyond explanation, some feeling of rejuvenation, or some mental openness to what God has to say? We are, after all whole people, mind, heart, body and soul. Indeed, the spiritual dimension of life in particular is always likely to be experienced, to one degree or another, in an altered state of consciousness. Doubtless, such an encounter can be expected to be more probable in someone who is a prayerful and faithful follower of Jesus Christ. However, Scripture also describes extraordinary, overwhelming experiences of God in those who have been far from the way – not least Saul on the Road to Damascus (Acts 9:1-9).

Research shows that, God apart, certain human situations and conditions make altered conscious states more likely:

1. Fasting. This slows brain function, causing the person fasting to feel more detached from data arriving through the eyes, ears and other sensory organs, but able to move more readily into a spiritually receptive frame of mind. Perhaps this is one reason why Jesus practised and encouraged the habit (Mt. 4:2; 6:16-18).
2. Reduction of sensory stimulation, e.g. total social isolation or withdrawal of other stimuli, such as light.
3. Increased sensory stimulation. When the nervous system is bombarded with light, sound, touch or extreme emotion, the brain can 'blow a fuse', becoming incapable of processing all the data presented to it. In such circumstances, it will often 'shut down' into an altered conscious state.
4. Increased alertness or concentration, e.g. when writing intensely or participating in sport. In such instances, the door bell often goes unheard, or an injury is not felt until after the match.

5. Decreased alertness or mental relaxation, e.g. in day dreaming, sunbathing or reflecting nostalgically on the past.
6. Body chemistry alterations, through, for example, drug-taking, alcohol ingestion, hyperventilation.

Once again, some or all of these factors may have operated in Toronto-style gatherings. The key question which then arises is whether their presence should necessarily be viewed as invalidating such gatherings from a biblical or doctrinal perspective. The answer to this question must surely be that they do not, even if we should be aware of their potential effects and even if we should realise that what passes for a genuine experience of God might, in fact, have a purely psychological basis.

Repetition of a familiar, much loved liturgical prayer, meditation on a beautiful stained glass window, watching waves breaking on the shore, solitary contemplation on a mountain-top – all these are widely regarded as helpful means to heightening spiritual awareness. Speaking in tongues also 'shuts down' the logical language part of the brain and encourages a mental switch, which may explain why so many charismatics find it helpful in facilitating a fresh awareness of God's presence. Jesus himself sought out contexts in which he would be best able to attune himself spiritually, whether in fasting, solitude, or mountain ascents (Mt. 4:2-4, 14:13, 23; 26:36-46; Mk. 1:35; 6:31; Lk. 5:16; 6:12).

Altered states of consciousness are, then, a normal part of everyday life in one way or another; they are an almost universal part of Christian experience, uniting believers from many different traditions and cultures. They provide both positive and negative explanations of some of the more puzzling aspects of events related to TTB. The age in which we live places great value on experiences that take us out of our normal view of the world and which thereby orient us to a more spiritual outlook. This cultural trend was clearly an important factor in the spread of the Toronto Blessing. In and of itself, however, it should be taken neither as a reason to damn the Blessing outright, nor to affirm it uncritically. Rather, the crucial test of the Blessing is this: what was the longer term (one to five year) impact on the Christian lives of those who claimed to have been deeply touched by it?

Longer Term Consequences

As we have seen, for the vast majority it appears that the intense perceived experience of God's presence in TTB was episodic and temporary, usually lasting an hour or two at a time over a period of days or weeks. Even so, it was taken to be strongly beneficial. Many have told me that in the years that have passed it has been more common for them to feel particularly empowered in prayer or Christian service.

Those whose experience of God was very acute commonly reported a sense of anti-climax in the months that followed their encounter with TTB. At the time, they knew that life could not carry on at such a pace, with the number of meetings and prayer times threatening to overwhelm other aspects of life. Nevertheless, when things settled down, people often felt a little low, and in the worst cases were disorientated, confused and left wondering what it had all been about.

In a small minority of cases, 'over-indulgence' in highly emotional meetings created a mental brittleness. I have seen a few 'spiritual junkies' who travelled vast distances and attended large numbers of meetings in a constant but ultimately doomed quest to relive a recent ecstatic state. Although it cannot be proved, anecdotal experience suggests that such people have since been at an increased risk of making uncharacteristic, foolish or precipitate decisions, rejecting aspects of their previous lives, and even (if rarely) their faith.

Sometimes entire churches lost focus, e.g. abandoning evangelism in the mistaken belief that the Blessing was itself sufficiently evangelistic. It does appear, however, that this balance is now being restored.

Almost universally among those impacted, there has come a recognition that receiving is for service. They have realised that God blesses his people in order to empower and equip them; they have resolved that since the season for receiving has passed, it is now time to work practically with renewed faith, energy, purpose and vision.

We live in a third-millennium culture that prizes life-changing experience above rational argument. Trying to reason someone to a point of commitment to Christ on the basis of the evidence for the resurrection is so 'last-century'. For some it undoubtedly still works very well, but for a growing number who believe first by intuition, it means little.

One lasting effect of TTB has been that tens of millions of believers around the world have shifted one step further towards a combination of Word and Spirit, a synthesis based on sound doctrine and spirituality. For others, already firmly committed to experience, the recent debates have been a healthy reminder that all Christian experience must be grounded in biblical truth.

Toronto polarised the church towards two extreme positions: it often appeared to force people to be either 'pro' or 'anti' emotional experience in church meetings. But both extremes are unrepresentative of the vast majority. It is rare indeed to meet an evangelical who upholds the centrality of scriptural truth while denying the importance of any experience whatever. It is also almost unknown to find one who has no interest in what the Bible says and is only interested in experiencing God's power.

The middle ground on which our unity rests is the recognition that we have been saved by faith as unworthy recipients of God's favour, forgiven through the sacrificial death of Christ, granted eternal life through the resurrection, given Scripture as a unique gift from God revealing his character and purpose, and offered an intimate relationship with God through faith in his Son. Our common and urgent calling is to spread the good news, make a difference and see God's kingdom come. This new millennium is a great open door. Life is far too short to bicker over secondary issues.

7

A Reconfiguration of Pentecostalism

Margaret Poloma

But a Pharisee named Gamaliel, a teacher of the law, who was honoured by all the people, stood up in the Sanhedrin and ordered that the men be put outside for a little while. Then he addressed them: 'Men of Israel, consider carefully what you intend to do to these men. Some time ago Theudas appeared, claiming to be somebody, and about four hundred men rallied to him. He was killed, all his followers were dispersed, and it all came to nothing. After him, Judas the Galilean appeared in the days of the census and led a band of people in revolt. He too was killed, and all his followers were scattered. Therefore, in the present case I advise you: Leave these men alone! Let them go! For if their purpose or activity is of human origin, it will fail. But if it is from God, you will not be able to stop these men; you will only find yourselves fighting against God.'

(Acts 5:34–39, NIV)

Introduction

As a sociologist who has been involved with TTB since late 1994, I welcome the opportunity provided here to reflect on it, now that the flood of discussion and controversy has subsided. Too much of the early material published on the Blessing failed to reflect the wisdom of Gamaliel's advice to the Sanhedrin. As I write this article, over six years have passed since the inception of the refreshing/renewal/revival that began in a small Vineyard church just outside the Toronto International Airport on 20th January 1994, and then so quickly spread to the UK and around the world. The time is now ripe for more serious reflection.

I write not as a theologian, but as a sociologist who attempts to use her research and perspective to contribute a kind of 'empirical theology' or 'theosociology' on our topic of interest. As a sociologist, I have played the role of a participant observer of the larger Pentecostal/Charismatic (P/C) movement for over two decades, and I view the latest happenings as waves that have once again revitalised the P/C movement. As an approach to Christianity that is heavily dependent on personal and corporate religious experience, the P/C movement requires ongoing revitalisation lest it lose its charisma. Yesterday's manna will not sustain the movement against the forces of routinisation that prowl the modern world. Providentially, the manna arrives with regularity at local churches around the globe, with some outbursts of charismata spreading far beyond any single locality. To switch metaphors, the waves of refreshing continue to come. It matters little for the purposes of this sociological discussion whether these waves are termed 'renewal' (as with TTB in North America), 'refreshing' (as in the UK) or 'revival' (as in the Pensacola Outpouring at Brownsville Assembly of God, which followed on from Toronto and which is detailed in the Chronicle which forms Part II of this book).[1] All these developments together represent the latest example of the revitalisation accompanying the major waves that have been part of P/C history since its founding nearly a century ago. TTB will undoubtedly take its place along side other revivals in P/C history, including the Azusa Street and Welsh revivals of the early twentieth century, the Latter Rain and Healing Movement of the mid-twentieth century, the spread of Pentecostalism in the mainline churches during the 1960s and 1970s, and the so-called 'Third Wave' which popularised a range of fresh experience during the 1980s and 1990s. It was out of this Third Wave, of course, that the river of renewal known as the 'Toronto Blessing' began its course.

The names of John Wimber and John Arnott are inseparably linked to TTB. It was Wimber, founder of the Association of Vineyard Churches (AVC), who proved to be the prominent voice in the so-called Third Wave of the P/C movement, whose style of worship and ministry helped to shape Arnott's own ministry, and whose earlier tilling of the P/C soil in the UK provided ground for TTB's rapid spread across the Atlantic. As a Vineyard pastor and regional leader in Canada, Arnott's quest for ongoing renewal, ministry style and P/C orientation reflected that of Wimber and the AVC. Wimber's later dissociation from the Blessing (after earlier endorsing John Arnott's book *The Father's Blessing*, parts of which were used later as 'evidence' against the Blessing) quenched some of the enthusiastic Third Wave support for it, adding further fuel to existing controversy surrounding the renewal.

Each revival movement carries within it the seeds of controversy and opposition, nurtured both by those outside the larger movement and by many predecessors within it. Nevertheless, I would suggest that it is precisely because the revitalising waves keep coming – regardless of the controversy and opposition – that the approach known as Pentecostal Christianity today has an estimated 500 million followers, comprising nearly 30% of the world's Christian population.[2] Each of the major waves, including the revivals of the 1990s in which the Toronto Airport Vineyard (TAV) – latterly Toronto Airport Christian Fellowship (TACF) – has been a key player, has contributed to the present vitality of the larger P/C movement. It is the intent of this article to discuss briefly some significant tributaries of the Toronto stream of the 1990s renewal, in order to assess what may be called 'Gamaliel's Test'.

Gamaliel's Test I: Social Psychological Data

When I first visited TAV in November 1994, I felt in some ways as if I had just entered a Methodist camp meeting of the nineteenth century, or had chanced upon a meeting of William Seymour on Azusa Street in the early twentieth century. Although I had been involved in the Catholic charismatic movement during the late 1970s, and had studied classic Pentecostalism in the 1980s, I had never witnessed anything like the strange manifestations I saw all around me. My earlier cynical evaluation of TTB as simply another hyped attempt to rekindle the fire from the cooling embers of an earlier wave of the charismatic movement, was immediately challenged. TTB was a happening of greater intensity and duration than anything I had yet experienced during my years of studying the P/C movement, and I wanted to research it for posterity. When I approached Toronto's pastor, John Arnott, with a plan to conduct a survey on pilgrims to the site, Arnott's immediate response was, 'What can I do to help you?' He seemed as eager as I was to secure some hard data with which to address the 'Gamaliel' issue.

In 1995 we conducted a non-random survey distributed through the August issue of TAV's *Spread the Fire* magazine, through the church's October 'Catch the Fire Again' programme, and through its November 'Healing School Program'. Questionnaires were returned to the author at The University of Akron, Ohio, with a place for the respondent to indicate whether he or she would be willing to participate in a possible follow-up study. A total of 918 usable responses were received from 20 countries, with the largest proportions coming from the USA (54%), Canada (26%), and England (11%).[3] Seventy-five per cent provided a usable address for the follow-up survey, which was conducted in May 1997 and which yielded data on 364 of the original respondents.

While such non-random procedures do not permit generalisations to the hundreds of thousands of persons who visited Toronto during the on-going renewal meetings, they do permit us to describe some of the possible effects TTB has had on the respondents – conclusions that could, with caution, be extended to thousands of others who did not fill out the surveys.[4] Responses to two sets of questions will be presented in this article: those concerning increases in personal empowerment, and those addressing increases in service and outreach.

Personal Empowerment

Although the doctrine and experience of glossolalia has been a focal point for many in the classic Pentecostal movement, the Third Wave (out of which TTB developed) has placed less emphasis on speaking in tongues and more on empowerment by the Holy Spirit. The preliminary and exploratory questions asked in the 1995 survey indicated that the vast majority of the respondents

(92%) had experienced the power of God, and that it lasted even after leaving TACF. Presumably it was this fresh touch of the power of God that led 90% of them to invite others to come to TACF and 82% to report that evangelism was more important to them now than it had ever been before. The follow-up survey secured additional information on experiences of empowerment.

More than half of the 1997 respondents indicated an increase in receiving prophetic words (62%), while almost half reported an increase in receiving words of knowledge (47%), prophetic inter-cession (48%) and prophetic dreams (41%). Similar figures were reported for an increase in empowerment in praying for the phys-ical and emotional healing of others since visiting the renewal in Toronto: 49 % replied that there was an increase in emotional healing, and 34% saw an increase in their efficacy in praying for physical healing.

In sum, it would appear that many pilgrims to Toronto did experience a fresh release of charismatic gifts, particularly in the realms of the prophetic and of healing, both of which are subjects of regular conferences conducted at TACF. On the basis of this survey, it would be safe to say that many individuals who have visited TACF believed they were moving in a much greater power of the Spirit in 1997 than they were in pre-renewal days.

Increase in Service and Outreach

Another area of questioning in the 1997 survey that is relevant to the Gamaliel Test is whether renewal participants were moved to action as a result of the Blessing. We have already seen that many purported to be more effective in charismatic ministry, especially in the areas of prophecy and healing. Other questions tapped an increase in service and outreach to the larger community.

Nine questions were asked to determine whether participants became more involved in outreach as a result of the renewal, with a mean or average of 3.6 and a median of 4. This statistic suggests that the model respondent increased his or her service for approx-imately four of the listed items. Those experiencing the Blessing reported themselves to be more likely to offer assistance to friends (64%) or acquaintances (57%) as a result of their Toronto experi-ence. They were also more likely to increase their service to the church (55%), to give financially to missions (44%) and to the poor (35%), to visit the sick (34%), to lead others to Christ (25%), to reach out to the poor and homeless (24%), and to be involved in other works of mercy (20%).

There appears to be a relatively strong relationship between experiencing an increase in empowerment and reporting an increase in outreach to others. Those who have been more effective in prayers of prophecy and healing are more likely to report an increase in works of service. While these are personal data and self-reports, they do suggest that there are countless individuals whose ministries have been enhanced as a result of their experience of TTB.

An appropriate sociological question to explore is how personal experiences and individual outreach have generated institutions that in turn provide resources for the revitalization and spread of the P/C movement. Assuming that institutions are the result of collective social behaviour, it is theoretically sound to expect that the recent experience of charismata through TTB would have been responsible for at least some reshaping and transforming of the P/C movement. In the next section I shall consider what can be called the 'institutional fruits' of the Blessing. These represent only a few of the ministries I have encountered which have been either birthed by or renewed through TTB.[5]

Gamaliel's Test II: Institutional Data

Religious experiences are central to the maintenance of P/C vitality. At the same time, religious experience holds a paradoxical position in its relation to institutional religion. (1) On the one hand, it is through religious experience that most religions come into existence or have been revitalised. This is certainly true of Pentecostalism, whose origins are commonly, but not exclusively, traced to the Azusa Street Revival of 1905-07 in Los Angeles. Religious experience was also central to the other waves of renewal which have revitalised Pentecostalism through the decades. (2) On the other hand, religious experiences are often problematic in their critique of, and challenge to, existing religious form. In short, whatever else it may be, religious experience is institutionally dangerous.

The P/C movement has been subject to endless critique for the role its followers have allegedly played in splitting churches and confusing doctrine. It should be no surprise that there are examples of Toronto spin-offs that have been institutionally dysfunctional. What is dysfunctional for one institution, however, may prove to be highly functional for another. Jesus' life and ministry, and the early church which developed from it, was hardly functional for institutional Judaism. Sociologists have long known that seeming dysfunctionality can be an instrument of social change, proving paradoxically 'functional' when approached from another vantage point.

There is not space here to address this conundrum of functionality and dysfunctionality, except in passing to note that I am aware that not all that has been done in the name of Toronto has been a 'blessing'. Rather, I have sought to provide illustrations of ministries and churches through which TTB seems to have been an important force for P/C revitalisation. There is little doubt that the P/C approach to Christianity itself has become a major stream in global Christianity within the past hundred years, now accounting for as many as one in three Christians worldwide; TTB represents but one of several renewals of the twentieth century that has contributed to the revitalisation and institutional reinvention of this larger religious movement. The ministries used in this account are illustrative and narrative, representing only some of the interesting 'institutional fruits' I have encountered during my research. I have grouped them to illustrate (1) the emergence of new 'denominations'; (2) the planting of new charismatic churches and the revitalisation of existing ones; and (3) the emergence of local networks for teaching, empowering, and evangelism. Together, they are forces that are helping to direct the course of some tributaries of a global religious movement.

Denominations in the Making

The history of the P/C movement has been rife with struggles against the institutional forces of denominationalism. It is significant that the Assemblies of God, a major worldwide Pentecostal denomination with well over 20 million members, born out of the Azusa Street Revival and formed in 1914, still denies (at least in American dress) that it is a denomination. The two denominations-in-the-making that have developed out of TTB, Partners in Harvest (Toronto, Canada) and Harvest International Ministries (Pasadena, California), display a similar ambivalence toward denominationalism. Both emphasise relational networks, in contrast to rigid structures, as basic to their respective operations. Both also purport to be 'new-wineskins' in which to hold the first fruits of renewal. Yet they are somewhat different in their respective articulation of purpose and structure, particularly as they relate to TTB.

Partners in Harvest / Friends in Harvest

It was in early 1996, just after the Toronto Airport Vineyard had been ousted from the AVC, that pastors of several churches affected by TTB asked John Arnott to provide them with ongoing spiritual support. Partners in Harvest – 'a family of churches and ministries pursuing renewal and revival' – was developed to meet such requests. As Arnott wrote in an open letter to pastors on the Partners in Harvest (PIH) web site:

> I realised after talking to several leaders in the Body of Christ that all of us have a need for our churches and ministries to have an identity as well as a desire to belong to something bigger than ourselves... We are discovering this to be true in terms of our own network of churches, Partners in Harvest. We are able to share resources with one another and strengthen each other's hand, in many and varied ways .... We want to present to you what we believe is a very effective and efficient 'new-wine-skin' for both growing and networking a renewal church that has a high value on wholeness, and a desire for outreach, evangelism and harvest.[6]

Some 73 churches and 14 ministries are now members of PIH. Most are located in the USA (35), Canada (25) and the UK (14). Another 198 churches and ministries belonging to mainline denominations, or simply wishing to affiliate more loosely with

PIH, have become members of Friends in Harvest (FIH). The network is served by 'Family Days' – gatherings held approximately eight times a year at TACF just prior to major renewal conferences, and particularly before the annual 'Catch the Fire' event. This allows pastors and ministry leaders of PIH churches to be 'encouraged and blessed' at the Toronto church. An elaborate Website and periodic e-mails provide the electronic means by which this 'relational network' is sustained.

The emphasis on an organisational structure that stresses relationships is a theme that John Arnott and Fred Wright, the International Coordinator of PIH/FIH, have borrowed from the late John Wimber's AVC. Both Arnott and Wright had served in leadership roles within the AVC before it severed ties with TACF – Arnott in Canada and Wright in the USA. The issue of whether or not to call PIH/FIH a 'denomination' is tackled on the FAQ section of the network's web site: 'If a denomination means an identifying name for a specific family in the broader church, then we are. If denomination refers to conformity to a tight pattern of insisting on firm control, then we are not.'

The primary expressed purpose of PIH/FIH is to keep the coals of renewal burning by encouraging and empowering leaders of churches committed to P/C Christianity. While attendance at nightly renewal meetings at TACF has tapered off, and although most local churches have been unable to maintain the momentum of local renewal gatherings, TACF conferences remain a time and place where charisma still freely flows. Through the holistic healing and empowering of its leaders, it is assumed that evangelism and the development of new church congregations will follow.[7] There are 73 churches and 14 PIH ministries in 11 nations, out of which have developed 21 new church plants. These have all joined together to become 'a family of churches and ministries pursuing renewal and revival'.

TACF has established an academic arm to complement its renewal meetings and conferences. The School of Ministry has reportedly 'prepared over 500 young people to minister in the power and love of God', in preparation for missionary outreach and evangelism. The recently established Ablaze Bible Institute serves those in a different life stage, offering 'a school of Biblical and Theological Studies, coupled with many practical "hands on" opportunities'. Ablaze Bible Institute is reminiscent of the Bible Institutes of an earlier era of Pentecostalism, many of which have been transformed into accredited colleges and universities over the decades. Students are promised that they will be 'dually prepared in the Scriptures and in the anointing, with the Word and the Spirit together'.

How successful PIH/FIH will be in maintaining a distinctive profile within the plethora of other P/C ministries, networks and denominational organisations is somewhat unclear at the time of writing. The fire of the renewal of the 1990s may have been reduced to glowing embers, but rumours of fresh wind, another downpour and new fire abound in some P/C circles.

Whether PIH/FIH can keep its coals hot, or even fan them into another revival flame, remains to be seen. Balancing charisma with organisation remains tricky business, at best.

Harvest International Ministries

Harvest Rock Church (HRC) in Pasadena, California is one of many independent churches that developed out of the renewal of the 1990s. Che' Ahn, founding pastor of HRC, had a Toronto-like experience that spiritually energised him to start the church in April 1994, following a conference held at John Wimber's own Anaheim Vineyard. After beginning his church plant, Ahn visited Toronto and quickly identified with the renewal taking place at TACF. HRC and Ahn catapulted to renewal fame after a visit by John Arnott in 1995. HRC soon became known as 'the Toronto of southern California' thanks to its nightly meetings, large conferences, and itinerant pastors who led events in other locations.[8]

Three other leaders, who brought their churches into HRC, joined Ahn in 1995. This resulted in an unusually effective example of pastoral teamwork. The integrated pastoral team, in which authority and responsibility is shared among five men, has allowed HRC to develop a strong organisational base while simultaneously freeing Ahn to pursue a vision that frequently takes him beyond the walls of the Pasadena church. Ahn and another pastor, Rick Wright, have been responsible for the development of a fledgling denominational structure known as Harvest International Ministries (HIM).

When TTB began to wane, HRC slowly shifted its identity from being the 'Renewal Center for the West Coast of the United States' (as claimed on its website in 1998), to becoming a 'new apostolic church', with Ahn declared both one of the new apostles and President of HIM. A thoroughly revamped website mirrors this shift in emphasis from a commitment to the free-flow of charisma to an organisation that brokers spiritual power and authority.[9] There is little evidence of the Toronto influence on its new website, save for the annual 'Catch the Fire' conference. This is not to say that HRC has ceased to play an important role in the revitalisation of the P/C movement, but rather that it sees itself moving beyond the Toronto experience. As Rick Wright, now Vice-President of HIM, commented in a recent interview, 'The Renewal made us visible to others looking for oversight in the U.S.' Like PIH, HIM promises to provide a 'relational network', conferences, and spiritual renewal to interested church leaders.

Where HIM differs somewhat from PIH is in its structural model, and in the articulation of its strategies and goals. Ahn's passion for world missions is the spirit of HIM; it takes flesh in a model provided by the leading Third Wave proponent C. Peter Wagner, particularly in the development known as a 'new apostolic reformation'.[10] Wagner, who was one of Ahn's professors at Fuller Seminary (where Ahn earned a doctorate in World Mission), is one of several leaders promoting the restoration of the apostolic age, 'spiritual mapping' to identify the geographical areas in need of special prayer (the so-called '10/40 window'), and worldwide evangelism. HIM has a reported priority for church planting and reaching the 'unreached peoples, especially those living in the 10/40 window of the world'. It is also committed to 'apostolic equipping', in which those with an apostolic anointing (like Ahn) recruit, screen and send skilled missionaries to these areas of the world. Like TACF, which has developed its schools, HIM has opened Harvest International School, with majors in either church planting or missions to train young people for the mission field.

The church website describes the purpose of HIM as follows:

> Harvest International Ministries is a voluntary association of churches, ministries and missionaries seeking to impact the nations. HIM gladly welcomes affiliation with local and international churches which demonstrate a heart for missions, a hunger for revival and renewal and fervency for sharing the gospel with the lost.

The site lists names and addresses for over 50 churches and ministries who share Ahn's vision for the establishment of a 'new apostolic church'.[11] Unofficially, in church sermons and during an interview with the writer, a much larger network is described, with a conservative estimate of 400 churches being involved in HIM. It would appear from all this that HIM is operating on two levels. At one level it is functioning as a group of independent renewal churches, primarily on the U.S. West Coast, who are coming together under Ahn's leadership. These are the usually small and independent churches that utilise their association for networking, receiving counsel and attending conferences, in exchange for a contribution of three to ten percent of the ministry's annual income to support HIM. On another level, there are 'apostles' in other countries, especially those in developing nations, who are joining with and bringing their churches under the HIM umbrella.

Ahn's voice is part of a chorus in the P/C movement who believe that apostleship is the last of the fivefold biblical offices presently being restored to the church (cf. Eph. 4:11-13). On this model, while the 1970s saw the restoration of the office of evangelist and the 1980s the prophetic office, the 1990s witnessed the beginning of the restoration of 'the apostolic'. Ahn is regarded as one of the emerging new apostles in the Pauline tradition; HRC claims the identity of a 'new apostolic church'. This vision, which is closely related to 'spiritual mapping' and its attendant controversies, is one that is gaining increased credibility among leaders, both in the P/C movement and in the larger evangelical world.[12] Given the ability of Ahn to retain a vision while changing course within the larger P/C movement, it is likely that HIM will continue its growth as an emerging denomination, albeit one with fuzzy boundaries that fits well with the larger worldwide P/C movement.

Church Planting and Church Revitalisation

One of the institutional fruits of the Toronto experience is the undetermined number of new charismatic churches established throughout the world due, at least in part, to the fact that their founders and/or ministers were personally touched by the Blessing. As already noted, HRC in Pasadena is one example of such a church plant. Another related fruit is the refreshing of established P/C churches whose own congregations and ministries have been revitalised as a result of the Blessing. In this section I wish to tell abridged stories of four churches in the greater Cleveland-Akron-Canton, Ohio area which have been impacted by TTB. These are churches that I have been tracking personally since the rise of the Blessing, through visiting several times a year, attending conferences, and talking informally with pastors and congregants. They are also in many respects representative of countless other churches I have encountered locally in the greater Cleveland area during my travels to other locations, and in surfing the Internet. Each narrative involves a modern entrepreneurial pastor whose pragmatism has been tempered by a life-changing mystical experience in Toronto. Their accounts of personal transformation flesh out the statistical reports from renewal pilgrims presented above, by matching faces and testimonies to the statistics on changed ministries. They also illustrate the process whereby a personal religious experience often has institutional consequences.

Case 1. Shiloh Church: Maintaining the Presence and the Spirit

I begin with the story of Shiloh Church, not because it is the 'greatest' of the four congregations I will briefly discuss, but because appearance would suggest that it is the 'least'. With an attendance of seven to twelve people on a given Sunday morning, it is unlikely to be selected as a feature for any of the multitude of magazines on successful church ministry. Meeting in a large but homely rented room in an office building on a quiet street in North Canton, Ohio (some 40 miles south of Cleveland), its obscurity makes Shiloh somewhat different from the other churches discussed in this section. Its lack of programmes and its minimal structure have created a kind of 'open space' in which the intense divine presence associated with TTB is still experienced in some measure at every gathering.

The name 'Shiloh' was 'given' to the young pastor, Jeff Metzger, as part of a larger vision for the church he felt he was called to plant. It seems a most appropriate name for a place where the presence of God can be experienced by both seasoned charismatics and those uninitiated into P/C thought and practices. A written paper is handed to newcomers instructing them simply to worship and seek God. In short order, even visitors unfamiliar with Toronto and the strange manifestations of the renewal meetings may find themselves laughing or sobbing uncontrollably, involved in strange bodily contortions or rendered motionless for hours as if in a trance. Unlike at TACF and other renewal venues, however, there has never been a programmed order of music, testimonies and preaching to precede the time of quiet prayer that is the focus of Shiloh's gatherings. With CD music playing in the background, some 40 or more people are likely to wander in and out during the main midweek gathering, which begins at 8pm every Thursday. Those who attend more regularly may approach others in the room, quietly asking them if they would like prayer. Often prayer in general is wordless, thus allowing the pre-programmed CD music to function as the invocation. There is no formal opening and no timed dismissal; it is not unusual for the last worshipper to leave after midnight. Each person seems to depart this free-form gathering with a sense of having encountered the presence of God.

When Metzger first visited TACF in June 1996, he went as part of a business venture, to assist in the production of the video *Go Inside the Toronto Blessing*. He describes his first Toronto experience as 'being glued to the carpet and filled with liquid love'. His life, he says, has never been the same since. Upon returning to his North Canton home, Jeff and his wife Beth prayed with a woman who was seeking counsel for her problems. Metzger had no wise advice or quick fix for the woman, only the offer of prayer, which she graciously accepted. Although Metzger often prayed with people, he had never experienced the power of prayer in a non-church setting as he did that night. The woman went under the power of the Spirit for several hours, later reporting that she was freed from the emotional baggage that brought her to the Metzger home. This scene was repeated time and again before Jeff and Beth opened their home on Thursday nights to anyone who wanted prayer. The Thursday meetings, now held at the new rented facilities, have been going on weekly for over four years. Many come only for a time, some just once. Although there is a core of those who attend more or less regularly, the periphery seems to change with the seasons. The small Sunday gathering, and the turnover on Thursday nights, could be discouraging, but somehow it is not. People phone regularly – even the one-time visitors – to share some blessing with Metzger, assuring him that the felt presence of God is not an illusion. Their personal accounts of the presence of God keep Metzger faithful to the gatherings, regardless of the relatively low numbers.

Shiloh remains a place where the essence of TTB can still be experienced. For many, if not most, the prayer time after the service at TACF, with its visible expressions of 'carpet time' and the other physical manifestations that became so controversially linked to it, was when the presence of God seemed most intense. The outward signs may have caught the attention of the media and first-time visitors, but they masked the inner experiences of God and the attendant healing that was occurring throughout the auditorium. For the present, Shiloh remains as it has for the past five years, devoid of organised ministry and programmes which might detract from this singular focus on the presence of God. It provides a kind of 'open space' which is in keeping with the ethos of the earliest stages of TTB – a space in which Mary's sitting at Jesus' feet is cherished over Martha's preparing a meal. In this regard, Shiloh evinces a quietism that may be unsettling to many, even those who might otherwise benefit from its ministry.

Metzger's own originally fundamentalist approach to P/C Christianity has changed a great deal since his Toronto experience. With God's love being so palpably felt each week as people gather, it is difficult to emphasise doctrine or form. Metzger still seems content to live out what he wrote after a Shiloh retreat in October 1998:

> Shiloh must remain a place in which people can find rest in the presence of God. Our emphasis is on truly *being* a Christian, allowing our *doing* to flow naturally from who we are. In the future, it cannot take

on any rigid form, but rather must remain free-form. In other words, we should remain simple and flexible in order to respond to his direction. We must allow fluidity in the midst of truth: not being preoccupied with the traditional way but not putting 'being unique' on a pedestal either.

Metzger continues to listen for direction for the church, but tries to resist the use of his entrepreneurial skills and training to facilitate growth. As he and his wife read the signs, God seems to be behind this call to provide a place where people can simply rest in the loving presence of God. Recently, Metzger found himself without a job, and with three young children to support. Before long, however, a new and lucrative business seemed to fall from nowhere into their lives, with little effort on their part. Metzger jokes that God seemed to give him this business to keep him from practising his entrepreneurial skills on Shiloh.

I suspect there are many Shilohs throughout the world that have developed out of TTB. At times I have heard warnings from the pulpits of more established churches where TTB was once was strong, advising people not to leave such churches for new breakaway home fellowships. I have also learned of intercessory prayer groups which have effectively become the vestiges of TTB in larger mainline churches. Most American believers are too used to a full-service congregation to be satisfied with a diet of contemplative prayer. Shiloh-like meetings will probably continue, but with little institutional consequence, save as a means of reminding believers of the essence of the Blessing.

Case 2. Akron City Vineyard Church: Taking the Blessing to the Streets

Like TTB itself, Mark Perry's story begins in the Association of Vineyard Churches. While still a schoolteacher in California, Perry began to feel called to plant a church, a call that was confirmed when the Vineyard where he started to serve on staff selected him to begin a new church in nearby Five Cities, California. After pastoring Five Cities Vineyard for three and a half years, Perry and his wife Cheryl 'felt called' to leave their growing church of 250 members, to begin another church in Akron, Ohio. Perry's 'Welcome to the Vineyard' letter introduces himself and the church with the following:

> In May of 1996, we moved our family to Akron, Ohio from the Central Coast of California, where we were pastors of a growing Vineyard church. Through his guidance, we believe God directed us to move to Akron to start this church. Since we've arrived, we have enjoyed the warmth of good people who have welcomed us and have helped us to build a really great church here in Akron. What started as a single family now involves dozens of families and individuals who have caught the vision. Our vision at Vineyard City Church is a family of happy, effective Christians loving our city into relationship with Jesus.

Perry's narrative is filled with prophecy, and with the divine serendipity that has guided his ministry. He and his family left a church and area of the country they loved as a result of a series of 'signs' that God wanted them to establish this church in Akron, a place neither had ever visited until Perry began to hear the call. One prophecy given to them just before they left Five Cities stated that at first Akron would be a desert-like experience, but that 'in three years you will be vindicated'. I interviewed Perry at the end of April 2000, when the spring rains seem to have fallen upon the new congregation. The church had finally grown to over 100 people who had caught Perry's vision that renewal and evangelism have to be wedded together.

Mark Perry remembers well his first visit to TACF in April 1994, a visit that came shortly after he planted his first church. It began on the Tuesday after Easter, with one of the leaders talking about repentance – and Mark wept. The next day he felt the Lord was telling him to drink freely as he experienced being 'drunk' in the Spirit. On Thursday he was hit with 'holy laughter', one of the most common signs during this renewal. On Friday Perry said he 'shook, crunched, and trembled', during which he felt he was 'given power'. Perry returned to Toronto six more times, with each visit having a well-remembered significance, including a meeting in January 1996 with two men from Akron, which provided another 'sign' of God's call to relocate.

Perry's experiences in Toronto, and with renewal on the Central Coast of California, left him convinced that renewal and evangelism had to be linked, that those in the renewal community 'needed to give away to the whole community what had been given to them'. His early desert experience in Akron was in part caused by the ups-and-downs of testing out ways to put flesh on this vision. His new church plant was in an area of the country that is quite different from central California – geographically, culturally and socially. Perry first got a vision of planting a church in 1993 while still in California. It was to be a church that would be relationship-based, with weekly services to celebrate relationships; its multi-ethnic and cross-class membership would minister to other churches in the city. Akron City Vineyard, with its cross-section of people and its commitment to the city, is finally beginning to take shape in accord with this vision. It is an unusual church whose worship time is not limited to the meeting room but includes 'going out and bringing church to people in the neighbourhood' (rather than waiting for them to come to church). Perry's approach continues to be one of taking renewal to where the people live, or as he puts it, taking 'the waters of renewal to the street'.

Mark Perry seems like a man who is at peace, even though he is uncertain as to what the next step will be. He still waits to 'hear from God', and listens carefully for confirmations to guide him. In December 1999 Perry received an e-mail from a prophetess in his old Five Cities Vineyard, who told him, 'The test is over. You almost didn't make it, but the next season will be fun. You will receive clear direction in the spring.' Another man, who knew nothing of these words, said to Perry, 'Have fun right now. The Lord will give you clear direction.' After nearly four years of ups-and-downs with this new church plant, Perry seems to be enjoying the vision that is becoming a reality.

Case 3. Metro Church South: Taking Nations and Cities

Steve Witt founded the Metro Church South, a congregation of some 200 adult members and another 100 children, in the southern suburbs of the greater Cleveland area. Witt, a former Vineyard pastor, church planter and regional leader of the Canadian AVC, founded the church on 13th September 1996, while he was involved in TTB. Although he had established two other churches, including one in the same area of Cleveland as his new church, prior to his Toronto experience, Witt describes this newest church plant as having a different quality from his earlier ventures.

Witt jokingly described his first visit to TACF, in April 1994, as a 'baptism into the spirit of "I don't care"'. He elaborated:

> I was stone drunk and hit with waves of laughter. I was leaning against the wall, laughing and laughing. The laughter was so deep in my stomach that I was aching. I used muscles in my face that were not used to exercise. The next morning my face was swollen from the laughter. I left Toronto feeling invincible. I was able to lay aside my concerns about security, numbers, public response, etc. I felt as if I had been baptized into God. One cannot be a God-pleaser and a man-pleaser. There was a washing off of all my cares and concerns – they were simply washed off!

This intense sense of surrender and abandonment is one that Witt has felt on five or six other occasions since that initial experience, allowing him a new freedom to minister.

As with the majority of the TACF survey respondents (90% of whom reported being more in love with Jesus than ever before), Toronto touched in Witt a moment of 'first love' – a love he compares to the description of the Church of Ephesus in Revelation 2:4. As Witt commented, 'The only thing that really matters is the Lord. That experience simplifies the reason why we are here. Only God matters. We can forget everything else.'

It was in this spirit of abandon that Witt and his family left their Canadian Vineyard for Cleveland to plant a church in the summer of 1996. Although Witt still has a high regard for the AVC, he chose to align his Cleveland congregation with Partners in Harvest and has visited some 15 countries 'fanning the flames of revival' as an itinerant speaker. The first meeting of Metro Church South brought in 92 people, many responding to the three 50-second spots that Witt took on Christian radio. In them he called for people who 'loved the Lord but who were dissatisfied with church'. The entrepreneurial church-planter 'knew' that such a call would probably bring malcontents who were unlikely to stay put in any fellowship, but the mystic felt that God was telling him to put out this call. Surprisingly, most of those who answered this early call are still with him. Witt comments, 'This is the first church I've planted out of renewal. The focus was on worship. There were no other ministries (no youth groups, Sunday school, etc.) for the first year. Our main reason for coming together was to worship.'

Although worship remains a prime reason for Metro's existence, other ministries are now in place to serve the mostly young families in the congregation. One ministry relevant to the spread of the P/C movement is Witt's own itinerant leadership, which he shares with teams from his congregation. He explained recurring trips to the Faeroe Islands, a group of islands with some 43,000 inhabitants in the North Atlantic, as 'practising nation-taking.' When asked what he meant by this phrase, Witt replied:

> We send ministry teams to bless and build a nation. Even if we don't build, we want to bless. Our team prays with people and gives prophetic words of encouragement to each person prayed with. We want to strengthen people, to encourage them, to help them in any way we can.

Metro teams are presently set to practise 'presence evangelism' in the United States, as well as abroad. Like Perry's Akron City Church, they take the renewal with prayer and prophecy to the streets of Cleveland. Led by Witt, they are also available to train teams in other churches and cities for low-key evangelism that focuses on blessing rather than tracts.

Case 4: St Luke's Episcopal Church: Reviving the Renewal

Although persons of many different denominations visited Toronto, the single dominant group involved in the Blessing has been independent/non-denominational congregations. Small independent churches and new church plants have less to lose in aligning themselves with controversy, whereas established congregations often fear division and loss of members. St Luke's Episcopal Church in suburban Akron, Ohio is one of the few mainline churches to have risked taking an active role in the Toronto revival. It did this by encouraging people to visit TACF, sponsoring renewal meetings and conferences, and opening its Sunday morning service to renewal experiences. When first hearing parishioners' reports about Toronto, Fr Roger Ames, Rector of St Luke's, would reply, 'You don't need to go to Toronto. Whatever they have, we have right here.' After finally making the pilgrimage himself, with other priests who serve the congregation, for the 1994 'Catch the Fire' Conference, Ames confessed upon his return: 'Brothers and sisters, I know what I said – and I have had to repent. I now say, whatever Toronto has, we want.'

St Luke's Episcopal Church (formerly of Bath and now Fairlawn, Ohio) has been a flagship for the P/C movement in mainline churches for nearly 30 years. Its founding pastor, Charles Irish, received the baptism of the Holy Spirit in the late 1960s during the height of the Charismatic Renewal Movement (CRM) and led his tiny congregation into the renewal.[13] The congregation grew and St Luke's eventually launched two other charismatic Episcopal churches, one of which still serves inner-city Akron. Unlike many other mainline churches touched by the CRM in the 1960s and 1970s, St Luke's remained a viable and growing church that retained a charismatic flavour. Over the years, charismata continued an ebb and flow within the church, being periodically revitalised through visiting speakers and special conferences. It was not without reason that Roger Ames could assume that the Toronto church had little new to offer his congregation. Moreover, TTB came at a time when St Luke's was planning to launch a fund-raising campaign for a new church building, to accommodate its congregation of about 400-450. Aligning with this new controversial movement could involve great risk.

Roger Ames took the risk and it seemed to pay off. The building campaign, the construction of the new church, and the transition to these new facilities on Pentecost Sunday, 1997 (all during the height of the experience of the Blessing at St Luke's) were successful beyond anyone's expectations. St Luke's now has approximately 650-700 people in attendance each Sunday in its new facilities – an increase of over 25% since the rise of TTB. Ames believes that the renewal has also heightened the mission emphasis of the church, not least through the adoption of 'sister churches' in the Ukraine and Brazil. He feels that short-term mission trips to poor countries overseas have 'helped this upper-middle-class congregation to better understand socio-economic issues. It has given us a higher consciousness about issues here in the United States.'

When Ames was asked to summarise what effect TTB has had on St Luke's, he responded:

> It has revitalized the old and given us new perspectives. It has increased our awareness of our early Christian roots. It has also increased intercessory prayer. The intercessors have become more contemplative. We will see if this spirit of contemplation moves into the Body. Intercession does undergird our mission work, our conferences, and our increased outward focus.

Harvest Net: Harvesting Northeastern Ohio

Moving behind the scenes of the institutional developments we have discussed, one usually finds an interesting P/C narrative, not only in personal lives, but also on local and regional levels. In the case of Northeastern Ohio (the greater Cleveland-Akron-Canton area), the saga begins with prophetic promises spoken about this region years ago and reiterated as TTB came into the vicinity. These promises point to a 'church of God's dreams' coming to Cleveland. A key prophecy was given in September of 1989 in Kansas City, Missouri, at a spiritual warfare conference. The prophetic team emphasised that this prophecy was for all believers in the Cleveland-Akron area, and that those present at the Kansas City conference were functioning as 'seed representatives of the entire local church'. An eyewitness to the prophetic word describes it as follows:

> The Holy Spirit gave these men many revelatory insights into certain situations in the city, insights that were quite miraculous and which attested to the veracity of the whole prophecy. The sense was that Psalm 18 was an inspired curriculum or training manual for the metropolitan Cleveland area, like a spiritual treasure map that would help the city church in finding the treasures of her inheritance. In a symbolic way what was received in that room on that day was received for the whole church in Cleveland. Not only that, but it was revealed

that to fulfil this word it was God's plan to bring other prepared vessels into the city, and that God would fulfil his wonderful promises to all of us together.[14]

Some caught the seedling vision of a Cleveland 'city church' that would transcend old and new denominational and congregational barriers. After prayer and fasting, some of the pastors began to gather a couple of times a month for prayer and once a month for lunch, to promote a pastoral unity that would be a foundation for the vision. As Tom Hare, one of the leaders of this movement and now director of HarvestNet Institute, commented: 'These individuals were sowing God's vision into the genetic code of this region.'

When TTB developed, Tom Hare was a pastor to the Church of the King (COTK), a non-denominational congregation in one of the eastern Cleveland suburbs. As early as June 1994, COTK experienced a minor Toronto-style outbreak. In October, the church began to host monthly 'refreshing' meetings patterned after TACF's renewal. In March 1995 a team from TACF came to minister to an overflowing crowd in the church's rented facilities, an event that led to COTK's hosting renewal meetings four nights a week. By late 1995 Hare began to feel that people were 'missing the point' about the renewal. As he noted, 'People were perceiving it only as a rain of refreshing. It is refreshing, but the purpose is to water the crop. It needed to grow in depth, purpose and magnitude.'

Hare was one of a growing number of leaders who began to agree that it was time to 'get off the carpet'. and to prepare for evangelism. By late 1995, in some sectors of the renewal there was less talk about experiencing personal intimacy with God, and more about gathering in the soon-to-come 'harvest' during a new 'wave' of 'revival'. The renewal at TACF was becoming old news as many charismatics were flocking to newer well-publicised sites, especially in Pensacola, Florida and Smithton, Missouri. With this shift also came more emphasis on the concept of 'harvest' as a development from the original emphasis on divine intimacy. It was out of this search for a structure with which to prepare for the harvest that HarvestNet emerged in 1997. Pastors of six churches, including Metro Church South, St Luke's Episcopal Church, and Church of the King provided initial support.

HarvestNet describes its mission as the training of workers for the harvest of souls that was coming to the area, a mission that would be pursued through the HarvestNet Institute. A publicity brochure describes HarvestNet as 'a training center based in Northeast Ohio ... to equip the next generation of leaders and workers for the massive harvest of souls that is coming, not only to the greater Cleveland area, but to the nation and the world'. HarvestNet leaders believe that local congregations must work together as a city-wide church to accomplish the task that is coming. Its booklet on HarvestNet Institute of Northeast Ohio offers the following explanation:

> The city-wide church is a formidable force of talent, diversity, gifting and anointing. In fact, it is within the city-wide church, throughout its local expression, that God has given 'some to be apostles, some to be prophets, some to be evangelists, and some to be pastors and teachers, to prepare God's people for works of service ...' (Eph. 4:11). It is in unity that the church has strength …. It is this common vision of unity, strength and anointing which birthed HarvestNet, a broad range of area churches representing thousands of people, coming together to meet the challenge to train workers in this region.

In certain respects, HarvestNet Institute bears resemblance to HIM's Harvest International School (HIS). Both have been shaped by Peter Wagner's call for a new paradigm for training that offers an alternative to the traditional seminary. Both offer training as well as theory about the range of the fivefold ministry, rather than the seminary focus on training pastors and teachers. The Institute calls for more than academic knowledge, promising a place where anointing can be imparted. It would appear that, at least at this initial stage, HarvestNet has been more successful in recruiting students within its regional network than HIS, which has sought a more international focus. The regional pastors who have come together in support appear to agree that HarvestNet Institute is one vehicle to express their Christian unity, despite the racial, socio-economic and denominational differences within and between their congregations.

As with Harvest International Ministries, there is talk about the rise of the apostolic in these 'last days' before the big harvest. The concept of 'city-church' itself implies the rise of the apostolic, although the apostle for HarvestNet is still more of a theory than a named individual. Perhaps all of the 16 pastors involved see themselves in some way in an apostolic role, but as yet an apostolic hierarchy has not emerged. Itinerant prophets ministering in the area have pronounced some pastors 'apostles', but the precise shape of this apostolic city-church has yet to emerge (if indeed it ever will).

HarvestNet Institute's purpose is to train locals for citywide mission and citywide church planting. At present, 16 churches are sponsor churches, including three Black churches, one Asian, and one Messianic Jewish congregation. Of the nine Anglo churches, only two are members of recognised denominations (one Episcopal and one Pentecostal). HarvestNet seems to offer another alternative to existing denominationalism for corporate renewal endeavours, as the continually changing P/C movement seeks new structures to balance charisma with institution. As with the other case examples presented, how much of its vision will be actualised remains to be seen.

Conclusion: Refreshing, Revitalisation, and Rest

Three of the key questions which Dr Hilborn asked each contributor to this volume to consider were:

1. To what extent do you now view the Toronto Blessing as the work of God?
2. What lessons can be learnt from the Blessing?
3. Does the Blessing have a future, or was it only 'for a season'?

This article has sought to offer empirical evidence with which to address Question 1, even while accepting that any attribution of divine activity to the data presented is ultimately a matter of faith and theology which goes beyond the sociologist's remit. What I am suggesting is that, like other major waves of P/C renewal in the twentieth century, TTB has borne institutional fruit that is revitalising the movement. As a medium for life-changing individual experiences, it has empowered many to begin new ministries and has revitalised old ones. (Another paper could be written to describe the many P/C parachurch ministries that have been launched, brought to greater visibility, or revitalised through the Blessing.)

In sum, I believe that TTB has been a significant revivifying force in the P/C movement through its use of, and teachings about, the charismatic gifts, especially different forms of prophecy and emotional, mental and physical healing. In addition, the experience of 'signs and wonders' within TTB has brought another generation of younger followers into the P/C movement, to complement the greying heads of the Baby Boomers who experienced the Jesus Movement and the charismatic renewal of the 1960s and 1970s.

It is only with great hesitance that I proceed to briefly address the second and third questions, those concerning lessons to be learned and longevity. Although sociologists have a pretty good track record for analysing the present, we usually prove to be dismal prophets. My own assessment is that renewals such as TTB have a limited life span before their charisma is transformed into more static institutions.[15] Charisma and institutionalisation are both needed for the continuation of a viable P/C movement, a relationship that is usually more of an uneasy alliance than a graceful dance. Despite rumours of new revivals, prophetic words about harvests and attempts to provide 'new-wineskins', it appears that the Blessing has run its course. It has offered a new crop of leaders and young followers to replace the ageing leaders of the earlier charismatic movement and its boomer-aged followers. Some continue to bathe in its afterglow, but the free-flowing, nameless-faceless 'Toronto Blessing' of 1994-5 has slowly but surely moved away from charisma toward institutionalisation.

I expect other renewals will come in the future, once again to revitalise the P/C movement. They will most likely and most commonly take the form of mini-renewals and revivals similar to those that occurred between the first, second and third Waves of the P/C movement prior to TTB, and which have taken place in its slipstream. Information about such mini-renewals and revivals will, however, be more quickly disseminated in this electronic age. Given the speed of communication and travel, and increased input from developing nations where the P/C movement seems less subject to the roller-coaster effect I have described, it may not take another generation for a major new Wave to develop.

Beyond such sociological observations is a word I have been hearing in prayer and in the reported prayers of others. It is a word of caution and invitation. The word of caution is to remain focused in the present. While much of Christendom either focuses on the past contained in its traditions, or apocalyptically looks to the future, TTB has provided those who chose to be refreshed by it a taste of the kingdom among us. Emmanuel had come to Toronto followers; God was with them. Retaining the focus on the present while looking to the vision of the kingdom that is yet to come has never been easy for Christians.

The word of invitation is to continue to rest in the (present) presence of God. One of the most important messages of the P/C movement is that God is indeed with us, in the ordinary and in the not-so-ordinary happenings of life and worship. God is not simply the giver of or the subject of propositional truths, but is the one in whom 'we live and breathe and have our being'. Living in the now, as illustrated in some of the narratives found in this article, is not easy. It is a challenge for those who have swum in the river of renewal, as well as those who have not. Perhaps the 'lesson' of Toronto can be found in reflection on Matthew 11:28,29:

> *Come to me, all you who are weary and burdened, and I will give you rest. Take my yoke upon you and learn from me, for I am gentle and humble in heart, and you will find rest for your souls. For my yoke is easy and my burden is light.*

Toronto was, at least in part, about learning to find rest for one's soul in God. Such Sabbath-rest (cf. Heb. 4:1-11) is an elusive and fragile gift, but one that was almost universally experienced during 'carpet time' throughout TTB. It remains to be seen whether those who have experienced this 'Blessing' can retain it and transmit it to others.

Notes to Chapter 7

[1] See entries in Chronicle for 18th June 1995; 11th-13th, 23rd November 1996; 25th January 1997ff.

[2] See A.H. Anderson and W.J. Hollenweger's edited collection entitled *Pentecostals after a Century. Global Perspectives on a Movement in Transition.*

[3] A compilation of the quantitative data from this survey and the qualitative data accompanying responses can be found in my own book *Toronto Report.*

[4] See my report, 'Inspecting the Fruit' which compares the two surveys.

[5] Information on these ministries was gathered through participant observation, personal interviews with leaders, and (where available) the organisation's website.

[6] See, www.partners-in-harvest.org.

[7] For a discussion of a model of healing found in the Toronto Blessing survey data, see M.M. Poloma & L.F. Hoelter, 'The "Toronto Blessing": A Holistic Model of Healing', *Journal for the Scientific Study of Religion* 37.2 (1998), pp.258-73.

[8] For an autobiographical account of the founding of HRC see Che'Ahn's *Into the Fire: How You Can Enter Renewal and Catch God's Holy Fire* (Gospel Light Publishing Co).

[9] www.harvestrockchurch.org.

[10] See P.C. Wagner, *Churchquake.*

[11] Approximately a dozen of these affiliates are in California, with another ten scattered throughout the USA. Twelve other countries are represented, with a half dozen being in Korea, where a former pastor associated with HRC is playing an apostolic role.

[12] For a brief discussion of spiritual mapping, see A. Moore, 'Spiritual Mapping Gains Credibility Among Leaders' in *Christianity Today* (12th January 1998).

[13] An autobiographical account of C. Irish's own conversion and guidance of his congregation into the charismatic renewal can be found in *Back to the Upper Room.*

[14] M. Gonzales, one of the men present for the Kansas City conference in 1989, has recently written a statement about the prophecy, together with relevant reflections on Psalm 18; see *Psalm Eighteen: The Warriors Psalm – A Word for Cleveland.* Available at Marcos@metrochurch.net.

[15] I have written about this phenomenon as the 'routinisation of charisma' in the following books and articles: *The Assemblies of God at the Crossroads: Charisma and Institutional Dilemmas*; and 'The "Toronto"

Blessing": Charisma, Institutionalization, and Revival', *Journal for the Scientific Study of Religion* 36 (1997), pp.257-71.

PART II

A Chronicle of the Toronto Blessing and Related Events

Compiled by David Hilborn

This part of the book summarises and synthesises news reports from the Evangelical Alliance's extensive press archive, from the various publications and articles cited in the footnotes and listed in the bibliography, and from pertinent sound and video recordings. Although similar 'logs' were compiled early on in the life of the Blessing by Dave Roberts, Patrick Dixon and others, what follows covers the whole span of influence, activity and comment related to the movement, from its 'pre-history', through its rise in 1994, its spread, and the critical response inspired by that spread, in 1995, to its decline and transmutation from 1996-2000. While there has clearly been editorial influence in the selection of material for inclusion, every effort has been made to offer a representative balance of events and opinions. To this end also, direct editorial comment has been minimised in favour of a straight, chronological, 'diary' format.

8

The Pre-history of the Blessing

1954

On the basis of a vision that will later be detailed in his autobiography, *Ploughboy to Preacher*, Strict Baptist pastor David Obbard implies that revival might break out in the year 1994. Obbard has been studying Ezekiel 37, and, as he will go on to recall, 'It came to me in this way; that as bone came to bone, so there would be a revival of interest in the doctrines of grace, which are surely the framework of the true church, but this would not bring revival itself. Also, as the sinews and flesh came upon them, so there would follow a revival of true biblical order and experimental spiritual life, but neither would these things bring revival. Following this there would be a mighty movement of the Holy Spirit, the breath of God, and the Church would be raised from its lifeless state to that of an exceeding great army.'

Obbard will go on to reflect that as this conviction came upon him, 'there was presented to my mind the figure of twenty-year periods; twenty years for the bones to come together, twenty years during which Bible-based churches of born-again believers would be established on a world-wide scale, and some time during the next twenty years [ie. 1994 onwards] a mighty outpouring of the Holy Spirit.'

Looking back on all this in the early 1990s, Obbard suggests that the ministry of the great Welsh evangelical preacher Martyn Lloyd-Jones might be construed as evidence for the first period of recovery in the doctrines of grace. He moves on to propose that the second predicted wave of renewed spiritual life [1974-94] could be related to the rise of the charismatic movement. He then looks to the period from 1994 as one in which true revival will arise.

As what will come to be called the 'Toronto Blessing' develops in the UK from June 1994, journalist Dave Roberts will re-present Obbard's words as a prophecy which might well have come to pass [1]

1966–68

Toronto-born John Arnott attends Ontario Bible College, but leaves in the final year without graduating.[2]

Late 1960s and early 1970s

Now running a travel agency and dealing in property[3], Arnott attends several meetings in his home city led by the healing evangelist Kathryn Kuhlman.[4] These meetings make a profound impression on Arnott,[5] and anticipate significant features in his own later ministry. From modest beginnings in the mid-West, Kuhlman has developed a prominent radio and TV ministry thanks to a contract with the CBS network. She is known not only for pinpointing specific ailments among members of her audience, but also for the fact that as she prays with them, many people fall to the floor or 'go under the power', a phenomenon more usually referred to in classical Pentecostalism as 'being slain in the Spirit'.[6]

1974 onwards

Israeli-born Benny Hinn develops a self-styled 'anointed' ministry based in the Ontario area. Pentecostal in approach, Hinn nonetheless claims to offer more power (or anointing) to those already baptised in the Spirit and speaking in tongues.[7] This emphasis, coupled with Hinn's flamboyant style, will attract growing controversy through the next two decades. Arnott, however, attends a number of Hinn's increasingly well-supported meetings and, as with Kuhlman, he is deeply moved.[8] Hinn himself has been strongly affected by Kuhlman and, following her death, will pay regular visits to her graveside, and that of another leading female evangelist, the Ontario-born Aimee Semple McPherson.[9] Not surprisingly, Arnott and Hinn form a close friendship during this period.[10]

1976

Kathryn Kuhlman dies, just short of her seventieth birthday. She and Benny Hinn have been dominant exemplars in Arnott's spiritual development. Recalling their impact on Arnott during this period, Arnott's future co-Pastor Guy Chevreau will later confirm that 'in significant ways they laid an imprint for the future direction and conduct of [Arnott's] ministry'.[11]

Around this time, Arnott's marriage ends in divorce. He will later recall this period as one in which everything 'seemed to go down the drain'. In the ensuing three years or so, he will say, 'I ended up with my two daughters kind of looking after dad.'[12]

1979

Arnott marries fellow divorcée and Ontarian, Carol. She brings her children into the partnership, along with Arnott's daughters. Arnott will later reflect that after the despair of his divorce, Carol 'literally loved me back to life'.[13] Speaking to Clive Price in 1996, he will say: 'We started over again – like the Brady Bunch.'

July 1979

Rodney Howard-Browne, an eighteen year-old South African, attends a prayer meeting, hungry for a personal touch from God. Raised in Port Elizabeth by devout Pentecostal parents, Howard-Browne will later testify to having been born again at the age of five, and to having been filled with the Holy Spirit when as young as eight.[14] Eager to move on in his faith, Howard-Browne will recollect in 1992 the words he shouted out at this 1979 prayer meeting: 'God, tonight is my night! Lord, either you come down here and touch me, or I'm going to die and come up there and touch you.'[15] After some time, he begins to sense what he has been seeking: 'It felt like liquid fire – like someone had poured gasoline over me and set me on fire. My whole body was tingling. The best way I can describe it is that it was as shocking as if I had unscrewed a light bulb from a lamp and put my finger in the socket. I *knew* it was God. When it hit me in the belly, I began to laugh uncontrollably ... Your head says, 'What are you laughing at?' Your head says, 'Shut up!' It bubbles. It was so over-whelming, I couldn't stop it, and I didn't want to stop it. It was joy unspeakable and full of glory ... The next minute, I was weeping for no reason. I got drunk in the Spirit, like the people on the Day of Pentecost.'[16] Howard-Browne remains in this condition for four days.[17]

1980

John and Carol Arnott go to Indonesia on a business trip. Opportunities to preach and minister while there prompt them to consider leaving their business commitments to embark on full-time ministry.[18] At first, however, they are unsure where they should pursue their calling. Arnott will later remember thinking 'I was willing to go any place on the earth ... [but] who would have us – I mean, what would we do?' Soon, however, they are called to plant an independent congregation in Carol's home-town of Stratford, Ontario.[19] Looking back, Arnott will say, 'It was like, oh man, I don't want to go there – this small town with [Carol's] ex-husband. But it was really God.'[20]

Rodney Howard-Browne begins a public ministry with Youth for Christ. As this develops, it is marked by various 'slayings in the Spirit'.[21]

1981

The Arnotts co-found the Stratford Church. Full time work there quickly becomes a reality thanks to the growth of the congregation.[22] As John Arnott will later recall it, 'we saw a mini-revival break out. Lots of young people were getting converted and saved and filled with the Spirit and there were wonderful things happening.'[23]

October 1981

Rodney Howard-Browne marries fellow South African, Adonica. Shortly after-wards, he enrols at Rhema Bible Training Centre in Johannesburg, and begins to serve as an associate of Ray McCauley at the massive Johannesburg Rhema Church. The 'Rhema' network is part of the so-called 'Word of Faith' movement pioneered by the Southern American preacher Kenneth Hagin, and now promulgated most notably by his protégés, the televangelists Kenneth and Gloria Copeland. 'Word of Faith' (or 'WordFaith') teaching draws heavily on the writings of William Essek Kenyon (1867-1948), and at the very least appears to draw influences from 'New Thought Metaphysics' – the sectarian New England Transcendentalism which, among other movements, spawned Mary Baker Eddy's Christian Scientists and Horatio Dressler's Church of the Higher Life.[24] Word of Faith teaching is distinguished by five key tenets. First, it promotes 'positive confession', the belief that the very act of uttering a desire, blessing or word of healing in true faith constitutes the basis on which the desire, blessing or healing in question will come to pass. The causal 'guarantee' implied by this approach has led to its being disparagingly labelled 'name it and claim it' theology. Second, and closely related to positive confession, WordFaith typically regards sickness and suffering as inimical to God's plan for human beings; as such, it posits a direct correlation between faith and healing. Third, it teaches that prosperity in its various forms – and not least material prosperity – is a definitive characteristic of the fulfilled Christian life. As with healing, it perceives a strong correspondence between prosperity and faith, often expressed in terms of 'reaping' and 'sowing'. The interrelationship between these second and third points accounts for the fact that WordFaith teachers are often described as promoting a 'health and wealth' gospel. Fourth, WordFaith teachers frequently espouse a 'little gods' doctrine which suggests that, because humans are uniquely made in God's image to have 'dominion' over the earth, they have a divine capacity to shape reality by their powerful words – a capacity related to God's verbal declaration, 'Let there be …'. Fifth, the Word of Faith movement has been significantly influenced by the view that Jesus' atonement was not completed on Calvary, but depended instead on his very literally 'becoming sin' for us in such a way that he died spiritually as well as physically, thus enduring the flames of hell and even taking on the nature of Satan, thereby becoming 'born again' in preparation for his resurrection and ascension to glory.[25]

Over the next few years, Rodney Howard-Browne will publish a number of writings that bear out his formation within 'Word of Faith' circles.[26] All the same, he will operate a common sense, plain speaking approach which somewhat mitigates the worst excesses of positive confession, unlimited prosperity and 'on demand' healing.[27] Like Benny Hinn, he will stress the centrality of 'the anointing', which he will go on to define as 'the power of God manifested' – that is, something 'tangible' and capable of transmission through the laying on of hands, as well as through such means as blowing (after Jn. 20:22) and touching a sanctified handkerchief (after Acts 19:12).[28]

1986

John and Carol Arnott attend conferences in Vancouver and Ohio led by the head of the Vineyard church network, John Wimber.[29] Along with the Arnotts, Wimber will become a central figure in the development of TTB.

A former rock musician and producer from California, Wimber and his Roman Catholic wife Carol were converted in 1963, whereupon they joined a Quaker congregation at Yoruba Linda. From 1970-73, John took a degree in

Biblical Studies at Azusa Pacific College while co-pastoring at the same church. In 1975, the couple moved from Yoruba Linda to Pasadena, where John enrolled on a church growth course at Fuller Seminary. Prof Peter Wagner, who would become a close friend, taught this course. Wagner's 1973 study, *Look Out! The Pentecostals are Coming!* had a major influence on Wimber at this time.[30] Wimber had previously held to a cessationist understanding of the New Testament charismata, but Wagner's work led him into a significant exploration of spiritual gifts. This also included study of work by the English Pentecostal Donald Gee and the Episcopalian charismatic Morton Kelsey. As a result of all this, Wimber became convinced that effective preaching and evangelism depended as much on demonstration as declaration. In the Gospels, he concluded, Jesus consistently matched his words with works of power such as healing, exorcism, resurrection and feeding the hungry; indeed, Wimber came to hold that the two ministries were inextricably linked. He concluded from further reading in missiology and anthropology that this emphasis on 'signs and wonders' was still evident in many vibrant Third World church settings, but had been lost in the modern West. Sensing that a recovery of such 'power evangelism' and 'power healing' could transform American Christianity, Wimber sought to put his ideas into practice with a new fellowship, which started to meet in his home in 1977 and which linked with Chuck Smith's group of Calvary Chapels.

By 1981, Wimber's congregation had already grown impressively when a young man who had given testimony prayed the simple invocation, 'Come, Holy Spirit'. At this, hundreds fell to the floor, weeping, wailing and speaking in tongues. There then followed a period of even more rapid growth before Wimber moved his church's affiliation in 1982 to a small network of congregations formed in 1974, overseen by Ken Gulliksen, and called the Vineyards. Gulliksen had become known in the late seventies for encouraging the legendary singer-songwriter Bob Dylan to embrace Christianity.[31]

Also in 1982, Wimber was invited back to Fuller to teach a course entitled 'The Miraculous and Church Growth'. Listed in the Fuller School of World Mission Catalogue as MC 510, this course ran on Monday evenings and started with around 130 students. By 1985, when it was discontinued amidst theological dispute in the seminary, it had become the most popular course in Fuller's history. Peter Wagner became one of its most enthusiastic supporters and contributed personally as a teacher on the course.[32] During the three years in which the course ran, Wagner developed the theory that it, and Wimber's church, were modelling a 'Third Wave' of modern renewal, which was dependent on, but distinct from, the first two 'waves' of Pentecostal and Charismatic Christianity. In contrast to the classical Pentecostalism developed from the Azusa Street revival of 1906-9, Wagner wrote that the Third Wave defined baptism in the Holy Spirit as coincident with conversion, rather than with a 'second blessing'. He also stressed, over against Pentecostalism, that the Third Wave saw speaking in tongues as neither particularly important, nor as 'initial evidence' of Spirit baptism. Furthermore, whereas the Charismatic Renewal movement which had sought to adopt Pentecostal spirituality into historic denominations from the 1950s could be prone to create friction with established structures and practices, Wagner followed Wimber in defining the new movement as dedicatedly assimilationist and ready to compromise on such things as tongues, raising hands in worship and methods of prayer, in order to maintain harmony. Moreover, Wagner underlined that the Third Wave was thoroughly committed to a corporate, 'every member' style of ministry, one that diverged markedly from the more individualistic, 'anointed man' model of Pentecostal leadership.[33]

By 1986, Wimber's church had accumulated around five thousand members and had taken up residence in a large warehouse building in Anaheim. Wimber himself had been groomed by Ken Gulliksen to take over leadership of the Vineyard, and had developed an extensive itinerant ministry through the specially formed organisation, Vineyard Ministries International (VMI). Crucially, he had already made his first main tour in the UK (in October 1984), at the invitation of David Watson. As vicar of the leading charismatic Anglican church, St Michael-le-Belfrey in York, Watson had been in touch with Wimber since 1981, and had helped him make a major impact on other Anglican congregations. These included St Andrew's Chorleywood, whose Vicar, David Pytches, was formerly Bishop of Chile, Bolivia and Peru, St Thomas Crookes in Sheffield, St John's Harborne in Birmingham and Holy Trinity, Brompton, in London.[34] The last of these centres would become especially significant in the development of TTB a decade hence.

As they catch up with his latest tour in Vancouver and Ohio, the Arnotts are deeply impressed by Wimber's character and methods, and are especially drawn to his emphasis on empowering every believer for ministry. As a result, shortly afterwards, they and their Stratford congregation begin informally relating to the Vineyard.

August 1986

Wimber speaks at a 'Signs, Wonders and Church Growth' conference in Auckland, New Zealand. Murray Robertson, Senior Pastor of Spraydon Baptist Church, Christ Church, is present.[35] Two years later, Robertson will recall in a book written by Wimber's associate Kevin Springer, that an unusual form of 'holy laughter' broke out in this meeting, and that he himself laughed and rolled around on the floor for 'four and a half hours'.[36] This laughing phenomenon will become the subject of intense debate in the context of TTB from 1994 onwards. It is not, however, entirely without precedent. In the eighteenth century, both John Wesley and Charles Chauncy had reported it occurring in revival meetings, although both had ascribed it to the work of the Devil. Others, however, had witnessed it and had taken a more favourable view.[37] In the early 1970s, the Church of God evangelists Charles and Frances Hunter (the 'Happy Hunters') are known to have presided over meetings at which 'holy laughter' sometimes emerged, while A.L. Gill, a missionary from California, will later claim to have seen it in his meetings from 1983.[38] As noted above, Rodney Howard-Browne has already experienced it for himself in a dramatic way in

1979; he will begin more actively to cultivate it in his own public ministry from 1989.

1987

The Arnotts' Stratford church officially joins the Vineyard network.[39] Arnott will in time become Vineyard Area Pastoral Co-ordinator of the Southern Ontario region.[40] The Stratford congregation continues to grow, and the Arnotts sense a call from God to plant a new fellowship back in John's home area of west Toronto. As a first step, they convene a 'kinship house group' there along with Jeremy and Connie Sinnott. This, too, begins to flourish. For the next four years or so, the Arnotts commute between their two fellowships in Stratford and Toronto.[41]

Also in this year, the British House Church network New Frontiers invite John Wimber to lead a four-day conference at the Brighton Pavilion. This attracts large numbers from a wide range of denominations, with a particularly large proportion of Baptist pastors being affected by events during the conference itself, or by gleaning its ministry model from friends and colleagues who have attended.[42]

Summer 1987

By now leading the seven thousand member Orlando Christian Centre in Florida, Benny Hinn speaks at the first Eurofire Conference – a Pentecostal celebration held in Frankfurt, West Germany. Reinhard Bonkke, the increasingly high-profile evangelist, is also due to appear, and it is he that Ken Gott, an Assemblies of God pastor from Sunderland, has primarily come to hear. It is Hinn, however, whose ministry affects Gott most profoundly. As Gott will later recall, 'I was standing at the back, as far from the platform as I could possibly be, when at some point during the prayer I found myself flat on my back on the floor. I had never been 'slain in the Spirit' before and was the only one in my section of the crowd to fall.'

On the last evening of the conference, Hinn calls all the English pastors to the platform. As Gott will remember it:

> In that moment I decided I was going for prayer, whether or not I liked this man's style of ministry, and I literally ran to the front, jumping over seats to get there … I [then] experienced one of the most unusual manifestations of the presence of God I have ever known! I can only describe it as like walking through a force field about one metre high. As he put his hands on me I crashed to the floor and became totally immersed in what felt like liquid anointing, and I felt myself shaking and vibrating … From a distance I heard Benny's voice say, 'Pick him up!' and I was hauled back to my feet. He prayed and blew on me, and once again I fell … I heard him say, and this time he looked right into my eyes and said, 'Young man, from this moment you will never be the same again!' And I wasn't! I received a mighty impartation of the Holy Spirit that night. My preaching was different; I was excited and alive. I was filled with the joy of the Lord. My heart was enlarged, and I discovered a new,

unqualified faith in God my Father. It was no longer a struggle for words when I met with my people. A power dimension had been added to the church. We were about to scale new heights of effectiveness ....[43]

The church in question is Sunderland Christian Centre, which Gott is in the process of establishing with his wife, Lois. From 1994 onwards, it will become one of the key British sites of TTB.

September 1987
The first British Vineyard congregation is founded in Putney, South West London.

December 1987
Rodney Howard-Browne moves his wife and children from South Africa to Orlando, Florida. He is stirred by reading about past North American revivals, and believes that there may be a role for him in the next one. As he will recall in 1991, his emigration is organised 'to fulfil what the Lord [has] told [me]. As America has sown missionaries over the last 200 years, the Lord [is] going to raise up people from other nations to come to the USA, and [is] sending a mighty revival to America.' Arriving with just $300 and a month's worth of engagements, Howard-Browne spends the next two years building an itinerant preaching ministry, but enjoys only moderate success.

3rd December 1988
At his Vineyard offices in Anaheim, California, John Wimber meets the increasingly high-profile 'Kansas City Prophet', Paul Cain. Jack Deere, a fellow-leader with Cain at the Kansas City Fellowship (KCF), has brokered the meeting.[44] It will prove to be a significant and controversial moment in the pre-history and provenance of TTB.

KCF has been running for five years, having been planted in 1982 by a 27-year old former Roman Catholic, Mike Bickle. It has since experienced considerable growth. The swelling numbers have, to a large extent, been attracted by the ministry of a team of prophets who began to gather around Bickle and KCF in 1983. As well as Deere, this team includes Bob Jones (not the southern fundamentalist leader), John Paul Jackson, and Cain, who joined in mid-1987.[45]

Cain's mother Anna fell pregnant with him in the 1920s, when aged 44 and dying of tuberculosis. According to Cain, during her pregnancy an angel visited her and said that she would be healed. She was apparently told to name her son 'Paul' because his ministry would reflect that of the apostle to the Gentiles. She was also told that she would subsequently live to an unusually old age. She died 60 years later at 104.[46]

As a young man in the 1950s, Cain toured the country with William Branham, the Pentecostal pioneer of the so-called Post-War Healing Revival – a movement also associated with Oral Roberts and Gordon Lindsay. Branham's ministry was

characterised by angelic visions, prophecies and 'words of knowledge' about specific individual healings and life-circumstances. Although aligned to the 'Oneness'
tradition of Pentecostalism, which disavowed the Trinity and insisted on baptism
in the name of Jesus only, Branham appealed to a wider range of Pentecostals
thanks to his support for the 'prosperity' teaching of Kenneth Hagin, and to backing from the influential Full Gospel Business Men's Fellowship.

Despite his popular profile, Branham went on to promote more controversial doctrines, which came to be regarded by many as heretical. These included
the teaching that Eve's sin involved sexual relations with the serpent in Eden,
so that those descended from this 'serpent's seed' were predestined for hell,
while others, who had benefited from Branham's ministry, were those predestined to become the bride of Christ. In this scenario, Branham allowed that
certain others might through their own freewill be saved out of denominational churches, but that they would have to pass through the Great Tribulation.
Denominationalism itself, however, was the 'mark of the beast' (Rev. 13:17).
Branham also declared himself to be the angel of Revelation 3:14 and 10:7, and
predicted that by 1977 all denominations would be assumed into a World
Council of Churches controlled by Rome.[47]

While working with Branham, Cain became especially known for his own
ability to pinpoint the names, ailments and problems of particular people in a
congregation without having ever met them. This also led him to perceive,
when engaged to be married, that his fiancée had done something that would
displease him. In response, Cain vowed to God that he would break off the
engagement and stay celibate for the rest of his life, as long as God took away
his sexual desire. Cain duly remained celibate from then onwards.[48]

In 1958, Cain grew disillusioned with the healing movement, some of
whose leaders had by then been damaged by allegations of pride, competition
and immorality.[49] He believed that God had already told him in 1956 that a
'new breed' of Christians would arise who would not be prone to such failings.
This 'faceless generation' would modestly ensure that all glory went to God.
They would, according to Cain, be known as 'Joel's Army' and would be devoid
of 'superstars'. Until this new breed arose, however, Cain would be 'taken aside'
into the 'desert'. He duly withdrew and adopted a lower profile, pastoring various small churches until eventually resuming more public ministry with KCF.[50]
Having met Mike Bickle at a prophecy conference in Birmingham, Alabama in
April 1987, he visited Kansas on 10th-12th May, became convinced he should
stay, and formally committed himself to the fellowship a short while later.[51]

With Cain now added to the team, the 'Kansas City Prophets' have been
attracting growing attention. Cain's 1956 vision of 'Joel's Army' seems vividly
to have complemented Bob Jones' own 1973 prophecy of an 'elect seed' whom
God would raise up to create a mega-church 'ten thousand times greater than
the church in the Book of Acts'.[52] Indeed, both men have now begun to prophesy that KCF will become the headquarters for a group of Christian pioneers
who will together spearhead preparations for the end-time harvest of souls and
the return of Christ.[53] Jones has been claiming to have had mystical visions in

which he has journeyed to heaven and hell, and has been recognised by the apostle Paul as an end-time prophet.[54] Bickle has augmented these predictions of an imminent pure end-time church by saying that it 'will take dominion over the Earth for ultimate presentation to Christ at his second coming'.[55]

In time, commentators will make comparisons and connections between such statements and those issued in 1948 by the 'Latter Rain' movement, sometimes also referred to as Restorationism.[56] This controversial variation of Pentecostalism emerged from the Sharon Orphanage and Schools in North Battleford, Saskatchewan, Canada in February 1948. It was driven by an interpretation of Joel 2:23 which took the 'former rain' of the text to denote the Day of Pentecost described in Acts 2, and the 'latter rain' to refer to an end-time revival, which Pentecostal leaders like George and Ern Hatwin, Herrick Holt and Milford Kirkpatrick believed had begun with a dramatic surge of spiritual activity in the town. Against this strongly eschatological background, 'Latter Rain' teachers like George Warnock and J. Preston Eby identified a band of new 'apostles', called 'Overcoming Sons of God' or 'Manifest Sons of God', whose task it would be to 'restore' the church to a state of purity, and thereby fit it as a 'spotless bride' for the return of her husband, the Messiah.[57] One key facet of this envisaged restoration was the recovery of the signs and wonders experienced by the early church – signs and wonders which, in Restorationist historiography, had declined sharply after the first apostolic age and needed to be fully reinstated as a prelude to the *parousia*. It seems hardly coincidental that such teachings developed after members of the Sharon staff had visited one of William Branham's healing rallies in Vancouver just three weeks prior to the North Battleford outpouring.[58]

Sanctioned by the General Council of the Assemblies of God in 1949 on various grounds, including potential elitism and an 'overemphasis on imparting spiritual gifts through the laying on of hands and prophecy', Latter Rain teaching has nonetheless influenced key figures, such as Bryn Jones, Gerald Coates and Terry Virgo, in the British 'House Church' movement of the 1970s and 1980s. Importantly, all of these men will become prominent in TTB from 1994 onwards.[59]

Bringing all these background influences with him to California, Cain has already conveyed through Jack Deere that an earthquake would mark his arrival at Vineyard Headquarters. Deere has also told Wimber that Cain expects another quake to occur when he leaves. On cue, Anaheim feels the San Andreas Fault tremor alarmingly just as Cain turns up.

Cain carries with him a warning for Wimber and the Vineyard. The essence of his message is that Wimber must give greater priority to holiness within the movement. For some time, the Vineyard has been struggling with internal organisation and discipline, so Wimber takes this a word from God, and decides from now on to forge a close association with KCF.[60]

7th-8th December 1988
As Paul Cain leaves California following his meeting with John Wimber, his prediction of an earthquake when he departs appears to be borne out by a devastating shock in Armenia.[61]

April 1989

At a series of meetings in Albany, New York, Rodney Howard-Browne begins to see his ministry gain a significantly greater impact. Later, he will recall this period as one in which 'many people began to fall out of their seats. It looked like someone was shooting them and in some places whole rows at a time would go down. They were laughing and crying and falling all over the place and looked like drunken people.' He will add that he tried to preach above the noise of all this, but could not do so: 'the glory of the Lord fell in such a wonderful way. Some were healed in their seats. The Lord then said to me, "I will move all the time if you will allow me to."'[62] Over the next five years, these occurrences will become increasingly common at Howard-Browne's meetings, and will have a profound effect on several of those who will go on to pioneer TTB.

1990

John Arnott finds rented accommodation for his and Carol's burgeoning Toronto congregation. It is the end block of a warehouse/office complex near the airport, by the intersection of Derry and Dixon Roads. Hence a new name: the Toronto Airport Vineyard (hereafter TAV).[63]

May 1990

Ernie Gruen, pastor of a large Pentecostal church in Kansas, issues a severe 233-page critique of KCF under the title 'Do We Keep Smiling and Say Nothing?' This accuses Mike Bickle's church of false prophecy and misconduct. Among many other charges, Gruen attacks Bob Jones for reporting five-to-ten 'bizarre visions' per night, and upbraids Bickle for promoting elitism through Jones and Paul Cain's 'elect seed' and 'new order' teachings (cf. 3rd December 1988). Writing about all this some time later, W.J. Oropeza will suggest that at best, Jones achieves no more than a 65% 'success rate' in his prophecies during this period.[64]

Shortly after Gruen's text is published, John Wimber seeks to mediate in the dispute that it inevitably causes. Jack Deere has already penned a defensive reply for the Vineyard magazine *Equipping the Saints*,[65] but Wimber adopts a rather more conciliatory tone. His intervention leads Mike Bickle to place KCF more directly under the auspices of the Vineyard network, and to re-name itself Metro Vineyard.[66]

September 1990

On the basis of a Paul Cain prophecy that revival would break out in the UK this autumn, John Wimber flies his team and family to London for a series of meetings at the Docklands Arena. Although the level of anticipation is high, the predicted outpouring does not appear to ensue. Initially, Wimber seeks to account for this by explaining that revival comes in stages, and that the earliest 'tokens' of it, in the form of a deepened emphasis on signs and wonders, have in fact been evident. His Kansas City Prophet colleagues also receive backing at this time in a signed statement from leading British charismatics including Gerald Coates (Pioneer), Graham Cray (St. Michael-le-Belfry), Roger Forster (Ichthus), Sandy Millar (Holy Trinity, Brompton), David Pytches (St Andrew's, Chorleywood) and Terry Virgo (New Frontiers). Jones, Cain, Bickle et al are described in the statement as 'true servants of God, men of sound character and evident humility [with a] radical commitment to the Word of God.' The signatories add they 'have no doubt about the validity of their ministry'. [67]

Despite all this, over the course of the next year, Wimber will be forced to re-evaluate his relationship with the Kansas group. By the summer of 1991, he will find himself on another London platform, apologising with Mike Bickle for their errors and excesses, while seeking to recover the original Vineyard emphasis on equipping and empowering church members for evangelism.[68] By Spring 1992, Bob Jones will have been expelled from his ministry because of 'serious sin', including allegations of sexual impropriety, manipulation, slander and divisiveness.[69]

By 1993, Mike Bickle will be admitting that 'God used the critique of Ernie Gruen to bring a deeper level of legitimate caution about prophecy to Kansas City'. He will also sign a declaration of peace with Gruen.[70] Also by this point, Jack Deere will have returned to his home base in Texas to develop an international teaching ministry.[71] Cain, meanwhile, will find himself controversially relating to Westminster Chapel, London, and its minister, R.T. Kendall, who will embark with him on a new initiative to recover a balance between the Word and the Spirit. Both Kendall and his church are noted for their Reformed reticence about charismatic ministry; when TTB begins to affect the UK in mid-1994, Kendall will be initially sceptical. In time, however, he will prove to be one of its most influential supporters (see 6th July and 1st October 1994). Indeed, the rise of TTB will maintain at least some traces of the 1988-91 period of KCF-Vineyard co-operation.

1991

During a tour of the USA, David Yonggi Cho, pastor of the world's largest church, the Yoido Full Gospel Church in Seoul, South Korea, prays for North America. As he does so, he is prompted to find a map. As he will later recall it, he then points to the city of Pensacola in the Florida panhandle and senses the Lord telling him, 'I am going to send revival to the seaside city of Pensacola, and it will spread like a fire until all of America has been consumed by it.'[72]

Spring 1992

Claudio Freidzon, the head of the Pentecostal Assemblies of God in Argentina, visits Benny Hinn at his church in Florida.[73] In the five years since he so affected Ken Gott at Eurofire 87, Hinn has gained equal measures of fame and opprobrium within and beyond the evangelical world, both for personal claims to extraordinary feats such as causing people to be hurled several feet when approaching him,[74] and for idiosyncratic doctrinal pronouncements such as the declaration that Adam could fly through space[75] and the claim (subsequently retracted) that there are nine in the Trinity.[76] His strongly autobiographical books *The Anointing* and *Good Morning, Holy Spirit* have become best-sellers, but have also been criticised for their theology. In the face of these criticisms, Hinn has recently moderated some of his views. In particular, he has sought to distance himself from the so-called 'Word of Faith' movement, the 'health and wealth' constituency pioneered by Kenneth Hagin, Oral Roberts and Frederick Price, and now led by Texas-based televangelist Kenneth Copeland. Although influenced to a large degree by this movement, Hinn has told Randy Frame in the preceding October's edition of *Christianity Today*, 'I no longer believe the faith message.' All the same, there are those who doubt the genuineness and extent of this disavowal, citing apparent contradictions of it made only weeks subsequently.[77]

Notwithstanding all this, Claudio Freidzon has come to Hinn, seeking a new anointing for what has become a notable ministry. Along with Carlos Annaconda, Ed Silvoso (brother-in-law of evangelist Luis Palau), Omar Cabrera, Hector Gimenez and others, Freidzon has emerged as a leading figure in a remarkable period of church growth in his country since the mid-eighties. Reports of this 'Argentinian Revival' recount miracles that include the raising of the dead, the replacement of removed bodily organs and the restoration of dental fillings. They also record outbreaks of 'holy laughter' at Freidzon's King of Kings church since 1987.[78] Although the King of Kings congregation has grown from modest numbers to some two thousand in a relatively short time, Freidzon senses that much more is possible. Hinn prophesies over Freidzon, who returns to see his church rapidly double in size, with the laughter becoming more prominent and large numbers 'falling under the power'.[79]

May 1992

Marc Dupont, a pastoral team member at TAV, has a detailed vision. He sees a mountain landscape in which a large amount of water is cascading onto a huge, heavy rock. He understands God to be telling him that 'Toronto shall be a place where much living water will be flowing with great power, even though at the present time both the church and the city are like big rocks, cold and hard against God's love and his Spirit.' The vision also implies, for Dupont, that this 'water of revival' will overflow the plains of Canada and extend much further afield.[80] Dupont will share a second vision with the TAV leadership in July 1993, which develops the themes introduced here. Later still, John Wimber will testify to having had a very similar picture (see Late July 1994).

Summer 1992

Work at TAV reaches the point at which both John Arnott and Jeremy Sinnott feel called to commit themselves there full time. Oversight of the Stratford congregation is duly passed to Jerry Steingrad, who had been one of the associate pastors there. The Arnotts move from Stratford and settle in Toronto. At this major crossroads in their life and ministry, the couple are keen to seek fresh empowerment from God.[81]

September 1992

Benny Hinn holds a series of meetings in Toronto's Maple Leaf Gardens.[82] His good friends John and Carol Arnott attend, seeking fresh 'anointing' for their ministry at the Airport Vineyard. John will later reflect on this quest, saying 'I knew that it took the anointing to really set people free. We'd seen it in Kathryn Kuhlman's ministry and that totally ruined it for us for settling for more traditional ministry models'.[83] They are greatly enthused by Hinn's approach, and are moved to see one thousand or so make commitments to Christ. They will later tell Guy Chevreau that they left the arena certain that 'Yes, we do have a mighty God. He is able to reach the city of Toronto. He can do it in power and might.'[84]

April 1993

Karl Strader, a pastor in the Assemblies of God, invites Rodney Howard-Browne to hold revival meetings at Carpenter's Home Church in Lakeland, Florida. The church can seat ten thousand, but at this point the congregation numbers less than two thousand. Strader arranges broadcasts of the meetings on radio and TV, and within a month, nightly services are attracting an average eight thousand people. Some such services last until 2.00 am. By the end of Howard-Browne's visit, it is estimated that one hundred thousand people have attended from a wide range of countries in Africa, South America and Europe. As a result of the meetings, some 2,260 will go on to be baptised.[85]

As with the 'Happy Hunters' and John Wimber in the previous decade, while conducting the Lakeland meetings, Howard-Browne presides over notable outbreaks of 'holy laughter'. Indeed, this phenomenon not only featured in his call to ministry in 1979; it has been a prominent aspect of his public meetings since 1989.[86] Following his stint at Lakeland, the laughter spreads, as those who have attended return to their own congregations. Among those radically affected are Paul and Mona Johnian's Boston-based Christian Teaching and Worship Centre; the Episcopal Church of Christ the King in Lakeland itself; Oral Roberts University and Rhema Bible College – both in Tulsa, Oklahoma.[87] The last of these institutions is especially significant given Howard Browne's spiritual formation within the Word of Faith constituency.

June 1993

During a trip to see John's daughters in Texas, the Arnotts attend their first Rodney Howard-Browne meeting. Held at Fort Worth, this gathering sees 248 people 'fall under the power'. John Arnott is impressed, but remains on his feet, as he has done previously at Benny Hinn events and on other such occasions. He takes this to be indicative of a block in his relationship with God: as Guy Chevreau will later describe it, 'repeatedly, [John] would wonder, "Lord, what's the issue of my heart?"'[88] A year on from here, Arnott will tell journalist Dave Roberts, 'My mind on these occasions slips into analysis and control.'[89]

July 1993

While visiting Vancouver, TAV leader Marc Dupont is struck by a 'sense of urgency'. He envisions a new power and authority coming to the Toronto churches by virtue of a dramatic move of the Holy Spirit. On his return to Toronto, Dupont shares the details with his fellow team members. There will, he says, be two stages: the first will be related to Ezekiel's vision of dry bones receiving flesh (Ezek. 37). This will be 'a prophetic stage, where the church and the leaders begin to seek the Father and cry out to him for grace'. The second will be 'an apostolic stage', and will 'include powerful signs and wonders, such as in the early days of the church in Jerusalem'. It will, he says, be trans-denominational, but will be conditional on prior operation of the full five-fold ministry specified in Ephesians 4:11.[90]

August 1993

Close to a nervous breakdown having pursued a tough but relatively unfruitful ministry at Vineyard Christian Fellowship in St. Louis, Missouri, Randy Clark attends a Rodney Howard-Browne meeting at Kenneth Hagin's Rhema Bible Church in Tulsa, Oklahoma. He is initially sceptical of both the laughter and the falling that characterise the event. He is also seriously troubled by the WordFaith context. Despite this, Clark senses God rebuking him and telling him, 'You have a denominational spirit. How badly do you want to be touched afresh?'[91] Clark soon ends up on the floor laughing. In a subsequent meeting at Lakeland, Florida, Howard-Browne ministers to Clark, who feels tremendous power come into his hands. The South African evangelist tells Clark, 'This is the fire of God in your hands – go home and pray for everybody in your church.' Clark duly does as Howard-Browne has instructed on his return to St Louis, and, according to his own testimony, some 95% of his congregation 'fall under the power'.[92]

4th October 1993

Marc Dupont meets for prayer and fellowship with the Arnotts, with fellow TAV team members Wes and Stacey Campbell, and with other Toronto area Vineyard leaders. Those present are reminded of Dupont's earlier prophecies about a great outpouring of God's presence from Toronto. TAV is at this point around 350-strong.

October 1993

At a regional meeting of Midwestern Vineyard churches held at Lake Geneva, Wisconsin, area overseer Happy Leman asks Randy Clark to share his recent experiences of renewal in St Louis. The meeting duly turns into a ministry time, with many being powerfully affected. Among these is Bill Jackson, Pastor of the Champaign Vineyard Christian Fellowship in Urbana, Illinois. The following Sunday, a number of people in Jackson's congregation are touched as he has been.[93]

By April-May 1994, Jackson and Champaign will have emerged as the first to define and publish formal teaching and practical guidelines on the new movement.[94]

Also in this month, a number of people at the West London Elim Pentecostal church, Kensington Temple, are affected by 'holy laughter' during worship.[95]

October/November 1993

At a Harvest Evangelism pastors' conference in Argentina led by Ed Silvoso, Claudio Freidzon prays over John and Carol Arnott and a ministry team from TAV.[96] A year later, Guy Chevreau will write of this encounter: '[Claudio] had gone to a Benny Hinn meeting [see Spring 1992] and came home powerfully anointed, something that John had been longing to do. Claudio was ministering to the Hispanics in Argentina, but [now] he prayed for all the visitors first. John and Carol went up, and as John puts it, 'Carol went flying'. He himself fell down, but instantly began to analyse things: 'Lord, was this really you, or did I just go with it because I want you so badly? What am I supposed to do? I don't know if I am supposed to stand, fall, roll or forget it.' After John got up off the floor, Claudio came over to him. John was standing with his hands up, posturing his openness to the Lord, and Claudio looked at him and said, 'Do you want it?' He said, 'Yes. I really want it.' Then Claudio said, 'Then take it!' and he slapped John on both of his hands. John fell again.'[97]

Also present at this conference is Roger Mitchell, of the London-based Ichthus network, which has been led for the past twenty years by Roger and Faith Forster. Mitchell carries news of the Argentine 'refreshment' back to the Ichthus community, which begins to experience some of the phenomena he had witnessed when with Silvoso, Freidzon and the Arnotts.[98]

November 1993

On his way back from Argentina, Arnott attends the annual board meeting of the Association of Vineyard Churches in Palm Springs. Regional overseer Happy Leman reports on the transformation of Randy Clark's ministry and congregation which has been wrought through Rodney Howard-Browne, and which has been demonstrated at the previous month's meeting of mid-Western Vineyards. Arnott swiftly contacts Clark and asks him to visit TAV in the coming January.

November 1993

In the UK, reports of the North American 'holy laughter' movement begin to spread as tourists and business travellers return home from trips across the Atlantic. Church services in Penzance have been overwhelmed with laughing. Others in the South of England are beginning to 'fall under the power'. Still others have apparently been struck dumb for days.[99]

5th December 1993

John Wimber senses God prompting him to 'stir up the gifts of the Spirit that our people may have a greater hunger for the giver, Jesus'. Wimber's Vineyard at Anaheim devotes its Sunday evening service to this theme. He tells them to 'prepare their hearts' for God.[100]

December 1993

A stranger visits John Arnott at the TAV church office. The stranger tells him that he has been 'running with the footmen', but that he will soon be 'riding with the horsemen'. A visiting speaker, Larry Randolph, then tells TAV that a great anointing is imminent. John Arnott will later reflect that these prophetic words are vital in 'catalysing my own faith'. Arnott and his wife Carol also begin to view Marc Dupont's earlier two-part testimony in more immediate terms.[101]

Notes to Chapter 8 (Pre-history)

[1] 'Rumours of Revival', *Alpha*, July 1994, p.46. The article in question is unattributed in the magazine itself, but Roberts, the editor of *Alpha*, later reveals himself to have written it; Roberts 'Toronto', pp.27-8.

[2] Oropeza, *A Time to Laugh*, p.21; A. & J. Fitz-Gibbon, 'God, Do What You Want to Do', *Renewal*, August 1995, p.15.

[3] Oropeza, ibid., p. 21; R. Hough, 'God is alive and well and saving souls on Dixon Road', *Toronto Life*, February 1995, p.3.

[4] Chevreau, *Catch the Fire*, p.21.

[5] Ibid.

[6] J.L. Sandidge, 'Kathryn Kuhlman' in S.M. Burgess et al (eds.), *Dictionary of Pentecostal and Charismatic Movements*, pp.529-30.

[7] B. Hinn, *The Anointing* (7th ed.), pp.23-7.

[8] Chevreau, *Catch the Fire*, p.21.

[9] B. Hinn, *Double Portion Anointing 3* (Audio) and *Praise the Lord* (TV programme), Trinity Broadcasting Network, 16th April 1992.

[10] Chevreau, *Catch the Fire*, p.22.

[11] Ibid., p. 21.

[12] C. Price, 'Fire in the Gulf', *Alpha*, April 1996, p.30.

[13] Roberts, 'Toronto'; A. & J. Fitz-Gibbon, 'God, Do What You Want to Do', *Renewal*, August 1995, p.15.

[14] Howard-Browne, *Manifesting*, p.5.

[15] Ibid., pp.13-4.

[16] Ibid., pp.16-7.

[17] Oropeza, *A Time to Laugh*, p.20; Roberts, 'Toronto', p.84.

[18] Chevreau, *Catch the Fire*, p.21.

[19] Ibid.

[20] C. Price, 'Fire in the Gulf', *Alpha*, April 1996, p.30.

[21] Roberts, 'Toronto', p.84.

[22] Chevreau, *Catch the Fire*, p.21.

[23] C. Price, 'Fire in the Gulf', *Alpha*, April 1996, p.30.

[24] For a detailed account of these connections see D. R. McConnell, *The Promise of Health and Wealth: A Historical and Biblical Analysis of the Modern Faith Movement*.

[25] For a more in-depth study of the Word of Faith movement see McConnell, ibid.; A. Brandon, *Health and Wealth*; R. Jackson, 'Prosperity Theology and the Faith Movement', *Themelios* 1, October 1989, pp.16-23.

[26] It must be said, however, that Howard-Browne's stance on 'little gods' and 'Jesus died Spiritually' teaching is unclear.

[27] This assessment is made by Oropeza, who remains highly critical of Howard-Browne's methods and theology, but who, unlike many of the South African's critics, has read extensively in Howard-Browne's own writings, and cites several disavowals of absolutist WordFaith teaching, as well as general commendations of Hagin, the Copelands and the basic Rhema ethos: Oropeza, *A Time to Laugh*, pp.30-50.

[28] R. Howard-Browne, *The Touch of God: A Practical Workbook*; and *The Anointing*, pp.3-4.

29 Chevreau, *Catch the Fire*, p.21.

30 P. Wagner, *Look Out! The Pentecostals are Coming!*

31 For a helpful biography and analysis of Wimber see Scotland, *Charismatics*, pp.200-18.

32 Ibid., pp.203-6.

33 C.P. Wagner, 'A Third Wave?' *Pastoral Renewal* (July-August 1983), pp.1-5; and 'The Third Wave', *Christian Life,* September 1984, 90; also 'Third Wave', in Burgess et al (eds.), *Dictionary of Pentecostal and Charismatic Movements*, pp.843-4.

34 Scotland, *Charismatics*, p.302.

35 Oropeza, *A Time to Laugh*, p.17.

36 Robertson, '*Power Encounter*', pp.149-57.

37 For a helpful account of the relevant sources here, see Oropeza, *A Time to Laugh*, pp.145ff.

38 Ibid., pp.15-6.

39 Chevreau, *Catch the Fire*, p.21, Roberts, '*Toronto*', p.63.

40 Roberts, ibid., p.63.

41 Chevreau, *Catch the Fire*, p.22.

42 Scotland, *Charismatics*, pp. 205-6; *Mainstream* (Baptist Charismatic Magazine), No. 26, September 1987.

43 Gott, *Sunderland Refreshing*, pp.52-6.

44 Oropeza, *A Time to Laugh*, p.53; Wright, *Strange Fire?*, pp.260-61.

45 D. Pytches, *Some Said It Thundered: A Personal Encounter with the 'Kansas City Prophets'*.

46 Oropeza, *A Time to Laugh*, p.53.

47 D.J. Wilson, 'Branham, William Marrion', in Burgess et al (eds.), *Dictionary of Pentecostal and Charismatic Movements*, pp.95-7.

48 Oropeza, *A Time to Laugh,* p.53-4.

49 P. Thigpen, 'How is God Speaking Today?', *Charisma*, Sept. 1989, p.52.

50 Oropeza, *A Time to Laugh*, p.53-4.

51 Pytches, *Some Said It Thundered*, pp.130-32.

52 J.A. Beverley, *Holy Laughter and the Toronto Blessing*, p.123.

53 Ibid.

54 Ibid.

55 Christian Research Institute, *Transcripts*, p.10, Wright, *Strange Fire?*, p.162, n.34 (p.342).

56 For example, Oropeza, *A Time to Laugh*, pp. 58-65; T. Tillin, 'But Is It A Blessing?' *Christian Herald*, 3rd December 1994, p.8; D. Forbes, 'From North Battleford to Toronto', *Prophecy Today*, Vol. 12, No. 1, Jan-Feb 1996, pp.14-5.

57 For a survey of Latter Rain teaching, see R.M. Riss, 'Latter Rain Movement', in Burgess et al (eds.), *Dictionary of Pentecostal and Charismatic Movements*, pp.532-4. See also Oropeza, *A Time to Laugh*, pp.58-65.

58 D. Forbes, 'From North Battleford to Toronto', *Prophecy Today*, Vol. 12, No. 1, Jan-Feb 1996, p.15.

59 For material on this link, see N. Wright, 'Restoration and the House Church Movement', *Themelios* 16/2 (Jan/Feb 1991), pp.4-8; and Oropeza, *A Time to Laugh*, pp.58-65.

60 Wimber's own account of this meeting with Cain is printed in the Vineyard publication *Equipping the Saints*, Fall, 1989. Also see Pytches, *Some Said It Thundered*, pp.135-6; M. Maudlin, 'Seers in the Heartland', *Christianity Today*, 14th January, 1991, p.21, and Oropeza, A Time to Laugh, p.53.

61 Pytches, *Some Said It Thundered*, p.135; Oropeza, ibid., p.53.

62 Quoted in Roberts, '*Toronto*', p.85.

[63] Chevreau, *Catch the Fire*, p.22; Roberts, ibid., p.62; Oropeza, *A Time to Laugh*, p.21.

[64] Oropeza, ibid., p.56.

[65] Cit. Beverley, *Holy Laughter*, p.132.

[66] Oropeza, *A Time to Laugh*, p.261.

[67] Scotland, *Charismatics*, pp.163-4, 221-22; Oropeza, *A Time to Laugh*, p.55; N. Wright, 'An Assessment', *Themelios*, 17 no. 1 (Oct/Nov 1991), p.20; J. Wimber, 'Revival Fire', in *Equipping the Saints*, Winter 1991, pp.10-13, 21.

[68] *Renewal*, August 1991, p.21.

[69] *Renewal*, March 1992; M. Moriarty, *The New Charismatics*, p.102.

[70] Beverley, *Holy Laughter*, p.133.

[71] Wright, *Strange Fire?*, pp.262-3; Beverley, ibid., p.133.

[72] Cit. I. McFarlane, 'Is This Revival?', *Baptist Times*, 28th November 1996, p.5.

[73] Oropeza, *A Time to Laugh*, pp.17-8.

[74] Hinn, *Anointing*, p.26.

[75] *Praise the Lord*, Trinity Broadcasting Network, 26th December 1991.

[76] *Benny Hinn* (TV programme), Trinity Broadcasting Network, 3rd/13th October 1990: 'Each one of them is a triune being by himself... there's nine of them.' This was later acknowledged by Hinn in an interview with the magazine *Christianity Today* to have been 'a very dumb statement' (R. Frame, 'Best-selling Author Admits Mistakes, Vows Changes', *Christianity Today*, 28th October 1991, p.44). Even so, Hanegraaff, among others, still doubts the orthodoxy of Hinn's view of the Trinity; see *Christianity in Crisis*, p.344.

[77] For sources on this see Hanegraaff, ibid., pp.343-4.

[78] Oropeza, *A Time to Laugh*, p.17.

[79] Ibid., pp.17-8

[80] For more detail see Chevreau, *Catch the Fire*, pp.28ff.; Roberts, 'Toronto', p.16.

[81] Chevreau, ibid., p.22; Roberts, ibid., pp.63-4.

[82] Chevreau, ibid., p.22.

[83] Quoted in Roberts, 'Toronto', p.63.

[84] Chevreau, *Catch the Fire*, p.22.

[85] Roberts, 'Toronto', p.88.

[86] Oropeza, *A Time to Laugh*, p.76.

[87] Roberts, 'Toronto', pp.89-90.

[88] Chevreau, *Catch the Fire*, p.23.

[89] Roberts, 'Toronto', p.64.

[90] Chevreau, *Catch the Fire*, p.32-5.

[91] 'Rumours of Revival', *Alpha*, July 1994, p.46.

[92] Oropeza, *A Time to Laugh*, p.22, citing R. Riss, 'History of the Revival, 1993-1995', unpublished paper (7th ed., 17th January 1995)

[93] B. Jackson, 'What in the World is Happening to Us?', in Dixon, *Signs of Revival*, pp.303-26.

[94] Jackson, ibid., p.303-26; B. Jackson and the Champaign Vineyard Christian Fellowship, 'Vineyard Champaign Suggested Ministry Tips', in Dixon, *Signs of Revival*, pp.327-9.

[95] Dixon, ibid., p.18.

[96] Chevreau, *Catch the Fire*, p.23; Oropeza, *A Time to Laugh*, p.22; Roberts, 'Toronto', p.31.

[97] Chevreau, ibid., p.23.

[98] Roberts, 'Toronto', p.31.

[99] Ibid., p.18.

[100] P. Goodman, 'The Evangelist Who is Refreshing Religion', *Sunday Telegraph*, 2nd October 1994, p.22.

[101] Roberts, '*Toronto*', p.20

9

1994: The Rise of the Blessing

16th January 1994

Wimber believes that God is giving him the word 'Pentecost'. During an evening meeting at the Anaheim Vineyard, he has a vision of 'young people in a certain set and order'. He duly invites the younger members of the fellowship to come forward. Later, he will recall this moment as one in which 'the Lord came, consuming them in a beautiful and powerful way', and which precipitated 'a significant increase of the out-flowing of power'.[1]

20th January 1994

Randy Clark begins a series of four evening meetings at TAV, having been invited to do so by John Arnott in November. This is a Thursday, and has been designated as a family night. Friday is set for a children's meeting, Saturday for youth and adults, and Sunday for the regular Vineyard worship service. At the end of this first meeting, Clark invites people forward for prayer. Virtually the whole congregation responds. This results in their exhibiting a range of manifestations including laughter, falling, prostration and various apparent weakenings of bodily control, which will soon collectively be dubbed 'drunkenness in the Spirit'. Several of the 80% or so of those who find themselves on the carpet report seeing visions and undergoing intense conviction and spiritual transformation. Deeply impressed by all this, Arnott persuades Clark to stay on, and he continues to lead what become daily meetings through to mid-March, when he is obliged to return to his home church in St Louis. During this period, testimonies to conversions and healings among family and friends of the TAV congregation become commonplace.[2]

February 1994

The Arnotts travel from Toronto to an out-of-town healing conference. As they begin to share what has been happening at TAV, people start laughing and manifesting phenomena similar to those that have been seen in the Arnotts' home church.

At the end of the month, the Arnotts fly to minister in Hungary, and see TAV-style phenomena break out there.[3]

March–April 1994

Following Randy Clark's return home to St Louis, TAV develops a pattern of daily ministry which will soon become standard for churches operating in the same vein. Guest preachers including Larry Randolph, and a team of Vineyard pastors comprising Mike Turrigiano, Happy Leman, Wes Campbell, Ralph Kucera and Ron Allen, join with the Arnotts and a specially trained prayer team of around thirty men and women. This leadership group works out a *modus operandi* which includes encouraging people to receive repeatedly from God, catching them carefully when they fall, urging them to stay on the floor and 'rest in the Spirit' if they have gone to the carpet, interceding enthusiastically for those who are manifesting the activities associated with the new movement and, where appropriate, explaining the spiritual significance of what is going on to those present.[4] This team leadership approach marks a significant departure from the classic Pentecostal 'anointed man' method promulgated by Rodney Howard-Browne, in which the minister prays for people one-by-one in a line. Although Howard-Browne has had a major impact on the Arnotts and Randy Clark, they are in this respect truer to the 'body ministry' ethos of the Vineyard and John Wimber.

As well as laughter and falling down, certain other phenomena are emerging as significant at the TAV meetings. Physical convulsions such as jerking and twitching, pogoing, bouncing and running on the spot appear regularly, along with shouting, weeping and roaring. In addition, prophetic words and pictures are commonly being 'acted out' in mimetic fashion by those who receive them.[5]

Champaign Vineyard, Urbana, Illinois, is also developing principles and codes of practice to deal with these phenomena at this time. Pastor Bill Jackson and his congregation first witnessed an outbreak of dramatic manifestations following the Vineyard Midwestern Regional meeting in October. However, their intensity grows markedly following an event led by Randy Clark at Marion, Illinois on 4th–5th March – an event which several Champaign members attend.[6]

Back at TAV, attendance at meetings swells to one thousand, a fourfold increase in just four months – and this with a considerably greater frequency of meetings than before. Also in this period, TAV sees the beginnings of what will become a mass 'pilgrimage' from far beyond the shores of North America. By the end of April, for example, the number of British visitors has increased from a handful to twenty or thirty per week.[7] Indeed, although only seven actual Vineyard fellowships have taken root in Britain up to this point, high-profile visits to the UK by John Wimber in the 1980s have ensured that many more congregations in a range of denominations have been strongly influenced by the Vineyard approach.[8]

April–May 1994

Having so profoundly impacted Randy Clark the previous autumn, Rodney Howard-Browne spends a month leading meetings in Clark's home city of St Louis, Missouri. These are at least as dramatic as those which have characterised his ministry for the past few years. Among the two thousand or so who attend each day are dozens from a church in nearby Columbia, currently being overseen by the Briton Terry Virgo, leader and self-professed 'apostle' of the New Frontiers International network. Ironically, Virgo has been on a ministry trip to Durban, in Howard-Browne's native South Africa. On arriving back in the USA, Virgo's wife Wendy tells him what has been happening, and Virgo goes straight from the airport to see Howard-Browne in action. As a prominent charismatic leader, Virgo has seen many of the manifestations on display before, but is somewhat disconcerted by the extent of 'holy laughter'. However, when he returns to his church, several in the congregation tell him of significant changes in their relationship with God, which they attribute to the anointing they have received at Howard-Browne's meetings. Also present at Virgo's church during this time is Dave Holden, a leading New Frontiers pastor in the UK.

A fortnight on, Virgo presides over a special church weekend marked by what he will later describe as 'paroxysms of joy and hilarious laughter'. Most of those attending fall to the floor, which leads to the abandonment of preaching. A number of men and women have to be carried home 'quite incapable of walking unaided and apparently totally "drunk"'.[9]

Virgo then flies back to the UK, where Alan Preston, an elder at his home church in Brighton, tells him of a recent trip to TAV. Preston had returned to the South Coast from Toronto full of enthusiasm for the new movement; this enthusiasm was infectious, because many in the congregation had then manifested Toronto-style phenomena. News of what is happening in Brighton spreads quickly to other parts of the New Frontiers network, and falling, laughter and apparent 'spiritual drunkenness' duly overwhelm a 250-strong leaders' meeting. Brighton NFI pastor John Hosier reports these developments with great enthusiasm; he will soon be quoted on what is happening: 'We are hearing many   testimonies … of a sense of encounter with God, an increase in prayer and Bible reading, a boldness in witnessing. We've seen our congregation double.'[10] Resisting the urge to define all this as 'revival', Hosier makes a suggestion which is beginning to characterise TAV teaching on the new movement: 'I would describe it more in terms of days of refreshing from the hand of the Lord [after Acts 3:19].'[11]

This description of the new movement is most influentially applied in a 'Vineyard Position Paper' written at the beginning of May by the Champaign Vineyard pastor Bill Jackson. Entitled 'What in the World is Happening to Us?' the paper recounts the evolution of the current wave of spiritual activity, from Randy Clark's encounter with Rodney Howard-Browne in August 1993, through his report to the Midwestern Vineyard regional meeting in October, to his visits to TAV in January and Champaign in March. It then proceeds to discuss the biblical basis of what has been occurring.[12]

Jackson begins by admitting that in Scripture 'there are no primary texts that clearly state that Christians are to fall down, shake or look drunk during seasons of divine visitation.' All the same, he avers, there are 'a number of secondary ... texts that illustrate that these were some of the responses people had during moments of divine visitation'. Where falling or 'resting in the Spirit' is concerned, Jackson suggests precedents in Abraham's deep sleep (Gen. 15:12); Saul's prone prophesying (1 Sam. 19); the temple priests' immobilization (2 Chr. 5:13,14); Ezekiel's prostration (Ezek. 1:28; 3:23), and Daniel's (Dan. 8:17; 10:9); the disciples' grounding (Mt. 17:6), the soldiers' felling in Gethsemane (Jn. 18:6), and the reaction of the guards to the angel at the empty tomb (Mt. 28:4). He also cites Paul's being knocked down in Acts 9:2-6, Peter's 'falling into a trance' (Acts 10:10), and John's lying 'as though dead' at the foot of God's messenger (Rev. 1:17). Jackson adds that such responses were recorded in the early 1740s at revival meetings in Northampton, Massachusetts by the great New England theologian and preacher Jonathan Edwards (1725-60), and a century or so later by the evangelist Charles Finney (1792-1875). Recognising that these biblical and historical references are largely concerned with falling forwards rather than backwards, Jackson nonetheless suggests that the current wave of 'resting in the Spirit' bears an affinity with past instances of God's putting people to sleep 'for the purpose of divine intervention, rest and healing rather than contrition'. He also quotes Francis MacNutt's 1984 study *Overcome By the Spirit*, which interprets falling backwards as a response to the heaviness (*kabod*: weight) of God's glory.[13]

As for shaking and trembling, Jackson finds corroboration in the reaction of Daniel's companions in Daniel 10:7, and in the earth's response to God's majesty at Psalm 114:7 and Jeremiah 5:22. Jeremiah's physical prophetic experience at Jeremiah 23:9 is also adduced, as is Habbakuk's (Hab. 3:16). The guards at the empty tomb are mentioned again (Mt. 28:4), and the shaking of the gaol in Acts 4:31, together with the shuddering of the demons at James 2:19, are brought into play. From church history, Jackson points to the example of George Fox and the Quakers, who derived their name from their tendency to tremble during prayer and worship.

'Drunkenness' in the Spirit is found, writes Jackson, at Jeremiah 23:9 and, most famously, on the Day of Pentecost (Acts 2:13). Here, he argues, the 120 'would not be accused of being drunk because they were speaking in other languages. They would have been accused of such because they were acting like drunks, i.e. laughing, falling, slurred speech by some, boldness through lack of restraint, etc. The analogy of the gift of the Spirit being 'new wine' would lend itself to the connection.' Jackson goes on to quote Ephesians 5:18: 'Do not get drunk on wine which leads to debauchery. Instead, be filled with the Holy Spirit.' While conceding that Paul is making a contrast at this point, Jackson contends that the present continuous tense of the Greek verb implies 'an analogy as well'. Being filled with God's Spirit, he infers, 'is similar to being drunk on wine. The difference is that the former is holy while the other is sinful.'

For crying, Jackson highlights God's approval of contrite weeping in 2 Chronicles 34:27; the Israelites' reaction to the reading of the law in Nehemiah 8:9, and the conviction of the crowd at Acts 2:37. He also quotes from John Wesley's Journal for 17th April 1739, which recounts a meeting in Bristol at which several 'cried out aloud, with the utmost vehemence, even as in the agonies of death'.

Laughter is found by Jackson in Sarah's reaction to the news that she is to have a child in old age (Gen. 18:12), in the very name of Isaac himself ('he laughs'), in Psalm 126:2, in Ecclesiastes 3:4, and in Jesus' promise of a 'full joy' in John 17:13. He also underlines Jonathan Edwards' description of those affected by the Northampton revival as people 'ready to break forth into laughter'. Laughter, concludes Jackson, 'fits within the general flow of Scripture. Christians can be so filled with the joy of the Lord that they are given over to fits of laughter.'

All these phenomena are said by Jackson to have a discernible purpose. First, he writes, they are 'signs of the Lord's presence'. Although God promises that his presence will go before Moses in Exodus 33:14-16, and although this presence abides continually in the Christian believer through the Holy Spirit (Jn. 14:17), Jackson nonetheless states that there are particular times when God 'allows us to see his presence to build our faith and show us where he is working'. Using familiar Vineyard parlance, he refers to this category of divine self-disclosure as the 'manifest presence' of God. Backing for this distinction is suggested in 2 Kings 6:17, when Elisha's servant is allowed to view heavenly horses and chariots of fire surrounding his master. As far as Jackson is concerned, the new movement is mediating the manifest presence of God as a 'a wake-up call' to the churches, that they may be better able to realise their responsibility. Although some of the current manifestations might appear foolish, Jackson favourably quotes the 'Kansas City Prophet' Paul Cain: 'God offends the mind to reveal the heart.' The issue, he continues, 'is one of control. God wants to know who among his people will be willing to play the fool for his glory.'

A second key purpose of the present outpouring, writes Jackson, is to confirm the need for anointing. Again, the Champaign pastor follows Vineyard understanding in relating this, through Ephesians 5:18 and 2 Timothy 1:6, to the ongoing need to experience the power of the Holy Spirit. There is, however, a caveat; the outward activities themselves can be no guarantee of anointing. 'When the Holy Spirit comes in power, he comes to make us like Jesus, to heal us and to empower us for our particular roles in the mission. The results are what he's after, not the phenomena.' Jonathan Edwards is again seen as instructive: Jackson quotes his advice that 'neither a negative nor a positive judgement should be based on the manifestation alone because the Scripture gives us no such rule'.[14]

Jackson next anticipates possible objections to the new movement, and seeks to provide biblically based answers.

To the charge that the new movement may owe more to demonic deception that divine blessing, Jackson responds by citing Luke 11:9-12 and Mark

3:24. God, he argues, would not allow one who sincerely asks him to answer prayer to be misled by Satan. A person whose prayers glorify Jesus is touched by the Holy Spirit rather than the Devil, who 'wants to slander Jesus' name, not exalt it'.

Lest some think that the unsettling and even frightening nature of certain manifestations should rule them out, Jackson retorts that 'visitations [of God] produce fear throughout the Bible'. For evidence, he turns to lightning, thunder and smoke on Mount Sinai (Ex. 19), Daniel's awestruck pallor (Dan. 10), the fact that Gabriel had to assure people not to be afraid because of his glory (Luke 2:10), and the fear which seized the whole church after the death of Ananias and Sapphira (Acts 5).

As for the potential divisiveness of the current wave, Jackson contends that 'when the kingdom of light clashes with the kingdom of darkness, it causes godly division. Jesus said that he had not come to bring peace but a sword [and that] a man's enemies will be the members of his own household' (Mt. 10:36). Adding that the inclusion of the Gentiles caused division (Acts 15), Jackson insists that 'Godly division is thoroughly historical.'

Jackson also realises that some will object to the more dramatic phenomena on the grounds that they override natural human faculties. He represents this view as being predicated on the assumption that 'God is always a gentleman and would never force anything upon us.' Jackson suggests, however, that the Bible says otherwise: 'God is God and he does what he wants. In Isaiah, God says, 'I say my purpose will stand and I will do that I please' (46:11). God overrode Balaam in Numbers 23 and caused Balaam to prophesy against his will. God overrode Saul and his men in 1 Samuel 19 and caused them to prophesy instead of killing David. Jesus blinded Paul on the road to Damascus against his will…' By the same token, writes Jackson, God allows his people to express 'a full range of emotion' in various ways: 'David danced, wept, fought. Jesus wept, was joyful, angry. Peter wept, rejoiced, felt convicted. God is emotional because we are. We have been created in his image.' Yet again, Jonathan Edwards is brought to bear: 'Nothing of religious significance ever took place in the human heart if it wasn't deeply affected by the emotions.'

Jackson admits that in any movement like the present one, there is a danger of narcissism and egotism. He is also adamant that good standards of discernment are essential. Even so, he urges on the basis of Matthew 12:33 and Galatians 5:22 that what is happening be judged according to its fruit, and not according to 'our personalities', or the prejudices which might stem from them.

In conclusion, Jackson says 'it is clear from what we are seeing and hearing from all over the United States and Canada, that we are in a sovereign move of the Holy Spirit.' He defines this as a 'time of refreshment' after Acts 3:19 – a time in which the church is 'learning to party in God again because the Spirit of the Lord has come among us'. He notes that many of those involved are reporting 'a return to our first love' [cf. Rev. 2:4]. Christians, he writes, 'are falling in love with Jesus in a whole new way, about a new love for the Bible, about being taken up into heaven in the form of visions and dreams'. There are also reports 'too numerous to count' of 'physical healings, deliverance from demonic influence and deep emotional wounds being touched'.

On a more restrained note, Jackson states that while there have been 'numerous salvations', they are 'not enough to characterize this as a genuine revival'. He does, however, confirm that 'those who have been on the vanguard of this move of the Spirit believe that its purpose is to refresh the church and to prepare it for the mighty and genuine revival that is on the horizon.'[15]

Alongside Jackson's biblical and historical survey, the Champaign Vineyard also publishes 'Suggested Ministry Tips' for those involved in the new movement (see Part III for the full text). This document urges leaders to encourage public testimonies from people who have been touched by the new movement. 'There seems to be a special grace for these people to receive another "drink" of the new wine when they are up front giving testimonies,' it notes. At the start of the ministry time, leaders are also prompted to focus on 'those who are most obviously anointed', as indicated by 'manifestations such as crying, shaking, laughing, etc.' In due course, however, the text emphasises that all those who wish to should receive prayer, with those who do not 'manifest' being assured that 'God works differently in different people.' Children are said to be often afraid until they see their parents 'receive', but the clear implication is that the current movement is for them, too.

The 'Ministry Tips' text goes on to ask that leaders refer 'these manifestations' as 'times of refreshing' after Acts 3:19, or as 'renewal', but not as 'revival'. 'Revival,' it states, 'has the connotation of touching the larger community.' In addition, the term 'resting in the Spirit' is preferred to the classical Pentecostal description 'slain in the Spirit'.

To provide assurance for those who might fall, the guidelines suggest that a 'catcher' or 'catchers' be positioned behind them, and that prayer should continue to be offered for them once they have gone to the ground. Short, biblically derived phrases are recommended for this purpose, including 'more, Lord', which the text relates to John 5:19, i.e. 'blessing what the Father is doing'.

Sunday 1st May 1994
Following his visit to Terry Virgo's church in Columbia, Missouri, last month, Dave Holden addresses a church in Cambridge, England, and begins to see the occurrence of the phenomena he has witnessed in the USA.[16]

Sunday 8th May 1994
After the Sunday evening service at Queen's Road Baptist Church in Wimbledon, London, a young woman remains on her knees in the sanctuary, deep in penitential prayer. The Pastor, Norman Moss, sees her and talks with her. He and his wife Margaret have themselves just returned from a visit to TAV, where they have 'spent more time on the floor than upright', and where Moss has developed a 'strange twitching in the stomach' whenever he has felt the Spirit moving.[17] The penitent woman explains that she has had a vision of the whole Queen's Road congregation kneeling in repentance. Moss relays this to

those now drinking coffee in the lobby of the church, and many return to the sanctuary to ask God for forgiveness. They later join hands and pray around the building; they close by celebrating communion together, and the unscheduled supplementary meeting ends just before 11.00pm.

This same Sunday, Gerald Coates, leader of the Pioneer People network of 'new' churches, speaks at the South West London Vineyard church in Putney. John and Eleanor Mumford lead the church, but Eleanor is currently away on a visit to TAV. After Coates has finished speaking, several in the congregation break out in laughter; others begin to shake, while some fall to the floor. Coates has been travelling extensively in the last few weeks and has seen similar phenomena beginning to feature at meetings in Geneva, Dublin and Orebro in Sweden.[18]

Tuesday 10th – Thursday 12th May 1994
The South London-based Ichthus fellowship holds its 'Building Together' conference for church leaders linked to its network. Among those present is Roger Mitchell, who attended the Harvest Evangelism conference in Argentina with Ed Silvoso, John Arnott and other Vineyard leaders in October-November 1993. Many who attend 'Building Together' are affected by Toronto-style manifestations.[19]

Sunday 15th May 1994
The Queen's Road congregation convene once more after the evening service. Worship leader Malcolm Kyte soon falls to the floor and does not get up again for a further hour and twenty minutes. Laughter, crying and shaking spread through the body. Within the next few months, Queen's Road will emerge as one of the key centres for the promulgation of the new movement sweeping in from across the Atlantic.

Tuesday 17th May 1994
Around two hundred New Frontiers leaders meet with Terry Virgo, who has just returned from the USA. The meeting is co-led by Dave Holden. The main focus is prayer and fasting, but many display Toronto-style phenomena.[20]

From the end of May, the new movement develops so rapidly in the UK that it becomes necessary to chart it virtually on a day-by-day basis.

Monday 23rd May 1994
Rob Warner, Minister of Herne Hill Baptist Church and a popular evangelical speaker, attends a meeting of the Younger Leaders Forum at the Evangelical Alliance in Kennington, London. After the meeting, he speaks to Peter Linne, Director of Training for the Christian charity Oasis. Linne tells Warner that he has just been to visit one of his placement students at Queen's Road Baptist Church in Wimbledon. While there, he says, he was prayed for and spent the

subsequent ninety minutes 'resting in the Spirit' on the floor. Warner is deeply affected by this testimony, and on arriving home, attempts to contact Norman Moss, Queen's Road, Pastor, whom he knows well. He is unsuccessful, but leaves a message explaining that he wants to learn more about recent developments at Wimbledon. Warner himself has been experiencing an increased vigour and urgency in his preaching since the New Year; he believes that Moss may help to put into perspective what Warner and the Herne Hill congregation have discerned to be a 'promise that God would make us like well-watered gardens'.[21]

Tuesday 24th May 1994

This proves to be as pivotal a day for the new movement in Britain as 20th January had been in North America. It unfolds as follows:

11.30am – Having visited TAV earlier in the month along with a growing number of British Christians, Eleanor ('Elli') Mumford of the South West London Vineyard recounts her trip at a meeting of church leaders held at her and her husband John's house in Kingston-upon-Thames. Among those present are Nicky Gumbel, curate of Holy Trinity, Brompton (HTB), and his wife Pippa. Gumbel has become well known as co-ordinator of the increasingly popular Alpha course – a thirteen week introduction to Christianity which will go on to be used by tens of thousands of churches worldwide.

When Elli Mumford prays for everyone to be filled with the Holy Spirit, the characteristic 'Toronto' manifestations take hold and a dramatic session continues uninterrupted through lunchtime.

2.00pm – Nicky Gumbel realises that he is supposed to have been present at a staff meeting back at HTB. He arrives just as the meeting is breaking up, apologises and gives a brief account of what has happened at the Mumfords'. With everyone keen to move on to other tasks, it is suggested that Gumbel say a closing prayer. As he does this, he invites the Holy Spirit to fill those present and, again, this has a powerful effect, with several falling to the ground; others working at the church become aware of what is happening and join in.

At one point, a staff member crawls on her hands and knees to telephone HTB Vicar Sandy Millar, who is away in a meeting at the Evangelical Alliance offices in Kennington. The Staff member in question is Glenda, Millar's Secretary. Millar is taken aback when told what is going on, but remains calm and returns to his meeting, at which various key church leaders are present, including the Alliance's General Director, Clive Calver. At the earliest convenient juncture, Millar leaves the meeting and returns to HTB. There he finds people still 'resting in the Spirit' past 5.00pm.[22]

After consultation with Gumbel, Millar decides that HTB should invite Elli Mumford to preach on the coming Sunday. She accepts the invitation.

Wednesday 25th May 1994

Rob Warner manages to speak on the telephone with Norman Moss. Moss recounts what happened at TAV when he visited, and what is now happening at Queen's Road Baptist Church. Although naturally cautious about new trends, Warner's only response on this occasion is 'When can I receive?' He will reflect later that at this time he 'felt as if God had been warming us up, preparing us for a fresh visitation of the Holy Spirit'.[23]

Thursday 26th May 1994

Peter Linne tells a joint elders and deacons, meeting at Herne Hill Baptist Church what he told Rob Warner three days previously at the Evangelical Alliance (see Monday 22nd). As he speaks, his right hand twitches in an unusual way. When he offers to pray for those present, Warner is first to accept. After a short while, he falls to the floor. This is the first time such a thing has ever happened to Warner, despite many years of charismatic church and ministry experience. A year on, he will recall being rendered quite unable to minister to others as a result of what takes place: 'Like many who spend a lot of time giving out to others, I need to learn more about receiving. That evening God took me right out of the action, rested his glory upon me, and obliged me to receive, not just for a minute or two, but for what seemed like hours.'[24]

Sunday 29th May 1994

This is the day that the TAV-based movement 'goes public' in Britain:

11am – In her sermon at HTB, Elli Mumford describes what she has seen at TAV as 'the power of God poured out in incredible measure'. In particular, she tells of 'many very weary pastors who turned up with their even wearier wives', and of how they were 'so anointed by the Lord'. She continues: 'God is sending us his joy and refreshing our spirits, just because he loves us. It's about his nearness to me and my dearness to him. It's contagious.' She then recalls having visited a Christian school in Clapham some days earlier: 'I talked to the children about the Lord, and I prayed for them. The Holy Spirit fell on those five-year-olds and they were laughing and weeping and crying out to the Lord. The teachers were affected and the parents were rolling around. I thought, "God, this is a glorious thing you are doing. This is fantastic."' Mumford also reflects on the ecumenical implications of what has been occurring: 'Jesus is breaking down the barriers of his church. We have been meeting with Baptist pastors, New Frontiers pastors and Anglicans; God is pouring his Spirit out on all of us. God is moving across London and England in a fantastic way. I cannot get over the excitement of being alive now, at this time in history … I was brought up during the last war. I always had what I needed, but I never had sweets or party dresses. I never knew joy. Jesus has given me joy in the last week, which has made up for all my childhood … The prodigal son went to look for parties but he discovered that the best party was in his father's house. Isn't that the truth?'[25]

At first, Mumford's words prompt a time of silence. Gradually, however, some of those present begin to cry, while others start to laugh. Mumford invites people to come forward for prayer, and many do so. As she and members of the

HTB team minister, scores of worshippers fall to the floor. The children return from their Junior Church meetings and begin praying for one another. Ministry is still taking place in the sanctuary past 1.30pm.[26]

Similar scenes unfold at Rob Warner's Herne Hill Baptist Church, with ministry continuing past 2.00pm.[27]

6.30pm – Elli Mumford speaks at the HTB evening service, again recounting her experiences in Toronto. As she asks the Holy Spirit to come; scenes similar to those that have occurred in the morning take place. About a hundred visitors to the church are prayed for. By 9.30pm, many rows of chairs have been removed to accommodate the large number of bodies lying on the sanctuary floor.

In view of the dramatic events that have unfolded, Sandy Millar resolves to visit TAV as soon as possible.[28]

At Herne Hill Baptist Church, Toronto-type manifestations and fervent prayer continue until 10.30pm.[29]

Tuesday 31st May 1994

The HTB office begins to receive reports of several churches in London that have begun to experience phenomena similar to those witnessed at HTB on Sunday.[30]

Sandy Millar flies out to Toronto with Pastoral Director Jeremy Jennings and Staff member Emmy Watson. In the evening, they attend the daily meeting at TAV and view the sorts of scenes they have witnessed just two days before.[31]

Wednesday 1st June 1994

The regular staff prayer meeting at HTB sees many deeply affected by Toronto-style manifestations.

The leading London Pentecostal church, Kensington Temple, holds a mid-week prayer meeting at which many are affected by Toronto-type phenomena.[32]

Over at TAV, Sandy Millar and Jeremy Jennings attend a meeting for overseas pastors, and are profoundly moved.[33]

Friday 3rd June 1994

Millar and Jennings fly back to London. Jennings goes on to lead the church's 'Alpha Weekend'. A concentrated section of the course is intended to encourage reception and filling of the Holy Spirit.[34]

Saturday 4th June 1994

Sandy Millar addresses the final session of a two-day conference for leaders of churches linked to the Ichthus Fellowship. There is considerable evidence of Toronto-style manifestations after he speaks.

Sunday 5th June 1994

11am – Leading morning worship at HTB, Sandy Millar invites Nicky Gumbel and various staff and church members to share testimonies of how they have been touched by the new wave of spiritual phenomena. Soon, many are falling, laughing and crying – to such and extent, in fact, that the Communion planned for the service does not take place.

6.30pm – HTB is completely full, with 1,200 or so in attendance. Testimonies again follow one after another; ministry is offered, and so many fall to the floor that the chairs are once again removed, with ministry continuing until after 10pm.[35]

Tuesday 7th June 1994
In a leaders' meeting at Kensington Temple, most find themselves falling to the floor and laughing vigorously.[36]

Friday 10th June 1994
Having obtained a copy of Elli Mumford's HTB sermon, Revd Ian McFarlane of Bookham Baptist Church, Surrey, begins to shake while gardening. He resolves to play the Mumford tape to his congregation on the coming Sunday.[37]

Sunday 12th June 1994
Elli Mumford's tape is played over the PA at the 200-strong Bookham Baptist Church. The pastor, Ian McFarlane, is 'slain in the Spirit' for twenty minutes. Others around him shake, laugh, cry and pray for one another.

Roger Forster of the Ichthus Fellowship preaches at Herne Hill Baptist Church. He reports that he has recently spoken at conferences in several countries where the Spirit has been moving in greater power, bringing 'repentance and conversions, joy and laughter, and … an increased level of healings'.[38]

By now, Elli Mumford's HTB sermon of 29th May has reached a considerable number of churches and reports of Toronto-style phenomena are arising from, to name but a few, HTB's sister congregation at St Paul's, Onslow Square; St George's, Ashtead; South St Baptist Church in Greenwich; Gerald Coates' Pioneer People network; Bryn Jones' Covenant Ministries constituency; King's Church, Loughborough; Loughborough Elim Pentecostal Church; NFI's Sidcup Community Church; Highdown Church, Worthing; and parts of the Salvation Army.[39]

Meanwhile, back at HTB, the in-house newspaper *HTB in Focus* details the remarkable events of the preceding two and a half weeks. In his vicar's column, Sandy Millar seeks to contextualise what has been happening by suggesting precedents in Scripture. Quoting the King James Version's rendering of Acts 2:16 – 'This is that which was spoken by the prophet Joel' – he argues that what has been happening at Brompton and elsewhere constitutes a re-evocation of the Day of Pentecost. Just as the disciples were mistakenly perceived as having drunk too much wine (Acts 2:13), so Millar contends that the 'extraordinary manifestations' of this new movement 'carry with them many of the symptoms of drunkenness'. Although he is quick to point out that Scripture finally *contrasts* the two states in Ephesians 5:18-20, he comments that 'you don't get accused of being drunk just because you speak in tongues'.

Extending his 'this is that' theme, Millar goes on to draw explicit comparisons between the current events and the experience of great revivalists in the past. He suggests that the renowned American evangelists Jonathan Edwards and Charles Finney, and the Scottish preacher Alexander Webster, sometimes witnessed scenes similar in intensity and strangeness to those now taking place, and that they either approved or allowed manifestations at least as unusual as those presently on display. As Toronto-style phenomena increase across the UK, such comparisons with the past will become a major bone of contention. Perhaps anticipating this, Millar sounds a more modest note when he states that for the time being, the movement is 'primarily towards God's people. Naturally we expect it to flow out and over into a movement that will affect the rest of the world but for the moment it's God's deep desire to minister to his church – to refresh, empower and prepare them for a wider work of his Spirit that will affect the world to which the church is sent.'[40]

Unsurprisingly, from this point onwards news about what is happening begins to filter through to the media.[41] Stories start appearing the local papers; the national press will soon pick them up.

Monday 13th June 1994
Rodney Howard-Browne commences a week of meetings hosted by Woodgates Assembly of God in the English West Midlands city of Birmingham. Several members of Ichthus and other new churches attend, and they are strongly affected. Among those present is Bryn Jones, leader of Covenant Ministries.[42]

Wednesday 15th June 1994
Bryn Jones gathers seventy of his leaders from across the UK for a meeting at Nettle Hill near Coventry. Pioneer overseer Gerald Coates has been asked to join them. Although Jones and Coates were once close colleagues in the fledgling House Church movement of the 1970s, they have not worked together like this for some time. Coates speaks in the morning and continues after lunch, concentrating on his recent experience at Putney Vineyard (8th May 1994). Many are deeply affected by Toronto-style manifestations.

In the evening, Jones and Coates take the other leaders to the Rodney Howard-Browne conference in Birmingham. Many experience falling, laughter and weeping; they carry what has occurred back to their own churches.[43]

Thursday 16th June 1994
St Andrew's Chorleywood, a prominent Anglican charismatic church, hosts a day conference on working in the community. This theme is followed in the morning, but in the afternoon, David Pytches, the vicar of the church and former South American bishop, relates details of a visit he and his wife, Mary, have just paid to TAV. Included in his testimony is an account of his having roared like a lion – something his wife will later interpret with respect to Hosea

11:10-11: 'They will follow the LORD; he will roar like a lion. When he roars, his children will come trembling from the west. They will come trembling like birds from Egypt, like doves from Assyria. I will settle them in their homes, declares the Lord.'[44] The press soon latch on to the image of an Anglican bishop writhing on the floor while making animal noises.

Friday 17th June 1994

The British Christian monthly *Alpha* publishes a lead article in its July edition under the title 'Rumours of Revival'. The magazine's editor, Dave Roberts, writes it. After supportive quotes from John Hosier of NFI's Christ the King Church in Brighton, Malcolm Kyte of Queen's Road Baptist Church and Gerald Coates of Pioneer People, Roberts traces the roots of the new movement in the Argentine revival, Benny Hinn and Rodney Howard-Browne. Like Sandy Millar, he also suggests parallels between what is happening now and what occurred in various historic revivals, including the Great Awakening of 1740-43 associated with Jonathan Edwards, the 1859 Ulster revival, and the 1804 Kentucky revival.

In the same article, Roberts makes much of the twenty year 'cycles of renewal' envisaged by Strict Baptist pastor David Obbard in 1954. Since Obbard had implied that a radical new outpouring of the Holy Spirit would occur in 1994, Roberts suggests that he may have foreseen what is now happening at TAV, HTB and elsewhere.[45]

This same day, the *Church of England Newspaper* carries a front-page article by James Lindsay headed 'Revival Breaks Out in London Churches'. Recounting the key events described above, Lindsay relies heavily on HTB's own record of what has happened, as published in its newsletter on 12th June. Towards the end of the article, Sandy Millar is quoted as sounding a warning which many will come to regard as prescient: 'At times of great excitement like this, the enemy can get in and start everyone fighting each other.'[46]

Saturday 18th June 1994

First reports of the new movement appear in the national British secular press.

In the *Daily Telegraph*, Damien Thompson focuses on events at HTB, quoting extensively from the church's own literature and interviewing a worshipper called Ronald Travis, who tells him, 'The first time I went down, I felt all the anger go and after that I felt that the Spirit was on me for the rest of the evening.' Thompson also reports that all this has led to 'speculation about a world-wide miraculous revival'.[47]

In *The Times*, Religious Affairs correspondent Ruth Gledhill adopts a decidedly more circumspect tone, referring to a 'religious craze' marked by 'mass fainting', which has 'crossed the Atlantic to cause concern in the Church of England'. Again highlighting HTB, and the apparent incongruity of 'MPs and young, wealthy people from the Chelsea and Fulham areas' laughing, shaking and falling to the floor in an Anglican church, Gledhill nonetheless points out that 'former topless model Samantha Fox is a recent convert'. She then quotes 'an insider' as worrying that 'there seems to be no control, with everyone doing their own thing'. She also cites Dr Laurence Brown of the Alister Hardy Centre for Research into Religious Experience in Oxford: 'There is nothing mysterious about this,' he says, 'the problem is how to understand it.' Beyond all this, however, Gledhill's piece will be remembered as the first to report that the new movement is being popularly referred to as 'The Toronto Blessing', after its 'city of origin'.[48] From now on, this sobriquet will occasionally be disavowed as misleading (either because, as we have seen, Toronto is not its sole geographical source, or because it is regarded as *God's* blessing). Overwhelmingly, however, it becomes the definitive term by which the movement will be known.

Sunday 19th June 1994

The *Sunday Telegraph* carries two reports on TTB. Fred Langan and Paul Goodman's extensively-researched article begins with words that will be much-quoted in subsequent months: 'British Airways flight number 092 took off from Toronto Airport on Thursday evening just as the Holy Spirit was landing on a small building a hundred yards from the end of the runway.' Their assessment of TAV is that 'in the world of charismatic evangelicalism, this is *the* place to be'. Alongside descriptions of laughter, falling and weeping, and of Bishop David Pytches roaring from the floor like a lion, Langan and Goodman quote Ewen Huffman, a British Baptist visitor from Carshalton in Surrey: 'I don't know why it's happening here in this grotty little church,' he says; 'I've never seen anything like this.' Jeremy Sinott of the TAV staff adds, 'We don't know why God picked our dumb little church among so many others.'

Langan and Goodman also chart events at HTB, referring to it as 'a cathedral of charismatic churchmanship'. They relay 'rising speculation … that what may be happening is more than a renewal, more even than a revival'. They add: 'The world, it is said, may in fact be on the brink of a fully-fledged awakening – something on the scale of the great Wesleyan movement that swept England during the early 19th century [sic].' Sandy Millar, however, is quoted as stating that such talk is 'premature', even though he 'obviously' has 'hopes'.

At the end of their piece, Langan and Goodman print extracts from an interview they have conducted with the General Director of the Evangelical Alliance, Clive Calver. He is broadly encouraging, but suggests that TTB must develop in relation to church unity and social transformation:

> I think that many British Christians want to enter deeper into their relationship with God, and make it a reality in their daily lives. This is [a] very internal and personal process – and will, obviously, be seen as an emotional one if accompanied by these phenomena, and viewed from outside. What is important is that this internal transformation is accompanied by a new commitment to social action – such as care for the poor and homeless. If this happens, it's nothing but good news.

Pointing to the Worldwide March for Jesus scheduled for the coming Saturday (June 25th), Calver continues: 'There will be lots of people on the march in

Britain who've been deeply affected by what seems to have started in Toronto, and there will be lots of people who haven't.'[49]

In the second, shorter *Sunday Telegraph* report, Nicholas Monson comments on a visit he has paid to HTB the previous Sunday (10th June). Veering between genuine perplexity and sarcasm, he compares the mass falling, laughing, shaking and shrieking he has witnessed to 'an episode of *The Twilight Zone* where everyone else in town is being taken over by aliens while you alone are evading them'. He recalls, though, that he eventually allowed a member of the ministry team to pray for him, which caused him to start giggling. His laughter was soon interrupted, however, by the screams of a woman undergoing deliverance from occult involvement. As the children returned to the   sanctuary from their classes, Monson writes that he wondered at the time what they would have made 'of their parents lying on the floor, comatose', but then reflects that he was 'too dazed to discover'. His article concludes by commenting on the fact that 'while bedlam continued around us', a curate tried to persuade him to join one of HTB's Alpha courses.[50]

Monday 20th June 1994

Tony Halpin reports on TTB in the *Daily Mail* under the headline 'Rolling in the Aisles at Church of Laughter'. As with all national, London-based press reports so far, his piece majors on HTB. Describing worshippers there as 'apparently possessed' and in 'religious ecstasies', he then quotes members of the congregation as stressing that 'they are neither fanatics nor prone to hysteria'. HTB regular Deirdre Hurst is cited as comparing the atmosphere to 'the huge wall of warmth that hits you when you go somewhere like Florida'. Curate Tom Gillum is also interviewed: 'We are fairly typical English people,' he says, 'we probably don't expect things like this to happen to us, [but] it is rather pleasant when they do.'[51]

In one of its humorous columns, the *Daily Telegraph* mocks TTB:

> There is nothing new about fainting in church. Convent girls have always done it, although usually in ones and twos, seldom *en masse* ...It would be a sad thing if, after generations of declining religious faith, we all decided that the whole basis of religion was so unlikely as to be preposterous, and burst into hysterical laughter every time we thought of it.[52]

Tuesday 21st June 1994

In a feature headed 'John Wesley Had Similar Experiences', The *Independent* publishes an analysis of TTB by its Religious Affairs Correspondent, Andrew Brown. This is distinguished by the fact that he has visited not HTB, but St Paul's Onslow Square in Kensington – although the latter is a 'church plant' from the former. Brown reports 'heavy thuds as congregants fainted and then sudden rapid drummings ... when people began to shake uncontrollably and beat their feet against the floor.' St Paul's leader Rev Nicky Lee is quoted as teaching that the current period is 'a season when God is refreshing his church

[by] pouring out his Spirit'. Brown also hears Lee tell the congregation that TTB has clear precedents in the revivals spearheaded by John Wesley and George Whitefield in the eighteenth century. 'This sort of ministry should become more and more part of the regular ministry of the church,' adds Lee, 'I hope that it will go on and on until the Lord returns.' Despite his studiedly neutral stance, Brown remarks of the St Paul's service that 'there is nothing of the hucksterish atmosphere of a Morris Cerullo or Reinhard Bonnke rally'.[53]

Thursday 23rd June 1994

Letters columns begin to carry responses to the various articles on TTB published at the weekend. The *Daily Mail* presents one correspondent 'for' and two 'against'. Keith Munday of Rushden claims that Toronto-style phenomena are biblical and 'have been happening in charismatic churches in this country for years'. S.C. Levy of Billingham, however, objects to the ostentation of the new movement, while Dorothy Flan of Edgware compares the current 'mass physical and mental turmoil' at HTB to the 'soothing and worshipful' atmosphere she enjoyed there as a youngster in the 1940s.

Writing to *The Times*, Colin Symes, an elder at Edinburgh City Fellowship, insists that 'anyone with a knowledge of church history will realise that such phenomena have been previously experienced in the Great American Awakening of 1740, the Wesleyan revival in this nation around the same period, as well as in the early days of the Salvation Army.' He goes on to suggest biblical precedents for 'falling under the power' in the fact that people were 'unable to stand in the awesome presence of God [at] the dedication of Solomon's Temple' and in the fact that 'St John in Revelation' fell on his feet before the glorified Christ [Rev. 1:17].

Friday 24th June 1994

Anglican weekly the *Church Times* summarises recent accounts of events at HTB and St Paul's, Onslow Square. Reporter Betty Saunders also includes fresh quotes from HTB's Director of Resources and Communications, Mark Elsdon-Dew. He has asked her to emphasise that 'this is not so bizarre or outrageous that sensible people won't want anything to do with it. We try to show commonsense and order, but if it is God it would be awful not to have all that he offers.'[54]

Monthly periodical *Evangelism Today* publishes the first articles by British evangelicals opposed to TTB. July's front page carries two articles on the new wave from Canada – one an editorial and the other by an anonymous recent visitor to TAV. The editorial quotes neutrally from Rick Oldland, a member of Queen's Road, Wimbledon, who implies that there are signs of revival in the events. It also re-presents enthusiastic comments made by Nicky Gumbel in *HTB Focus* on 12th June. Then, however, the piece takes a more critical turn: 'What seems certain is that such manifestations will create a hunger to run hither and thither, and increase the trans-Atlantic traffic as some find their curiosity gets the better of them.' Commenting on the comparisons that have begun to be made with past revivals, the leader concludes that such parallels 'seem hardly fitting'. The manifestations associated with George Whitefield's ministry, it says, 'followed the preaching of the Word', whereas the current manifestations 'seem to follow little more than a very shallow summary of 'what we saw in Toronto'.

The second, unsigned article is more directly negative. The writer is identified only as 'a beloved colleague, highly respected for his own ministry and an active member of a local charismatic church'. He reports that from the start of a meeting that he attended at TAV on 18th June, 'a number of women … were arm and/or hand-waving and/or shaking, rapidly, even violently and continuously'. He comments that 'this looked very much self-induced and did not seem to be for any purpose'. Then, as people were invited forward for prayer, he adds that 'we were treated to a performance of uncontrollable laughing, jerking and shaking. Each [person] was interviewed but little was said that I could describe as glorifying the Lord – indeed, some were unable to speak intelligibly due to the jerking, shaking and laughing.' The article continues in the same aggrieved vein: 'What we witnessed was described by the leaders as being 'drunk in the Spirit' and despite the fact that they have stated that this is renewal not revival, they, on this evening, used the word 'revival', stating 'the soft, gentle and sweet approach is not going to work', but 'God is going to hit the world in the face'.' The writer is particularly upset by 'men roaring in a great voice like lions' – a phenomenon which he says lacked any explanation – and by the fact that laughter continued all through a reading of the solemn text Isaiah 55. He concludes: 'I wish I were wrong, but I have to say I don't think I witnessed renewal or revival on 18th June.'

Saturday 25th June 1994
The London gathering of the Worldwide March for Jesus offers charismatics a chance to exchange news about what has been happening in TTB. Many talk enthusiastically of their 'refreshment' from God, and there are signs of 'holy laughter' along the route of the march.

At the Kensington Temple evening service, many experience falling and laughter.[55]

Sunday 26th June 1994
The *Sunday Telegraph* reports that the Archbishop of Canterbury, George Carey, has turned down the chance to visit TAV while on an official trip to Toronto. Carey has been in the Canadian city since Tuesday 21st June, but a Lambeth Palace spokesman is quoted as saying that he has 'a very full programme' and cannot 'drop everything' to call in on the Vineyard. 'The Archbishop does not want to downplay what is going on but there are many ways that God's Spirit manifests itself,' adds the spokesman; 'he has to be careful about identifying himself with one form of charismatic manifestation.' Although Dr Carey is said to 'privately' be delighted by the possibility of revival, Canon Michael Green, a leading Anglican charismatic who has co-directed the Archbishop's

Springboard programme for the Decade of Evangelism, says 'it would be very helpful and significant if he went along'.

Thursday 30th June 1994

Baptist Times reporter David Dewey tells readers that it is not only HTB and St Paul's, Onslow Square which have felt the impact of TTB. Detailing the experiences of Norman Moss and his congregation at Queen's Road, Wimbledon, Dewey goes on to discuss dramatic 'times of refreshing' at Herne Hill and Bookham, Surrey. He also quotes Mike Wood, Minister of Lewin Baptist Church in Streatham, South London, who tells him, 'It is as though God wants to redevelop the people as well as the building [here] ... This is not revival, but we hope it is preparation for one ...the test will be in the fruit – whether this leads to conversions and whether the church is renewed.' Rob Warner of Herne Hill concurs: 'I have never experienced such a profound outpouring,' he tells Dewey, 'but this is not yet a revival ... the acid test will be whether it leads to conversions.' Dewey ends by quoting from an interview he has conducted with Rev Dr Nigel Wright, lecturer in theology at Spurgeon's College, London and a respected scholar of the charismatic movement. Wright accepts that this is a genuine 'time of refreshing' after the pattern of Acts 3:19, and adds that what is currently happening should not be despised. Neither, however, does he think that it should be 'overvalued'. He expresses concern that TTB might be too much associated with 'certain church networks', and that those outside such networks might feel alienated or unduly confused. He concludes that TTB is best seen as a 'wave' and adds that by their nature, such waves 'pass'. The point, he says, is to look beyond the outward phenomena to 'the deeper thrust of what God is seeking to do'.[56]

Friday 1st July 1994

The *Church of England Newspaper* reports that Rev Alan Morrison, Pastor of Crich Baptist Church in Derbyshire, has just published a leaflet denouncing TTB. Entitled *We All Fall Down*, some thirty three thousand copies of the leaflet will be distributed over the next three months. Morrison co-ordinates *Diakrisis*, a ministry established in 1990 'to acquaint believers with the importance of Christian apologetics, to provide commentary on topical, doctrinal and pastoral issues, and to hold out a hand of rescue to those who are caught up in psychological and spiritual bondage in the religious scene'. In the leaflet, Morrison casts TTB as a pagan New Age cult in disguise, and draws parallels between the manifestations associated with it and the practises of mesmerism and spiritism. He concludes that 'there is no biblical support for this experience as normative for the Christian believer ... its true origins lie either in the realms of suggestion and hypnosis, as proffered by Western psychotherapy, or in the Possession-Trance of ancient Shamanism ... The spirit by which these people are being 'slain' is not the Holy Spirit of God but some other spirit, for 'God is not the author of confusion but of peace' (1 Cor. 14:33). The churches which practise this phenomenon are being swept up into a supernatural tide of evil, where they become shipwrecked on the rocks of ignorance – ignorance of church history, ignorance of Scripture, and ignorance of the true work of God the Father, Son and Holy Spirit.'

As TTB develops, Morrison will step up his campaign of opposition with further tracts, teaching videos, conference addresses and meetings at his church.

Wednesday 6th July 1994

The regular 'London Leaders' meeting for key evangelicals in the capital convenes at Westminster Chapel. London Leaders is co-ordinated by Evangelical Alliance UK Director Joel Edwards and the Director of the evangelical charity CARE, Lyndon Bowring. The meeting focuses on TTB. Rob Warner reviews the events of the past few weeks and then invites Norman and Margaret Moss to recount their experiences at Queen's Road Baptist Church. Norman Moss concludes by praying for and laying hands on his wife, who soon starts shaking and falls to the floor with a sigh. Sandy Millar then tells of what has been happening at HTB.[57]

Realising that some will be disturbed by what they have just seen and heard, Edwards and Bowring announce a 'comfort break', to allow those who wish to do so to leave. Some duly depart, but the majority remain for further prayer and ministry. Writing a year later, Rob Warner will recall the rest of the meeting as follows:

[It] may well prove to have been the most significant prayer meeting in London for several decades.

The Spirit came upon the room in great waves of power. Brethren and Pentecostal, Anglicans, New Church and churches of every other stripe of evangelicalism were represented, and upon leader after leader the Spirit brought the awesome presence of God. It is always difficult to estimate such things, but it looked to me as if about two thirds of those present ended up on the floor at some stage. As Norman Moss moved around the room, Roger Forster caught his attention and asked for prayer. Norman promptly fell to his knees saying he would rather Roger prayed for him. Roger began to pray but as he did so, the Spirit fell not on Norman but on Roger, who stumbled forward into Norman's arms. Norman laid him out on the carpet and continued to pray for him. At one stage I was talking with Gerald Coates and R.T. Kendall. Gerald spoke about the immense impact this new wave was already having in Pioneer. RT stated his clear conviction that this was a genuine work of God and that the outward signs could be recognised as the hallmarks of previous times of refreshing and revival. Some leaders who had always been very wary of charismatic renewal began to receive from the Spirit of God that morning....

… As for me, at first I felt a little detached from the ministry time, then the Spirit of God began to come upon me. It was like the rising tide, wave upon wave of the warmth of divine love. Nicky Gumbel prayed for me: 'The Spirit of God is upon you, Rob.' As I rested on the floor there was a twin focus to what God was doing in my life, pouring out his love into my heart and anointing me with joy. Once again God was granting richly undeserved blessing. However, I could not help but notice how much less comfortable it is to fall on an uncarpeted floor.

Once back on my feet, I joined the coffee queue. Even there we were not immune to the overwhelming presence of God. One man had just reached the front of the queue when, without warning or receiving prayer from anyone else, he collapsed on the floor and rested there in peace. Sipping my coffee I marvelled at the astonishing power of God breaking out upon London leaders. Not just in one church or stream, but right across the board. God was turning up the heat. I believe this amazing prayer meeting demonstrated that God is beginning to do things beyond anything seen in our land for generations. Oh, Lord that we might see you come in revival power!

When Lyndon Bowring pulled himself together sufficiently to set off for his next appointment he left me a message. 'Isn't it wonderful! Tell Joel I am leaving him in full charge,' he said, beaming. Joel Edwards, meanwhile, was lying flat on his back, his face tranquil, his attention fixed not on earthly things but on peace in the heavenlies.[58]

Friday 8th July 1994

The *Church of England Newspaper* publishes three views of TTB from three prominent Anglican evangelicals.

Decade of Evangelism Officer Robert Warren is positive. On the question of whether TTB is of God, he says '"Yes" … Or rather, "Yes, thank you", and "Yes, please"'. He explains: 'The capacity to laugh and relax is at the heart of being truly human.' While warning against the temptation to use it as 'a fad or the latest technique for getting your church to grow', he insists that 'if such an experience comes our way we are to receive it with thanksgiving and integrate it into our whole experience of life. God's gifts come both to draw us to Christ, and to make us more Christlike.'

David Prior, Vicar of St Michael's, Chester Square, is similarly supportive of the new movement. The joy and laughter associated with TTB are, he writes, 'a gift and activity of God himself'. When confronted with even a foretaste of God's glory, he remarks that it is quite understandable that 'our physical bodies cannot cope. Many fall down under its weight and tremble, many look drunk and are filled with laughter.' Convinced that the present phenomena represent 'times of refreshing from the Lord', Prior nonetheless counsels on the basis of 1 Thessalonians 5:16-22 that all spiritual manifestations are to be tested. This, however, is to be a testing based on 'involvement, not detachment; presence, not hearsay; sensing as it happens, not deciding in advance'.

Demurring from all this, General Synod Board of Education member Professor Arthur Pollard condemns TTB for its 'mass emotionalism', 'mindless laughter' and 'exhibitionism'. Pollard laments the 'debasing' of 'the intellectual dimension' in charismatic circles whilst stressing that John Wesley actually discouraged the overvaluing of 'feelings and inward impressions'. Approving Alan

Morrison's sharp critique of the new wave, he pleads for a return to the 'order, decorum and dignity' of Anglican liturgy as prescribed in the *Book of Common Prayer*.[59]

On this same day, the Cor Lumen Christi group holds a rally for Roman Catholic charismatics in Guildford, Surrey; around 350 attend. Some of those present are aware that Toronto-style manifestations have been witnessed at the Hillsborough Bible Week in Northern Ireland, held over the preceding few days. As the Holy Spirit is invoked, many shake, weep and laugh.[60]

Thursday 14th July 1994

The Evangelical Alliance's UK Director Joel Edwards drafts a six-paragraph position statement on TTB. This is approved by his fellow Senior Managers and defines EA policy on the new movement for the time being (the full text of the Alliance's Preliminary Statement is reproduced in Part III). The statement confirms that the Alliance has 'attempted to keep abreast' of TTB and begins by urging that 'all spiritual phenomena' should be measured 'by biblical criteria' and by the extent to which they issue in 'holiness, prayer and witness'. The statement goes on to recognise that 'the current phenomenon is not new', drawing parallels with events which occurred during the ministries of Jonathan Edwards, John Wesley, George Whitefield and the early Pentecostal pioneer Stephen Jeffreys. Also, however, the text concedes that such events attracted their own share of 'controversy and blessings'. The Alliance is said to 'rejoice with those who testify to a deeper level of commitment and joy', but equally, urges them 'to avoid excessive behaviour which may discredit the gospel' and to refrain from 'indiscriminate enthusiasm'. At the same time, the statement warns against 'condemnatory behaviour which dismisses all unusual events out of hand'. The text then advocates the 'Gamaliel Principle', namely, 'If the phenomenon is genuinely of God it will certainly bear lasting fruit' [Acts 5:38,39]. In conclusion, the Alliance expresses its 'hope and sincere prayer' that evangelicals 'will not allow the issue to polarise and divide our witness at a time when it is most acutely needed'.

Saturday 16th July 1994

Dr Andrew Walker, a sociologist of religion at King's College, London and author of *Restoring the Kingdom*, the definitive history of the house church movement in Britain, comments on TTB in an article for the weekly *Christian Herald*. He wonders whether this new movement is not simply one more wave of pre-millennial expectation, and whether it might not eventually leave only 'tremors of disappointed excitement'. Having taken a straw poll of charismatic postgraduates at King's, he reports them as having 'mixed feelings about the present situation'. He adds: 'Two American missionaries, both studying for their doctorates, felt both positive and blessed by recent 'laughing' experiences at a London conference; but another student who visited Holy Trinity, Brompton, during a Toronto 'fall out' was untouched by the whole affair and could not wait to get home. A Bible-based Baptist was worried that the recent waves of excitement seem to have stemmed not initially from Toronto but from theo-logically dubious 'health and wealth' sources. None of these students assumes that the recent excitement heralds a world revival.'

Ultimately, Walker tends toward the view that the spectacular physical phenomena associated with TTB 'may have no spiritual significance' one way or the other. 'Christians,' he writes, 'are not immune from fashion, crowd hysteria, auto-suggestion, or simply being plain daft.' Even so, he adds that such phenomena 'should not be ruled out of court simply because they are odd'. If they are genuinely signs of a coming revival, he concludes, they will lead soon enough to 'conviction of sin, tears of repentance and love of neighbour'.[61]

Sunday 17th July 1994

Rob Warner and his wife Claire attend an evening meeting at Queen's Road Baptist Church, Wimbledon. It is the day of the World Cup final, but the meet-ing attracts over 200 people. Warner will later describe his experience thus: 'when my turn came for prayer I felt instantaneously drunk. I staggered a couple of steps, and fell to the ground. My hands began to twitch and shake, and then my whole body trembled as if I had been linked up to a high voltage cable. I heard the voice of God saying to me, "This is a revelation of my power. Not all of it, but as much as you can take right now."'[62]

Thursday 21st July 1994

The letters page of the *Baptist Times* for this week shows a generally hostile response to TTB from correspondents. Catherine Shephard of Abergeveny is given the most space for her complaint that the new movement is as likely to scare off non-believers as attract converts or genuinely refresh existing Christians.

Wednesday 27th July 1994

The Times carries a letter from Peter Howarth of Corpus Christi College, Oxford. He assures readers of the newspaper that those who had wondered whether weeping or sustained laughing in services would be exclusively confined to evangelical churches 'need not worry':

> The well-known fundamentalist Erasmus described such a service in his *On the Amiable Concord of the Church*: 'Sometimes the spirit of Christ can be seen to be present in the hearers. Some sigh; some burst into tears; the faces of some grow happy. In short, you would say that they had all been transfigured.'

Friday 29th July 1994

Alpha magazine follows it's July issue's report on TTB with an August leader advising that it cannot yet legitimately be described as 'revival', but may well be 'preparation for revival' after the model of 2 Chronicles 7:14. If so, writes editor Dave Roberts, there ought to be an increased emphasis in the coming weeks and months on repentance. 'Another mark of every great revival,' says Roberts, 'has been its effect on the whole community.' It is too early, of course … to see this distinctive feature. A comment, however, from one of those closely involved is, 'If, in six months time, we don't see the fruits, this isn't revival.' The leader closes by urging readers to 'learn the lessons and heed the warnings', calling them to be 'open to whatever the Holy Spirit would do in us and through us.'[63]

Roberts contributes two further articles on TTB to this month's edition. The first offers a summary of what has happened thus far, with fresh quotes from a number of key figures. Many of these quotes emphasise ways in which the new movement is bearing tangible evangelistic fruit. Various conversion stories from Bryn Jones' Covenant network are followed by Gerald Coates reporting that 25 people have come to salvation at a recent Pioneer meeting, and by Malcolm Kyte of Queen's Road Baptist Church stating that since May, 30 have come forward in response to the preaching of the gospel – either to make re-commitments, or to declare faith in Christ for the first-time. Roberts also quotes Steve Long of TAV saying that an average of two people are giving their lives to Christ at each of the daily meetings now being held there.

Roberts also refers in this first feature article to Bill Jackson's papers on TTB for Champaign Vineyard Church (April-May 1994). He comments that these texts have rapidly been conflated to function as a 'handbook for understanding' in the movement as a whole.[64]

In his second feature, Roberts takes up the comparison now being made by a number of spokespeople, between TTB and great revival experienced in New England under the ministry of Jonathan Edwards between 1740 and 1742. Referring particularly to Edwards' text *The Distinguishing Marks of a Work of the Spirit of God*, Roberts underlines the great theologian's openness to emotional expressions of faith and commitment. While making clear Edwards' insistence on the primacy of Scripture, Roberts quotes him as stating that 'what the church has been used to is not a rule by which we are to judge.' Roberts goes on to show Edwards as a preacher for whom Pentecost-type scenes were only to be expected as God pours out his Spirit 'in the latter ages of the world'. Edwards, we are told, did not suppose that there was a need to 'express Scripture for every external, accidental manifestation of the inward motion of the mind', but that he nonetheless found biblical parallels for the manifestations he had seen at Northampton in the falling and trembling of the Philippian jailer (Acts 16:29), and the crying out of the disciples during the storm (Mt. 14:26). Furthermore, although Roberts finds Edwards clear about the importance of discerning the fruit of believers' experiences and the general 'root and course' of their life, he cites his dictum that 'A thousand imprudences will not prove a work to be not of the Spirit of God.'

Roberts characterises Edwards' writing on revival as having been driven by a 'militant pursuit of balance'. He then concludes by quoting Edwards' summary of the five main 'positive fruits' to be looked for in any spiritual experience:

- An honouring of Jesus.
- A detachment from selfish pleasure or gain.
- A hunger for the Scriptures.
- A dwelling on truth.
- A deepening of mutual love.

Roberts also derives from Edwards various 'practical warnings and encouragements':

- The need for wise leadership.
- Caution before criticism. Gleaned by Roberts from Edwards' promotion of the 'Gamaliel Principle', i.e. the idea that an apparent work of God is best assessed according to whether or not it thrives in the long run (Acts 5:38-39).

- Get off the fence.
  Inferred by Roberts from Edwards' suggestion that wilful disengagement from spiritual outpourings is 'a kind of secret opposition'.
- Stay humble.
- Care in censuring of others. Rebuke is seen as legitimate, says Roberts of Edwards, but should be confined to the specific matter in hand, and not extended to wholesale denunciations of others' character. Roberts also find it helpful that Edwards warned 'friends of revival' not to treat their less enthusiastic critics with 'angry zeal'.[65]

These criteria and guidelines will be much-repeated and much-debated over the next weeks and months, as will the more general relevance of Edwards to TTB.

The same issue of *Alpha* also carries Terry Virgo's reflections on what has been happening in his NFI churches, and a reprinted version of Sandy Millar's testimony from the June 12th edition of *HTB in Focus*.

Also on this day, *Evangelicals Now* editor John Benton publishes a feature on TTB in which he states that 'the jury is still out for us'. Benton quotes George Whitefield writing to John Wesley with concern that the 'convulsions' seen at some of Wesley's meetings might 'take people from the written Word' and make them more dependent on experience than on 'the gospel'. Citing a friend, Benton concludes that Christian experience 'can be likened to a road which leads to God':

Running along one side of the road is the hedge of biblical beliefs. Along the other side is the hedge of biblical behaviour. Any experience which takes us through the hedge and off the road is spurious. But any experience which keeps us between the hedges, and propels us to love God more, and more zealously walk the road to him, can be taken as from the Lord.[66]

The *Evangelical Times*, which will prove to be one of TTB's severest detractors, prints a summary of Alan Morrison's broadside, *We All Fall Down*. Morrison's paralleling of TTB with mesmerism is given special attention.

Saturday 30th July 1994

The Christian Herald publishes Gerald Coates' response to its previous week's article on TTB by Andrew Walker. As leader of the Pioneer People network, Coates declares, 'I have never seen so many confessions of sin, letters of apology and witnessed acts of reconciliation as I have in the last few months.' Challenging Walker's non-committal stance, Coates expresses surprise that the sociologist failed to see strong comparisons with earlier evangelical revivals, such as the Northampton revival of 1740-42 associated with Jonathan Edwards, and the Everton revival of 1758-59 spurred by the ministry of John Wesley. He also applies the late conservative evangelical preacher Martyn Lloyd-Jones' words on these and other revivals to TTB: 'Why should the Devil suddenly start doing this kind of thing? Here is the church in a period of dryness and drought; why should the Devil suddenly do something which draws attention to religion and Jesus Christ? If this is the work of the Devil, well then, the Devil is an unutterable fool. He is dividing his own kingdom; he is increasing the kingdom of God.' Coates concludes by expressing his belief that 'we are on the edge of what could be the greatest thing to hit our nation this century.'[67]

Late July 1994

Having been prompted to do so by his friend Wesley Richards of the King's Church, Slough, Ken Gott of Sunderland Christian Centre flies down from the North East at short notice for a leaders' meeting at HTB. Initially unsettled by the Anglican ornamentation of the sanctuary, and by the upper middle class ethos of the church, Gott is prayed for by guest speaker Bishop David Pytches. Along with Richards and others from the King's Church, Gott is struck by what, in his own words, 'seemed to be a divine thunderbolt', and falls to the floor. Then he and his companions start to laugh: 'I was rolling first one way and then the other, holding my sides, which were aching with laughter. I had rolled under the baptismal font and every time I looked up and saw it I laughed even louder. Infant baptism was not part of my tradition, yet nothing seemed to matter.'[68] Gott relays all this to an evening meeting at his home church the next Sunday and, as he will later recall, 'hilarious laughter broke out, affecting some of the most unlikely people – one woman, a magistrate, was almost under her chair laughing. Many people were deeply touched.'[69]

Across the Atlantic around this time, writing in the in-house journal *Vineyard Reflections*, John Wimber recalls experiencing a vision very similar to that shared by Marc Dupont in May 1992. Fresh water runs down a mountainside into a plain of vineyards below, where labourers dig irrigation channels. 'I got the clear impression of a co-labouring,' writes Wimber. 'God was pouring out his blessing. But if we don't dig the channels, if we don't go out into the highways and by-ways, if we don't put evangelism forward, if we don't do the things God calls us to do, revival won't spread ... In other words let's begin organizing ourselves to give this blessing away.'[70]

Again in the last days of July, the main New Frontiers International Bible Week at Stoneleigh sees around fourteen thousand people from 30 countries experience or witness TTB on a larger scale. NFI leader Terry Virgo will later recall this as an event at which 'the power of God came flooding in. Literally thousands of stories can be told of lives touched and transformed, people saved, bodies healed and people falling in love with God in a way that they had never known before.'[71]

During the last week of July, some four thousand young people gather for the music and teaching event 'Soul Survivor'. Linked to the Anglican charismatic 'New Wine' festival, which will take place a short time later, this gathering shows clear evidence of the impact of TTB, with the characteristic manifestations on display.[72]

Thursday 4th August 1994

The *Daily Mail* reports that 'at least 40 of the 100 worshippers' at St James, an evangelical Anglican church in Bream, Gloucestershire, 'have collapsed writhing, weeping or giggling in services during the past month.'[73]

Thursday 4th – Sunday 7th August 1994

HTB and its church plants hold their annual holiday and study conference, 'Focus '94', at Morecambe Bay in Lancashire. Not surprisingly, TTB is the dominant theme, although the United Reformed Church theologian and retired Church of South India Bishop Lesslie Newbigin also speaks on 'The Gospel as Public Truth', and evangelist J. John teaches on 'Confidence'.

Two vicars in the HTB network, John Irvine of St Barnabas, Kensington and Jeremy Crossley of St James-the-Less, Pimlico, bear enthusiastic witness to the effect of TTB on their congregations. At this stage, however, Irvine cautions that it is better to talk in terms of 'a time of refreshing' than of 'revival': '"Time of refreshing" is a good biblical term,' he says, referring to Acts 3:19; 'let the historians later call it revival or awakening if that's what happens.' Meanwhile, HTB Churchwarden Ken Costa recounts how his initial scepticism turned to acceptance when trying to teach from Ephesians and finding himself unable to do so because of uncontrollable laughter. Soon after this experience, he says, he visited TAV and found himself 'bouncing up and down like a pogo-stick'. Costa relates all this to C.S. Lewis's description of having been 'surprised by joy'.[74]

In the Sunday evening main session, Evangelical Alliance General Director Clive Calver shares his latest thinking on TTB with the Focus audience. As when he spoke to the *Sunday Telegraph* on 19th June, he is keen to stress the imperative of social transformation:

> Today, if we are seeing a move of God it will not rest easily with the religious establishment. God always rocks the boat. He rarely does what I say he is going to do. That's why he is so uncomfortable.

When you look around today, something is happening. Just after this move of God started I was in a set of churches and they said, 'Is this an awakening?' And I said 'No'. An awakening is what God does in the world when he turns society around as he did in the eighteenth century.' They said, 'Is this a revival?' I said, 'I don't think so. Revival is what God does when he brings the world into the church.' They said, 'Is it a renewal?' I said, 'Yes, definitely. It's as important as this: you have never had an awakening in history that hasn't started in renewal and revival.' Now I want to see an awakening. I want to see God touch our nation and to see God turn our society upside down and inside out. But he won't start in society. He'll start with the people of God.

If this is an end in itself, I've got to confess to being slightly disappointed, because I've spent the last 20 years waiting for God to turn society round. This is the beginning. God is after a people broken before him. God forgive those who've condemned this as a work of the Enemy. I believe that God starts with us. But we don't want it to finish here, do we? I like laughing, but I'd like our world to laugh too ....

... God wants a people who will offer themselves so totally and completely that he can blow by his Spirit in a way that we have never seen. This is just a beginning – and as God gets surrendered lives, he wants to take us out to make a difference. It's a call to repentance. It's a call to follow Jesus. It's a call to surrender ourselves. When we do that we'll stop waiting for God and find that God's waiting for us. And when he's found us, I believe he's going to use us to change this nation in a way we haven't seen since Wesley and Whitefield.[75]

Saturday 6th August 1994

Ken and Lois Gott begin a week-long visit to TAV. A special offering collected by their congregation in Sunderland has funded their trip. As worship takes place, John Arnott prays for them. As they will later record, Lois begins 'bobbing up and down and shaking from head to foot', eventually falling to the floor. Ken bends forwards with arms and legs outstretched and fists clenched: 'it seemed like my insides were growing and growing and trying to burst out'. Some time later, he will reflect that the early Pentecostal leader Smith Wigglesworth 'described such an experience himself, saying he felt about ten times bigger on the inside than on the outside'. While all this is going on, Gott sees a vision of revival fires being lit all over the North of England. This is his first such vision, and leads him to shout out 'I can see it, I can see it'.[76]

Under the heading 'Are We in Revival?', the prominent prayer leader Brian Mills writes in today's *Christian Herald* that although 'many of us hoped we would be in a state of revival by now', this has not yet occurred. While some are seeing genuine marks of revival their fellowships and immediate communities, he says, this trend is 'not general – it is still very local'. Hoping for an increase in the present momentum, he calls people to the sort of corporate prayer currently being fostered by the Evangelical Alliance-backed Quarterly Prayer Initiative (QPI).[77]

Monday 7th August 1994

Ken Gott tells the TAV morning meeting about the history of revival in Sunderland, focusing especially on the ministry of Alexander Boddy, the Anglican Rector whose explorations of revival in Wales, Norway and elsewhere led All Saints Parish Church, Sunderland, to become a key site of Pentecostal renewal in the early twentieth century. Gott concludes: 'Just as Alexander Boddy travelled to Wales to see revival and brought it back to Sunderland, I am in Toronto to taste revival and refreshing and take it back with me.'[78]

The Gotts experience the remainder of the week as a time of 'soaking in the Spirit', marked by 'laughter, weeping, shakes and jerks', but most of all by 'deep repentance'.[79]

Saturday 5th – Friday 12th August 1994

The annual 'New Wine' week takes place at the Royal Bath and West Showground in Shepton Mallett. Originally a church weekend away for the congregation of St Andrew's, Chorleywood, New Wine has expanded into a large-scale, mainly Anglican charismatic festival which also attracts members of other denominations, including Roman Catholics.

Against the background of TTB, this year's New Wine highlights the subject of 'ministering in the Spirit'. Speakers include Sandy Millar and David Pytches. Event co-ordinator Joyce Wills tells the *Church Times*, 'A great many people have been touched by the Holy Spirit here. Some have been going out in the Spirit and having a wonderful, real experience of the presence of Jesus. There has been some exaggerated physical movement and lots and lots of laughter. Not every-body has been able to understand it, but David [Pytches] is marvellous at put-ting it in its biblical context. People are certainly hungry to learn about it.'

Sunday 7th – Friday 12th August 1994

The annual 'Scotland Aflame' festival in Blair Atholl sees hundreds affected by Toronto-style manifestations. The Covenant Life Church in Glasgow, who have organised the event, tell the London *Independent* that this is part of a global movement which may be set to emulate the Wesleyan revival. The *Independent* itself reports that 'more than two hundred and fifty thousand people, including many Europeans' have visited TAV since January.[80]

Friday 12th August

Best-selling Christian writer Joyce Huggett reflects on TTB in an article for The *Church of England Newspaper*. Now domiciled in Cyprus, she has yet per-sonally to experience the distinctive phenomena associated with the new movement. Even so, word of what has been happening has, she writes, led her to re-examine her own devotional life and to discover a fresh sense of God's assurance. As for the phenomena themselves, she urges concentration on their fruit, which, she says, 'is often best examined by asking a series of searching questions like: Are those who are claiming a fresh touch being reminded of the things Jesus said and did? Is our love for the written Word and the Living Word being rekindled? Are our prayer lives being transformed? Are our lives changed? As we enjoy more intimacy with God, do we find ourselves filled with self-sacrificing compassion for the poor and the marginalised? Do we have a heart for mission?' [81]

In the *Daily Telegraph's* 'Sacred and Profane' column, Clifford Longley suggests that TTB might well be explicable on purely socio-psychological grounds. He thinks it significant in this regard that the Toronto phenomena have been affecting agnostic journalists as well as dedicated charismatics; he then draws parallels with similar manifestations in other religious traditions.'Just how infectious emotional seizures can be in a religious setting,' he writes, 'is well documented from earlier centuries, from Eastern religions and even from the infamous Sun Dance which had such a destructive effect on the morale of American Indian tribes 100 years ago.'

Longley notes that TTB could be regarded as one more outworking of the well-developed 'appetite for experiences, particularly new ones' which has marked evangelicalism in the post-war period: 'In the 1960s, speaking in tongues became the fashion; in the 1970s, exorcisms and ritual healings; in the 1980s ... a more communal sense of joy; since earlier this year, it seems, the 1990s are set to become the decade of spiritual laughter.' Longley goes on to set these trends in a wider cultural context: 'The demand for signs and wonders is all part of a world where the deferment of gratification, whether for moral or spiritual purposes, has given way to the demand for instant satisfaction.' Furthermore, challenging the widely promoted test according to 'fruits', Longley writes that 'increased devotion and dedication, the reform of life and renewed commitment to one's fellow men' can be just as readily apparent after 'conversion to Buddhism or Scientology'. Such things, he says, 'prove nothing about the thing committed to, or the cause of the increase'.

Despite all this, Longley concludes on a somewhat more open note, based on a decisive commitment to truth as the final criterion of authenticity:'When faced with the claim that gales of involuntary laughter in church are a sign of a special visitation of God and a special sign of his favour and purpose, it still matters whether that is or is not in fact the case. If it is, we should all join in. And if it is not, then it is indeed a form of madness and should be seen as such.' [82]

Sunday 14th August 1994

On their return to Sunderland Christian Centre from Toronto, Ken and Lois Gott tell the congregation about their experiences at TAV. Ken struggles to remain on his feet while preaching and, on praying for people at the end of the service, sees many Toronto-style manifestations take place.

Following the service, it is decided that Sunderland Christian Centre will adopt a TAV-type schedule of daily meetings, at least for the ensuing fortnight. This pattern in fact continues through to October, when the programme shifts to four nights per week with a monthly rally. Attendances at these daily meetings will range between 150 and 400. [83]

Friday 19th August 1994

The conservative Protestant newsletter *English Churchman and St. James's Chronicle* refers dismissively to TTB as 'an outbreak of psychic phenomena in the London area in places of worship', and recommends Alan Morrison's critical leaflet *We All Fall Down* to its readers.[84]

Monday 22nd August 1994

The *Daily Telegraph* reports that various Roman Catholic groups have begun to experience TTB. As well as Cor Lumen Christi, who saw three hundred or so affected at a meeting in Guildford, Surrey on 8th July, Damian Thompson, Religious Affairs Correspondent, also mentions The Upper Room, a Catholic community in St Albans, Hertfordshire, which 'first experienced the Toronto Blessing three weeks ago after a visit by a pastor in the Vineyard Fellowship', and which has witnessed the characteristic manifestations on each occasion it has met since.[85]

Friday 27th August 1994

The Comment column of the *Evangelical Times* offers a denunciation of TTB which typifies its avowedly anti-charismatic stance:

> There is a real sense of *déjà vu* every time we hear of some new charismatic experi-
> ence which someone has received. In the past we have had speaking in the spirit, slain
> in the spirit [sic] and even breathing the spirit, but giggling, this will be new to many
> readers. This sense of 'already seen' is however not restricted to the actual manifesta-
> tions. The whole process is so well trodden that one can almost anticipate what the
> next marvellous revelation will be before it happens. Fairly regularly over the past
> twenty-five years … the charismatic movement has been indulging itself with claims
> of supernatural phenomena which just happen to occur in the last place anyone
> would ever imagine, and spread like wildfire among those churches which one would
> least expect … We do not doubt that there is an attraction about this kind of
> sensual activity. People in the world pay good money for a buzz or a trip or a high.
> Couple the sensationalism with some tweaking of the emotions and a sensitive sea-
> soning of superior spirituality and the cocktail becomes quite intoxicating … There
> is a peace that passes understanding [but] it is not found in lurching from the last
> amazing experience to the next. There is a joy which runs higher than giggling in
> the spirit. Possessing the righteousness of Christ brings peace with God and eternal
> happiness in the company of our Saviour. It also has its consolations for the here and
> now.[86]

In the same issue of *Evangelical Times*, John Legg presents a reading of Jonathan Edwards that contrasts markedly with that offered by Dave Roberts in the August issue of *Alpha* on 29th July. Insisting that Edwards is being 'wrongly quoted' in defence of TTB, Legg argues that far from endorsing physical and emotional responses to the gospel such as those experienced in Northampton in 1734-35 and 1740-43, Edwards in fact disapproved of them, and held merely that they could not, in and of themselves, be taken to rule out an under-lying work of God. Thus, 'Edwards's argument was that the mere occurrence of physical effects proves nothing one way or the other ... While [he] would probably say that current events do not of themselves deny that the Spirit is truly at work, he would also say that they do not prove that he is. I am sure he would categorize the things themselves as "wildfire", to be discouraged not relied upon.' Legg concludes by suggesting that Edwards would have asked 'very serious questions about the positive content' of the meetings associated with TTB: 'Falling down because of bodily weakness under a great awareness of sin in the presence of a holy, sin-hating God is one thing; collapsing and being 'slain' by just the touch of a mere man is another.'[87]

On a milder note, Peter Anderson and Derek Cleave urge readers of the September edition of *Evangelism Today* to grasp the authentic marks of revival before applying the term too hastily to TTB. They write:

> Revival always leads to the overwhelming success of the Gospel in the community ... It always produces a heightened awareness of sin. It certainly produces serious-minded Christians. What is important to notice is that revival comes out of the powerful preaching of the Word of God and an increased thirst on the part of the hearers to hear more. It certainly cannot be reproduced automatically and exactly the same in any part of the country as in the current manifestations, for revivals have never been uniform or predictable.[88]

Saturday 28th August 1994

In the September–October edition of the magazine *Prophecy Today*, editor Clifford Hill voices profound concerns about TTB. Contrasting the 'hysterical and even maniacal' laughter recounted by various sources with true 'joy in the Lord', he adds that 'throughout the Bible, the great majority of references to laughter are associated with scorn, derision or evil'. Hill is disturbed by the animal noises he has heard about, and by the 'heavy beat music', triumphalism and lack of biblical focus at a meeting in Brighton which a 'Pentecostal pastor' has reported to him.

He also objects to the 'pilgrimage' aspect of TTB, with so many now travel-ling to TAV in order to 'catch the blessing and take it back with them'. Echoing Alan Morrison, Hill likens the effect of 'resting in the Spirit' to 'the Hindu practice of using group laughter as a means of control to bring worshipers under the power of the guru'. Despite all this, Hill concludes by accepting that 'there are a few details given in Acts of the manifestations accompanying the outpouring of the Holy Spirit'. Therefore, he says, 'It would be unwise ... to rule out any manifestation unless it was blasphemous, destructive or sinful ... There are good things happening as well as bizarre.'[89]

Wednesday 31st August 1994

The *Daily Telegraph* reports that children 'claim to have seen Satan' during the New Wine festival held earlier in the month. Damian Thompson, Religious

Affairs Correspondent, quotes Rev David Gardner of Burwell Baptist Church in Cambridgeshire as saying that during the event a nine-year old boy fell to floor and had visions of 'heaven, angels, Jesus and "Satan in a cage"'. Gardner in fact recalls that many of the one thousand or so children in attendance fell to the floor, rested in the Spirit, and, while doing so, 'heard the voice of Jesus and saw pictures and visions'.

Thompson goes on to record that the Bishop of Coventry, Simon Barrington-Ward, has just approved a new book called *And For Your Children*, written by Styvechale vicar Rev John Leach with his wife, Chris. It suggests that children should be taught to receive charismatic gifts from a young age, on the grounds that they are prone to satanic attack from infancy. Leach will go on to apply this approach explicitly and enthusiastically to TTB (see 23rd December 1994). By contrast, Thompson quotes the reaction of the well-known radical Anglican priest, Rev Donald Reeves of St James's, Piccadilly, who says that it is 'quite irresponsible to attempt to manipulate the emotions of people at that age'.[90]

Thursday 1st September 1994

John Wimber convenes a meeting of the Association of Vineyard Churches (AVC) to review TTB. John Arnott, Randy Clark and Wes Campbell attend. It is agreed that AVC should urge restraint in the promotion of the phenomena associated with the new movement, whilst recognising that the movement itself is an authentic work of the Holy Spirit. A memorandum, to be issued on 14th September, is drafted to this effect.[91]

Sunday 4th September 1994

The *Observer* carries a report on TTB by Martin Wroe. He has just visited Queen's Road Baptist Church, and writes that the congregation there have been 'rolling and weeping and laughing and sometimes just lying there, moaning, wailing but in no pain'. Although he did not witness animal noises on this occasion, he recounts that elsewhere Christians are 'occasionally barking, crowing like cockerels, mooing like cows, pawing the ground like bulls and, more commonly, roaring like lions'. Bishop David Pytches is quoted: 'The Book of Micah talks of 'howling like a jackal and moaning like an owl'. What God is doing is shaking people physically and shocking people mentally, drawing attention to himself, like a parent shaking a child which wants to run across a busy road.'

Wroe goes on to write that Sunday attendances at HTB now stand at 'more than two thousand', with 'queues of five hundred outside by 5.30' for the 6.30pm evening service. For all this enthusiasm, however, he suggests that TTB may owe a great deal to 'pre-millennial tension or mass hysteria'. Even so, for balance he quotes Dr Simon Wessley, senior lecturer at King's College School of Medicine: 'This religious experience appears to be cathartic. The people feel rather good about it and appear to go for the purpose of group ecstatic experience. It is not mass hysteria or any form of mental disorder – it may be rather un-English, but there is nothing sinister about it at all.'[92]

Monday 5th September 1994
The *Western Mail* quotes Barry Napier, head of the Swansea-based Christian Research Ministries, as saying that TTB is 'a cancer in the Church'. A 'qualified psychologist and psychiatrist', Napier complains that the Blessing is 'going through the Church of England like a dose of salts and [is] now hitting churches and chapels in Wales'. Napier's colleague, James Wadell, dismisses the Toronto phenomena as 'familiar sights in hypnotism stage acts' and expresses sadness that those affected include 'intelligent, professional medical people whom I respect'. In a 12-page paper, Christian Research Ministries are reported to have called TTB 'demonic with a covering of human psychological hysteria'.[93]

Friday 9th September 1994
The prominent charismatic pioneer Michael Harper offers his assessment of TTB in the evangelical-Catholic magazine, *Directions*. Once an Anglican but now a Bishop in the Antiochian Orthodox Church, Harper confesses to having first been 'a little sceptical' about early reports of the Blessing. On visiting TAV for himself, however, he reports that 'from the moment I stepped inside the door I knew God was there, and the rest didn't really matter'. Despite remaining unimpressed by the music and feeling that the preacher 'went on far too long', Harper says it was clear to him that 'something extraordinary was happening [which] was due not to the human factors, but to the divine presence and power.' Praising the 'complete absence of "hype" at the meeting', Harper goes on to reflect that God's choice of 'an unknown 'storefront' church' as the key conduit of the new movement bears out his biblical tendency to choose the weak to confound the strong.

Harper continues to wonder in his piece whether the more intrusive bouts of laughter, and the 'grotesque' animal noises, are doing more harm than good. He also questions why people have to fall backwards rather than forwards, as is 'more normal in the Scriptures'. Such things, he writes, only point up the need for thorough explanation and interpretation, so that ordinary Christians can understand 'what God is saying' through TTB. In the end, however, he commends the Blessing as 'a sign of hope, when there is not much else to cheer about'.[94]

Monday 12th September 1994
The Times reports that HTB is now attracting so many visitors to its services that it is set to issue tickets 'for worshippers who want to ensure they get a seat for Sunday services'.[95]

Tuesday 14th September 1994
AVC issues a memorandum stating that TTB constitutes a genuine move of the Spirit, but that restraint should be shown in the promotion of the phenomena associated with it (the full text of the AVC Guidelines is given in Section III).[96] Seeking to offer guidelines on the pastoral administration of the physical

phenomena associated with TTB, the AVC Board urge that such things should generally be allowed to happen, but should not enjoy any special 'stimulation' or 'endorsement'. While some are acknowledged to bear biblical precedent (e.g. in Dan. 8:16-18,27; 10:8-10; Mt. 17:6,7; Rev. 1:17), the statement insists that others should not be 'explained' by 'inappropriate proof-texting'. In particular, the Board underlines that 'Biblical metaphors (similar to those concerning a lion or a dove, etc.) do not justify or provide a proof-text for animal behaviour.'

On the search for historical validation, the Board notes that 'people like Jonathan Edwards are helpful in that they give us examples of how godly men, who submitted themselves to the Scriptures as their final authority, sorted our similar issues.' Even so, they go on, 'in fairness to them, we don't know exactly what they would say about the current phenomena'.

Beyond such detail, the Board stresses the need to focus on 'the main/plain issues of Scripture', which it defines as 'witnessing, healing, demon expulsion, ministering to the poor and widows, etc.' Neither is it keen on 'theologizing' on the basis of manifestations themselves.

Moving on to eschatology, the Board guidelines disavow 'linking the present work of the Spirit to any precise eschatological scenario, e.g. Hal Lindsey[97] or the Latter Rain Movement, etc.' (cf. 3rd December 1988). Rather, it suggests that it would probably be 'wiser' to 'maintain the loose pre-millennial views held by the vast majority, but not all – namely, that we have been in "the last days" since Pentecost and we don't know when the precise last moments of time are.' Consequently, it advises, 'we don't know if this current renewal is "the last big one" or not.'

Reiterating established Vineyard 'key values', the statement encourages proponents of TTB to inculcate a passion for evangelism, to maintain simplicity, to do nothing for effect's sake (i.e. to hype or manipulate), to equip the saints, and to respect individual privacy and dignity. It also points to 1 Corinthians 14 as the 'main guideline' for the conduct of meetings, and highlights Paul's concern there for clear explication of spiritual phenomena and the edification of the whole body. In conclusion, the Board state that they 'desire to embrace all that is good about this renewal while correcting that which is excessive, long-term hurtful or contrary to biblical mandates'. In particular, they point out that they are 'committed to "power evangelism" not just "power"', and to '"signs and wonders and church growth", not just "signs and wonders."'[98]

Thursday 15th September 1994

TAV Associate Pastor Marc Dupont, on a visit to the UK, addresses a meeting of three hundred or so at John and Elli Mumford's Putney Vineyard church. He speaks of having recently witnessed the Blessing at work in India and mainland Europe, as well as in Britain and North America. 'When transition hits and the Spirit begins to move,' he says, 'sometimes people are taken by surprise.' He warns that those on the cutting edge of God's activity can be prone to spiritual pride, and urges humility and generosity among those who are spearheading the work of the new movement. Later, journalist and author Mike Fearon will recall that during the ministry time at this meeting, around fifty people end up on the floor and many others manifest the by now common phenomena of shaking and weeping. Fearon will also report this as his own first experience of 'the notorious lion noises', which emanate from those called forward to receive an anointing for prophecy.[99]

Writing in this week's edition of the *Baptist Times*, mental health chaplain Nigel Copsey presents a psychological analysis of TTB. Declaring himself from the outset to be 'very sympathetic' to the Blessing, he suggests that it offers 'a holistic experience of God [which] is to be welcomed'. For many, he goes on, it has also provided a chance to discover 'the healthy "child within" which has either been lost for many years or has never been experienced before because of a damaged childhood'. On the other hand, he warns that the greatest possible danger from the psychological viewpoint is the potential for 'hypnotic induction', which can be fostered by the 'use of music, relaxation of the body, tone of voice [and] atmosphere'. Seeking to recommend a pastorally and theologically balanced model of ministry for TTB, Copsey proposes the following guidelines:

1. Repeated reinforcement of certain suggestions should be avoided.
2. Meetings should not be 'hyped up', but instead there should be a real openness to God's Spirit.
3. As well as spontaneous prayer for one another, there should be available mature Christians who are experienced in spending time ministering to people.
4. There should be clear teaching beforehand on the movement of the Holy Spirit, covering the full range of experiences, e.g. silence as well as laughter, standing as well as falling.

Copsey proceeds to warn against the potential for 'in group' behaviour arising from TTB, whereby those who have 'received from God' define themselves over against the rest, and thus risk dividing the body. He encourages responsible and sensitive pastoral care for 'those who are not touched', noting that as things stand, the Blessing is still largely associated 'with a particular network of charismatic churches' and will appear to many in 'mainstream' or 'mixed' denominations to be a quite exotic form of devotional response.[100]

Friday 16th September 1994
Picking up *The Times'* report of 12th September on HTB now being 'ticket only', *The Church of England Newspaper* quotes vicar Sandy Millar as warning that the Toronto-style phenomena are 'not intended to be part of some spectacular in which they're observed, analysed, dissected and become the subject of instant judgement at a boo/hurrah sort of level'.[101]

Tuesday 20th – Friday 23rd September 1994
John Wimber leads a series of meetings at Wembley Conference Centre under the heading 'Let the Fire Fall'. Approximately eight hundred attend the daytime

meetings on church planting, with about one thousand two hundred present each night for the main celebrations.[102]

Friday 23rd September 1994

In a widely researched review of TTB, *Church Times* reporter Colin Moreton interviews and cites various leading figures on how things have been developing.

Disavowing the term 'revival', Sandy Millar tells Moreton that 'all we're safe to say is that God is refreshing his Church'. The manifestations, Millar reflects, have mostly been seen before, but are now 'more vivid'. Echoing what other key figures have said about the background and motivation of many who have been affected, he continues: 'the body of believers has been discouraged, and in many cases is totally weak. These manifestations are restoring us to the intimacy with God for which we cried out when we first became Christians.'

While agreeing that the Toronto phenomena have re-ignited a passion for reconciliation and generosity within his 100-church Pioneer group, and within the wider New Church network he helps to represent, Gerald Coates sounds a cautionary note: 'If these are meant to be times of refreshment,' he asks, 'how come many of the leaders I have spoken to are already exhausted? Something must be wrong. Also, we must be careful not to become a ministry of manifestations, otherwise it's not long before you're judging the value of meetings by whether people are laughing or crying, roaring or bellowing, or on the floor.'

Moreton goes on to report John Wimber's 'Let the Fire Fall' meetings, held this week at Wembley Conference Centre. Wimber is said by Moreton to have corrected the TAV leadership for giving 'inappropriate interpretations' of Toronto phenomena, and his quoted comments certainly seem somewhat restrained:

> What we have is a birthing process. The Holy Spirit has chosen to visit and revitalise the Church, and with that there are all kinds of noises and activities that would be best done behind closed doors. I'm a little puzzled myself by some of the things that God chooses to reveal publicly. But I love the after-effects. I've talked to hundreds of people now, and they tell me they love the Lord more, they read the Bible more, they're giving more and praying for the sick more, and they're operating in new gifts. Frankly, if someone's got to make an animal noise to do that, I don't care.

Moreton has also spoken to Eric Shegog, head of communications at Church House, who says that the Church of England has no official policy on TTB: 'People's reaction to it will vary ... but there has been no formulated response.' Shegog then quotes the Bishop of Newcastle, Rt Rev Alec Graham, who chairs the Church of England's Doctrine Commission, which reported on the Holy Spirit in 1991:

> There has been a history of spiritual manifestations in every century since the New Testament. It is very appropriate that these should be received in a low-key manner,

not sensationalised … A lot of people have particular revelations in their prayers, and so it is not entirely surprising if these things are corporate from time to time. One has to ask the traditional questions: Do they build up the Church? Do they show the fruits of the Spirit: love, joy, peace and all that? Are they edifying and upbuilding, or selfish and destructive? By their fruits shall ye know them.[103]

Saturday 24th September 1994

In the October issue of *Evangelical Times*, Alan Morrison's Diakrisis organisation advertises an audiotape he has produced on comparisons between the handling of physical manifestations during the Great Awakenings of the eighteenth century, and their treatment by proponents of TTB. The tapes expand the arguments presented in Morrison's previously published Diakrisis pamphlet, *We All Fall Down*, and his soon-to-be issued critique, *Falling for the Lie* (see next entry).

Friday 30th September 1994

The *Evangelical Times* prints extracts from Rev Alan Morrison's new critique of TTB. Entitled *Falling for the Lie*, this is a follow-up to his widely distributed leaflet, *We All Fall Down*, published in late June/early July. Continuing in the combative vein of the earlier paper, Morrison attacks TTB for its 'frivolity', its misappropriation of 'drunkenness' imagery in Acts 2 and Ephesians 5:18, its likeness to occult ritualism, and its 'deceptive' parallels with historic revivals:

> …when any phenomena occurred in the revivals of earlier eras – such as the Evangelical Awakenings in the UK and the US in the eighteenth and nineteenth centuries – they always took place as a result of powerful preaching of the cross from the Bible, an overwhelming sense of one's foulness in the face of an infinitely holy God, the shocking realisation of the impending reality of eternal punishment in hell, and a desperate desire to be free from the scorching blaze of God's wrath. In genuine revivals, any 'falling down' which occurred was the result of a sense of horror at one's sin and grief at the offence caused to an omnipotent God – certainly not an experience one would want to be repeated. In complete contrast to this, the current phenomena that we are seeing in churches today are completely unconnected to any of these contexts and are, at best, the outworking of a childish and hysterical mimicry; at worst, they are the result of something far more sinister.

Morrison concludes that those who are promoting TTB are siding with a 'false church' that is threatening the true body of believers through its emphasis on 'personal revelations, fashionable ideas and subjective experiences'.[104] In today's edition of *Evangelicals Now*, Morrison's Diakrisis ministry also markets a new 2-hour taped talk he has done entitled 'The Hallmarks of Genuine Revival; How These Phenomena Were Handled in the Great Awakenings; The True Origins of the "Toronto Blessing"'.

On this day also, the October edition of *Alpha* magazine carries an article by Gerald Coates in which he defends TTB against 'the Pharisees' who have begun to attack it. In stark contrast to Morrison, Coates draws a number of positive parallels with previous revivals, from the Wesley-Whitefield movement of the 1730s and 1740s, through David Brainerd's remarkable work among the Delaware Indians in 1745-6, to the Ulster revival of 1859. He also enlists Martyn Lloyd-Jones for support, quoting his observation that 'it comes near to being the rule that in revival phenomena begin to manifest themselves' – an observation which defines such phenomena as including fainting, falling to the ground, physical convulsions and trances. In conclusion, Coates issues a dramatic challenge: 'should we be privileged, as I believe we could be, to live through a time of sustained revival, we need to put this moment into perspective. It will shape our eternal destiny.'[105]

Saturday 1st October 1994

In the charismatic *Renewal* magazine, Wallace Boulton interviews R.T. Kendall, the Reformed minister of London's Westminster Chapel, and successor to Martyn Lloyd-Jones. Although Kendall has for some time been promoting co-operation between conservative evangelicals and charismatics, he admits to deep initial scepticism about TTB: 'If you had put me on a lie detector when I first heard about it, and asked me if I though this was of God, I would have said no.' Despite this, he now tells Boulton that he has since had to make a 'public climbdown'. Kendall explains his reasons:

> I saw one of my closest friends, who wasn't all that open to it, fall flat on his face for 10 or 15 minutes when he was prayed for in my vestry. The man who prayed for my friend had come to pray for me, which he did. But my friend said he would allow himself to be prayed for, not expecting anything to happen. He had only heard of Toronto that morning from me. He was the one who fell flat on the floor, not me. That impressed me.

Kendall recalls that the next day he had lunch with HTB warden Ken Costa, and became convinced by Costa's testimony that TTB 'had to be of God'. This has led him, he says, to do something he 'never thought' he would have to do: 'I have publicly affirmed what is happening at Holy Trinity, Brompton.' Having given this endorsement from the pulpit of Westminster Chapel, Kendall tells how he then invited Sandy Millar and other HTB staff to minister to his family, his deacons and their wives: 'My wife joined us as they were praying for me. After about two minutes she was on the floor. I had never seen such a radiant smile on her face. She wept, she laughed and she said to me later that if this was what being slain in the Spirit was, she could see why people wanted it.' Kendall himself was less immediately touched, but goes on in the interview to describe how, in time, he was also strongly affected: '...my mind became so relaxed. The nearest I can think of to describe it was when I had sodium penathol years ago when I had major surgery. Yet I wasn't unconscious. I felt myself falling forward ... For me it was so humbling. I think God was wanting to teach me to be humbled, to look stupid and to be a fool. There I was on the floor in front of all my deacons and their wives.'[106]

In the same issue of *Renewal*, Gerald Coates, 'with help from Bryn Jones, Sandy Millar, David Pytches and Vineyard USA', publishes a 750-word set of Guidelines on how to minister in TTB (the full text of these Guidelines is published in Part III). The joint document begins by defining four key principles:

- Make a swift response to the work of the Spirit, even if it means changing structures, programmes and agendas.
- Respond with humility and faith (cf. Mt. 7:9,10).
- Take responsibility for what is happening, giving due account of what is occurring.
- Ensure proper oversight and administration of what is going on, especially with regard to fostering an evangelistic, rather than an introspective, ethos.

The Guidelines then more specifically warn against developing 'a ministry of manifestations', and urge 'expectancy' rather than 'hype'. Children are encouraged to take part in meetings on the basis that most 'believe this to be a little like heaven and are much more responsive than some adults'. It is deemed acceptable to arrange special 'catchers' for those who fall over, and to create floor space in advance for the same purpose, 'even if it means moving chairs'. Extended cross-gender ministering is discouraged, however, as is 'manipulation' of the Holy Spirit through such activities as 'pushing people over, or saying things that amount to triumphalism or pure fantasy'.

A good deal of the text is devoted to handling criticism. Holding that 'there has never been a move of God which hasn't faced serious opposition', the authors go on to acknowledge that when journalists or other Christians go on the attack, 'it is easy to be reactionary, cynical, dismissive or superior'. Even so, they say, it is important to 'remain calm, rational and reasonable', and 'to disagree without being disagreeable'.[107]

In its October-November issue, *Aware* magazine carries an interview with HTB Communications Director Mark Elson-Dew, in which he reflects on the dramatic changes in the Knightsbridge church over the past few months: 'For years, at the end of services, we've been inviting the Holy Spirit to come – and he has – though not necessarily in a way that would be obvious! What's happening now is new in the sense that you can't miss it!' Elsdon-Dew emphasises that the church's commitment to sound teaching is still paramount, but notes that 'the programme's gone out of the window! Instead of preaching on the subjects planned – perfectly good and important subjects, by the way – we're deciding week by week what needs to happen next.' Elsdon-Dew confirms that HTB's close relationship with John Wimber and the Vineyard network, which goes back to the early 1980s, meant that to some extent a way had already been smoothed for reception of the Blessing. He also stresses that HTB is hardly the only church to have been affected. Even so, he tries to explain why it, above all other congregations in Britain, has become synonymous with 'Toronto': ' … we're a large Anglican church, and the press – including the national press – is known to me, and to the church. We're seen as a large church, so people watch what we do in a way that other churches aren't watched.'[108]

The weekly *Christian Herald* carries prayer leader Brian Mills' latest reflections on TTB. He reports that Kensington Temple, an Elim Pentecostal fellowship and 'Britain's largest church', cancelled all 'normal' activities during the month of September 'in order to seek God'. He also notes that his own church 'put on a regular, mid-week meeting during August and found an unprecedented two hundred plus turning up to seek God and to worship him'. Despite this, Mills refrains from designating TTB as a 'revival' on the basis that it has yet to develop a sufficiently profound or thoroughgoing dynamic of repentance, holiness and prayer.[109]

Christian Herald also reports today on a new critique of TTB which has just been published by a Derbyshire housewife, Tricia Tillin. Distributed by Banner Ministries, Tillin's study, *Looking Beyond Toronto: The Source and Goal of Pentecost*, alleges that TTB is dangerously rooted in the 'heretical' Canadian 'Latter Rain' movement (cf. December 1988). Tillin goes on to echo criticisms already levelled by Alan Morrison and others as she questions the 'pilgrimage' mentality of the many who have flocked to Toronto, the shrine-like status of TAV, the apparently coercive nature of ministry offered, the prevention of preaching by laughter and the abandonment of worshippers to physical sensations which might 'unwittingly fulfil the conditions of demonic activity'. With respect to the epiclectic character of much TTB prayer, she adds 'There is no warrant for calling upon the Holy Spirit or praying to him; our relationship is with the Father in Christ Jesus.'[110] Significantly, Dr Andrew Walker, a scholar of the charismatic movement who voiced tentative concerns about TTB in *Christian Herald* on 16th July, is now quoted as saying that while some of Tillin's analysis is speculative, 'it is at least 70% accurate'.

Around this time, the anti-cult organisation Reachout Trust publishes its Winter newsletter. Director Doug Harris reports that in the past few months he has received 'a full postbag concerning the Toronto Blessing'; if Reachout were to believe everything they have read they would by now be 'schizophrenic':

> The morning post brings a clear presentation that everything is of the Devil. The next post shows equally clearly that this is of God. This situation is a cameo of the division and confusion that are found within the Church in Britain at this time. Reading many of the articles received, speaking to people involved and observing various activities I feel it's clear that there is a mixture manifesting itself in the country. Mixture can be detected by the fact that sometimes God has clearly moved and changed the lives of his people. Alternatively there have been manifestations that do not bring any glory to God at all either at the time or in the life of the person afterwards. In summary we feel that there is both a genuine move of God and a counterfeit. The copy has emerged where the flesh has been stirred up and is manifested instead of the Holy Spirit of God. Of course, this leads to a dilemma where we have to decide which is genuine and which is not. This is not just a useless mental exercise because in all our work we need to be able to discern what is truly of God.[111]

Sunday 2nd October 1994
The *Sunday Telegraph*, prints an interview with John Wimber, conducted by Paul Goodman.[112] Touring Britain to observe and encourage churches involved in TTB, Wimber appears more upbeat about the new movement than in previous interviews. He tells Goodman, 'This recent happening ... is as intense as anything we've seen, but much more pervasive and rapid. I see it as a quickening – an awakening in the heart of the Church.' Although careful not to claim undue credit for what has been happening, Wimber recalls that whilst recovering from cancer in late 1993, God communicated to him that 'a season of new beginnings was about to start', which his Vineyard colleagues understood to be 'a refreshing'. Describing how the Holy Spirit fell 'sovereignly and powerfully' on his own congregation at Anaheim on 16th January, Wimber reflects that the rapid spread of the movement since then owes a great deal to 'the network of relationships' he and other Vineyard leaders have built up over '16 years on the road'.

Wimber is clear that the TTB cannot yet be defined as revival, but is hopeful that it might be 'the initiation of what can become a revival'. A key condition of this, he concludes, would be 'a *deepening* ...a heartfelt and wholesale repentance in the church'.

Friday 7th October 1994
The *Church of England Newspaper* reports that Gerald Coates' Pioneer network has had such great success with its Toronto-oriented 'Event in a Tent' meetings in Cobham, Surrey, that they have extended the run until Christmas. A total of more than 2,500 are said to have attended, with 850 present on a single night for a visit by John Wimber. Wimber himself is said to have been 'puzzled' by the manifestations, but is quoted as taking a relatively neutral, matter-of-fact line: 'I don't see much difference between [them] and soccer fans making all the strange and exotic noises they make when they get excited,' he says; 'Nor do I see [them] as something that ought to be endorsed, embraced, affirmed or accepted by the Church.' His overriding hope is that TTB will lead to 'a major revitalisation of the Church', with hundreds of thousands converted.

Wednesday 12th – Saturday 15th October 1994
TAV hosts a special four-day conference for church leaders, designed to help them 'experience the fire of God and then take it home'. Speakers include John Arnott, Randy Clark, William DeArtega, Wes Campbell, Jeremy Sinnott, David Ruis, Richard Riss and Guy Chevreau.

Monday 24th October 1994
London publisher Marshall Pickering launch TAV pastor Guy Chevreau's new book *Catch the Fire*. This has been rush-printed and enjoys the distinction of being the first title from a mainline Christian publisher about the TTB. Many others will soon follow.

Written as it is by an 'insider', *Catch the Fire* is predictably positive about TTB. It begins with an account of the 'pre-history' of the Blessing, focusing particularly on the influences that shaped John and Carol Arnott's ministry. It then moves on to offer a biblical apologetic for the new movement. Falling to the ground, says Chevreau, finds precedents in the spiritual experiences of Abraham, King Saul, Ezekiel and the apostles Paul and John (Gen.15:12; 1 Sam. 19:24; Ezek. 3:23; Acts 9:4; Rev. 1:17).[113] While Chevreau accepts that none of these examples can necessarily be treated as *pre*scriptions for responding to God today, he argues that Daniel's flat-out, trembling trance (Dan. 10:4ff.) constitutes 'probably the fullest *des*cription detailed in the Scriptures, of "God showing up", a favourite Vineyard expression'.[114] Holy laughter is set in the context of the 'unfettered enthusiasm and joy' of the early church, as recorded in texts like Acts 2:46, Philippians 4:4 and 1 Peter 1: 6, 8.[115] Citing James Dunn and Johanes Weiss on the diverse nature of spiritual experience in the Christian communities of the New Testament period, Chevreau defends TTB as an outworking of this diversity in the present day. While it might seem 'messy' to some, he argues that such apparent messiness represents more often than not a challenge to expand our 'operative theologies' and re-examine the 'status quo' of tradition.[116] In the final major section of the book, Chevreau draws extended parallels with the experience and reflection of Jonathan Edwards, on whom he has been conducting postgraduate research. Chevreau argues that appreciation of Edwards' work reveals TTB to be a reiteration of much of what happened in the Great Awakening, rather than an unprecedented deviation from evangelical faith and experience.[117]

Chevreau's biblical interpretations are paralleled in a piece published today by Gerald Coates in November's *Alpha*. Under the headline '"Toronto" and Scripture', Coates asserts that 'there is plenty of biblical material covering these manifestations of the Holy Spirit and reactions to his presence'. Insisting that 'the Bible is not a text book but a test book', he stresses that 'between those things [God] specifically approves of, and others he specifically disapproves of, we are given liberty to develop a wide range of activities broadly to reflect things he approves of.' The same liberty, says Coates, applies to 'manifestations of the Holy Spirit's presence'. Hence trembling or shaking is lent 'more than sufficient evidence and endorsement' by its mention in Psalms 2:11 and 119:120, and by Paul's reference to it in 1 Corinthians 2:3 and Philippians 2:12. Its periodic development into a loss of bodily strength is then related to the effects wrought by divine visitations in Exodus 19:16, Daniel 10:11 and Acts 10:10. Weeping can be justified, according to Coates, from texts such as Ezra 10:1, Nehemiah 8:9, Jeremiah 31:9 and Joel 2:12. Drunk-like states and 'trances' are validated by the appearance of Hannah at 1 Samuel 1:13, and by Luke's Pentecost narrative at Acts 2:13 and 15. The holy laughter associated with the Blessing finds precursors, writes Coates, in Psalms 2:4; 37:13 and 126:1-3. It is also a natural corollary of the 'overflowing joy' of 2 Corinthians 7:4 and the 'inexpressible joy' of 1 Peter 1:8.

While Alan Morrison has already criticised this sort of exegesis in his leaflets *We All Fall Down* and *Falling for the Lie*, it is also questioned around this time by David Forbes, in the November/December issue of *Prophecy Today*. Echoing various sceptical correspondents to the Christian weeklies, such as Tony Haynes in the *Baptist Times*[118], and Geoff Chapman in *Christian Herald*,[119] Forbes argues that the sometimes dramatic physical manifestations described in Scripture occur spontaneously in reaction to the preaching of the gospel and deep conviction of sin and, as such, bear little connection to 'what is currently happening to Christians when a time of ministry is scheduled specifically so that the manifestations might appear'. Forbes' doubts are reinforced by his unease at the provenance of the Blessing, which he sees stemming in part from the controversial Pentecostal Latter Rain movement of the late 1940s (see 1st October).

At this juncture, too, the leading American evangelical magazine *Christianity Today* (*CT*) reviews the development of TTB. Noting that the Blessing's advocates range 'from dispensationalists to Presbyterians to Roman Catholics', it reports that 'Ontarian exports of spiritual outpouring' have impacted churches in 'Atlanta, Anaheim, Saint Louis, several Canadian cities, Cambodia, and Albania'. Moreover, so many Britons, it says, are now flocking to TAV that 'direct flights from London to Toronto are sometimes sold out for days'. John Wimber is quoted: 'Nearly everything we've seen,' he suggests, 'falling, weeping, laughing, shaking – has been seen before, not only in our own memory, but in revivals all over the world'. *CT* also speaks to John Stackhouse, Associate Professor of Modern Christianity at the University of Manitoba. He is generally approving: 'It seems to me,' he says, 'that people are enthusiastic about Jesus and are happy to be Christians, and there doesn't seem to be an oversupply of that in North American Christianity today. If you don't like the idea of holy laughter that breaks out in a church service, then what kind of laughter do you believe in?'

Canadian Vineyard member John White, a psychologist who has written several best-selling books about sexual mores, and who in 1988 published a major apologetic for John Wimber's 'signs and wonders' ministry called *When the Spirit Comes with Power*,[120] is depicted in the same article as 'enthusiastic yet cautious'. His main concern is the potential for self-indulgence: 'Certainly one of the by-products of Toronto is extreme pride in some at having had the experience.' The tendency of some people to focus on 'my physical state, how I'm making it' is liable to detract, says White, from 'the sanctifying grace of God and our declared righteousness'. John Arnott himself appears to concur with this warning as he tells *CT*, 'I'm always on the lookout for someone who would have a "we-have-it-and-you-don't" attitude.'

The *CT* piece concludes by reporting that a new interdenominational group has formed in Toronto as a result of events at the Airport Vineyard. Even so, Peter Moore, Rector of downtown Toronto's Little Trinity Anglican Church, observes that 'there is more talk about the Airport Vineyard in England than here.'[121]

Wednesday 26th October 1994

Having flown to Britain for a brief visit, John Arnott speaks to a packed leaders' conference hosted by Sunderland Christian Centre. *Joy* magazine journalist Charles Gardner will later describe the scenes following Arnott's address as 'extraordinary'. All over the auditorium

> people were spontaneously breaking out into bursts of rip-roaring laughter, which appeared to come on them in waves, rising and receding ... There were shouts, shrieks, women prophesying, people shaking, some tearful and other jerking or flailing their arms about like a windmill ... Hundreds, meanwhile, were falling down after prayer until the floor was virtually covered with bodies.[122]

Friday 28th October 1994

Continuing his prolific output on TTB, Dave Roberts, the Editor of *Alpha*, warns in the November issue of his magazine against various forms of 'intolerance and impatience' which appear to be arising in relation to the new movement. Specifically, he cites four cardinal faults:

- Snap judgements derived from wariness about the past record of key participants. 'Dismissing something on the basis of old history,' says Roberts, 'makes no allowance for change and process ... Would we leave the Corinthian church, the wild men of their day, to their heretical devices, or like Paul, acknowledge their fervour and seek to bring gentle reproof?'
- Unresearched judgements, which are arrived at through misconstrual or distortion of primary sources.
- Unrighteous judgements, which proceed without recourse to those vilified and refuse to engage pastorally with them.
- Legalistic and illogical judgements predicated on 'theological perfectionism' and 'guilt by association'.

Roberts also contributes a distinctly personal reflection on TTB, citing his interwoven experiences in 'the Reformed heartlands of Leicester' and the New Church movement as formative in his current desire to 'bless what God is blessing and ... root out that which undermines and destroys'. This 'middle line' is, however, something which Roberts is finding it increasingly difficult to sustain: 'It is no easy task', he reflects, 'being open, thoughtful, biblical, spiritually sensitive, open to the supernatural and God's disruption of our normal patterns, all at the same time.'[123]

The news pages of *Alpha* today also report that Gerald Coates' Cobham-based Pioneer People network met every night for a fortnight in the latter part of September, with over five thousand five hundred attending. What is more, Sunderland Christian Centre 'has met every night except Mondays since mid-August ... with crowds in excess of six hundred attending every night, and as many as 30-50% being newcomers.[124] In addition, Kensington Temple has recently been seeing 'over eight hundred a night pack the church'. 'KT' Pastor Colin Dye is quoted as commending TTB as something that can 'lead us closer to the Lord'; in an article for the coming month's *Direction* magazine, he expands on this as he draws parallels with Isaiah 35. Just as Israel is promised revival after a period of spiritual dryness, so Dye sees the Blessing as an opportunity to reverse the systematic removal of 'God and his values from almost every level of society' over 'the past 50 years'.[125]

On a busy day for coverage of TTB, the *Church of England Newspaper* carries a profile of TAV's Guy Chevreau, who is in Britain to promote his book, *Catch the Fire* (see 24th October). In the profile, Andrew Carey explains that Chevreau is a Baptist pastor, but that he was driven out of his last church in Oakville, Ontario, because of 'opposition to his commitment to the unchurched': 'I experienced open accusation, malice and gross distortion,' says Chevreau. 'I was accused of spending too much of my time in frontline evangelism.' Despite this background, Chevreau sees no reason why TTB should be viewed as intrinsically divisive. To those who are wary of the new movement, he says, 'Get your very legitimate questions answered as best you can. Figure out what it is you expect to happen. Don't target any particular manifestation – just show up. Allow God to bless you.'

Disarmingly, Chevreau admits that TTB may be no more than a fad. But, he quickly adds, there may be another possibility: 'This may be building on the renewal of worship, on the healing ministries that have arisen in recent years. If that's true, we're trying not to screw it up.' Like many others at the forefront of the Blessing, he is cautious about labelling it a revival at this stage: 'If what you mean by revival is mass conversions of whole towns, we're not seeing that ... yet. At the moment it is the revival of churches. Many Christians have had a hard time living out their faith. They have had a hard dry time spiritually. The Toronto blessing brings a new vibrancy.'[126]

Saturday 29th October 1994

The Territorial Commander of the Salvation Army in Britain writes on TTB in his regular column for *The Salvationist*. He begins by advocating 'the Gamaliel principle' as derived from Acts 5:38: 'If this counsel or this work be of men, it will come to nought: But if it be of God, ye cannot overthrow it.' (KJV) This fruits-based test leads him in turn to write that in his view 'a human or diabolical origin could not explain the positive spiritual benefits that occur'. Urging his readers to talk to those who have experienced the Blessing, he notes that such people 'are certain that God's Holy Spirit has come to them, even though they are often mystified as to why they and not the person next to them have been singled out'. What most worries the Commander about the new movement is not so much pneumatological as ecclesiological: his chief concern, he writes, 'is about the danger of division and diversion'. As he explains it, 'I would not want to embrace anything that divides the Army. Neither can there be any place for elite spiritual cliques ... God is the Spirit of unity. I cannot countenance anything that diverts this Army of ours – raised up by God for a worldwide mission to the unconverted – from its basic purpose.' Even so, the Commander is more than willing to trace parallels between the manifestations associated with TTB and events reported by the renowned Victorian Salvationist Bramwell Booth in his book *Echoes and Memories*. Booth is recalled as describing a prayer meting at which 'here and there among the audience people would be observed to fall to the ground'. In Harold Begbie's classic biography of Army founder William Booth, Bramwell is also quoted as reporting that during meetings in London led by his father, 'men and women would suddenly fall upon the ground, and remain in a swoon or trance for many hours, rising at last so transformed by joy but that they could do nothing but shout and sing in an ecstasy of bliss'.[127]

Also published today, the generally pro-TTB *Renewal* magazine prints a report from St James', Bream, an Anglican church in rural Gloucestershire. During the past five weeks, writes Helen Terry, the vicar Alistair Kendall and his congregation have seen 'a massive change of scale with anything up to 40 being affected simultaneously' by the distinctive manifestations of the new movement. Toronto-style ministry is now being offered at every service, and has attracted the attention of both local and national media. Elsewhere in the same magazine, Mike Breen, the new Rector of St Thomas' Church, Crookes, Sheffield, finds that biblical light is shed on the Blessing by Ezekiel's vision of a rising river flowing through the Jersualem Temple and eastwards into the Dead Sea (Ezek. 47:1-12). 'To follow the renewing life of God's Spirit,' writes Breen, 'means getting into deeper and deeper water until our feet are off the bottom and he is fully in control.' This text will soon become a favourite reference-point for those teaching on the significance of TTB (cf. 3rd December 1994; 10th July 1995).[128]

In the same issue of *Renewal*, Jane Grayshon, a popular author best known for her *Confessions of a Vicar's Wife*, writes of the need for sensitivity towards those who cannot or do not feel able to participate in Toronto-style experiences.[129]

On a much harsher note, the November edition of *Evangelical Times* today launches another damning blast against TTB, this time in its editorial column. Identifying the proponents of the new movement as 'impostors' who have 'stolen the clothes, the language and the structures of the old evangelical Christianity', the article goes on to suggest sardonically that such people should be re-named 'Wavangelicals', on the basis that they are 'pseudo-evangelicals who look for waves – new waves, third, fourth and fifth waves, arm waves, airwaves and waves of emotion'. The piece concludes by accusing these 'Wavangelicals' of presenting 'a false Christ to the unbelieving world', after the manner of the deceivers mentioned by Jesus in Matthew 24:24.

Seeking a somewhat more even-handed approach, the new edition of *Evangelicals Now* carries two features, one expressing a generally positive view of TTB and the other a strongly critical assessment. The first takes the form of an interview with Epsom Downs Baptist minister Roger Welch, who recounts that after feeling increasingly tired out by church activities, he went, 'almost in desperation', to the after-service meetings that Queen's Road Baptist Church had begun to hold in May. He then travelled to TAV and came back sure that a 'time of refreshing' was at hand. While wary of some of the names associated with the early formation of the Blessing, and while 'neutral' on the phenomena after what he sees is the model presented by Jonathan Edwards, Welch nonetheless senses 'greater depth' coming to the movement, 'especially in repentance, obedience and righteousness'. All this, he says, 'stirs my heart, my mind and my spirit to go on seeking God for a mighty outpouring of his Spirit in revival that will touch us all'.[130]

By contrast, the second article sees in the origins of TTB, and particularly in its links with the Word of Faith movement, the operation 'not ... of the Holy Spirit, but some other spirit'. Stephen Sizer, Vicar of St John's Church, near Guildford in Surrey, writes the piece (Sizer's updated reflections on Toronto appear in Part I of this book). Rehearsing the development of TTB through Rodney Howard-Browne and Benny Hinn to the Vineyard, Sizer sees this as a 'false' and 'heretical' lineage that is enough, in itself, to condemn the Blessing as something that might well 'open ... believers to demonic deception'.[131]

Alongside the Welch and Sizer features, the letters page of *Evangelicals Now* sees Evangelical Alliance UK Director Joel Edwards respond to N. Murray of Woodford Green. Mr Murray suggested in the October issue of *EN* that the London Leaders meeting convened by Edwards and CARE Director Lyndon Bowring on 6th July had, by its inclusion of Toronto-style ministry, confirmed a 'charismatic take-over' of the Alliance. Edwards writes that those who planned the meeting were seeking to recognise 'the significant impact that the "Toronto Blessing" is having on many churches in the capital'. He continues:

> After careful reflection we felt it appropriate to make room during the latter part of the meeting for leaders who felt comfortable to participate in a time of ministry, as well as those who were not fully persuaded but who wished to take part.

> Evangelicals should make every effort to measure all spiritual phenomena by biblical criteria. The devotional hallmarks of holiness, prayer and witness provide reliable in-dicators of authentic moves of God. I respect the accounts of those who testify to a deeper level of commitment and joy as a result of their experience. But equally I would urge them to avoid excessive behaviour which may discredit the gospel or distance those who genuinely seek an encounter with God. Indiscriminate enthusiasm can alienate, but so can condemnatory reactions which dismiss all unusual events out of hand.

> Mr Murray asks about the danger of a charismatic 'take-over' of the Evangelical Alliance. The Alliance remains committed to reflecting the broad spectrum of its membership across its varied ministry. The noticeable presence of charismatic streams within EA should not detract from this on-going commitment. Phenomenon [sic] like the 'Toronto Blessing' present a potential cause of division. They should not eclipse the goal of evangelical unity across denominational and theological boundaries.[132]

Friday 3rd November 1994
Kingsway publish *Alpha* editor Dave Roberts' book, *The 'Toronto' Blessing*. Collecting and supplementing his numerous articles of the past few months, the

book takes a largely supportive view of the new movement, but suggests that it still has some way to go before it can genuinely be compared to the socially transforming evangelical revivals of the past.

Friday 11th November 1994

Eagle publish journalist Mike Fearon's 258-page survey of TTB. Entitled *A Breath of Fresh Air*, this is based substantially on interviews with a wide spread of evangelical Christian leaders, ranging from keen Toronto advocates like Gerald Coates, Sandy Millar and David Pytches, to more cautious observers like Andrew Walker, Tom Smail and Dave Tomlinson. While Fearon generally lets his interviewees speak for themselves, it is not hard to detect more sympathy for those who are 'risking' involvement with TTB, than with those who have already dismissed it out of hand. Indeed, he describes himself as 'personally convinced' that TTB is authentically of God, even while being 'deeply suspicious of some of the teaching associated with it'. 'Perhaps,' he concludes 'in the next century, people will re-read these words from the vantage-point of a major Awakening, and wonder with amusement why so many Christian leaders were so cautious at the beginning of a revival!'[133]

Also published this week, and promoted in the Christian press today, is Pioneer People leader Patrick Dixon's analysis of the Blessing. Entitled *Signs of Revival*, it is more comprehensive than the books written by Chevreau, Roberts or Fearon, containing as it does a detailed history of the present movement, and extensive comparison of it with historic revivals and outpourings of 'emotional faith' (Patrick Dixon's updated reflections on TTB are presented in Section I of this book).[134] Dixon highlights the 'Everton revival' presided over by John Wesley, the Ulster revival of 1859, the London meetings addressed by William Booth around 1878 and the proto-Pentecostal Azusa Street meetings of 1906 as times when intense physical manifestations of spiritual activity were numerous, with falling, shaking, laughter, roaring and convulsions similar in appearance to those now associated with TTB.

Most significantly and distinctively, however, Dixon's professional work as a medical doctor prompts him to assess the new movement in terms of 'altered states of consciousness' or 'ASCs'. Rejecting the suggestion made by Alan Morrison and others that the Blessing mediates mass hysteria, mesmerism and auto-suggestion, Dixon defines ASCs within an essentially neutral category of human experience – one that may be quite compatible with biblical faith and authentic theological anthropology. ASCs, says Dixon, can help to explain Isaiah's vivid vision in Isaiah 6, Peter's trance in Acts 10, Paul's description of one caught up into 'the third heaven' in 2 Corinthians 12:2, and the revelations given to St John the Divine. They are marked by shifts in patterns of thinking, changed notions of time, some relinquishing of control, fresh emotional expression, new body image perceptions, a sense of the ineffable and feelings of rejuvenation. None of these, argues Dixon, are necessarily suspect from a Christian point of view, although ASCs can certainly also predispose people to more dubious conditions of hypersuggestibility. In the end, however, he argues that Christians not only voluntarily open themselves to ASCs through special disciplines like fasting, but may also experience ASCs in the course of relatively routine Christian activities:

> Many Christians would agree that all ASCs are likely to open doors, but the question is, open them to what? An ASC in the middle of a séance or during a voodoo ceremony could be highly dangerous. However, an ASC during an act of Christian worship could be a helpful and healing experience which is life changing and long lasting in its beneficial effect on body, mind and spirit. Some may find this whole discussion uncomfortable, denying that they have ever had an ASC. But who has not knelt at the communion rail and felt something outside themselves? Who has not sat in a place like King's College, Cambridge and not been transported to a sublime height with the soaring ethereal notes of the choir? Who has not for a moment imagined they have caught a glimpse of heavenly glory itself in a fading sunset, or been aware of the presence of God in the instant between sleep and wakefulness?[135]

Dixon's summarises his book in an article for *The Church of England Newspaper*, which also generates a front page story from his warning that those affected by TTB should not drive cars while under its influence.[136] This story is repeated in tomorrow's *Daily Telegraph*.[137]

In the same issue of *CEN*, Mike Fearon's interview with Graham Cray is extracted from *A Breath of Fresh Air*, with new, unpublished material added. Cray is now Principal of the evangelical Anglican theological college Ridley Hall, Cambridge, but was previously Vicar of St Michael-le-Belfrey, York – the Anglican church from which David Watson did so much to promote charismatic renewal in the 1970s. Cray readily admits to having experienced Toronto-style manifestations at the August New Wine festival: 'I found myself swaying,' he recalls, 'and I don't remember starting. After a while I began to laugh from the depths of my gut.' All the same, Cray emphasises that he never thought that his sense of self-control was being overridden: ' I always felt that what was happening had not been initiated by myself, and that I could have stopped it had I wished, but I could find no reason to stop. There was a deep sense of personal liberation.' Subsequently, Cray says, tears have also followed as he has been led into a deeper understanding of the world's brokenness. He is well aware of the potential of TTB to fall prey to the power of suggestion, but, he adds, 'even taking that as the worst-case scenario, what is the difference between someone saying, 'Come, Holy Spirit' and it actually happening, and someone using the power of suggestion? The Spirit of God has to come along the same path. There's such a fine line. I think 'it can be of God' even if the people up the front are not very wise.'

During the course of the interview, Fearon notes that beyond his own assessment that two thousand churches have now experienced TTB, Gerald Coates has recently put the figure closer to four thousand.[138]

Thursday 17th November 1994

John Horner reviews Guy Chevreau's *Catch the Fire* in the *Methodist Recorder*. Although he praises Chevreau for making 'valuable points' about revival phenomena, the personal dynamics of renewal and the possible relation of the manifestations to God's sovereignty, Horner remains suspicious: 'It seems to me,' he concludes, 'that if God wants to prove his presence in this world, he would do much better to raise up a host of latter-day Elijahs to work miracles with cruses of oil and barrels of meal in countries where people are starving, than to promote all this carrying-on in Toronto, Brompton and elsewhere.'[139]

Friday 25th November 1994

The December issue of *Alpha* extracts Dave Roberts' chapter on Rodney Howard-Browne from his book *The 'Toronto' Blessing*. While documenting Howard-Browne's controversial links with the WordFaith movement, Roberts argues that the Pentecostal evangelist has nonetheless displayed a commendable 'independence of mind' in giving short shrift to associated teachings on heavy shepherding, tongues fanaticism and extreme spiritual warfare. 'Dismissal of him as a Word of Faith extremist', is, says Roberts, 'not adequate.'[140]

The same issue of *Alpha* also reproduces Patrick Dixon's analysis of past revivals from his book *Signs of Revival*.[141]

Saturday 3rd December 1994

In a major feature for the *Daily Telegraph* Saturday magazine, Mick Brown reports on a visit to TAV's recent 'Catch the Fire' conference. Along with two thousand five hundred others, Brown recalls having heard Randy Clark expound on TTB and having watched 'drips of laughter ...become a torrent'. Soon, recalls Brown, a ministry team 'moved among the laughing, the tearful and the merely stunned, laying on hands, causing them to fall backwards to the ground, as if struck with electric cattle prods'. After an account of the history of the Blessing to date and its possible precursors in historic revivals, Brown returns to the scene at TAV. Despite being an agnostic, Brown testifies to a startling experience of the Blessing: 'I found myself beside John Arnott,' he writes. 'I didn't even see his hand coming towards me as it arced through the air and touched me gently – hardly at all – on the forehead. "And bless this one, Lord..." I could feel a palpable shock running through me, then I was falling backwards, as if my legs had been kicked away from underneath me. I hit the floor – I swear this is the truth – laughing like a drain.'[142]

Also today, Trisha Tillin reviews Chevreau, Fearon, Roberts and Dixon's books for *Christian Herald*. Concluding that they are 'in varying degrees useful and readable accounts of an emerging phenomenon', she nevertheless says that none of them offers adequate biblical and theological analysis of how to test spirits, exegete key 'Toronto' texts like Joel 2 and Ezekiel 47, assess the practice of 'calling down the Spirit', deal with biblical warnings against deception on the one hand and quenching God's work on the other, and offer pastoral advice to those hurt by what has been going on.[143]

Tuesday 13th December 1994
The Canadian newspaper *Christian Week* reports that because of the extraordinary attendances at TAV, the church will soon be moving to what has been known as the Asia Trade Exchange, 'a cavernous conference and exhibition centre on Atwell Drive – still near the airport'. Respected evangelical historian George Rawlyk comments in the same article that it is intriguing that the Blessing has occurred where it has: 'certainly,' he reflects, 'if you want to affect the Christian church throughout he world, you want it by an international airport.' While recognising from his professional academic perspective that very little in TTB is really new, Rawlyk still warns that 'the real danger in this whole business is if experience becomes paramount and the head isn't part of the religious experience at all.'[144]

On a brief tour of the UK, Rodney Howard-Browne leads a meeting tonight at the Wembley Conference Centre (see also 14th and 28th January 1995).

Monday 19th – Tuesday 20th December 1994
The Evangelical Alliance convenes a meeting of 23 key evangelical leaders at the Ibis Hotel in Euston, London, to discuss TTB. The attendees are as follows: Clive Calver and Joel Edwards, respectively General Director and UK Director of the Alliance, Dave Cave (then Convenor of ACUTE), David Abernethie (Above Bar Church, Southampton), Robert Amess (Duke Street Baptist Church), Matthew Ashimolowo (Kingsway International Christian Centre, Hackney), Tony Baker (Bishop Hannington, Hove), John Butcher (Pentecostal), Gerald Coates (Pioneer), David Enoch (a psychiatrist), Faith Forster (Ichthus), Alan Gibson (British Evangelical Council), Philip Hacking (Reform), Phil Hill (Baptist), Gordon Hills (Assemblies of God), Professor Tudur Jones, R.T. Kendall (Westminster Chapel), Bryn Jones (Harvest Time), Philip Mohabir (Alliance of Asian Christians), Paul Perkin (St Mark's, Battersea Rise), Stephen Sizer (St John's, Guidford), Derek Tidball (London Bible College) and Rob Warner (Herne Hill Baptist Church).

The meeting begins with three short talks on revival. R.T. Kendall expounds Acts 2 as the cardinal text on this matter. Tudur Jones then speaks of revival in church history, and Derek Tidball continues with a reflection on the tensions that have often challenged the church at such times. There is then a period of open response and discussion before the meeting divides into four groups, each of which expresses a variety of views on TTB.

Later on the first day, Stephen Sizer and Rob Warner are asked jointly to draft a statement that might reflect the theological consensus, mood, hopes and fears of those present. They work on this into the early hours of the next day, and eventually present a 12 paragraph, 800-word text to the meeting. Under the guidance of Clive Calver, the great majority of those present adopt this. Indeed, only one person declines to endorse it.

The statement (which is reproduced in full in Part III) itself begins by stressing the need 'not only to evaluate' TTB, but 'also to make to make clear distinctions between primary and secondary convictions among us as evangelicals, even though we differ in our initial interpretations of these experiences'. It proceeds to define agreed primary convictions as the authority and divine inspiration of Scripture, the atoning work of Christ, the 'vital need' for personal conversion, and the prerogative of active witness and service in the world. It then rejoices that God has poured out his Spirit in revivals, and that these are 'intrinsic to the evangelical heritage we share'.

The text moves on to emphasise the need for a unity of Word and Spirit in evangelical life and action. With particular concern for the outworking of this unity in the evangelical context, it acknowledges that in the past, evangelicals have sometimes failed adequately to listen to one another, and 'to denigrate and caricature those with whom we disagree'. In the Euston consultation, the statement declares, 'we have sought to ask questions of ourselves and one another, without compromising the integrity of our consciously held differences.'

Dealing particularly with the manifestations related to revivals, the statement notes that they must be seen as 'secondary'. In and of themselves, it explains, 'they cannot … prove that a movement is or is not a work of God'. The final test must be 'the lasting, biblical fruit'. Acknowledging that the Toronto experience 'is not yet integrated with theological reflection', clause 7 rejoices with those who have known 'genuine life changing encounters' as a result of it, while regretting that 'some have neglected the discipline of biblical preaching in the face of current manifestations'.

Warning against the dual dangers of imbibing 'the existentialist spirit of our age' along with TTB, and dismissing it out of sheer 'enlightenment rationalism', the text urges that the 'absolute truth of the gospel' be guarded 'without compromise'.

The Euston statement closes by deducing that the church in the UK is not presently experiencing revival, but accepts that many during recent months have known significant 'enrichment'; this encourages 'hope that we may be in a period of preparation for revival'. Concluding that any evaluation of the present phenomena can only be 'provisional' since it is 'too early for definitive judgements', the text calls for a group within the Evangelical Alliance 'to continue to provide evaluation and theological reflection on these developments within the church'. It suggests that this group should report back one year hence, and encourages it and other assessments of TTB to apply Jonathan Edwards' classic tests for a genuine work of God: exaltation of Christ in people's understanding; undermining of Satan's purposes; a fostering of greater regard for Scripture and truth; a cultivation of seriousness about the things of God, and of greater love for God, fellow Christians and the world as a whole.

The meeting and statement are not officially publicised until 12th January, after which they receive extensive press coverage.

Friday 23rd December 1994

The *Church of England Newspaper* reports Coventry Vicar John Leach keenly applying the principles of his book on charismatic ministry among children to TTB (cf. 31st August 1994). 'As children have seen and heard bizarre sights and sounds', he says, 'there has not been a hint of fear.' Rather, he adds, they 'are having fun in the church in ways which just wouldn't have been their experience a few months ago.' In opposition to this view, Rev David Streater of the Church Society warns against regarding children as any less prone to the influence of sin and deception in the new movement than adults.[145]

Friday 30th December 1994

Ron Davies, Director of the Postgraduate Centre at All Nations Christian College in Ware, writes on Jonathan Edwards for the January issue of *Renewal*. Suggesting that one of those most profoundly affected by the weakening, falling, weeping and joy of the New England revival was Edwards' own wife, Sarah, Davies argues that the Northampton theologian would have encouraged those debating TTB today 'not to dismiss a movement out of hand because there are unusual and often inexplicable physical manifestations accompanying it. Nor, on the other hand, should we focus on or encourage the extreme and bizarre accompaniments. Rather, we should emphasise and seek fellowship with the Lord, a closeness to him and the practical outworking in holiness and love.'[146]

This last week of December also sees the Evangelical Alliance send out the January-March edition of its members' magazine *Idea*. One of its main features – written by Joel Edwards, UK Director (later to become General Director) – is on TTB. As in the initial Alliance statement on the new movement that he drafted on 14th July 1994, Edwards expresses deep concern for the preservation of evangelical unity. Acknowledging that 'Toronto' has great potential for destructiveness as well as for blessing, he quotes John 17:23 to underline the need to 'do everything possible to resist an evangelical Cold War'. Hopefully, he goes on, 'we will be able to disagree without becoming disagreeable', even if 'our evident disagreements will undoubtedly be tested in the months ahead'.

Perhaps conscious of the predominantly 'neutral' view on physical manifestations taken by Jonathan Edwards (no relation!), he writes, 'you can argue either way about [their] appropriateness ... but it's very hard to prove whether or not they are from God. Even if you conclude that they are surplus to biblical requirements, does that make them unbiblical?' Responsible testing will be vital, he implies, as evangelicals approach TTB with 'open Bibles, hearts and minds'. But this must all be done, concludes Edwards, with a clear understanding that there is a common enemy, the Devil, 'whose commitment is to kill, steal and destroy'.[147]

Notes to Chapter 9 (The Rise of the Blessing)

[1] Roberts, 'Toronto', p.20.
[2] Roberts, ibid., p.21, L. Hurst, 'Laughing all the way to heaven', *Toronto Star*, 3rd December, 1994, Wright, *Strange Fire?*, p.31.
[3] Chevreau, *Catch the Fire*, p.26
[4] Ibid., p.27.
[5] Ibid., p.27.
[6] Jackson, 'What in the World is Happening to Us?', p.304.
[7] Roberts, 'Toronto', p. 21.
[8] Ibid., pp.21-2.
[9] Virgo, *A People Prepared*, pp.13-4.
[10] Cited in Roberts, 'Toronto', p.23.
[11] Ibid., p.23.
[12] Jackson, 'What in the World is Happening to Us?', pp. 303-26.
[13] Ibid., p. 309; F. MacNutt, *Overcome by the Spirit*.
[14] Jackson, 'What in the World is Happening to Us?', pp. 316-7.
[15] Ibid., pp. 316-26.
[16] Dixon, *Signs of Revival*, p.19.
[17] Warner, *Prepare for Revival*, pp.2-3.
[18] Dixon, *Signs of Revival*, p.19.
[19] Ibid., p.20.
[20] Ibid., p.21.
[21] Warner, *Prepare for Revival*, pp.1-7.
[22] Roberts, 'Toronto', p.25; 'A Day By Day Diary of What We Have Seen', *HTB in Focus*, 12th June 1994, p.3; Fearon, *Fresh Air*, pp.115-6.
[23] Warner, *Prepare for Revival*, p.4.
[24] Ibid., p.9.
[25] Mumford, 'Spreading Like Wildfire', pp.17-9. For a fuller transcript, see 'A Mighty Wind from Toronto', *HTB in Focus*, 12th June 1994, pp.4-5.
[26] 'A Mighty Wind from Toronto', *HTB in Focus*, 12th June 1994, pp.3.
[27] Warner, *Prepare for Revival*, p.9.
[28] 'A Mighty Wind from Toronto', p.3.
[29] Warner, *Prepare for Revival*, p.9.
[30] Roberts, 'Toronto', pp.31-3.
[31] 'A Mighty Wind from Toronto', p.3.
[32] Dixon, *Signs of Revival*, pp.26-7.
[33] 'A Mighty Wind from Toronto', p.3.
[34] Ibid.
[35] Ibid.
[36] Dixon, *Signs of Revival*, p.22.
[37] Fearon, *Fresh Air*, p.16
[38] Warner, *Prepare for Revival*, p.10.
[39] Roberts, 'Toronto', pp.30-37; Dixon, *Signs of Revival*, p.24.
[40] *HTB in Focus*, 12th June, 1994, p.2.
[41] Fearon, *Fresh Air*, p.16; Roberts, 'Toronto', p.31.
[42] Dixon, *Signs of Revival*, p.24.
[43] Ibid., p.25.

[44] P. Nodding, 'The Holy Spirit in Our Midst', in W. Boulton (ed.), *The Impact of Toronto*, p.32; Fearon, *Fresh Air*, pp.98-9.

[45] Roberts, 'Rumours of Revival', *Alpha*, July 1994, p.46.

[46] J. Lindsay, 'Revival Breaks Out in London Churches', *Church of England Newspaper*, 17th June 1994, p.1.

[47] D. Thompson, 'Evangelical Congregation Shows Signs of the Spirit', *Daily Telegraph*, Saturday 18th June 1994.

[48] R. Gledhill, 'Spread of Hysteria Fad Worries Church', *The Times*, 18th June 1994, p.12.

[49] F. Langan, and P. Goodman, 'Faithful Fall for Power of the Spirit', *Sunday Telegraph*, 19th June 1994, p.5.

[50] N. Monson, 'Congregation Rolling in the Aisle', *Sunday Telegraph*, 19th June 1994.

[51] T. Halpin, 'Rolling in the Aisles at Church of Laughter', *Daily Mail*, 20th June 1994.

[52] 'What's So Funny?', *Daily Telegraph*, 20th June 1994.

[53] A. Brown, 'John Wesley Had Similar Experiences', *Independent*, 21st June 1994, pp.2-3.

[54] B. Saunders, 'Spirit Wind Perceived at London Churches', *Church Times*, 24th June, 1994.

[55] Dixon, *Signs of Revival*, p.27.

[56] D. Dewey, '"Toronto Blessing" Hits Baptist Churches in London', *Baptist Times*, 30th June 1994, p.2.

[57] Warner, *Prepare for Revival*, pp.13-4.

[58] Ibid., pp.17-8.

[59] 'Testing Toronto', *Church of England Newspaper*, 8th July 1994, p.7.

[60] Roberts, 'Toronto', pp.38-9.

[61] A. Walker, '...But is it Revival?', *Christian Herald*, 16th July 1994, p.3.

[62] Warner, *Prepare for Revival*, pp.19-20.

[63] D. Roberts, 'From the Editor: When the Holy Spirit Comes', *Alpha*, August 1994, pp.10-11.

[64] D. Roberts, 'Revival Call', *Alpha*, August 1994, pp.14-7.

[65] D. Roberts, 'The Finger of God', *Alpha*, August 1994, pp.32-4.

[66] J. ('JEB') Benton, 'Laughter at Toronto', *Evangelicals Now*, August 1994, p.18.

[67] G. Coates, 'A Mighty Convulsion', *Christian Herald*, 30th July 1994, p.9

[68] Gott, *Sunderland Refreshing*, pp.81-5

[69] Ibid., pp.85-6.

[70] *Vineyard Reflections*, July/Aug 1994, 7.

[71] Virgo, *A People Prepared*, pp.14-6.

[72] '"Lots of laughter" Heard at a Westcountry Worship Holiday', *Church Times*, 12th August 1994, p.3.

[73] 'Blessed are the fallen at St James', *Daily Mail*, 4th August 1994, p.7.

[74] *HTB in Focus*, 14th August 1994, pp.9-12.

[75] *HTB in Focus*, 14th August 1994, p.10.

[76] Gott, *Sunderland Refreshing*, pp.93-5.

[77] B. Mills, 'Are We in Revival?', *Christian Herald*, 6th August 1994, p.7.

[78] Roberts, 'Toronto', pp. 54-5; Gott, *Sunderland Refreshing*, pp.97-103.

[79] Gott & Gott, *The Sunderland Refreshing*, p.102.

[80] J. Price, 'Airport Church Lands Converts', *Independent*, 12th August 1994, p.6.

[81] J. Huggett, 'Have You Had a Fresh Touch of the Spirit Recently?', *Church of England Newspaper*, 12th August 1994, p.13.

[82] C. Longley, 'Once Upon a Time We Were Told Not to Laugh in Church', *Daily Telegraph*, 12th August 1994, p.17.

[83] Roberts, '*Toronto*', p.55.

[84] 'Slain in the Spirit', *English Churchman and St James' Chronicle*, 19th & 26th August 1994, p.4.

[85] D. Thompson, 'Roman Catholics Affected by Toronto Blessing', *Daily Telegraph*, 22nd August 1994.

[86] 'Comment', *Evangelical Times*, September 1994, p.2.

[87] J. Legg, 'What Would Jonathan Edwards Say?', *Evangelical Times*, September 1994, p.12.

[88] P. Anderson and D. Cleak, 'Laughter in Church', *Evangelism Today*, September 1994, p.11.

[89] C. Hill, 'Toronto Blessing – True or False?', *Prophecy Today* Vol. 10 No. 5 (September-October 1994), pp.10-11.

[90] D. Thompson, 'Children See Vision of Satan after the "Toronto Blessing"', *Daily Telegraph*, Wednesday 31st August 1994, p.10.

[91] Cit. Wright, *Strange Fire?*, p.28.

[92] M. Wroe, 'A Drop of the Holy Spirit Has Them Rolling in the Aisles', The *Observer*, 4th September 1994.

[93] S. Dube, 'Holy Spirit "Blessing" Dismissed as Demonic', *Western Mail*, 5th September 1994.

[94] M. Harper, 'What is Happening in Toronto?, *Directions*, Issue 17, 9th September 1994, pp.1-2.

[95] 'Ticket to Worship', *The Times*, 12th September 1994.

[96] Wright, *Strange Fire?*, p.28.

[97] H. Lindsey's 1970 book *The Late, Great Planet Earth* became the biggest-selling Christian paperback in the USA, with 15 million copies in print by 1992. Reflecting a premillennial eschatology, it linked various apocalyptic prophecies in Scripture to contemporary events, notably the rebirth of the nation of Israel in 1948, the growing dominance of the USSR, which Lindsey cast as the 'Gog' of Ezekiel 38, and the rise of the European Community, which he associated with the Fourth Kingdom of Daniel 7; see H. Lindsey, *The Late Great Planet Earth*.

[98] Association of Vineyard Churches, 'Board Report: Sept/Oct 1994': Summary Report on the Current Renewal and the Phenomena Surrounding It'. Published on TAV web site, 14th September 1994, and again as part of material relating to the eventual disengagement of TAV from AVC, 12th December, 1995.

[99] Fearon, *Fresh Air*, p.15.

[100] N. Copsey, 'Touched by the Spirit', *Baptist Times*, 15th September 1994, p.8.

[101] 'London Church is Now Ticket-Only', *Church of England Newspaper*, 16th September 1994, p.3.

[102] Dixon, *Signs of Revival*, p.17, n.7.

[103] C. Moreton, 'Restoring the Intimacy with God We Cried Out For', *Church Times*, 23rd September 1994, p.7.

[104] A. Morrison, 'Falling for the Lie (Extracts)', *Evangelical Times*, October 1994, p.15.

[105] G. Coates, 'Revival and the Status Quo', *Alpha*, October 1994, pp.8-9.

[106] W. Boulton, 'Humbled by the Holy Spirit', *Renewal*, October 1994, p.13.

[107] G. Coates, et al, 'What Should Leaders Do When the Holy Spirit Comes?', *Renewal*, October 1994, pp.14-5.

[108] 'We're Just Going to Keep on Going', *Aware*, October-November 1994, pp.16-17.

[109] B. Mills, 'Revival – the Missing Elements!', *Christian Herald*, 1st October 1994, p.7.

110 'Toronto: Links with "False Movements" Alleged', *Christian Herald*, 1st October 1994.

111 'Toronto Blessing', *A Time for Discernment*, Winter 1994, p.2.

112 P. Goodman, 'The Evangelist Who Is Refreshing Religion', *Sunday Telegraph*, 2nd October 1994, p.22.

113 Chevreau, *Catch the Fire*, pp.45-6.

114 Ibid., pp.46-7.

115 Ibid., p.61.

116 Ibid., pp.58-69.

117 Ibid., pp.70-144.

118 'Biblical Falling Was in Abject Terror', *Baptist Times* 13th October 1994, p.12

119 'Lewis on "Toronto"', *Christian Herald*, 26th October 1994, p.15.

120 J. White, *When the Spirit Comes with Power: Signs and Wonders among God's People*.

121 'Is Laughing for the Lord Holy?', *Christianity Today*, 24th October 1994, p.78-9.

122 C. Gardner, 'Tears of Joy in Sunderland', *Joy*, January 1995, pp.26-7.

123 D. Roberts, 'Renewal: What God Desires', *Alpha*, November 1994, pp.2-5.

124 'Churches Meet Nightly', *Alpha*, November 1994.

125 C. Dye, 'After the Rain', *Direction*, November 1994.

126 A. Carey, 'The Toronto Experience: Blessing or Baloney?', *Church of England Newspaper*, 28th October 1994, p.13.

127 Showers are 'Strong Meat', *Salvationist*, 29th October 1994.

128 M. Breen, 'Flow, River, Flow', *Renewal*, November 1994, pp.18-21.

129 J. Grayshon, 'What About Those Who Feel Left Out?' *Renewal*, November 1994, pp.22-3.

130 'Positively Toronto', *Evangelicals Now*, November 1994, p.8.

131 S. Sizer, 'Toronto – Cautions', *Evangelicals Now*, November 1994, p.9.

132 J. Edwards, 'EA Charismatic Take-Over?', *Evangelicals Now*, November 1994, p.17.

133 Fearon, *Fresh Air*, p.253.

134 Dixon, *Signs of Revival*.

135 Ibid., p.227.

136 P. Dixon, 'Revival: The Church's Secret Service', *Church of England Newspaper*, 11th November 1994, p.7; '"Toronto" Drivers Warned', *Church of England Newspaper*, 11th November 1994, p.1.

137 D. Thompson, 'The Blessed Shall Not Drive Cars', *Daily Telegraph*, 12th November 1994.

138 M. Fearon, 'Principal of Laughter', *Church of England Newspaper*, 11th November 1994, p.8.

139 J. Horner, 'The Day I Went to Brompton', *Methodist Recorder*, 17th November 1994, p.17.

140 D. Roberts, 'Rodney Howard-Browne: The Joyful Power Evangelist', *Alpha*, December 1994, pp.5-7.

141 P. Dixon, 'Signs of Revival', *Alpha*, December 1994, pp.2-5.

142 M. Brown, 'Unzipper Heaven, Lord; Ha Ha, Ho Ho, Hee Hee…', *Daily Telegraph* (Magazine), 3rd December 1994, pp.26-30.

143 T. Tillin, 'But Is It A Blessing?' *Christian Herald*, 3rd December 1994, p.8.

144 D. Koop, 'Airport Vineyard Still Flying High', *Christian Week*, 13th December 1994.

145 '"Toronto" Put to the Children Test Proves Genuine', *Church of England Newspaper*, 23rd / 30th December 1994.

[146] Ron Davies, 'Physical Manifestations in Revival', *Renewal*, January 1995, pp.28-30.
[147] Joel Edwards, 'Peace, Not War', *Idea*, January-March 1995, pp.16-7.

10

1995: The Spread and Critique of the Blessing

Thursday 5th January 1995

Baptist Union General Secretary David Coffey writes on TTB in the *Baptist Times*. He begins by focusing on practical outcomes. 'Whatever Baptists may personally feel, and whatever questions they may want to ask,' he says, 'the evidence is that there are many Christians in local churches who have been touched by this blessing.' Coffey has observed situations in which, since TTB has emerged, 'repentance and reconciliation has transformed the life of a fellowship', in which ministers have discovered 'a new dimension to their pastoring and preaching', and in which local churches have rekindled their concern for evangelism. Despite all this, he acknowledges that the movement has also caused 'disturbance and concern', not least over its biblical validity, its potential for division and the place of children within it.

Seeking a way through the debate, Coffey presents guidelines that he hopes will be heeded by Baptists and others as the movement develops:

1. We may disagree on the 'Toronto' phenomenon but Scripture is plain that we should be very careful not to judge other groups of Christians without searching our own hearts. Luke 6:37-44 and Luke 9:49,50 have something to say to all of us.
2. We should respect the integrity of those Baptist leaders whose churches are experiencing the 'Toronto' blessing and in return expect that their claims and expectations will be in the spirit of 1 Corinthians 12-14.
3. All of us need to be aware of the danger of claiming that there is something ultimate and complete about our current religious experience or discovery. There is constantly more light and truth to break forth from God's Word. We need time to assess what is happening and what God may be saying to us. We need to recall that the current manifestations were not unknown in those revivals which all of us now regard as hallowed memories.
5. Those who believe they have experienced a 'time of refreshing from the Lord' (Acts 3:19) will no doubt bear witness to a repetition of the Acts experience of deepened fellowship in the local church, open-hearted generosity and a greater awareness of their spiritual inheritance. But they

will surely be asking 'Where now?' In Acts the experience also included open-air preaching with conversions and baptisms, miracles in the 'market square', imprisonment as a penalty for preferring to obey God and daring to oppose the state, the least likely people in the community confessing Jesus as Lord, and fresh insights for the church into the new paradigm for God's missionary activity.

6. [The] societal dimension has not been the major feature of the various streams of the renewal movement during the past few years but it could be a major fruit this time.

Coffey goes on to suggest that there are 'lessons from history which may speak to our present situation'. Citing Graham Tomlin on the Wesley-Whitefield revivals of the 1730s and 1740s, he sees significance in the fact that that movement met people on neutral ground, i.e. in fields and town squares rather than simply in churches; that it took lay leadership seriously; that it recovered the experience of intimacy and assurance as central in the Christian life; and that it saw a return to theological roots, most especially the Lutheran doctrine of justification by faith. Coffey ends by hoping that TTB might lead on to a similar transformation – once which marries spiritual with intellectual refreshment, and which recognises that 'when God blesses his Church he speaks to the world'.[1]

Saturday 7th January 1995
Christian Herald editor Bruce Hardy warns his readers that TTB could entrench divisions between charismatics and 'traditional evangelicals'. Siding with the traditional view, he writes: 'The events of 1994 have made a rapprochement less likely. I am not surprised, because thoroughgoing, extreme charismatic, Toronto-prone believers are sure traditional evangelicals are wrong and desire no accommodation.'

Thursday 12th January 1995
The Evangelical Alliance issues a press release on the consultation it hosted on TTB at Euston on 19th-20th December. The press release concentrates on the statement produced by those who attended, but also quotes Joel Edwards, the UK Director of the Evangelical Alliance: 'The "Toronto Blessing"', he says, 'has provoked less division than could have been the case. So it is crucial that we build on the unity we have by listening and understanding one another.'

Saturday 14th January 1995
In his regular column for *Christian Herald*, the prominent Anglican evangelical Tony Higton reviews a Rodney Howard-Browne meeting he and his wife have recently attended at Wembley Conference Centre. Higton is less than impressed. 'After an eight-minute talk on 1 Kings 17 to introduce the collection (the only Bible teaching)', he writes, 'Rodney Howard-Browne sang a long, repetitive solo to a jazz rhythm. "I'm drunk, I'm drunk. Every day of my life I'm drunk. I've been drinking down at Joel's place. Every time and every

day, I'm drunk with new wine.'" Higton is alarmed at Howard-Browne's encouragement of the audience to 'get out of your heads and into your spirits', and is clearly disturbed by the pogoing, the 'frantic disco dancing', the 'loud, hysterical-sounding laughter' and the 'corporate singing in tongues in a loud monotone', which he likens to a Hindu Om chant. Howard-Browne's practice of patting people on the forehead and shouting 'Fill' before they (mostly) fall to the floor reminds Higton of 'those hypnotists on TV who quickly wave their hands near people's foreheads, sending them into a hypnotic trance'. The Anglican rector is offended by Howard-Browne's labelling of those who leave the meeting early as 'religious dead-heads', and says that he is worried by 'the over-defensive, angry response of some pro-Toronto Christians to their critics'.

Higton's concluding remarks strike a somewhat softer note, but he is still plainly upset by what he and his wife saw: 'It seems that the event encouraged people to be open to God and to expect blessing (two laudable attitudes) and so God blessed them. He regularly blesses despite our spiritual state or circumstances. And he only has imperfect leaders and techniques to use. But that does not justify the excesses we saw that night.'[2]

Monday 16th – Thursday 19th January 1995

The Centre for Contemporary Ministry at Bawtry Hall, South Yorkshire, hosts a special consultation on TTB. Bawtry Hall is the base for the ministry of Clifford Hill and the magazine *Prophecy Today*. Both Hill and *PT* have been critical of TTB over the past few months, and the 35 leaders assembled for this meeting mainly comprise charismatics who have expressed serious concerns about the new movement.

The results of the discussions, which take place over these four days, will soon be edited and published in an eighteen-page report entitled *Charismatic Crossroads*.[3] This report records the consultation as concluding that TTB is giving rise to a 'mixture' of spiritual phenomena. It acknowledges that there have been 'many beautiful testimonies among believers of lives changed', but adds that alongside the work of the Holy Spirit, 'there are some very worrying signs of counterfeit which are confusing the situation'. The document confirms that much of the conference is taken up with reviewing the past 25 years of charismatic renewal, and assessing how and why it has led to TTB. Links are traced back from TTB, through the Restorationist theology of the House Church streams which emerged in the 1970s, to the 'heretical' Latter Rain movement that spread from Canada in the late 1940s, and which, in turn, influenced several of those now at the forefront of TTB in Britain, including Gerald Coates, Bryn Jones, Terry Virgo, Roger Forster and Roger Mitchell (cf. 1st October 1994). The Bawtry report is concerned by these links and sees them as largely responsible for a misguided 'triumphalism', and for the stoking up of false expectations within the charismatic constituency:

In Britain the House Church movement in the 1970s began to embrace 'restorationism', which taught that the church will do most of the work of the kingdom before the second coming of Christ. The Church will conquer the nations, controlling all [their] major institutions, and the 'sons of God' will be manifested and take the land[s] for Jesus. This was in reaction to extreme dispensationalism. This triumphalism is reflected in many charismatic songs but it is false teaching, based upon false biblical exegesis. It is not centred upon the cross. Sin and repentance, persecution, failure, trials and tribulations and suffering are all absent or minimised because the elect will be triumphant and will enjoy health, wealth and prosperity. This teaching has been given at Bible weeks and celebrations for the past 25 years, causing great excitement, with … promises of extraordinary power … and authority over the nations, [which] have put increasing pressure upon leaders to deliver. Fresh promises and fresh waves of excitement have therefore had to be generated in order to stem the tide of disillusionment and avoid mass desertions. The Toronto Blessing is the latest in these waves of excitement and promises of extraordinary power. It is being accompanied by the teaching that we should not use our minds to question anything that is happening, we should simply receive any of the spiritual power that is on offer. This is highly dangerous teaching and leaves believers open to deception.[4]

The conference expresses concern that trends such as these might show 'sections of the charismatic movement drifting towards cultism' and suggests that TTB might well accelerate this drift. Rodney Howard-Browne is singled out for particular concern. After watching video clips of the South African with Kenneth Copeland, 'clowning on stage using a strange tongue' and allowing children to 'fall under the power', the conference expresses 'unanimous agreement' that he 'does not appear to be ministering in the power of the Holy Spirit'.

More generally lamenting a loss of 'sound biblical teaching' to 'spiritual pragmatism', the conference concludes that 'the present crisis in the charismatic movement [is] at least as great and possibly a greater threat to the future of evangelicalism than was ever mounted by the impact of modernist or liberal teachings'. Internal corruption, it suggests, is 'always a more potent force for the disintegration of a movement than external attack'.

Finally, the Bawtry meeting resolves to urge the Evangelical Alliance 'and all charismatic leadership bodies' to recognise the 'seriousness of the present situation', and to realise the need for 'urgent consideration' of its analysis.

Thursday 19th January 1995

Hodder and Stoughton publish Rob Warner's book on TTB, *Prepare for Revival*. In the Foreword to the book, HTB Vicar Sandy Millar commends Warner for an 'extraordinarily helpful and well researched' account; Warner presents the Blessing as one of a number of 'new shoots springing up' which promise to reinvigorate the Church. As part of the re-engagement of laity in ministry, the recovery of charismatic gifts and the move away from denominationalism, TTB represents for Millar 'a new and real hunger for God'.

Warner's analysis begins with a history of Blessing seen particularly through his own eyes and those of close friends and colleagues. He then draws parallels between what people have experienced in the new movement and various 'power-encounters' recorded in Scripture, e.g. Saul's promised meeting with the ecstatic prophet band in 1 Samuel 10:5ff., David's supernatural protection from Saul's assassins (1 Sam. 19), Isaiah's vision (Is. 6:1-10), the weeping of the Israelites at the reading of the Law in Nehemiah 8, and their public confession of sin (Neh. 9), the Jews' transformation at Pentecost and the subsequent fervour of the early Church, and Cornelius' and his household's extraordinary response to Peter's preaching (Acts 10). Following this, Warner reviews the history of revival, and notes that its greatest proponents and practitioners have been remarkably alike in having gained the impetus for their work in intense 'crisis' experiences of God's in-breaking power. As for manifestations, Warner notes that Edwards' preaching occasioned tears, trembling, groans and loss of strength, that Whitefield and Wesley prompted and condoned profuse weeping, crying out and (despite initial reservations from Whitefield) fainting. The pioneering Welsh revival preacher Howel Harris, notes Warner, described himself in 1735 as 'acting like a drunk man' under the influence of the Spirit.

Warner goes on to recount his own dramatic visit to TAV the previous summer. Although wary of jumping on fashionable spiritual bandwagons, Warner points out that 'visiting the place of an outpouring to learn and receive is not new'. Jonathan Edwards, he points out, wrote in *A Narrative of Surprising Conversions* of 'men visiting Northampton, Massachusetts on business who ended up taking revival home with them.' Hindered by broken teeth, eye infections, car-hire stress and lost luggage, Warner and his wife are nevertheless profoundly affected by their time at the Airport Vineyard. As well as resting in the Spirit, Warner recalls being prayed for by one of the ministry team as an experience 'countless times greater' in force than an electric shock he had received as a teenager. He writes: 'It seemed that the scales were falling from my eyes and the Spirit was restoring my first zeal for Christ.'

Prepare for Revival proceeds in more detail to investigate the phenomena associated the TTB, mounting sustained biblical and historical defences of the tears, joy, laughter, falling and shaking. Warner is alive to the dangers of manipulation, mass hysteria, deliberate imitation and satanic counterfeit, but assigns them to the sinful intent of their perpetrators in any specific instance, and neither confines nor connects them in any necessary sense to the phenomena associated with 'Toronto'. Indeed, he is particularly dismissive of critics who make an undifferentiated causal link between the manifestations and the deceptions of Satan. Such people, writes Warner, are 'ignorant of both the Bible and the history of revivals'.

As the title of his book suggests, Warner is not ready to define TTB as 'revival', but expresses great hope that it may pave the way:

> We praise God for the times of refreshing we have been enjoying, but our plea must be that they are no more than a prelude. We long to see the glory and power of the living God sweeping across the face of the earth as never before. A global revival to prepare the world for Christ. Send revival, Lord, and send it in our day![5]

Also today, the *Baptist Times* and the *Methodist Recorder* both pick up the Evangelical Alliance's announcement of its Euston Consultation and Statement of 19th-20th December.

Friday 20th January 1995

One year on from the 'start' of TTB at TAV, the *Church Times* reports on the Evangelical Alliance's Euston Consultation and Statement.

Saturday 21st January 1995

Under the front-page headline 'Toronto: Call to Keep the Peace', *Christian Herald* informs readers of the Evangelical Alliance Euston Consultation.

Sunday 22nd January 1995

Chris Robeson, a student at Howard Payne University in Texas, publicly confesses his sins to the congregation of nearby Brownwood Baptist Church. This prompts many there to stream down the aisles to pray, repent and restore relationships. Subsequent services at Brownwood extend to three hours or more and are characterised by similar scenes.

There is another consequence back at Howard Payne, as a series of meetings led by Southern Baptist pastor Henry Blackby prompts 35-40 students to confess sins of lust, and two hundred in the campus church congregation to make commitments or rededicate their lives to Christ.

None of these events are marked by distinctive 'Toronto' phenomena, but they will be soon be connected to the Toronto movement by those seeking to trace a pattern of worldwide revival.[6]

Saturday 28th January 1995

A very Toronto-heavy day in both the Christian and the secular press.

The *Independent*'s Religious Affairs Correspondent, Andrew Brown, reports that a 'bitter row' has broken out over TTB in the Church of England. In his preface to the new *Church of England Yearbook*, The Dean of Worcester, Very Rev Robert Jeffrey has, writes Brown, denounced the new movement as 'an expression of hysteria' which could lead to 'a ghetto mentality, and the undermining of an intellectually respectable expression of faith'. The article goes on to quote the response of HTB's Sandy Millar. 'For the Dean of Worcester to make these sort of blanket comments is mischievous', says the Knightsbridge vicar. 'Our experience of the so-called Toronto Blessing is that it is a work of the Holy Spirit, bringing many hundreds of people to renewed faith in Jesus Christ, a greater depth of repentance, and a fresh desire to pray and read the Bible.' Millar then commends the Evangelical Alliance for conducting 'a detailed study of the TB recently' and for publishing 'a clear response' to it.

Importantly, Brown's piece also reveals the first signs that the pace of TTB may be slowing somewhat. An unnamed spokesman for HTB is quoted as acknowledging that the outward manifestations of the Blessing are now diminishing 'after their peak in the summer and autumn'. The spokesman adds, 'we are not interested in the outward manifestations in the slightest, because what matters to us is the change is people's lives.'"[7]

This weekend also, the February editions of *Evangelism Today* and *Evangelicals Now* reproduce the Evangelical Alliance's Euston Statement in full. By contrast, with a minimalism and negativity which bears out its hostile view of TTB and its often critical stance towards the Alliance, *Evangelical Times* devotes just seven lines to the Euston Consultation in its 'News in Brief' column. 'Leaders of charismatic and other churches throughout the UK', it says, 'remain divided as to the value of the phenomenon of laughing, weeping and falling over known as the Toronto Blessing. A two-page report issued by members of various groups attempts to explain irreconcilable differences by splitting them into "primary" and "secondary" beliefs.'[8]

The February issue of *Evangelicals Now* carries an intriguing interview with agnostic *Telegraph* journalist Mick Brown, whose review of TTB on 3rd December had included details of his 'falling under the power' when ministered to at TAV. Conducted by Mike Taylor, the interview sees Brown still unwilling to endorse evangelical Christianity, despite his experiences in Toronto and the fact that he appreciated the warmth and friendliness of those he met at the Vineyard. 'There are aspects of [it] which I don't buy into, and don't particularly like,' he says, 'for instance … the idea that knowledge of God is somehow the exclusive prerogative of the Christian religion … I don't believe that myself. I think that every culture and every religion expresses an understanding of God or the divine, in their own particular way, and the divine does not discriminate between different cultures, between different religions.' Taylor concludes his feature by posing a question: 'Could it be that we are witnessing what in the majority of cases is an essentially non-Christian experience, which some Christians are trying their best to assimilate into their view of the Christian life? If so, this could be a very significant turning-point in the history of our current evangelicalism.'[9]

In the same newspaper, Tim Thornborough recounts a recent visit he has made to TAV. Although he is concerned that some of the biblical apologetic offered for TTB lacks coherence, and suggests that group expectations are prone to manipulation in such a context, he is happy to accept that TTB's rock-style worship band, together with its encouragement of immediate experience and overt emotional expression, 'are all things that echo resoundingly with the life experiences of the age group it seems principally to address'. He is also dismayed by the jibes of a pastor who seems only to have come to snipe at the whole event. Despite this, Thornborough goes to wonder whether TTB is not 'more akin to revivalism than revival' – a modern form of 'Pentecostalism, with better marketing'.[10]

Renewal magazine carries a strongly autobiographical piece on TTB by Gerald Coates. A new story emerges here concerning the impact of TTB on London Bible College, one of the leading evangelical training centres in the UK. Coates recounts that he was recently invited to address two prayer meetings at the college, which each attracted more students than expected. 'After sensitive worship I spoke for twenty minutes', he writes, 'and the Holy Spirit then came upon the gathering in power. Chairs were hastily moved as the scene began to resemble a battlefield. There was the crying of repentance and the laughing of release.' One student, says Coates, had been writing a dissertation sharply criticising the new movement, but subsequently re-wrote it from favourable perspective. Coates also recalls a Salvation Army evangelists' conference in July, at which officers manifested a wide range of 'Toronto' phenomena.[11]

Renewal this month also surveys the spread of TTB in Scotland. Churches which have featured prominently include King's Centre, Motherwell; City Church, Aberdeen; Riverside Church, Banff; King's Fellowship, Inverness; and Fort William Christian Fellowship. It is also important to note that this article focuses at least as much on the growth of Alpha courses in these and other Scottish churches. Alpha is the 'Introduction to Christianity' course developed at HTB, and is now being used in an increasing number of congregations, both in the UK and abroad. Arguably, it will go on to eclipse even TTB in global impact.[12]

Evangelicals Now prints a detailed dissection by Mike Taylor of the Rodney Howard-Browne meeting held last December 13th at Wembley Conference Centre. From the outset, Taylor writes, he objected to the verbal control Howard-Browne appeared to exert over the audience, as he ordered them by turns to sit, stand, raise their hands, chant repetitively after him and, in Taylor's terms, to 'obey his voice'. As far as Taylor is concerned, this amounted to 'manipulative behaviour … typical of many American churches, whether they are Fundamental, Pentecostal or charismatic'. Similar techniques were in play, suggests Taylor, when the evangelist later repeated 'trigger words' such as 'this is that' to emphasise his message.

Taylor reports that Colin Dye, Pastor of Kensington Temple, was present at the Wembley meeting and soon fell face downwards. Gerald Coates was also on the platform, and, according to Taylor, told the crowd 'This is perhaps the greatest outpouring of God in our land ever.'

Taylor recalls that after an offering, Howard-Browne preached a sermon 'entirely concerned with outward manifestations', taking as his text 2 Chronicles 5:13,14.

Following the address, lines of people came forward to be 'anointed' by the South African, who 'started at his left, working his way round, saying in a loud voice, "Fill!" and touching each person in the mid-chest'. Catchers had been put in place ready to break the fall of those overpowered by all this. Taylor cannot help remarking, however, that 'only certain people, for whom it was expedient to do so, actually fell over. For instance, RHB never fell. The cameramen and staff never fell.' Taylor concludes by asserting that the meeting was 'clearly' designed to 'bypass the mind' by majoring on 'sub-rational phenomena'. He had gone to the event expecting some kind of spiritual atmosphere, he writes, 'but there was nothing at all – it was neither of God nor demonic; it was totally flat. The entire thing was most similar to stage hypnotism. Indeed, I was actually surprised by my extreme boredom.'

Monday 30th January 1995
The *Guardian* follows Saturday's *Independent* with a piece on the Dean of
Worcester's denunciation of TTB, and Sandy Millar's response (28th January
1995). In addition to comments quoted in the earlier article, journalist Owen
Boycott has Millar claiming that TTB is 'bringing many hundreds of people to
renewed faith in Jesus Christ, a greater depth of repentance and a fresh desire
to pray and read the Bible'. He also poses a question: 'How can the church in
its current state afford to disapprove of movements for God at this time? This a
movement of the Spirit designed to help us as a church.'[13]

Friday 3rd February 1995
The *Church of England Newspaper* prints articles on TTB by two leading British
evangelical Anglicans – Canons Tom Smail and David Atkinson.

Smail, who was Director of the key interdenominational charismatic body
The Fountain Trust in the 1970s, begins by comparing his task as a committed
Christian theologian with that of Gamaliel in Acts 5. 'We both are trying to
reach conclusions on the same sort of question', writes Smail: 'he about
whether the new Christian movement is of God, I about whether and how far
the recent so-called 'Toronto Blessing' can be recognised as an authentic movement of the Holy Spirit for our own time.' Beyond this, however, Smail perceives significant differences. Gamaliel, he argues, 'does not believe in the gospel
he is trying to assess, whereas I write as a believer in Jesus Christ who, although
he has not been touched by 'Toronto', appeals for a verdict both to the New
Testament Scriptures and to my own experience of the Holy Spirit working in
his charismatic mode.' In addition, Gamaliel's criterion of mere durability – 'If
it lasts God must be in it' – would, says Smail, 'authenticate Buddhism and
Hinduism even more than the gospel because they have lasted longer'. Rather,
he suggests, the new movement must be tested against the witness of the New
Testament gospel as a whole.

Smail notes that 'asking theological questions does not come easily to charismatic enthusiasts, who want to rejoice in what God has done for them and get on
with witnessing about it to others'. Such urgent pragmatism has also tended, in
Smail's view, to make proponents of TTB 'impatient with those who insist on raising awkward issues'. All the same, he writes, 'they need to remember that discernment is one of the gifts of the Spirit that is most needed and most neglected'.

With these preliminary points established, Smail proceeds to raise three areas
of questioning for his '"Toronto" friends'. The first concerns the fruit of the
Blessing; the second has to do with the noise it generates, and the third is about
the physical manifestations associated with it.

Firstly, in terms of fruit, Smail acknowledges that TTB is offering 'considerable and impressive' results. Even so, he is concerned to distinguish 'a temporary
holiness that has its basis in strongly roused emotion, from a covenant holiness
that involves the commitment of the whole person – mind, will and heart – to
God and his cause'. In defence of this distinction, he cites Jesus calling his disciples in John 15:6 to bear fruit *that will last*. What matters, urges Smail,

is not what happens in the glorious meetings or in the months which immediately follow when the glow is still upon us, but on how faithful we shall be when the great moment has passed, when the feelings have dulled and when the Spirit shows himself not in our passionate praise but in our dogged endurance.

As for the 'noise' of the Blessing, Smail feels compelled to plead for less emphasis on 'endless singing, roaring lions, uncontrollable laughter and hallelujahs all over the place', and more on the Lord 'who is not in the wind, the fire or the earthquake, but speaks in a still small voice'. Holding that some, including himself, have had more than their fill of 'that kind of frantic religion', Smail writes of the need for 'Toronto' advocates to realise that 'the same sense of God's presence, speaking and power can be given in a silent eight day retreat'.

Thirdly, Smail wonders how apparently 'regressive' phenomena like shaking, leaping, falling and laughing square with God's desire that we should 'attain ... to mature manhood, measured by nothing less than the full stature of Christ' (Eph. 4:13). It could be, he reflects, that God's healing operations 'sometimes require some anaesthesia for their performance'. Very soon, however, the Spirit 'will want us off the carpet and into action: "Son of man, *stand on your feet* and I will speak to you" [Ezek. 2:1]'.

In conclusion, Smail says 'I stick to what I have long thought about ... many other Christian movements besides – they are about two-thirds phoney and one third God, *but a third, with God in it, is a lot!*'[14]

As Chancellor of Southwark Cathedral and a leading evangelical pastoral theologian, David Atkinson not surprisingly focuses on the lessons to be learned from Jonathan Edwards. Stressing the New England pastor's concern for good fruit, Atkinson points out that Edwards saw this demonstrated by a profound increase in soberness, church commitment and repentance. Atkinson also finds particular resonance for contemporary evangelical debates on TTB in Edwards' insistence that revival should produce an aversion to judging other professing Christians of good standing in the visible church, and should stimulate a heightened sense of social responsibility. All this, says Atkinson, offers 'a good place from which to start evaluating Toronto'.[15]

Also today the *Church Times* prints a letter on TTB from the highly respected missiologist, Bishop Lesslie Newbigin. Newbigin has been teaching at HTB on John's Gospel for some time, and is upset at the Dean of Worcester's dismissal of the Blessing (28th January), calling it 'mistaken'. Newbigin continues:

It is, of course, true that for those (like myself) shaped by the pliant conformity of the mainline churches to the prevailing culture, some of he manifestations of the movement seem odd. John Wesley's contemporaries had the same problem. But one still has to ask two questions: is the genuine fruit of the Spirit present? And second, do those involved remain at the stage of mere emotional excitement? The answer to the first of these questions is yes, and to the second, no.

Newbigin writes that TTB induces 'the feeling that one gets when the monsoon breaks after a very dry summer'. It would be a shame, he adds, 'if the response of churchmen were to be to shut the doors and windows'.

Saturday 17th February 1995

English Churchman reports that the Chairman of the German Evangelical Alliance, Rev Rolf Hille of Tübingen, has denounced TTB. Rejecting the idea that the manifestations associated with the Blessing have a biblical foundation, he adds, 'religious madness was never propagated in the Scriptures'. While not going so far as to call the new movement anti-Christian, Hille is quoted as calling it 'a longing for which there [is] no biblical promise'. Hille is, notes the report, a member of the Theological Commission of the World Evangelical Fellowship.

Friday 24th February 1995

The March edition of *Alpha* magazine reports on the Evangelical Alliance Euston Consultation and Statement (19th-20th December)

Saturday 25th February 1995

Evangelical anti-cult group Reachout Trust updates its readers on TTB. Reachout worker Mike Thomas reflects on attending a Rodney Howard-Browne meeting held in Swansea last November. Stressing that 'RHB' could not be taken as representing the Toronto movement as a whole, and repudiating those who, 'in a personal crusade against all things charismatic have, through ignorance or mischief, misrepresented … the Toronto Blessing group and their leaders', Thomas is nevertheless very sceptical about the provenance of Howard-Browne's ministry: '[He] believes what he is teaching, I have no doubt … He is personable in his own way … I believe, however, that he is wrong.' The key error, for Thomas, lies in Howard-Browne's development within the Faith Movement, exemplified by the two years he spent as an Associate Pastor at Rhema Church, Johannesburg. Thomas claims to have detected plenty of residual WordFaith teaching at the Swansea meeting, including a characteristic use of 2 Corinthians 8:9 to justify the pursuit of wealth, and the notion that Job's suffering was due primarily to his own 'negative confession' (Job 3:25). On these grounds, Thomas is at least prepared to raise the possibility that Howard-Browne might be a heretic.[16]

In today's March issue of *Evangelism Today*, Dr Tony Sargent of Worthing Tabernacle considers how Jonathan Edwards and the great twentieth-century evangelical expositor Martyn Lloyd-Jones might have dealt with TTB. Regretting what he perceives to be the often 'irrational' nature of the Blessing, Sargent writes that 'the practices of some of [its] proponents are not just a long throw from Edwards, they are utterly unrelated'. Sargent goes on: 'any similarity is at a *phenomenal* not a *theological* level and only partially the former. Neither Edwards nor Lloyd-Jones subscribed to the suspension of critical faculties; quite the contrary. Certainly, Dr Martyn Lloyd-Jones conceded that there are experiences that surpass the mind. But surpassing and bypassing are not the same thing either!'

Sargent adds, in a clear reference to Rodney Howard-Browne, that the 'thought of dispensing the Spirit as though he were akin to a bartender's liquor would be totally unacceptable.' Edwards' ministry, he writes, was free from 'catchers, drugging music and (thankfully) [the] microphone'. As for Lloyd-Jones, 'even though his London pulpit knew great blessing, neither spontaneity in worship nor phenomena were its hallmark. The main point in Sargent's critique, however, concerns the likely ephemerality of TTB. 'Few', he suggests, 'would doubt that we are living in days when an extraordinary phenomenon has swept over thousands of churches. But this is in the wake of several other emphases which have come and gone – Spiritual warfare and Exorcism; Signs and Wonders; Terrestrial Spirits and Spiritual Mapping; the Kansas City Prophets and theatrical displays of the Word of Knowledge … Is this the latest craze? More kindly, is it yet another tendency of evangelicals to zoom in on one aspect of biblical teaching and distort it through overemphasis…?'

In closing, Sargent contends that there is a vital deficit in TTB which prevents it from qualifying seriously as 'revival', and that is 'a wide-scale evangelistic push'. For the church to be looking inward while forgetting its mandate to go out and win disciples of all nations, says Sargent, 'might suggest at best a failure in priorities or at worst a malevolent strategy causing Christendom to fiddle while a lost world burns'.[17]

A very similar version of Sargent's article will also appear in the April issue of *Renewal* magazine.[18]

Wednesday 1st March 1995

John Avent, Pastor of Brownwood Baptist Church near Howard Payne University, speaks at South Western Baptist Seminary on the dramatic events that have taken place in his congregation, and on the campus, since 22nd January. His address initiates seven hours of confession and prayer by students and staff. Further lengthy meetings follow at the seminary.[19]

Sunday, 19th March 1995

The Pierce Chapel of Wheaton College, Illinois, hosts the weekly campus service of the World Christian Fellowship. Famed as the college that trained international evangelist Billy Graham, Wheaton is one of the leading centres of evangelical higher education in the USA. The weeks preceding this meeting have seen a significant stirring of spiritual life among individuals and groups. This does not, however, appear to owe much to TTB: Wheaton is a relatively conservative college not known for a particularly charismatic outlook.

As students, staff and others gather for worship at 7.30pm, the programme includes testimony from two visitors – James Hahn and Brandi Maguire. Hahn and Maguire have come to describe a recent 'revival' that has been taking place among their own student body at Howard Payne University in Texas. After they finish speaking, the microphones are left open for the congregation to share their burdens and confess their sins.

There follows an outpouring of repentance so intense that the meeting does not eventually adjourn until 6.00am the following morning. Chaplain Stephen Kellough will later describe a stream of public admissions to 'pride, lust, sexual immorality, cheating, dishonesty, materialism, addictions and self-destructive behaviour'; this all issues in 'tears', 'smiles', 'singing' and 'healing'. He will reflect: 'It was biblical. It was Christian. It was orderly. It was sincere. And it honoured our Lord.'

Monday 20th March 1995

Following the remarkable events of the night before, nine hundred Wheaton students convene in the Pierce Chapel for prayer and worship. Four hundred are still present when the last confession is made, and even then, there are still many waiting for their turn at the microphone.

Tuesday 21st March 1995

In order to honour scheduled events in Pierce Chapel, a new venue, College Church, is pressed into use for another Wheaton campus 'revival' meeting. By 9.30pm, 1,350 people have arrived. By 2.00am, the lines waiting at microphones for the confession of sin are still long and another session is arranged for the following evening.

Wednesday 22nd March 1995

A capacity crowd of 1,500 gathers in College Church. By this point, the Wheaton College staff have decided that the new campus movement is significant enough that they should give guidance and teaching on it to the student body. Professors Litfin, Dorsett and Beougher duly address the meeting.

Thursday 23rd March 1995

More faculty, staff and members of the local community join students at College Church for an evening of praise and testimony. Teaching focuses on the wider challenges presented by what has been happening at Wheaton during the past few days. Those present are urged to move on to new levels of commitment in their love and service of God. The closing section of the meeting includes an invitation for those sensing a call to Christian ministry to go forward for a prayer of dedication. Many kneel at the front of the sanctuary to dedicate themselves to pastoral and missionary leadership.

It is decided that this will be the last of the 'plenary' sessions for the new outpouring. Instead of maintaining a schedule of large nightly meetings, the community is encouraged to direct their new sense of commitment and fellowship into evangelism and practical social action.[20]

Friday 24th March 1995

In the April-May issue of its magazine *Idea*, the Evangelical Alliance prints the full text of the Euston Statement. In addition, three of those who attended the Ibis

Hotel meeting are quoted. London Bible College Principal Derek Tidball says: 'we need to overcome misunderstanding, to destroy rumours, to increase our appreciation of how God works and above all to find that, whatever our differences, we have a common commitment to the Lord, his gospel and the authoritative Word'. Anglican Reform leader Philip Hacking also reflects positively: 'I appreciated the value of the consultation because of its prayerfulness and it openness. It is vital for Christians who differ to meet in honest debate. I am even more concerned today that we do not paper over the cracks to suggest a unity that is not real.' Gerald Coates adds that 'fellowship mellows judgement', while lack of it creates caricatures. Many such caricatures were, however, broken down at the Euston meeting, he says: 'we heard and understood one another to a greater degree than previously'.[21]

Saturday 25th March 1995
In the April edition of *Healing and Wholeness*, William Davies, the former Principal of Cliff College, surveys instances of ecstatic manifestations that occurred during the revival ministry of John Wesley, and compares Wesley's approach with that which has come to distinguish TTB. While not actively encouraging them, Davies shows that Wesley witnessed and largely tolerated falling down, trembling and even roaring in his meetings. Laughter, however, appears to have been a different matter and, when uncontrolled in the public context, was assigned by Wesley to the Devil. In such cases, writes Davies, it was seen as something that required deliverance.[22]

The Pentecostal periodical *Joy* reports that four thousand British churches have now been affected by TTB. Former Kensington Temple Pastor Wynne Lewis writes, 'I believe we could be in the early stages of revival if we handle it right. I am convinced that this move glorifies God and exalts Jesus. It can only be of the Holy Spirit.'[23]

Friday 7th April 1995
Wheaton College chaplain Stephen Kellough reflects on the extraordinary events which have been taking place on the Illinois campus since 19th March. 'The personal sharing within the body of Christ here', he says, 'has been spiritually sensitive and biblically grounded. The depth and breadth of the confession, repentance, and reconciliation point to a divine initiative. Every factor seems to confirm that we are experiencing an authentic work of the sovereign Lord who has chosen to visit us in a powerful way.'[24]

Saturday 8th April – Saturday 22nd April 1995
The annual Spring Harvest festival at Minehead and Skegness in the UK sees TTB in evidence at a number of worship sessions and workshops. Special 'receiving' meetings are held for teaching and ministry related to the new movement.[25]

Saturday 15th April 1995
Christian Herald reports on a recent three-day consultation on TTB, which has just been held at the Centre for Contemporary Ministry, Bawtry Hall, in South

Yorkshire. This was a follow-up to the earlier conference held there between 16th-19th January. Speakers included Peter Fenwick, Clifford Hill, David Noakes and the popular Bible teacher and author, David Pawson Those attending included the Evangelical Alliance's UK Director Joel Edwards. As in January, the consultation has issued a unanimous statement calling for caution, renewed study of Scripture and consultation. It states that those gathered at Bawtry Hall 'are not convinced that we are currently seeing the beginning of the longed-for revival', and urges that all experiences be tested against Scripture 'in order to avoid deceptions that distort the purposes of God, and may divert the Church from its calling'. The conference also expresses concern at 'the possibility of unnecessary division within the Body', and calls for 'urgent dialogue among leaders holding different views of contemporary developments' (the full text of the Second Bawtry Hall Statement is given in Part III).

Thursday 20th April 1995
The *Baptist Times* reports on events at Wheaton College over the past month. Chaplain Stephen Kellough is quoted as saying that he would prefer to define the campus movement as a 'spiritual awakening' rather than a 'revival'. The article points out that similar college and seminary 'awakenings' have taken place before: 'one in the 1950s led to one student, Jim Elliot, sensing a call to an unreached tribe in Ecuador at whose hands he was martyred'.[26]

Friday 28th April 1995
Canadian Christian periodical *Faith Today* reports that the recent 'Wheaton Awakening' is now being mirrored on campusues in Texas, Illinois, Alabama, Massachusetts and Kentucky. 'At Olivet Nazarene University in Illinois', says the article, 'a video clip on the 1970 Asbury College (Kentucky) revival turned into seven hours of praying, sharing, singing and exhorting one another to live holy lives.'

Also today, *Alpha* magazine prints a major feature that seeks to answer the question 'Has the Toronto Blessing Run Dry?' Despite suggesting that more than four thousand churches, or 'almost ten per cent of all churches from virtually every stream nationwide', have received TTB, it is concerned to ask, 'Where do we go from here?'

In order to address the issue, Clive Price canvasses opinions from Gerald Coates, Rob Warner, Sandy Millar, Ken Gott and Bryn Jones. Recognising that these men have been key supporters of, and apologists for, the Blessing, he also summarises the views of those who have been more sceptical, e.g. the Bawtry Hall Conferences, Doug Harris and the Reachout Trust, and Tony Higton.

Gerald Coates tells Price that two central questions have emerged in respect of TTB. They are, he says, the same questions that were asked on the Day of Pentecost: 'What does this mean?' and 'What should we do?' Coates sees a coherent response emerging as affected churches turn to 'intercession for the nation' and evangelism: there is, he says, 'a trickle of reports of people coming to faith'. He adds, 'it's time for God's people to be together in true Christian fellowship – and we want to give birth to something. You can call it revival or a great awakening.' Terminology aside, he stresses that such a move of God will be marked by tears, acknowledgement of inadequacies and 'a fresh humility with our Lord'.

For his part, Rob Warner reports on recent dramatic demonstrations of TTB at conferences run by Mainstream and GEAR – the renewal organisations associated with the Baptist Union and United Reformed Church respectively. He also reflects on the wider social significance of TTB. 'Our culture has been rationalistic', he says, 'so that everything has operated within the confines of scientific understanding.' Now, though, says Warner, this paradigm has begun to break down – something evidenced by the growth of New Age beliefs. More positively, he also argues that prevailing cultural rationalism has been challenged by the charismatic movement, with its openness to 'overwhelming encounters with the presence of God'. This has helped many realise, says Warner, that 'God refuses to be domesticated' and 'is restoring to us an understanding of his awesomeness and his might'.

Considering whether there might be more than one 'time of refreshing' for the churches, Warner says that this is quite possible:

> Prior to the Great Awakening, in Jonathan Edwards' church there were several periods of mini-revival. It was rather like the tide coming in. A series of waves came and things seemed to recede a bit, came and then receded, until eventually the full flood of high tide came crashing in. We can't say God must work in that way, but we certainly say from history [that] God can well work that way.

From his vantage-point as Vicar of Holy Trinity, Brompton, Sandy Millar expresses some weariness with the media 'hype' which has attended TTB, and with the 'megaphone hurling of almost snap judgements' by some of the new movement's detractors. 'Those of us on the ground have to live from day to day', he says, 'but there's no doubt at all … that we are in an unusually wonderful move of God's Spirit.' Many hundreds, he notes, have a renewed Christian faith, a greater depth of repentance and a fresh desire to pray and read Scripture. He accepts, however, that the next step involves a major impact on the world. 'I think that's happening', he states, 'but it's early days'.

Ken Gott is still overseeing meetings at Sunderland Christian Centre six nights a week. Indeed, Price writes that SCC has come to be regarded as the '"Toronto" of England'. 'The hallmark of what we're seeing up here', says Gott, 'is more of the manifest presence of God … You're just aware that the place is saturated with the presence of God.' In seeking to develop the Blessing, Gott reports that SCC has been considering how to reach the inner-city district in which the church is situated: 'We're looking to release some mercy projects and just be glad to do that because of the way God has touched our hearts.' Gott and his wife Lois will soon write up their experiences more fully in a Hodder paperback called *The Sunderland Refreshing*. This will be published later in the year, on 16th November.[27]

Bryn Jones tells Price that he is trying to stress that the benefits of the Blessing need not be location-specific, and rather than encouraging his congregations to visit Toronto, has been keen to see them 'drinking constantly' with God as their source. 'We've seen people "going down"', he recalls, 'and as they've done so, their shouts alone have indicated where they were unchurched! When they've got up they've been terrifically saved. And they're going on with God, too.' Jones' Covenant Ministries network has reported a range of 'Toronto' phenomena, along with more unusual manifestations such as oil flowing from hands during worship, a sweet fragrance filling the air, and nearly 40 people seeing a cloud fill a worship-space. Despite all this, Jones insists that if things are handled in a godly way, 'the external manifestations will quickly assume their proper place behind the far more important issue – and that's the purpose of God for our time'.

As for the critics of TTB, Price quotes from the Bawtry Hall Conference's *Charismatic Crossroads* statement, and from Reachout Trust's newsletter. He also speaks to Tony Higton, who tells him that he believes God is at work in the new movement, and that 'there is a baby with the bathwater, and the baby mustn't be thrown out'. Even so, he says that he has 'quite strongly-held cautions about the whole thing', not least the animal noises, the over-defensive attitude of some Toronto advocates, and the 'absolutely dreadful' techniques employed by Rodney Howard-Browne in the Wembley meeting which Higton attended in December and reviewed in *Christian Herald* on 14th January.[28]

The end of April also sees the launch by Monarch Books of *The Impact of Toronto* – a collection of articles from *Renewal* magazine edited by Wallace Boulton. Contributors include Eleanor Mumford, Nicky Gumbel, Terry Virgo, R.T. Kendall and Gerald Coates. In his preface, Boulton writes: 'God's Spirit is moving among us, with refreshing and releasing power. Momentous though this is, it is not, however, the longed-for revival which would shake and change the nation. It could be a preliminary, a preparation. We are at a critical stage.'[29]

Friday 5th May 1995

Christian Herald picks up on the 'campus awakenings' which have begun to take place in the wake of events at Howard Payne University in Texas and, most notably, Wheaton College, Illinois (see 19th March). At Eastern Nazarene College in Quincy, Massachusetts, President Kent Hill is quoted as saying, 'it's almost blasphemous to convey in words the power sensed in the remarkable openness of the students. There is nothing voyeuristic about it.' Hill adds that they 'were talking about the most important issues in their lives, the things they're ashamed of, afraid of, or struggling with'. College chaplains and deans, says the report, 'are forming accountability and Bible study groups and making themselves increasingly available for counselling'. John Woodbridge, Professor at Trinity Evangelical Divinity School in Deerfield, Illinois, is also quoted:

Students are glowing over the experience and the mood of anticipation fills the campus. My hope is that pastors all over the country will invite students into their churches to let them speak about reconciliation. Lack of reconciliation holds back the evangelical church. These young people are leading the way.[30]

Thursday 17th May 1995

Around ninety New Zealand Christians from various denominations attend a screening in Dunedin of a new video on TTB fronted by Alan Morrison. Entitled *A Different Gospel: The Origin and Purpose of the Toronto Blessing*,[31] the 150-minute film includes footage of a lecture given by Morrison in his home congregation, Crich Baptist Church, on 12th November 1994, and is illustrated with clips from meetings led by Kenneth Copeland and Rodney Howard-Browne in the United States.

Morrison states at the beginning of his lecture that he desires to see true revival, but that purported moves of God's Spirit must be tested in accordance with 1 John 4:1. The key criteria to be applied in such testing are, he says, whether what occurs bears out the teaching of Christ and the apostles, and whether it displays the reverence due to a holy God. Outlining the origins of TTB in the ministry of Rodney Howard-Browne and, by extension, the Faith movement with which he has been associated, Morrison shows a 30-minute video segment from a meeting led by Howard-Browne and Kenneth Copeland at Fort Worth, Texas. Both men quote Acts 3:19 in suggesting that the church is beginning to experience 'times of refreshing'. Copeland refers to Joel's prophecy of the 'former and latter rain' (Joel 2:28), and applies it to the current movement. For some time, both men address one another on the platform not in English, but in tongues. Towards the end of the clip, the meeting moves into a time of ministry. Amidst a good deal of laughter, Howard-Browne can be heard voicing phrases such as 'Fill 'em up, Jesus', 'Let the bubble out of your belly' and 'Go get 'em, Lord'. Eventually, Howard-Browne himself is ministered to by Copeland, and falls to the floor.

After the clip is finished, Morrison explains that the sort of teaching and ministry represented on the tape constitutes an important root of TTB. He also relates this to other strands of charismatic activity, such as the ministry of Kathryn Kuhlman, William Branham and E.W. Kenyon, and, as a result, questions its pedigree. He also draws parallels with New Age and occult practices like Mesmerism, Shamanism, New Thought and Gnosticism.

The Crich pastor then shows a second extract on video, this time from a Rodney Howard-Browne meeting. Here, three pastors are interviewed about their experience of TTB, but are unable to articulate it because they either shift into tongues or are struck dumb. Howard-Browne is shown describing such phenomena as 'signs' and 'wonders'. Morrison is predictably scathing about this closing of preachers' mouths, suggesting that it cannot be God's desire to block the preaching of his Word.

Morrison concludes that TTB threatens the church on at least eight fronts: by distorting Scripture to justify false manifestations; by eradicating the centrality of doctrine; by undermining the importance of evangelism; by ostracising those who would not participate; by offering a 'higher form of salvation'; by confusing pietism with true spirituality; by mediating occult-style practices, and by exhibiting the hallmarks of the great end-time deception of the saints prophesied in Scripture.

Despite all this, the video ends with Morrison hoping that TTB might spur biblical Christians into greater vigilance, and to diligence in their biblical study, the better to sift the true from the false.

Friday 19th May 1995
Writing in *The Church of England Newspaper*, Charlotte Hails surveys developments in a number of key evangelical Anglican churches, and in certain prisons. At St Mark's Battersea Rise, a church plant from Holy Trinity, Brompton, vicar Paul Perkin tells Hails that since TTB arrived, his congregation has 'a greater awareness of the vital importance of evangelism, a stronger desire to meet in prayer together and a heightened expectation of God's ability to do whatever he likes – a heightened awareness of the surprising intervention of God'. Meanwhile, Rev Sue Hope of St Margaret and St Thomas, Sheffield, comments that 'people are more in love with the Lord ... In Toronto I had the experience of roaring like a lion [and] I hear that [other] people have had extraordinary long-term experiences relating to the "lion". For me, inwardly this was a profound and prophetic experience ... [it] helps me to preach and teach more effectively and to pray more.'

David Betts, rector of the high-profile charismatic church St Nicholas, Nottingham, speaks of wide-ranging fruit: 'There is a greater spiritual love for God and awareness of him. There is renewed zeal and commitment to Christ and a love of prayer and worship.' In church meetings, he says, 'there is a deeper intensity and the interest in prayer and Bible study has increased.'

At Exeter Prison, Rev Bill Birdwood, a Chaplain, says that after a series of Bible studies in Mark's Gospel, 'we prayed for about fifteen of the eighteen there and about ten to twelve were on the floor'. This has combined with an Alpha course to bring about a powerful upsurge in evangelism, he says. Likewise, at Lewes Prison, Rev David Powe has seen 261 become Christians since he arrived in April 1994, with the keynote being repentance.

The past week has also seen some 25 ministries within the charismatic movement joining forces to issue a 500-word statement welcoming 'the current work of the Holy Spirit' and calling attention to 'the beneficial changes that have taken place', including numerical growth and the resolution of longstanding conflicts. Among those approving the statement are Pioneer, Salt and Light, Ichthus, Cornerstone and New Frontiers International. The text laments 'certain extreme statements that have been made in books and articles about the Toronto Blessing and these Times of Refreshing'. Most such critiques, it continues, 'have been made without any serious investigation' and have been 'based on hearsay'. The statement concludes with a pledge to accept God's further and future blessing 'so that the heart of the nation will be touched once more with the Good News of Jesus Christ.' It also applauds the work of the Evangelical Alliance in bringing together charismatics and non-charismatics to debate

TTB; it then calls for 'further conferences for those who are having difficulty with what is taking place as well as those who are at the centre of what they regard to be an outpouring of the Holy Spirit'.

This statement will subsequently be published in *Evangelism Today* (it is reproduced here in Section III).[32]

Friday 26th May 1995

The June issue of *Alpha* magazine updates readers on the 'college revival' that has emerged over the past two months in the USA. Reportedly, at the Wheaton plenary meetings, students filled five bin-bags with bottles of alcohol, pornography and secular music. Chaplain Barbara Woodburn confirms that counselling has been arranged for those affected: 'There are students', she says, 'who needed help in unravelling some very personal things that had complicated their lives.'

Saturday 27th May 1995

Writing in the May–June edition of *Prophecy Today*, Johannes Facius reports on a recent visit he has made to TAV. His assessment is that 'while some people seemed to have a kind of physical experience of great peace and joy, others appeared dominated by demonic manifestations'. He adds that 'there were those who were simply putting on a show and trying to fake a spiritual experience'. Facius does not believe that anything got seriously out of hand, but stresses that he is not impressed by what occurred.

In an article for *Renewal*, charismatic Anglican theologian Mark Stibbe warns of the potential 'pitfalls' of TTB. One of the greatest dangers, he writes, is that churches might neglect their 'outward-directed, mission focus' and seek 'blessings for their own sakes'. We need constantly to remind ourselves, he adds, that 'the power of the Holy Spirit is given in order that we may be Christ's witnesses (Acts 1:8)'. Furthermore, says Stibbe, 'demonstrations of the Spirit's power are mainly to accompany the proclamation of Christ crucified (1 Cor. 2:1-4). Signs and wonders attend and accredit the preaching of the gospel to the unsaved.' Rather than preaching on manifestations themselves, asserts Stibbe, Wesley, Whitefield and Edwards 'declared the life-changing truths of the gospel in public places, and the phenomena which we are witnessing today attended and followed that preaching'. Stibbe then wonders how many churches affected by TTB are viewing revival phenomena like falling, crying and laughing in the context of preaching the gospel to the unchurched. 'Manifestation without mission', warns Stibbe, is unacceptable.

Stibbe goes on to present a thesis which is expounded more fully in his soon-to-be-published book on Toronto, *Times of Refreshing* – a book for which this article serves as a 'trailer'. Defining contemporary Western society as 'addictive', he argues that in such a context, 'there is always a danger of quick-fix spiritualities – of people going to religious meetings in order to get high on experience'. Comparing this current situation with the ethos of the early British charismatic movement of the 1960s, Stibbe remarks that whereas emotionalism and outward display were then handled with great caution and reticence, there is now a real danger of people becoming 'addicted to ecstatic experiences of the Holy Spirit', thereby overlooking God's priorities of repentance, holiness, healing and renewal. Noting that despite their dramatic effect at the time, both the Welsh Revival of 1904 and the Azusa Street outpouring of 1906 faded for lack of focused Bible teaching, Stibbe worries that the same fate may befall TTB.[33]

On this day also, *Evangelicals Now* prints a 3,000-word analysis of TTB by the highly respected conservative evangelical preacher Roy Clements. This thoroughly researched piece is informed by a visit Clements has paid to TAV earlier in the year. Having described the structure and content of a typical evening meeting at Toronto, Clements declares, 'I find myself both less hostile and less euphoric than some whose opinions on the "Toronto" phenomenon I have read and heard.' It is 'quite irrefutable', he writes, that people 'are being helped in ways that seem spiritually positive as a result of "Toronto"-style meetings'. He perceives that the number of direct converts at TAV meetings is small, but admits that ministers whose churches have been affected by TTB 'often report extraordinary rates of church growth and greatly-increased evangelistic zeal among church members'.

Perhaps surprisingly, Clements states that the meetings he observed in Toronto were 'theologically orthodox' and conducted in a 'reasonably responsible fashion'. No serious error was being taught, he stresses. He reports that he did not detect 'undue psychological pressure or emotional manipulation from the leadership'. He adds that 'the atmosphere of expectation, was, if anything, 'being generated from within the congregation'.

Comparing the Toronto manifestations with those experienced in the revivals associated with Wesley, Whitefield and Edwards, Clements accepts that what is happening in TTB is 'not new'. He notes similarities with various kinds of non-Christian mysticism, from Hindu cults and New Age spiritualities to mesmerism. He also comments that 'infectious hysteria' is common in varieties of psychotherapy which practise 'body work', including primal therapy, psychodrama, bio-energetics and Ericksonian hypnotherapy. Despite such parallels, however, Clements underlines that the presence of such manifestations does not, in and of itself, prove anything. Citing Edwards, he takes the view that they cannot intrinsically confirm 'either positive or negative' assessments of a spiritual experience. The key, Clements implies, must lie in the motivations and intentions of those who manifest the phenomena in question. 'Are they laughing out of delirious relief at being saved?', he asks. 'Or is the emotion much less focussed than that? Is it simply the release of pent-up feelings arising from a general sense of inner tension and unresolved frustration?'

All in all, Clements suspects that the Toronto experience is 'a very mixed affair'. Some, he accepts, may have come to the meetings with many years of Christian understanding and biblical background behind them; they may well have related such knowledge constructively to what they found in the Blessing. Clements fears, however, that others with less maturity might simply have seized on TTB as 'a permissive context for "letting go" of repressed emotions', without finding that their devotional life or appreciation of Scripture has been advanced as a result. Within this somewhat vague set of emotional reactions, Clements expresses concern about the 'sexually suggestive' nature of the 'physical shaking and gyrating' he has witnessed. In the end, however, he strikes a neutral note which again takes its cue from Edwards: 'It is important', he writes, 'that the *diversity* of what is going on spiritually and psychologically at these meetings should be acknowledged. The manifestations observed are common to the whole range of human experience. Laughter can be a healthy and appropriate expression of intense feelings. But it can also be unhealthy, hysterical or even demonic.'

Outlining practical responses to TTB, Clements suggests a need for better counselling, given that some who manifest intensely may be *acting out* a trauma rather than *working it through*, and better teaching, since the Toronto meetings he has attended do not seem to be providing the sort of 'thorough and wide-ranging' exposition that is really demanded. Reflecting on the place of TTB within evangelicalism, Clements looks back thirty years to gain perspective and sound a warning:

> In many respects the Toronto blessing poses the same questions for us as did the wave of enthusiasm for the gift of tongues when the neo-charismatic movement began in the 1960s. Then, too, debate raged about whether this manifestation of spiritual renewal was a supernatural work of God, a demonic counterfeit or a self-manufactured psychological state of ecstasy. The same dangers are evident in the two movements also: mindless subjectivism; self-indulgent introversion; most of all, there is the peril of division among evangelical Christians. Ironically, the Toronto blessing is currently proving divisive within the charismatic constituency, as well as among those who have always been cautious about such manifestations of enthusiasm.

In conclusion, Clements personally finds 'no reason to oppose' TTB. Neither, however, will he 'shed any tears' if it 'fades into oblivion, like so many other fads that have ephemerally obsessed the neo-charismatic movement'. Moreover, he writes, 'whether I speak in tongues or fall on the floor in delirious laughter is a matter of very little consequence to me indeed'.[34]

Tuesday 30th May–Thursday 1st June 1995
Alan Morrison's Diakrisis organisation co-ordinates a conference – called 'Strange Fire?' – on TTB. The event, which takes place at High Leigh, Hoddesdon in Hertfordshire, attracts over a hundred and is addressed by Peter Fenwick, minister of Central House Church in Sheffield, Stanley Jebb, pastor of New Covenant Baptist Church, Dunstable, Brian Edwards, President of the Fellowship of Independent Evangelical Churches, church historian Nick Needham, and Morrison himself.

As he did at the Bawtry Hall consultation on 15th April, Fenwick insists that TTB has neither warrant nor precedent in Scripture. In a stinging critique, he asserts that twenty-five years of 'unfulfilled prophecies', a growing acceptance of Wimberite 'power evangelism' and of 'kingdom now' teaching, together with a 'dangerous pride', have left the charismatic movement in general, and its Restorationist wing in particular, 'wide open to every new thing'.

Jebb argues that over a number of years the charismatic movement has exhibited a range of dubious traits that have now made it susceptible to the distortions of Toronto. These traits are identified as: raised expectations, the elevation of questionable experiences, frequent exposure to such experiences at large meetings, preaching with little biblical or doctrinal content, crediting pictures as divine revelation and excusing the misapplication of scriptural truth.

Needham for his part objects to what he sees as a misappropriation of Jonathan Edwards by those seeking an apologetic for TTB. Stressing that Edwards regarded physical manifestations as incidental details of revival that cannot, in themselves, either validate or invalidate spiritual experience, Needham contends that whereas for Edwards bodily effects were secondary to the effect of the Holy Spirit upon the mind, in TTB, 'the power operates directly on the body'.

Brian Edwards bases his critique of TTB on Isaiah 62. The Blessing, he says, has defaced the image of God in humanity and has actually discouraged prayer for revival. Indeed, he is convinced that one of the greatest hindrances to genuine revival is the charismatic movement as a whole.

Morrison repeats many of the points made in his Diakrisis pamphlets, *We All Fall Down* and *Falling for the Lie*. As well as exhibiting numerous occult and New Age characteristics, TTB is seen by Morrison as doctrinally defective with respect to its models of revelation, pneumatology, sanctification and eschatology.

The High Leigh conference also gives several of those attending the chance to tell of their alienation and ostracism from churches where TTB has come to the fore.

The conference is subsequently reported in the *Baptist Times*,[35] *Christian Herald*,[36] *Evangelicals Now*,[37] *Evangelism Today*[38] and *Evangelical Times*.[39]

Friday 2nd June 1995

The Evangelical Alliance hosts a second major consultation on TTB, following up its Euston Conference of 19th-20th December 1994. This meeting is held at the Alliance's offices in Kennington, South London, and attracts some 60 leaders. Speakers on the day are Baptist Union General Secretary David Coffey, Marlow Christian Fellowship lay leader David Noakes, Ichthus Fellowship founder Roger Forster, Westminster Chapel minister R.T. Kendall and Dr Andrew Walker of King's College, London.

Setting the scene for the consultation, Andrew Walker traces the provenance of TTB in Britain through 'four main entry-points': the South-West London Vineyard and HTB, Queen's Road Baptist Church, Terry Virgo's New Frontiers network and Rodney Howard-Browne's visits to the UK in June and December 1994. Walker is particularly keen to highlight the difference between the 'Howard-Browne' version of the new movement, which he associates with the 'pump it up', classical Pentecostal tradition of his own childhood, and the more 'Wimberite' version that has spread mainly through HTB. 'There is clearly potential here for conflicts of style and social class,' he remarks. 'Perhaps more significantly, there is also potential for conflicts over theology.' Walker adds that he thinks TTB is moving, on analogy (though only on analogy) from an 'Acts 2' phase to an 'Acts 15' phase – 'from the first phase of blessing to the church council phase of reflection'. The Alliance Consultation, he implies, represents an important development in this respect.

David Noakes then proceeds to present TTB as a severe challenge to the charismatic movement. Suggesting that charismatics, of which he is one, have now 'lost our way somewhat', Noakes recounts a visit he has recently paid to Toronto. Disturbed by the 'deafening' music and 'rock concert' atmosphere, he describes the scene as one in which 'anyone prone to easy hypnosis might have ended up in a trance.' In addition, he detects many of the manifestations as being 'demonic', with several women 'unmistakably in a state of high sexual excitement'. Reporting that he heard instruction being given in Toronto that 'discernment was unnecessary, that God was totally in control and Satan could not get a look-in because the power of God was so great', Noakes comments that he 'cannot imagine a more deadly piece of advice'. Having examined the biblical arguments in favour of TTB, Noakes rejects their exegetical foundation, and concludes that 'the boundaries of safety which Scripture establishes are being torn down in order to justify the acceptance of new experience. This spells utmost danger for God's people.'

Roger Forster suggests that the new movement is not yet worthy of the term 'revival', but that it can legitimately be seen as a 'time of refreshing'. He believes that most of the manifestations can be shown to have biblical precedent and points out that Scripture can at times appear even more radical in this sphere than what has been occurring, e.g. in the levitation of Ezekiel. He concedes that animal noises are usually signs of demonic activity, but even here he urges that critics 'wait to judge, without being too quick to jump'. He can, he says, countenance the idea that 'the occasional roar or two … might sound like God roaring from heaven'. Through it all, however, Forster is clear that the phenomena should be interpreted and explained, lest the movement fall foul of mystical obfuscation. He accepts that there has been a degree of anti-intellectualism, libertinism, manipulation and self-indulgence. All the same, he is content to regard TTB as a sign of preparation for 'the end time' and pleads that the church does not throw away a 'God-given opportunity for world evangelism' before the end finally arrives.

R.T. Kendall surprises some by testifying that although he had been initially hostile to TTB, the personal transformations of his wife and son while sitting under the ministry of Rodney Howard-Browne have forced him to revise his opinion. 'It just so happens', he says, 'that I believe Rodney is a man of God. God uses crude men who are not so literate … and who stick their foot in it.' Recognising the use which is being made of Jonathan Edwards on both sides of the Toronto debate, Kendall points out that in his sermon 'True

Grace as Distinguished from the Doctrines of Devils', the New England theologian showed that the one thing the Devil cannot do is to produce a true love for the glory of God. Kendall is ready, he says, to affirm that such love and such glory are present in the new movement. One aspect of the manifestation of God's glory which is evident in TTB, says Kendall, is that 'God may choose to turn up in a way that offends the mind ... If I were forced to choose one verse as a theological rationale for what we are talking about it would be 'God has chosen the foolish things of the world to shame the wise' (1 Cor. 1:27).

Summing up, David Coffey appeals to Matthew 18 as he calls for a deeper examination of the theological issues at stake in TTB and a strengthened commitment to evangelical unity. The latter prerogative is vital, he says, at a time when political and social commentators are offering no clear solutions to society's loss of confidence.

The consultation ends with a request from those present that the Alliance Commission on Unity and Truth among Evangelicals (ACUTE) undertake more thoroughgoing biblical and theological analysis of TTB. ACUTE Co-ordinator Dave Cave agrees to take this forward.[40]

Also today, in an article for *The Church of England Newspaper*, Charlotte Hails questions whether anything approaching a 'theology of Toronto' has begun to emerge. The keynote of Hails' piece is struck in a quotation from Mark Stibbe. She has asked him whether, as a post-biblical phenomenon, TTB is generating 'a new theology of the Holy Spirit'. He answers:

> The question implies that there is an old theology of the Holy Spirit that we all agree to. I don't think this is so. People have only started to create one in recent years. The danger is that our experience might dictate our theology, but there has got to be a circle in which experience and biblical theology go together.[41]

In a corresponding article, East London University Chaplain John Richardson argues that experience is still running far too far ahead of theology where TTB is concerned. As such, it is, he charges, being constructed on sand rather than solid ground. The new movement does not, contends Richardson, derive from the message of 'Christ crucified', nor does it develop that message: 'What is preached are the phenomena. It is a 'Gospel of the Spirit' where Christians are focused on what is claimed to be the Spirit's work, instead of having the Spirit focus them on Jesus' work.' Richardson goes on to assert that 'there is nothing whatsoever in the New Testament that would suggest we should expect or seek any of the phenomena currently accompanying the "Toronto Blessing"'. Furthermore, 'Attempts to justify them from isolated incidents in the Old Testament are totally unsatisfactory since, unlike the biblical examples quoted, the experiences of the "Toronto Blessing" are usually detached from any corresponding cause. People laugh when there is nothing funny. They fall down when there is no manifestation of God.'[42]

Monday 5th June 1995
The Evangelical Alliance issues a press release on the 'Toronto' consultation held last Friday. The text summarises the contributions made by speakers at the event, and adds that delegates 'requested the Alliance Commission on Unity and Truth (ACUTE) … to look at how the Bible should be interpreted in the light of the "Toronto Blessing"'. ACUTE Co-ordinator Dave Cave, who organised the event with other Alliance staff, is quoted: 'There has been some theological firing from the hip over the "Toronto Blessing". We hope to produce an in-depth response to some of the issues being raised. Our aim is to preserve unity without sacrificing truth.'

The consultation, with its call for further research, is duly reported in this week's *Baptist Times* and *Church of England Newspaper*, and in the July issue of *Evangelical Times*.[43]

Wednesday 7th June 1995
New Zealand's leading Christian newspaper, *Challenge Weekly*, devotes this week's issue to a number of articles from various perspectives on TTB. In global terms, New Zealand churches have been among the most receptive to TTB since it emerged. In a leader, publisher and chief editor Henk Kamsteeg urges readers to observe five principles as they come to terms with the new movement:

1. Beware the sensationalism of the media;
2. Test everything;
3. Avoid the prejudice which dismisses anything new;
4. Learn afresh about discernment;
5. Toronto or no Toronto, seek greater holiness and devotion to Scripture.[44]

Sunday 18th June 1995
Today is Fathers' Day in the USA, and the Brownsville Assemblies of God Church in Pensacola, Florida, has invited the Texas-based evangelist Steve Hill to preach at their morning service. The church's minister, John Kilpatrick, is tired and weary, and is therefore pleased to have a visitor take the sermon. The congregation has been praying for revival since May 1993, but has never witnessed anything approaching what occurs when, after preaching, Hill issues an altar call. Hundreds among the two thousand or so present come forward for prayer, some manifesting Toronto-style phenomena.

Steve Hill himself has developed from working in *The Cross and the Switchblade* author David Wilkerson's Twin Oaks leadership academy, where Nicky Cruz taught him evangelism. After cutting his teeth on the streets of Dallas, he travelled to Argentina, where he came into contact with leaders of the 'Argentinian Revival'. Significantly, he has also paid a recent visit to Holy Trinity, Brompton. Later, he will recall what he experienced there in the following terms:

I read in *Time* magazine how God was moving. I had been to London several times, and I thought, 'I've got to see this. I've got to see God moving in an Anglican Church because I can't imagine it.' The article said they were laughing, they were falling, and I had a very critical spirit. I wanted a little private visit with pastor Sandy Miller [sic] to see what was going on.' When I visited Holy Trinity Brompton there was a conference going on. I walked into the stately Anglican church in downtown London right by Harrods, the richest area of town, and stepped over about 500 bodies, people shaking all over the place. I had seen things like that before, but I'm an evangelist, so I'm after souls. If I can't see hundreds and hundreds of people getting saved, then I'll leave. The Lord spoke to my heart and said, 'You don't need to talk to Mr Sandy Miller. Just have him pray for you.' I walked up to him and said, 'My name is Steve.' He says, 'Look what's happened in my church.' He laid his hands on my head and it was over. I mean, I went down under the power of the Holy Spirit.[45]

From today for the next fifteen months, Hill will concentrate his ministry at Pensacola, and will see some 1.4 million people attend services arranged on a four-night-per-week schedule. In the same period, it will be estimated that around seventy-seven thousand people will make professions of faith. In keeping with the classical Pentecostal ethos of the Brownsville Assembly, the emphasis at these meetings is generally perceived to fall more obviously than at Toronto on holiness, repentance and the preaching of the cross.[46]

Friday 23rd June 1995
Canon Michael Green, a leading Anglican charismatic now co-ordinating the Springboard evangelistic initiative, writes on TTB for the *Church of England Newspaper*. He is favourably disposed towards the 'Gamaliel Principle' of testing the Blessing by its longer-term fruit and durability, and rejects a number of arguments which, he feels, have 'muddied the water' in respect of the new movement. First, he writes, although Rodney Howard-Browne's links with Rhema and WordFaith are cause for concern, they need not in themselves detract from the validity of TTB. As Green sees it, 'An enormous amount of "the blessing" is taking place among all sorts of people who have never heard of Howard-Browne, been to Toronto, or had anything to do with Holy Trinity, Brompton. It can be and often is a spontaneous happening, quite unsought.'

The second 'misapprehension' noted by Green relates to the hotly disputed issue of manipulation. In response to those who accuse Toronto proponents of this, Green retorts: 'I challenge any clergy to get large numbers of a typically Anglican congregation to lie upon the ground of their church. I have not infrequently been praying for people myself and have been surprised when I looked round to find they had fallen to the ground.'

A third 'canard' singled out by Green is the Vineyard origin of the new movement. He accepts that this is a significant factor, but insists that the Vineyard is only one among several 'streams by which this phenomenon [has] hit Britain'.

Fourthly, Green questions the argument, mooted by Mark Stibbe and others, that TTB is a response to the addictive, experientialist culture of the postmodern West. Whilst conceding that we do indeed live in an experience-oriented age, Green's own observations lead him to submit that those most helped by the Blessing 'have not constantly returned for another dose, but have demonstrated a new love for Christ which they date to the profound experience of God they received while semi-conscious on the floor, or as laughter or tears broke through the inhibitions which had crippled their emotional life for years.' Sociologically, however, he is prepared to interpret TTB as reflective of a more general shift of worldview:

> In an age which is beginning to rediscover the right side of the brain, and reacting against Enlightenment rationalism, there is an understandable cult of experience. You see it in the addiction to music, the TV etc. But experience is what the church has been very short of. Plenty of talk about God, but not a lot of life-changing encounter with God. Is it so reprehensible, then, if God should determine in this day and age to offer a powerful experience of his presence and his power? Surely not.

Turning to Scripture, Green finds ample corroboration of 'Toronto'-style manifestations in the Old and New Testaments. On falling down, he cites Genesis 15:12; Ezekiel 3:23; Daniel 8:17; 10:9; Acts 9:26 and Revelation 1:17. On shaking, he draws attention to Daniel 10:7, Psalm 99:1, Habakkuk. 3:16 and Acts 4:31. On 'drunkenness', which he interprets as 'being so full of the Spirit that the limbs are uncoordinated', he finds parallels in Jeremiah 23:9; Acts 2:13 and Ephesians 5:18. Crying and laughing are present, says Green, at Nehemiah 8:9; 2 Chronicles 34:27; Acts 2:37; Psalm 126; Ecclesiastes 3:4 and John 17:13. All these phenomena are thus biblical, Green avers, and he can see 'no *a priori* reason why they should not happen today as they did in Bible times'. Furthermore, he defends them as signs of God's presence, rebukes to the this-worldliness of much of the church, and potential challenges to the 'rationalism that has dogged much of our theology for 200 years'.

Green follows Jonathan Edwards and the contemporary author John White in emphasising that the manifestations cannot intrinsically guarantee anything and should not be 'hunted' for. Even so, he is more than prepared to view them as spurs to 'greater Christlikeness of life and community'.[47]

Saturday 24th June 1995

The July edition of *Evangelical Times* publishes a letter written in late May by Diakrisis Director Alan Morrison to the Evangelical Alliance, explaining why he would not be attending the Alliance's special consultation on TTB on 2nd June. 'You are holding a meeting purportedly to uphold unity among evangelical churches,' he says. 'However, it is the people who have promoted the so-called "Toronto Blessing" itself who have brought division, deception and damaging practices into the church. I cannot possibly involve myself in an alliance with those responsible for this.' Quoting the favourite separatist text

Romans 16:17,18, Morrison justifies his absence on the grounds that Toronto is a dangerous departure from apostolic doctrine. Among its faults, he repeats the core accusations made in his address to the 'Strange Fire?' consultation at the beginning of the month, namely that TTB promotes extra-biblical revelation, false salvation, arrogant leadership claims, theological double-talk, defective Christology, erroneous pneumatology, unjustified scriptural proof-texting, vicious denunciation of detractors and syncretism. Dismissing the now familiar 'argument from fruits', Morrison asserts that the same results as claimed by Toronto proponents could be achieved 'from attendance at Erhard Seminars Training, a course in Silva Mind Control or becoming a sannyasin in the society for Krishna consciousness.' Morrison confirms that he is himself 'a veteran of the New Age movement and Eastern mystical sects', and that prior to his conversion, he would have seen TTB as just 'one more of the many cults that I experienced in over twenty years of spiritual searching'. Cults must not be negotiated with, he suggests, but must be rejected as deceptions. Hence, he writes to Joel Edwards, the Alliance's UK Director: 'I regard your meetings on this subject as one more pitiful episode in the downgrade which has so characterized professing evangelical churches in the last decades of the twentieth century.'[48]

In an editorial comment following Morrison's letter, *ET* remarks that 'of course, those involved know that anything short of unqualified rejection of the 'Toronto phenomenon' will be construed as a vindication of the whole sorry mess.' The Alliance's efforts at reconciliation in this matter are thus seen as merely perpetuating the root problem, rather than solving it. EA's call for more theological work is written off as 'just a fudge', while the Whitefield House Consultation's stated intent to 'look at how the Bible is to be interpreted in the light of the "Toronto Blessing"' is dismissed as 'the theology of liberalism, not of evangelicals'. By contrast, the comment concludes, 'The Toronto issue must be interpreted in the light of the Bible, not the other way around.'[49] Joel Edwards and Dave Cave will reply to all this in the August copy of *ET* (29th July 1995). Morrison will respond in his turn in September.

Also at the end of June, Kensington Temple Pastor Colin Dye writes in *Joy* magazine that 'this fresh move of the Spirit threatens the powerless and back-slidden body of Christ represented by Saul [cf. 1 Sam. 15]'. By the same token, he suggests, the movement can also be viewed in terms of the anointing which passed from Saul to David. As with the humble shepherd-king, writes Dye, 'today it will be the insignificant, unnoticed people who will do the greatest exploits for God.'[50]

The same July issue of *Joy* carries an interview with Mary Audrey Raycroft, Ministry Team Trainer at TAV. She emphasises the central place given to account-ability at the Airport Vineyard: all team members wear badges and directional prophecy is discouraged. There is a pool of around 150-170 trained team members, from whom she says she draws between 12 and 50, depending on the attendance.[51]

This late-June period also sees the publication of two critiques of TTB from Day One – the theological books arm of the Lord's Day Observance Society and a platform for largely conservative evangelical authors who are sceptical about the charismatic movement. Leigh Belcham's *Toronto: The Baby or the Bathwater* claims to be the work of 'an ordinary Christian' from a charismatic background who is concerned that TTB might be more negative than positive for the Church. Over thirteen brief chapters, he argues that advocates and proponents of the movement have thus far failed to present adequate evidence that it is truly of God.

Jebb's study is more detailed; it is partly based on the author's personal visits to some of the major British 'centres' of the Blessing. All the same, he reaches similar conclusions to Belcham. While prepared to accept that TTB covers a 'mixture' of experiences, Jebb argues that God, in spite of Toronto, may simply have touched those who have been positively blessed, 'because they are hungry'. God's grace can bypass the kinds of 'deception' that he believes are being mediated through the new movement.[52]

Both titles sell out within the first month of publication and are reprinted in August.

Thursday 29th June 1995

The annual Methodist Conference, meeting this year in Bristol, considers a motion on TTB proposed by Rev Paul Newman of Darlington and seconded by Rev Christopher Mabb of North Wales. It asks conference, 'in the light of the world-wide move of God sometimes referred to as the Toronto "blessing"', to 'welcome every genuine work of the Holy Spirit, holding to the words of Scripture: "Do not quench the Spirit, do not despise prophesying, but test everything."' Christopher Mabb indicates that the purpose of the motion is threefold: to legitimise those who feel called to minister in such things, to give a positive directive to those who have only heard the critical side of the debate, and to encourage others to feel able to minister in the mode of TTB.

In the ensuing debate on the motion, Rev John Cooke urges that while Methodism is a religion of the heart, new charismatic movements such as TTB can veer into triumphalism and should therefore be approached with caution. Rev Neil Dixon, Secretary to the Faith and Order Committee, acknowledges that the motion is carefully worded, but says that it seems to have done its testing already, and found a congenial answer – that TTB is clearly 'a worldwide move of God'. He does not believe that it is appropriate, he adds, for the Methodist Church either formally to welcome, or to reject, TTB. On this basis, he proposes that the motion is not voted on. This proposal is defeated, however, and the debate moves forward when Revs Martin Turner and Paul Smith present an amended notice of motion which deletes the phrase 'worldwide move of God' and adds a clause calling on the Faith and Order Committee to prepare for next year's Conference a report on the Blessing, which will incorporate responses from ministers and members of local churches. Conference duly accepts this revised notice of motion.[53]

Monday 10th July 1995

Marshall Pickering launch a major new assessment of TTB by the charismatic Anglican theologian Mark Stibbe. Entitled *Times of Refreshing*, the book is divided into five chapters.

Chapter 1 seeks to set TTB within its historical context. Stibbe proposes that the Blessing carries with it the 'first hints' of a 'fourth wave' of modern Holy Spirit renewal. Taking his cue from the taxonomy first proposed by Peter Wagner in the mid-1980s (1986), he identifies the 'first wave' of this renewal with the development of Pentecostalism, from the Azusa Street revival in Los Angeles in 1906 to its current presence in over two hundred countries among some two hundred million or more people. The 'second wave' is defined as the outflow of Pentecostal spirituality into the historic mainline denominations – a process which began in the early years of the century but which gained serious momentum in North America in the late 1950s, spreading to Britain and Europe in the early Sixties. The 'Third Wave' is associated with the 'signs and wonders' emphasis of John Wimber and the Vineyard (see 1986). Now, suggests Stibbe, 'Toronto' can be regarded as the 'sea fret' of a new swell of divine activity – activity which he predicts will lead on to nothing less than 'global revival'. Citing a famous prophecy given by the Pentecostal pioneer Smith Wigglesworth in 1947, Stibbe anticipates that this revival will stem from a profound re-integration of emphases on the Word and the Spirit.

What especially distinguishes Stibbe's analysis here is his relation of this historical schema to the vision of Ezekiel (Ezek. 47:1-12). This is the passage in which the prophet pictures four 'waves of blessing' flowing from Temple and going on to heal and restore the land. As Stibbe recognises, it has become a 'favourite passage' for proponents of TTB (cf. 29th October 1994; 3rd December 1994). For his part, he acknowledges Sheffield rector Mike Breen as the one who first alerted him to the potential of the text for understanding the different phases of twentieth-century renewal. As a reputable New Testament scholar, Stibbe readily admits the problems that go with using Scripture in such a way. He acknowledges that many Old Testament experts would regard any direct application of this ancient Hebrew document to twentieth-century church history as at best anachronistic and at worst downright misleading. 'Both liberals and conservatives', he notes, 'would argue that interpretation is a matter of discovering the objective meaning of a text using the scientific methods associated with historical criticism. Both would agree that Mike Breen's kind of exegesis is extremely subjective…' Despite this, Stibbe insists that such historical critics need to appreciate that people affected by Pentecostal spirituality have 'a different approach to hermeneutics'.

Stibbe dubs the approach in question the 'This is That' model of interpretation. The phrase is taken from the Authorised Version of Acts 2:16, in which Peter preaches to the crowd on the Day of Pentecost and says of the dramatic scene unfolding around him, '*This is That* which was spoken by the prophet Joel' [Joel 2:28-32]. Just as with Peter on this occasion, so with Pentecostals and charismatics today, Stibbe asserts, 'The primary task of exegesis involves perceiving what the Father is doing right now amongst us (like Jesus in John 5:19) and then allowing the Holy Spirit to lead us to Bible texts that elucidate that work.' He adds:'the important thing is "contextualized exegesis" – understanding our own communal story in the light of the overarching story of Scripture.' Contending that this approach is in fact closer to the use made of the Old Testament by the New, and is thus in significant ways more 'biblical' than historical-critical methods focused on the original intent of the author, Stibbe nonetheless urges that prophetic interpretations like Mike Breen's need to be tested. Even here, however, the most appropriate milieu for such testing is seen to be the church community. Interpretative validity thereby becomes substantially a matter of corroboration. Or as Stibbe himself puts it, 'Is the same thing being said by others?' Since many are gaining insight at this time from Ezekiel 47, and since the 'four waves' analogy appears to be widespread, he infers that it is likely to be from God.

Beyond the broad historical pattern he gleans from the text, Stibbe also finds in Ezekiel 47 eight 'marks' of revival which he expects will characterise the coming 'forth wave' of the Holy Spirit. These are: great sacrifice (vv.1-2); profound spirituality (v.5), Biblical integration (v.7), supernatural signs (v.8), massive growth (v.5), extraordinary variety among converts (v.10), practical compassion (v.7) and divine judgement (v.11).

In Chapter 2, Stibbe elaborates on these 'tests' for true revival by suggesting further criteria by which authentic movements of God's Spirit can be discerned. Most fundamentally of all, he highlights three essential checks which must be invoked. Quoting 1 John 4:1, he defines the first of these as the 'Test of Christology' – that is, whether a spiritual manifestation serves to exalt Christ. The second, after 1 John 3:23, is entitled the 'Test of Character'; it concerns whether a purported work of the Spirit binds believers together more closely in love. The third test is called by Stibbe the 'Test of Consequence'; it is derived from Jesus' advice in Matthew 7:15,16 that prophets should be known by their fruit.

In applying these and other criteria to TTB, Stibbe is persuaded that it is well on the way to qualifying as a genuine revival. It is, he says, 'not a planned event but an unplanned, sovereign work of God', one which has majored on the centrality of Christ and which has fostered reconciliation between churches and individuals. There is already much good fruit, he suggests, although he cautions that 'what we are not seeing at this stage is [the] centrifugal, evangelistic character of [previous] revivals'. In connection with this, he also concedes that deep levels of mass repentance have yet to be witnessed. Returning to Ezekiel 47, he concludes that 'the river of the Spirit is still confined to the Temple courts – that is, to the churches'. If the present movement is to develop into a revival, he writes, 'we must allow the Spirit to burst out of the closed doors of our churches and to carry us out into a world lost in the darkness of the Arabah.'

Chapter 3 of *Times of Refreshing* propounds another provocative theory in relation to the Blessing. Here, Stibbe attempts to account for the new movement in sociological terms. He suggests that in this instance, as throughout history, God is adapting his purposes to 'the needs of the hour'. Where TTB is concerned, says Stibbe, God can be seen to have provided a sanctified means of sublimating the 'addictive culture' that is the postmodern West. Following the psychologist of religion Howard Clinebell, Stibbe argues that as they face the stresses and confusions of the post-industrial world, increasing numbers of people are turning to 'ecstatic, mood-altering and escapist activities' in order to 'blot out the realities of life'. Whether through drugs, food, shopping or sex, they are seeking tangible experiences which are, in effect, serving as substitutes for direct, mystical, numinous encounters with God. By allowing itself to become 'pale and anaemic' in capitulation to Enlightenment rationalism, Stibbe submits that the Church has lost much of its capacity to attract such people. TTB is therefore God's way of meeting this deficit; it is the 'divine alternative' to ephemeral intoxication, an explanation for which Stibbe finds clear warrant in Ephesians 5:15-20.

In Chapter 4, Stibbe offers biblical and historical backing for the laughter associated with TTB. While generally sanguine about its validity, he accepts that some of the laughter mentioned in Scripture is mocking rather than truly joyful. He also writes that ecstatic expressions of laughter can be 'a potentially addictive experience'. Like eating, he says, 'it releases natural painkillers (endorphins) in the structure of the brain, creating a temporary anaesthesia and even euphoria. As such, this experience can, if we are not very careful, become an end in itself.' All the same, he urges that this should not be viewed as a reason to suppress it outright, and warns against the twin dangers of cultural captivity and controlling leadership for those who are inclined to impose a blanket ban on it.

In his final chapter, Stibbe is bluntly honest about the fact that many Christians have embraced TTB as an antidote to exhaustion and disillusionment with the Church. Indeed, he writes that prior to visiting TAV on the advice on David Pytches, he was himself 'desperate' – caught up in a cycle of 'performance rather than reality'. Having encountered God afresh through the Blessing, he has, he says, been led through a 'desert experience' that has challenged him about the need to overcome charismatic egoism, exhibitionism and escapism. Stibbe stresses that the Church as a whole must follow the same wilderness path if it is to progress to revival. As it does so, like Jesus himself (Mt. 4:1-11), it must, he says, steep itself once more in the Word of God.[54]

In early 1998, Stibbe's book will be subjected to sustained critique by four of his colleagues in the Sheffield University Department of Biblical Studies (see 16th January 1998).

Thursday 13th July 1995
Following the Methodist Conference's call for a report on TTB, Neil Dixon, Faith and Order Secretary, advertises in the Methodist Recorder for submissions on the new movement, and for nominations to the working party which will be set up to write the text.

Saturday 15th July 1995

The Wirral-based prayer ministry Intercessors for Britain hosts a meeting attended by around five hundred people at Westminster Chapel, London. A four-point declaration is presented, which denies that TTB is a genuine move of the Holy Spirit, deplores the widespread search for experience in preference to self-denial, and calls on churches to 'restore reality [in place of] excessive triumphalism'. Several of those attending have either actively opposed TTB, or have felt obliged to leave their congregations as a result of it. On the platform, alongside Intercessors for Britain leaders, is Peter Fenwick, who addressed both the second Bawtry Hall consultation and the Diakrisis conference at High Leigh at the end of June (see 15th April and 30th June respectively). Also present is Jo Gardner of Adullam Register – a network that has been established for those who have departed from their fellowships over the Toronto issue.[55]

Also, in today's *Christian Herald*, Peter Glover lambasts TTB as one more example of 'power' religion to be placed alongside recent evangelical trends like 'the obsession with spiritual gifts, power healing, the healing of memories, power evangelism, words of knowledge' and 'rampant, unaccountable prophecy'. He goes on to plead that evangelicals learn to sift the wheat from the chaff, and reject such emphases as distractions from true revival. 'I am sure', he adds, 'if the apostle Paul were here, he would hold his head in his hands in exasperation after all of the warnings from him and other New Testament writers about the end-times.' Citing Matthew 24, he stresses that these last days will be marked by 'a great apostasy from the faith', which will arise from 'within [the Church's] own walls'. Glover's implication is clear: TTB may be part of this coming attack.

Monday 17th July 1995

Darton, Longman and Todd publish a collaborative academic study of TTB entitled *The Toronto Blessing – Or Is It?*, which is edited by Stanley E. Porter (Professor of Theology and Religious Studies at the Roehampton Institute) and Philip Richter (a lecturer in sociology of religion who also works at Roehampton).[56] As well as contributions from these two, it features chapters written by John Kent (Emeritus Professor of Theology at the University of Bristol), Royse Murphy (a general medical practitioner with an interest in psychiatry and psychotherapy) and Wendy Porter (a professional musician).

Richter's opening essay draws on the work of French sociologist Daniele Hervieu-Léger to propose that TTB is a largely middle-class phenomenon whose participants have found in it a way of responding to the increasing marginalisation of religious discourse in contemporary western culture. 'If intellectual middle-class evangelicals are finding that the Gospel does not seem to be 'speaking the same language' any more', he writes, 'one solution is to adopt the inarticulate meta-language of glossolalia, another is to embrace the non-verbal Toronto Blessing.' Both solutions, according to Richter, 'avoid head-on engagement with the language of modernity'. In this way, he concludes, 'the Blessing can be seen as helping to mediate the acute contradiction between [the middle classes'] religious "cultural capital" and the day-to-day realities of living and working in the 1990s.'[57]

The next contribution is by Porter; he examines the claims to biblical precedent and warrant made by proponents of TTB. Emphasising that there is a significant difference between something being 'in the Bible' and something being 'biblical', he works through the key texts that have been adduced in favour of the new movement in general, and its associated manifestations in particular. The use of the phrase 'times of refreshing' to describe the Blessing is criticised on the grounds that in Acts 3:19 it most probably refers to the season of Christ's future return, and then more distinctly to the relief from trials and tribulations which this will bring to penitent Israel. Hence, in Porter's terms, 'To take it as a reference to one of several periodic times of renewal in the Church is a misapplication of the passage.' He adds that if such 'a crucial conceptual passage' has been wrongly applied, 'perhaps other passages have been misconstrued as well.' In analysing these 'other passages', he is no less sharp in his critique.

In Acts 2:13-15, says Porter, there is no positive parallel with drunkenness; rather, the text presents a radical *contrast* between alcoholic inebriation and the experience of the disciples at Pentecost. 'The apostles were doing something phenomenal which some *misattributed* to drunkenness,' he writes. 'However, Peter quickly refuted this, instead of encouraging it.' Likewise, Porter avers that Ephesians 5:18 must be read alongside clear prohibitions on drunken behaviour in Romans 13:13 and 1 Thessalonians 5:6-8: 'It simply does not follow that a clear denial of a practice, because it is recounted in the Bible, becomes a scriptural basis for it.'

Neither is Porter especially impressed with the apologetics so far offered by Bill Jackson, Gerald Coates and others, for 'uncontrollable laughter'. First, he contends, to construe this particular form of laughter from general references to joy and/or gladness is overly speculative and thus 'inadequate to make a case'. Secondly, even if it could be shown that Jesus' disciples broke out in spontaneous and possibly uncontrollable laughter (which Porter believes it cannot), this would not necessarily mean that what they did should be normative for the church today, nor that the laughter associated with TTB is necessarily of the Holy Spirit. Thirdly, Porter points out that James 1:2,3, together with 2 Corinthians 7:4-7; Philippians 2:17,18 and 1 Peter 1:8 confirm 'an uncomfortable equation of Christian joy with adversity, not with uproarious laughter.'

On trembling and convulsion, Porter dismisses passages like Jeremiah 5:22, Daniel 10:8-10, Psalms 2:11, 99:1 and 114:7, Habakkuk 3:16 and Acts 4:31; 7:32 as 'completely irrelevant for establishing a precedent for bodily shaking as an indication of reception of the Holy Spirit by a person'. Likewise the references most often used to defend 'resting in the Spirit', which are dismissed either on the basis of being 'pre-Pentecostal', on the grounds that they speak of prostration rather than falling backwards, or because Paul's experience is 'anything but representative of normative Christianity'.

Animal noises are given even shorter shrift by Porter. Hosea's reference to a lion's roar (Hos. 11:10,11) is, he says, descriptive of a divine rather than a human action. From the context, which compares the timid response of the Israelites to the might of God, Porter suggests that 'if anything, they should be like birds and doves [and yet] this does not mean that cooing is commended, but that they should be like animals before an awesome beast'.

Porter ends by hoping that the Vineyard's avowed openness to biblical correction will be heeded in the light of exegesis such as that which he has offered.[58]

Royse Murphy's contribution to the book explores the psychology of the Blessing. Stressing that it is 'inappropriate' to regard distinctions between psychology and spirituality as clear-cut and exclusive, he draws on the work of William James, Alister Hardy and Gerald Priestland to show that many more people claim religious experiences than are adherents of particular religious groups, and that the majority of such people are relatively balanced and healthy in psychological terms. This has two main consequences from Murphy's point of view. On the one hand, it means that it is most unlikely that all those who have experienced TTB are subject to mass neurosis; on the other hand, it means that the ecstatic phenomena associated with the new movement need not always bear an authentic Christian provenance.

Murphy accepts that many who have received TTB have reported 'improvements in their lives', but wonders whether this is not at least partly down to predispositions of personality. Invoking the Jungian Myers-Briggs model – now often used in Christian circles – Murphy suggests that 'ecstatic experience [such as that associated with TTB] may be the preferred means of relating to God for those who have an extraverted, feeling and sensation-based psychology, whereas for thinkers the rational approach is preferred, and for introverted intuitives meditation and reflection may be of greatest benefit'. But Murphy then adds a caveat, based on Jung's analysis of the religious significance of the 'shadow' side of people's personalities – namely that 'the lesser used spiritual expression may hold the greatest power for crisis'. Thus, 'an introverted thinker (while rejecting absolutely the subjective) may, through deeper spiritual need, have an unexpected ecstatic experience which may be of a deeply converting nature'.

The 'deeper spiritual need' which may have led many otherwise sober, reflective people into TTB could, writes Murphy, have a socio-cultural dimension. Echoing Hervieu-Lèger, Richter and Stibbe, he suggests that like many charismatic waves in the past, the Blessing has arisen 'at a time when levels of individual and social stress, and a disillusionment with society, have affected large numbers of people'. He explains: 'When the accepted social language and values exclude religious belief in favour of technology and self-promotion, the only way in which people can explore their spiritual needs may be within the context of disinhibition and emotional outpouring.'

Again paralleling Stibbe, Murphy suggests that this ecstatic reaction to postmodern ambivalence can be either constructive or destructive: 'The 'rave' experience', he submits, 'is a real disinhibition without foundation in reality and with no lasting benefit. On the other hand, participants may be finding a safe place emotionally to discharge accumulated anxiety and trauma in a cathartic way and therefore be open to real insight and spiritual growth.'

Less positively, Murphy remains concerned about the potential in TTB meetings for manipulation of the 'group effect' – the tendency for suggestibility and authoritarian leadership techniques to increase in proportion to the size of an audience or congregation. He is also wary of the fact that the Champaign Vineyard's 'Ministry Tips' document appears to prioritise those who are most clearly 'anointed' – that is, those who are manifesting outwardly – and that this could foster 'us and them' divisions within the church community, with the physical phenomena themselves becoming badges of 'true membership'. Murphy also warns that some who believe that they have been healed in a single meeting because of a significant outward release of emotion may still, in fact, need long-term psychotherapeutic help.[59]

John Kent's essay offers a church historical perspective on the Blessing. He remarks that the phenomena associated with it, and the claims made for its orthodoxy and importance, 'look familiar to the historian who has done work on Protestant revivalism and similar movements in other contexts'. Present attempts to subsume TTB under the evangelical understanding of revival fit, says Kent, into a characteristically 'quasi-Hegelian theory of human history, in which the sinfulness of humanity is opposed by the activity of the divine Spirit'. Furthermore, although for Kent it is arguable that the Spirit thus perceived has made 'little observable progress, especially in the twentieth century', there remains in this evangelical scenario 'the comfort of the assurance that at the end of history the Spirit will prove to have overcome sin in such a way that contemplation of the whole process will reconcile the redeemed to the past history of creation.' By contrast, Kent himself doubts whether the most commonly cited example of this model – the supposed sublimation of violent revolution in eighteenth-century Britain by the Wesley-Whitefield revival – can actually stand up to close scrutiny. 'No doubt', he writes, 'the Revival … played a vital part in a Protestant recovery which itself proved vital to the healthy survival of Christianity, but the shift of political and economic power, and the self-confidence which this gave to the ruling elites in Britain right down to 1945, did more for that Protestant renewal than the growth of evangelicalism….'

In addition, Kent resists making strong parallels between the events surrounding TTB and the British Revival of the 1730s and 1740s, because while one can 're-enact past events and rituals … one cannot recreate them'. In the case of Wesleyanism in particular, Kent argues that 'one is often dealing with the virtually unknown citizens of eighteenth-century Britain'. As for Wesley himself, although authors like Dave Roberts and Patrick Dixon have been quoting passages from his *Journals* which seem at least to condone certain physical phenomena, Kent insists that Wesley was essentially ambivalent about such things, and that they, and revival itself, were for him 'a means and not an end' – a means, that is, to thoroughgoing reform of Church and society. Thus,

The energy which was generated in Wesleyanism owed little to visions or more physical reactions to religious and personal pressures ... the influence on the public of
physical phenomena, similar in kind though different in context to those which have
distinguished the 'Toronto Blessing', seems to have been slight. They were regarded
as ambiguous, rather than decisive.[60]

The closing essay by Wendy Porter examines the worship of TTB and
presents a sharp indictment of it. Contending that it has downgraded essential elements in the liturgical traditions of baptistic, charismatic, evangelical
and sacramental traditions alike, she upbraids it for a general lack of Christ-
centredness and an unhealthy egocentrism. Specifically, she suggests that
whereas Baptist worship has been oriented towards winning converts and
leading them to baptism, churches caught up in TTB are now focused on
offering believers another dose of 'ministry time'. Whereas Pentecostals and
neo-pentecostals have traditionally looked to tongues or other biblical charismata as evidence of being Spirit-filled, Porter alleges that TTB is now
making its characteristic manifestations the key test. Whereas evangelical
churches have made the preaching of the Word the central plank of the
service, says Porter, 'Toronto'-style worship reaches its climax in the media-
tion of 'outward emotive manifestations'. And whereas sacramental traditions
have helped congregations remember the core events of the gospel narrative
through the celebration of the Lord's Supper, she maintains that the Blessing
has superseded this in importance in many of the churches where it is being
cultivated.[61]

Reviewing *The Toronto Blessing – Or Is It?* for *Christian Herald* shortly after
publication, Toronto detractor Stanley Jebb writes that it 'stands out from the
crowd of Toronto blessing literature' and praises it for its 'objective description
and restrained, but highly effective, criticism'. By contrast, the December
edition of *Renewal* will carry a review by Mark Stibbe, in which he chides the
authors for taking little or no account of testimonies from those who have
actually been affected by the new movement. He also wonders whether any of
the five contributors have been to TAV, and argues that the picture of Toronto-
style worship presented in the book is distorted and unfair. Although Stibbe
acknowledges some 'timely cautions' in the study, he complains that it offers no
constructive or decisive conclusion.[62]

Saturday 29th July 1995
Pentecostal magazine *Joy* reports on R.T. Kendall's recent 'climb down' over
TTB (cf. 2nd June).[63]

The August edition of *Charisma* notes that TTB has led several churches in
Florida to work more closely together than ever before. In the Melbourne area
on the Space Coast, charismatics have joined more traditional Presbyterians,
United Methodists and Southern Baptists for nightly interdenominational
prayer meetings at the 1,000-seat Tabernacle Church – meetings whose fervour
is leading many to speak of revival.[64]

Meanwhile, the August edition of *Woman Alive* magazine announces in a major article that since 'the snow has melted and the wind died down', it is 'time to balance opinion on "the Blessing"'. Three assessments are duly printed from divergent perspectives.

Patricia Higton's comments echo those already made by her husband, Tony, who has expressed concern about the movement in his regular column for *Christian Herald* and elsewhere (see 14th January and 28th April 1995). Referring to the Rodney Howard-Browne meeting which they both attended at Wembley in December 1994, she reflects on 'two hours of crazy crowd behaviour and ministry unworthy of the description "Christian"'. She also describes the 'cackles, roaring, screeches and groans' on a tape of a Toronto-style meeting she has acquired as sounding 'like something from the pit of hell!'

Regretting an insufficient balance between Word and Spirit in recent charismatic developments like the Third Wave and the Kansas City Prophets, she concludes that 'while we should seek the Lord with all our hearts, we should determine to be scriptural rather than gullible'.[65]

More positively, Rev Sue Watterson of the Isle of Man recalls a visit to TAV as a time of healing and anointing which has inspired in her 'a fresh hunger to read and study the Bible'. The worship sessions there, she writes, 'seemed to come together in a beautiful way', with Word, praise and ministry maintained in a dynamic balance. She concludes: 'Often, people who have only experienced the manifestations inappropriately, as spectators – particularly on video – will express distaste. But with such a movement of the Spirit, it seems appropriate to heed the counsel of the Pharisee Gamaliel: 'If it is from God you will not be able to stop these men; you will only find yourselves fighting against God (Acts 5:39).'[66]

An anonymous 'theological educator', who recounts a series of bitter disputes and divisions in his/her local fellowship over TTB, writes the final piece in the feature. 'The manifestations themselves became the important part of the meetings', s/he writes: 'love for the brethren and the unsaved was almost non-existent'. A once 'thriving' church has, s/he complains, been split in two by the new movement, which 'divided families too; wives happy with it but husbands not, and five teenagers now refusing to go to fellowship meetings'. A breakaway group has now joined with a sister church that has resisted TTB, and has, according to the writer, been able as a result to recover an emphasis on love for God and care for others.[67]

Also today, *Evangelical Times* publishes a response to Alan Morrison's attack on the Evangelical Alliance in last month's edition of the paper (24th June 1995). Joel Edwards, EA's UK Director, and Dave Cave, the co-ordinator of the Alliance Commission on Unity and Truth among Evangelicals (ACUTE), jointly write this. It reads as follows:

We were surprised to learn that the headline: 'EA Toronto consultation "a confusion"' (July *ET*) was based on the opinions of Alan Morrison, who did not even attend the event! May we offer some clarification in response to Mr. Morrison's published letter?

It is regrettable that Mr. Morrison feels that he 'cannot possibly involve myself in an alliance' with leaders who promote the Toronto Blessing. We can assure him that the consultation was not seeking alliances, but rather brought together leaders who fiercely disagree about the phenomenon to speak without compromise face-to-face, in a spirit of humility. Many of the concerns about the 'Toronto Blessing' which so worry Mr. Morrison were, in fact, aired at the meeting.

Mr. Morrison's contention that the 'Toronto Experience' is a cult has serious implications. It poses the question: Is the gospel so delicate that a significant proportion of Christians, who prior to 'Toronto' were considered to be orthodox, can become cultic overnight? Certainly we did not sense that we were dealing with members of a cult during our day of discussion and debate.

The Evangelical Alliance is committed to working for unity among evangelicals, but not at the expense of biblical truth. On this point we are happy to confirm that EA's original news release did contain an error and that the Toronto Blessing must be scrutinized in the light of the Bible and not vice versa! But it is sad that Mr. Morrison missed an opportunity to put his views directly to those he criticizes by declining to attend the consultation.[68]

The August edition of *Alpha* magazine, which is launched today, reprints a major assessment of the Blessing by John Wimber. Originally published in Wimber's leadership letter, *Vineyard Reflections*, this four-page piece essays biblical, theological and historical consideration of the new movement. Reiterating the core Vineyard emphasis to which he returned after the Kansas City Prophets episode in 1988-91, Wimber stresses that his chief concern with respect to TTB is 'whether [it] will contribute to or hinder our ability to achieve our goals of evangelism through church planting'. The making of new converts must, says the Vineyard leader, be the 'measuring rod' and 'destination' of any renewal activity. On this basis, he adds that if the renewal in question is 'merely a flashy explosion in the sky, or if it causes a change in the trajectory of the rocket', he must, out of obedience to God, 'bring correction to it so we do not go off course'.

Addressing the physical phenomena associated with TTB, Wimber insists that they have occurred in most revivals since the time of Wesley, and thus cannot be deemed, in and of themselves, to invalidate the Blessing. Even so, he adds, they must not become the 'main focus', but ought to be viewed as 'signs' pointing to the ongoing mission of God, and 'marching orders' from him on how that mission should be fulfilled by his people. Wimber goes on to deny that TTB can yet be described as 'revival'. This, he says, is characterised by mass conversions, sanctified lives, measurable social impact and the inculcation among believers of a 'Great Commission conscience', or 'power for service'. Such things, writes Wimber, have yet to flow clearly from the Blessing. Similarly, whereas Wimber underlines that 'the phenomena are not central to church life', he defines the essential marks of an authentic Christian community as teaching from the Word of God, administration of the sacraments, committed pastoral care, solid discipling, godly worship and evangelism. Lest this set of priorities is not clear, Wimber continues with a warning: 'In my opinion, any Vineyard pastor who neglects the above to pursue or give too great a place to phenomena long-term is making a potentially fatal mistake, as far as that local congregation is concerned.'

On the relevance of Jonathan Edwards for TTB, Wimber again highlights the evangelistic prerogative: 'Edwards would say we cannot discern what is really happening to someone based solely on what is happening to their body. This being the case, bodily reactions were not the end or the goal for Edwards; conversions were ... Conversion was the most important manifestation to Jonathan Edwards!'

Wimber, citing 1 Thessalonians 5:19 on 'not putting out the Spirit's fire', suggests that this is most probably an injunction not to cease the ongoing imperatives to which he has been referring. The same text also prompts him to reflect on the negative impact of his relationship with the Kansas City Prophets (1988-91), and the dangers of a similar distraction occurring as a result of the current movement. 'Here in the Vineyard', he writes, 'many of us have had some negative experiences with prophecy and various manifestations of the Holy Spirit. These disappointments can easily result in "putting out the Spirit's fire". With all that is within us, we leaders will strive not to make that mistake. But neither will we let the Spirit's fire be used in destructive ways. Following all the relevant biblical mandates will help us "keep the fire in the fireplace", where it is productive, and not on the carpet, where it could spread and burn down the house!'

Wimber closes by commending the example of John Wesley, who, he says, combined an admirable maintenance of spiritual fervour with an unswerving commitment to evangelism and cultural transformation. Wimber recalls,

> By his death at 83, Wesley had founded over 12,000 new groups/churches and had been a true social reformer. God changed the face of England through this determined, Spirit-filled man, who was brilliant as organisation. Wesley was 'ignitable' and found a way to keep the Spirit's fire burning hot in very biblical and productive ways. My prayer is that historians will be able to say similar things about us when our lives are over.[69]

Although it may not be immediately apparent, Wimber's rallying-call to refocus on evangelism will be seen, in hindsight, as a warning to TAV and TAV-influenced Vineyards to move away from their current models of ministry (cf. 13th December 1995 ff.)

Wimber's concerns about TTB also feature today in an interview which Andy and Jane Fitz-Gibbon have conducted with John Arnott for the August edition of *Renewal* magazine. After reflecting on the rapid rise in TAV's profile over the past 18 months, Arnott admits that despite his more general support, 'John Wimber wasn't too thrilled at first about the idea of catchers.' Even so,

Arnott claims that 'Nine out of ten Vineyard churches are doing the same as we are.'[70]

Saturday 5th August 1995

The Evangelical Fellowship of New Zealand convenes a national forum on TTB at the Greenlane Christian Centre.[71]

Monday 7th August 1995

The Evangelical Alliance UK makes available to its members an annotated book list on TTB. This includes titles already published by Mike Fearon, Patrick Dixon, Dave Roberts, Guy Chevreau, Rob Warner, Stanley Jebb, Wallace Boulton, Mona Johnian and Stanley Porter et al.

The list also includes a recently released video on the Blessing. Produced by Nelson Word Ltd. and presented by Gerald Coates, this is a 90-minute examination of TTB which features proponents such as John Arnott, Paul Cain, R.T. Kendall and Terry Virgo, 'cautious but open' figures like Clive Calver and James Jones (Bishop of Hull), and declared sceptics like Stephen Sizer, Brian Edwards and Stanley Jebb. It also includes interviews with various local church members who have been positively touched by TTB.

Coates begins the film by stating that around four thousand churches in the UK have now been affected by the Blessing. Subsequently, he confirms that the tape has been edited down from '15 to 20 hours of footage' comprising many more testimonies and analyses than appear in the final version. After film of testimonies from a Rodney Howard-Browne meeting in the US, comments are offered by a wide rage of key evangelical leaders.

Advocacy of TTB is led by John Arnott, who claims that TAV has seen 'over five thousand make decisions for Christ' since the Blessing began. Most of these, he admits, are re-commitments, but he nonetheless places what is happening in continuity with historic Christian revivals as he declares later on the tape, 'When you look into church history, all this stuff happened.' Rodney Howard-Browne also emphasises the evangelistic potential of the movement: 'I really believe', he avers, 'that God is going to bring in millions of backsliders ... This is only the beginning.' Bryn Jones, Covenant Ministries overseer, describes Howard-Browne as a man whose ministry he initially questioned, but whom he in time came to view as marked by 'integrity, sincerity and purity'. Ken and Lois Gott of Sunderland Christian Centre report that ministry at their church has 'exploded'. Ken Gott adds, 'It has to go to revival. [We are] daring to believe that this could be the last move of God before revival.' Wendy Virgo takes a similar view: 'We could', she says, 'be on the outskirts of a great harvest.'

As General Director of the Evangelical Alliance, Clive Calver expresses concern about the capacity the current movement might have to divide evangelicals at the very time when they have achieved greater unity and influence than for some while. Even so, he says, 'We could be on the brink ... of seeing revival in this country.' James Jones suggests that TTB may be a means by which God has managed to 'open people's eyes' to his kingdom, and adds that whenever the Holy Spirit is truly at work, there will be elements of unpredictability and 'adventure'.

More negatively, Stephen Sizer comments that although individuals do seem to be having genuine encounters with God through TTB, it also bears certain characteristics of psychological conditioning and 'epidemic hysteria'. He goes on to voice concern about elements of 'heresy' that are present in some circles, and warns that these might open doors to demonic influence. Stanley Jebb agrees, observing that while some may well have been blessed, the conduct of TTB has been such that 'the devil is muddying the waters'. He is also disappointed that the new movement has been so apparently lacking in the dimension of repentance. Quoting John 16:8, he emphasises that this will be central in any genuine move of the Holy Spirit. Similarly, Brian Edwards bemoans what he regards as a dearth of holiness in the Blessing.

Predictably, much of the debate featured in the film concerns the physical manifestations associated with TTB. There is a general consensus among those interviewed that while certain physical phenomena will occur in renewal and revival, they should not become the centre of attention. Terry Virgo insists that the current Blessing is not about outward displays, but 'about lives changed dramatically'. Paul Cain suggests that rather than dwelling on manifestations, those who experience them should move swiftly into prayer and fasting. Tony Sargent reiterates Jonathan Edwards' teaching that phenomena in themselves prove nothing. Beyond such general agreement, however, there is considerable dispute about how to view the specific phenomena associated with Toronto.

Gerald Coates quotes from Patrick Dixon's *Signs of Revival* to argue that the current manifestations are in continuity with those seen in previous revivals. The evangelist Don Double recalls that such things occurred 40 years previously in rallies led by the Pentecostal pioneer Stephen Jeffreys, even if the present wave of activity is 'more intense'. Repeating arguments already published in his various written articles on the Blessing, Coates also suggests a number of biblical precedents for what has been happening. By contrast, Brian Edwards contends that the characteristic Toronto phenomena are 'neither biblical nor historic in relation to revival'. Stanley Jebb submits that those who are presently falling to the floor are experiencing 'nothing to do with what John went through on Patmos'. Aware of such objections within his own Reformed constituency, R.T. Kendall calls critics to bear in mind that whereas many regard intense emotional and physical phenomena as intrinsically occultic, the occult is, in fact, a *counterfeit* of genuine Christian experience. Thus the point, he adds, is not so much the manifestations themselves, as their source and application. They may, in fact, be indications of God's sovereign work and majesty: 'Evangelicals should never be threatened by the glory of God …[and] should not dictate the manner in which he chooses to show up.'

In conclusion, Gerald Coates declares that although TTB appears to have made a great impact already, there is a good deal more still to be achieved: 'We have sown much', he says, 'but we have reaped so little.' The extent of the harvest, he suggests, depends on the continuing faithfulness of those who have received the Blessing during the past year. Bob Cheeseman agrees: 'The thought of this fading out is awful,' he remarks. 'But I believe this is the start of something profound.'[72]

Saturday 26th August 1995

Tony Higton appears publicly to have softened his stance on TTB. In his column for *Christian Herald*, he rehearses the more dubious provenance of the Blessing from the Latter Rain and WordFaith movements through the ministry network of Benny Hinn. Even so, he suggests that a fair proportion of the statements made by those associated with these movements may result from a lack of formal theological education rather than malicious heresy. Besides, he adds, 'I have no evidence that any "Toronto" leaders hold to any of these wrong views.' Hinn, he says, has apologised for some of his earlier doctrinal errors, while Rodney Howard-Browne 'has distanced himself from the views of the Faith teachers (though not from the people themselves)'.

In discerning the validity or otherwise of TTB, Higton reflects that it is vital to distinguish the 'roots' of the movement from its fruit. Quoting Matthew 7:15-27, he argues that Jesus' picture of a bad tree relates to 'the ministry of an individual prophet, not a school of thought'. Furthermore,

> the picture concerns the heart and ministry of that individual or his overt identification with a heretical movement. Scripture makes clear that we are to judge the roots by the fruit, not the fruit by the root. The question is whether the person is a doer of the Word – imperfections in a ministry do not invalidate the ministry. But a lifestyle or teaching that extensively contradicts the Word does.

As for demonic or occult influence, Higton appeals to 1 Corinthians 10:25-27 for confirmation that this cannot be passed on simply by contact.

In conclusion, Higton appears more sympathetic than in his previous pronouncements on the new movement: 'When I see that, whatever the fleshly imperfections, the Holy Spirit is using the "Toronto blessing" to bring about deep repentance, renewed love for and intimacy with God, renewed power in ministry, renewed love for others, I dare not dismiss it as a temporary fad.'[73]

In an exclusive interview with the Assemblies of God monthly *Joy*, Rodney Howard-Browne tells Charles Gardner his life-story, and recounts the events in his ministry which have led up to TTB. Addressing the situation in Britain, he says: 'I believe the general sweep of the move of God here is going to be preserved and will lead to something totally glorious.'[74]

September's *Evangelical Times*, out today, grants Alan Morrison an opportunity to respond to Joel Edwards' and Dave Cave's reply to his letter declining their invitation to attend the Whitefield House Consultation held on 2nd June (24th June, 25th July 1995). Morrison's central accusation is that the Consultation, like the Alliance in general, was run by and for charismatics, rather than for the benefit of 'genuine evangelicalism'. As such, he says, it was concerned only with 'skilfully-crafted damage limitation' on behalf of a constituency which he regards as 'scandalous', having long been characterised by 'bogus words of knowledge, false prophecies and the pagan power-pat known as being "slain in the Spirit"'. The real reason for the meeting, alleges Morrison, was 'the fact that the TB has caused great division in the charismatic movement and thus could hinder the progress of their so-called "Renewal"'. Claiming that the Alliance has been 'virtually taken over by those pursuing a charismatic agenda', Morrison insists that all this was obvious to him as soon as he saw the agenda for the Whitefield House event, and that its 'blatantly tendentious' ethos was not one with which he could possibly have associated himself. 'One simply cannot have Christian unity', he writes, 'with those who are pro-[T]TB and those who are against it. It is naïve in the extreme to think otherwise.'[75]

The Comment column of the same issue of *Evangelical Times* goes further even than Morrison as it seeks to implicate TTB in a Romish threat to evangelical Protestantism. 'It might seem a long way from London's Westminster Cathedral to Toronto', runs the editorial;

> In fact it is not so far at all. The continuing enthusiasm for the so-called Toronto Blessing is lamentable. Essentially the charismatic with his open view of prophecy and ongoing revelation of the Divine is searching for the same thing as the Romeward-bound Anglican. Once again, for them, final authority seems elusive. Ask not 'What does the Bible say?' but 'What does the Bible say to me?'[76]

Also critical of TTB is Clifford Hill. In an editorial for his Centre for Contemporary Ministry's magazine *Prophecy Today*, he states his belief that 'the time has come to recognise that what we are seeing is not a major move of God leading either to the renewing of the church or to widespread revival'. Rather, he writes, 'This kind of experience, however sincere the desire for a "move of God" among the participants, can only lead to disappointment.' Although Hill reflects that he has attended several meetings and consultations with leaders across the spectrum of opinion on the Blessing, it would be better to look for signs of hope in the 'college revival' which has gathered pace in the USA since mid-March.[77] In an accompanying piece later in the magazine, Hill contemplates the future:

> The Toronto experience is already fading away in many churches, although others are still highly involved, but will another wave come along in two or three years time? We have had the healing wave, the spiritual warfare wave, the prophecy wave. Now that we have had the laughter and animal noises wave, what will it be next? Will it be 'out-of-body' experiences, or levitation, perhaps? Or will there be a maturing of those who believe in the presence, power and activity of the Holy Spirit in the church today within evangelicalism? It is not only the future of the church that is in the balance, but the future of the western nations in which the forces of decay and moral corruption are already far advanced. Only an evangelical revival can save the nation. Revival, however, is a sovereign act of God. It cannot be engineered by human beings, however spiritually sincere and enthusiastic.[78]

Saturday 9th September 1995

Declaring 'dismay' at Tony Higton's softened attitude towards TTB (26th August 1995), Sheffield Central House Church leader Peter Fenwick accuses him of having questioned the 'more peripheral objections' to the new movement whilst avoiding 'the real issues which [it] has raised'. Writing in today's *Christian Herald*, Fenwick stresses that doctrinal truth and divine mercy must always be held together, and he contends that Higton's article played down the crucial matter of testing. 'It may well be', he writes, 'that dubious roots do not of themselves invalidate [T]TB, but where are the positive arguments that validate it? From the proposition "quality X does not invalidate movement A" we cannot leap directly to the conclusion that "movement A" is therefore fully validated.' Fenwick also criticises Higton for failing to produce adequate evidence for his assertion that the Holy Spirit is using TTB to bring about repentance, love and authentic power in ministry.[79]

Monday 11th September 1995

The American periodical *Christianity Today* takes stock of TTB. Confirming that there are still '500 to 1,000' attending TAV meetings on a nightly basis, James A. Beverley quotes John Arnott giving a by now well-known retort to his critics: 'We need to have more faith in God's ability to bless us than Satan's ability to deceive us.' He also notes that Arnott has had 'significant interactions with leading pastors in many denominations, including the Pentecostal Assemblies of Canada and the Fellowship of Evangelical Baptist Churches.' These interactions, writes Beverley, have revealed 'disagreements', but 'not about the central claims of the gospel'. Beverley goes on to quote Canadian academic Clark Pinnock and televangelist David Mainse as broadly supportive of TAV, and of TTB in general.

By contrast, however, Beverley goes on to cite recent pronouncements by Steve and Cheryl Thompson, two former members of TAV who have begun to suggest that TTB can mediate demonic possession. He also draws attention to the work of Hank Hanegraff and the Christian Research Institute, whose 1993 book *Christianity in Crisis* presented a fierce condemnation of the Word of Faith movement. Although the book did not mention Rodney Howard-Browne, Hanegraff is now quoted as stating that the South African evangelist's links with prosperity teaching, and his subsequent influence on Vineyard pastors in general, and on TAV in particular, could represent 'something extremely dangerous that could be a road to the occult'. Beverley also reports that the high-profile Reformed preacher John MacArthur has attacked TTB in his most recent book, *Reckless Faith*, and that Warren Smith of the Spiritual Counterfeits Project has submitted that the Blessing might, in fact, be a 'strong delusion' from Satan.

Ominously in view of what will unfold from December 13th onwards, Beverley also notes that the wider Vineyard network itself is less than entirely convinced about what has been occurring at TAV:

> While John Wimber, international director of the Association of Vineyard Churches, has endorsed the Blessing, he has done so with some reserve. A year ago he called a

special board meeting at the Vineyard's headquarters in Anaheim to address problematic issues about personal prophecy, and the making of animal sounds in worship.
This past January he sent two advisers to Toronto to monitor the renewal and give
some strong guidance to local Vineyard leaders about perceived weaknesses.

One of these advisers, Vineyard national co-ordinator Todd Hunter, is then
quoted: 'The human reason so many Christians have gone to Toronto', he says,
'is because of the enormous trust they have in the leadership of Wimber.' Even
so, he adds that 'if John thought the Airport Vineyard were hurting the body of
Christ, he would shut things down in a second.'[80]

Saturday 16th September 1995

St Andrew's Baptist Church in Cambridge hosts a day conference entitled
'Toronto Blessing? It's OK to Ask Questions!' Speakers for the event are Martyn
Percy, Chaplain of Christ's College, Cambridge and author of a detailed critique
of Vineyard theology and practice which will be published next year as *Word,
Wonders and Power*[81]; East London University Chaplain John Richardson; David
Armstrong and Philip Foster, both vicars in Cambridge, and Chris Hand, for-
merly pastoral assistant at Queen's Road Baptist Church, but now sceptical
about TTB and linked to more conservative Reformed networks.

Friday 29th September 1995

Although the Vineyard effectively dissolved its three-year connection with the
Kansas City Prophets in mid-1991, the October edition of the TAV magazine
Spread the Fire confirms that one of the Prophets, Paul Cain, is still to be regarded as someone who 'functions in the office of a prophet' and who, as such, 'not
only receives prophetic revelation, but … has a divine level of authority'. Even
so, the same issue carries a declaration that TAV is 'adamantly against words of
"direction, correction, dates or mates"'.[82]

Saturday 30th September 1995

Writing in the October edition of *Evangelicals Now*, Tony Payne contends that
the theology of TTB has been too much influenced by dualism. Whereas advocates of the Blessing have often appeared to privilege the realm of supernatural
feelings, emotional epiphanies and extraordinary prophecies, Payne argues that
God in fact operates in these spheres no more significantly than in the 'gritty
and grubby realities' of life, and has confirmed this supremely through the
incarnation and the cross. 'It is not as if [God] is "upstairs" and our problem is
being stuck "downstairs"', writes Payne. 'Nor is our problem a lack of spiritual
feeling … Our real problem is the separation in relationship from God because
of *sin*. The difficulty facing us is not breaking through or rising above the normal stuff of creation so as to experience the Spirit. The difficulty is our rebel-
lion.' As we overcome such sin, Payne avers, it is necessary to realise that if God
works in all aspects of creation and not especially in the realm of feelings, and
if this work includes Christ's work of atonement on Calvary, 'then this too will

be the work of the Spirit'. Indeed, 'It is not as if the Spirit is separate or tangential to all this. The Lord is the Spirit (2 Cor. 3:17). He is active in he world, working in and through the creation to achieve his purposes.' As a result of this Payne suggests, quoting Galatians 5:22,23 and 2 Timothy 1:7,8, that 'self-control, rather than self-abandon or loss of control' will mark the Spirit's presence and work.[83]

In somewhat similar vein, the renowned evangelical statesman John Stott gives his first public comments on TTB as part of an interview with Roy McCloughry for *Third Way* magazine. Remarking on the place of emotional experience in general, Stott attests that he has often undergone 'profound' encounters with God, involving tears and intense appreciation of the glorified Christ. Even so, he disassociates these from 'traditional charismatic experience', and in particular, from speaking in tongues. Moreover, he says,

> They have not been dissociated from the mind. In 1 Corinthians 14, Paul is all the time saying, 'You mustn't let these experiences bypass your mind'. The mind is involved, though the experience goes beyond it. But I know what Paul meant in Romans 5 about the love of God being shed abroad in our hearts. I also know what he meant in Romans 8 about the Spirit bearing witness with our spirit that we are the children of God.

On Toronto itself, Stott insists that he would never want to criticise anything which people claim 'has been a blessing to them in terms of a greater awareness of the reality of God, or a profounder joy, or an overwhelming love for him and for others, or a fresh zeal in evangelism'. Despite all this, however, he goes on to raise three 'major questions' in respect of the Blessing. First, he says, 'it is a self-consciously anti-intellectual movement'. In relation to a tape on which a TTB advocate has said 'don't analyse, don't ask questions; simply receive', Stott comments: 'I think that is both foolish and dangerous. We must never forget that the Holy Spirit is the Spirit of truth.'

Secondly, Stott declares that he 'cannot possibly come to terms with those animal noises'. It grieves him very much, he adds, that 'as far as I know, no charismatic leaders have publicly disassociated themselves from them'. The whole Bible confirms, he stresses, that 'we are different from the animal creation; it rebukes us when we behave like animals and calls us to be distinct'.

Thirdly, 'all the falling' troubles Stott. Even charismatic leaders have acknowledged, he states, that 'on the few occasions in the Bible when people [fall] over, they ... all [fall] forwards on their faces and [do] so *after* they have been granted a vision of the majesty, the holiness and the glory of God'. By contrast, in the Toronto experience 'people fall backwards, without any previous experience of God.'[84]

Monday 2nd October 1995

Monarch publish Andy and Jane Fitz-Gibbon's account of the impact of TTB on Sunderland Christian Centre, *Something Extraordinary is Happening*. The narrative of the book is close to that of Ken and Lois Gott's *The Sunderland Refreshing*, which will be published just one month hence, on 16th November. The Fitz-Gibbons make much of the fact that Sunderland was the focus of one of the first Pentecostal-style renewals in the UK, under Alexander Boddy at All Saints Parish Church in 1907. Otherwise, their account presents and reflects on the more recent events at SCC, which we have reported above (see Late July 1994, 6th, 7th, 14th August 1994, 26th, 28th October 1994, 28th April 1995 and 6th August 1995).[85]

Saturday 7th October 1995

ACUTE co-ordinator Dave Cave places an advertisement in *The War Cry* and various other Christian newspapers, asking for material and comment on TTB to assist in the research he has been asked to conduct on behalf of the Evangelical Alliance and those who attended the Alliance's Whitefield House Consultation on 2nd June: 'If any readers have relevant first-hand experiences (positive or negative), I would be grateful to receive them. I would also like to hear of any biblical/theological analysis which would help take the debate forward.'

Saturday 28th October 1995

As a follow-up to the Greenlane meeting it hosted on 5th August, the Evangelical Fellowship of New Zealand (EFNZ) convenes a forum on TTB at the Takapuna Assembly of God in Auckland. Dirk van Garderen of Avondale Reformed Church and Pastor Geoff Smith of Auckland Bible Church speak against the movement, while the Ven. Max Scott of St Margaret's Anglican Church, Hillsborough and Pastor Hamish Divett of Christian City Church speak in its favour. Theological comment is offered by Dr Stephen May of the College of St John the Evangelist, and Pastor Brian Hathaway of Te Atatu Bible Chapel chairs the event.

As a means of facilitating discussion and debate at the meeting, the EFNZ distribute a revised version of the UK Alliance's Euston Statement, incorporating certain 'refinements' which the EFNZ leadership have made as they have assessed the impact of the Blessing in New Zealand (the full text of the EFNZ version of the Euston Statement is reproduced in Section III). The Trinity and the Second Coming are added to the list of 'classic evangelical convictions' at the beginning of the Statement. There is more explication of the meaning and outworking of revival, and of the dynamic interaction and authority of the Word and the Spirit. Detail is also added in respect of physical and emotional phenomena, with greater stress being placed on their neutral status vis-à-vis the validation or refutation of a spiritual movement. There is also an added warning about the danger of manipulation: 'The power of God is always ministered for people', it says, 'and never over them, so that none are to be abused, coerced or dominated by any spiritual authority. Divine power invites, human power pushes.'[86]

Also today, the November issue of *Charisma* devotes a number of articles to the current state of TTB. Although some of the reports remain overwhelmingly positive, there are significant indications of discontent in certain charismatic and Pentecostal quarters.

The magazine's special *Eurocharisma* insert carries a front-page story which quotes John Wimber as having conveyed his 'reservations' about the modus operandi of TAV to the church's leadership. These reservations bear out comments made by Wimber in his recent Vineyard newsletter and re-published in the August issue of *Alpha* (29th July 1995). Although Wimber is 'thrilled' by what the Holy Spirit is doing, he reports having warned the TAV team against a 'come and get it' approach which might detract from the full message of the gospel. He also recounts having said that TAV model of ministry could be 'injurious to equipping', specifically in relation to dealing with those who fall to the floor: 'God didn't call everyone to be a "catcher". It is all right to catch somebody if they are falling, but let's get people praying for those that fall. I don't care if you need to move the chairs back, but it's not valid to designate a group as "catchers" while you are the divine instrument, walking through and touching everybody.'

Wimber is also deeply concerned about the potential for division according to degrees of 'anointing'. He is reported as having told the TAV staff

> We are making first and second class citizens. We are saying this person [the one doing the praying] is more anointed than others. So here's what I want you to do: I want you to strengthen the message. I want you to ask people to come and get and give it. So take them out on the streets. Let them feed the hungry, visit the aged, go minister to the lost, go into the streets and witness. Do whatever is necessary but get them out so that when they go home they can say 'Yes, I quacked like a duck for three days, but I went and visited this 84 year-old who was starving and we filled her pantry, prayed for her and her rheumatic condition has improved, and we led her to the Lord'.[87]

In addition to all this, the same magazine carries a report by J. Lee Grady on the recent 17th World Pentecostal Conference in Jerusalem, which reveals that several leading Pentecostals are uneasy with the Blessing. Ray Hughes of the Church of God (Cleveland, Tenn.) expressed from the Chair a concern with 'those who have left the mainstream of the purpose of Pentecost and have focused on the spectacular'. David Yonggi Cho of Yoido Full Gospel Church in Seoul, Korea emphasised that if God can grant holy laughter, the Devil can counterfeit it. German Pentecostal Reinhold Ulonska tells Grady that the Vineyard is 'not Pentecostal' because it downplays speaking in tongues as evidence of baptism in the Holy Spirit. Australasian representatives are, however, somewhat more sanguine. Grady notes that TTB has been promoted there especially by the Assemblies of God. R. Wayne Hughes of New Zealand confirms that he has invited John Arnott to preach at his Auckland Assembly, while top Australian AOG official Andrew Evans happily recounts having introduced his denomination to the ministry of Rodney Howard-Browne during its biannual conference in Brisbane. 'There are some things about [his] style that people don't like,' says Evans of Howard-Browne, 'and some older Pentecostal people have had a hard time with it.' Even so, he adds, some six hundred people have been converted in his local church since Howard-Browne's visit. 'I'm not a wild Pentecostal who just grabs the next thing that comes along', reflects Evans. 'But I'm determined not to be a Pharisee.'[88]

Charisma also carries a more thoroughly positive article by Daina Doucet, who reports that TTB has now spread to Indonesia, Russia and remote villages in South America. Furthermore, writes Doucet, 'In June, 300 Korean Christian leaders "soaked" in God's presence at the Toronto Vineyard [and] more than 500 Japanese church leaders have visited Toronto, as well.' Meanwhile, at Sunderland, 'the number of stolen cars has decreased by 44 per cent' and 'local police call Sunderland Christian Centre for prayer'.[89] Also in the UK, Clive Price presents a survey of the Blessing that puts the number of congregations now affected by it at 5,500. His piece includes interviews with Ken and Lois Gott of Sunderland Christian Centre, Terry Virgo of New Frontiers International, Gerald Coates of Pioneer and Sandy Millar of Holy Trinity, Brompton. The Gotts declare that the last year has been 'the best year of our lives', although sheer exhaustion has led them to cut the number of evening meetings per week from six to three, and the need for more support has drawn help from members of local Baptist, Pentecostal, Anglican and Methodist congregations. Virgo tells Price that 'Expectation is rising, and with it, an ever-increasing passion to pray and intercede.' Millar states that the development and flowering of TTB during the past five years is 'quite the most remarkable work of God in this country since the eighteenth century'. Meanwhile, the high-profile apologist Ravi Zacharias has apparently told Gerald Coates, 'If you go on like this, you'll change the nation.'[90]

As for Coates himself, he has just visited TAV for the first time, and reports on his 10-day visit for the November edition of *Alpha* magazine. Coates commends the measured and responsible way in which the leaders conducted meetings: 'The last thing you could accuse them of is showmanship,' he writes. He also refutes the widely levelled accusation that teaching and preaching have been neglected. 'The Scriptures were opened every night,' he insists, and of a John Arnott sermon he comments, 'it was so straight-down-the-line evangelical, you wonder how on earth this man could be remotely called a "controversial figure"'. Coates also takes up the 'animal noises' debate: 'I didn't see any dogs, lions or chickens. Neither did I hear anyone mimicking them either. Yet stories would have one believe that every dog in North America, every chicken in the pens of Arkansas and Tennessee had passed through. Not while I was there.'

Elsewhere, *Evangelism Today* prints an interview with the radical American evangelical Tony Campolo. Well known in the UK for his appearances at Spring Harvest, Campolo says that his first visits to the festival in the 1980s had given him great hope that revival might be imminent, and that it might cross the Atlantic. Latterly, however, he confesses that his enthusiasm has waned, and that this is partly down to TTB:

What I fear … is that the British community is getting side-tracked and becoming preoccupied with signs and wonders, the Kansas City Prophets, the Toronto Blessing and whatever comes next. It's no wonder that Jesus, in nine cases out of ten, told those he healed to keep quiet about it because he feared people would miss the point, that they would get fascinated by signs and wonders. Of course they draw the crowds and we can put on great seminars. But signs and wonders are just a sideshow.

Even more sceptical about TTB is Chris Hand, who questions the movement in an article for the November–December edition of *Prophecy Today*. His critique is of special interest because until November 1994, he was an elder and pastoral assistant at Queen's Road Baptist Church, Wimbledon – one of the centres of the Blessing in Britain from its earliest days. Although Hand is generous in acknowledging that Queen's Road did maintain biblical preaching and other 'normal' ministry once TTB had been introduced, he adds that his five months amidst the Blessing 'left me unconvinced that I was witnessing an authentic move of the Holy Spirit'. He goes on: 'What I was seeing and hearing, including the many testimonies I heard, left me unsatisfied when I compared accounts of historic revivals and the words and warnings of Scripture.' Indeed, he alleges that '80% of testimonies could be subsumed under [the] categories of "empty" or "contentless" experience'. As a result, he says, he left the fellowship after 'much soul-searching' and prayer: 'Concluding sadly that the situation more closely approximated a church in deception than revival I decided to withdraw.' Stressing that 'it is not "blasphemy against the Spirit" to examine and test things', Hand assures readers that 'there is no shortage of churches, charismatic and non-charismatic, which have not embraced the "Toronto Blessing", that are able to offer safe sanctuary and good counsel, and where there is plenty of good fruit and "love for Jesus".'[91]

Prophecy Today also carries an article by Jewish Christian teacher Jacob Prasch, repudiating the way in which TTB has appropriated the language of 'anointing' and the practice of laying on hands. While admitting that Mark 10:16 provides an isolated linkage of laying on hands with blessing, he nonetheless maintains that 'there are no biblical grounds to connect the action with the transmission of a "mantle", "calling", or "anointing" from one person to another, let alone undefined experiences'. Rather, he writes, the primary means by which God blesses people is through his Word – that is, verbally. In consequence, Prasch concludes, 'The real issue is whether or not there is a biblical basis for the Toronto "blessing", since neither the Bible's teaching on anointing nor the scriptural principle of laying on of hands can validate it.'[92]

Thursday 2nd November 1995

Hodder & Stoughton publish David Pawson's much-anticipated analysis of TTB, *Is the Blessing Biblical?*[93] Although he admits that he has neither been to Toronto nor even 'as far as the floor', Pawson says that the book has demanded to be written because so many have sought his advice on the movement; the Blessing has spread so widely and so quickly that it has become 'impossible to ignore'.

Over ten closely argued chapters, Pawson very deliberately concentrates on biblical exegesis and interpretation, consigning a brief historical review of revivals to an appendix so as to demonstrate that Scripture must always take first place in such matters. Indeed, he comments that it is unlikely that so many would be discussing Jonathan Edwards if a biblical rationale for TTB had been convincingly demonstrated.[94]

Decrying the existential spirit of much contemporary Christianity, Pawson disavows the notion that one cannot critique a movement like TTB without having personally experienced it. This idea, he writes, 'is as old as the Garden of Eden. Adam and Eve fell for it, though they already had God's Word telling them all they needed to know.' Furthermore, if this were the case, 'I was wrong to write a book about heaven and hell, since I've never been to either.'[95] Whilst accepting that many may have had very 'real' experiences as a result of TTB, Pawson counsels that these need not thereby be defined as divine in origin: 'They may be genuinely from God', he writes, but they may alternatively be 'a fleshly substitute from man or a subtle counterfeit from Satan'. Moreover, while emphasising that such experiences must be discerned and tested, Pawson questions the common idea that such assessment must be confined to the 'fruit' rather than the 'root'. Despite often being quoted to defend this distinction, Pawson argues that Matthew 7:20 is about 'discerning false prophets, not experiences', and cannot therefore be applied directly to TTB. Insofar as the true roots of any legitimate move of God will be found in Scripture, Pawson encourages readers to interrogate the 'roots' along with the fruit, lest a purely pragmatic approach be allowed to obscure their analysis.[96]

Like Jacob Prasch (28th November 1995), Pawson stresses that the usual means by which God and human beings bless one another in Scripture is not through the Toronto-style person-to-person 'ministry', but through 'word of mouth'.[97]

The central part of Pawson's study examines the manifestations associated with TTB. Falling, he says, certainly occurs in Scripture, but whether in the case of Ezekiel, Paul, John or 'many others', is 'invariably an involuntary response to an overwhelming and awesome "manifestation" of the first or second person of the Trinity in visible and/or audible form'. Furthermore, writes Pawson, 'It is never associated with the Spirit and is never interpreted as his work.' Indeed, he adds, citing Ezekiel 1:28 and 2:1, there is more direct warrant for levitation as a manifestation of the Spirit than for falling. Pawson also contends that trembling is not 'ever attributed to the Holy Spirit' and is 'never associated with blessing'. It is, rather, a 'reaction of the nervous system to shock or stress, at its simplest a sign of nervous tension (as seems to be the case with Paul in Corinth; [1 Cor. 2:3])'.[98]

In a detailed biblical taxonomy of laughter, Pawson suggests that Scripture countenances humorous, happy and haughty laughing, but that it does not refer to 'hysterical' laughter. Furthermore, he submits, 'we notice no justification for using such a phrase as "laughing in the Spirit"'. Thus, while the Bible indicates that there is often 'good reason to laugh ... helpless laughter without an adequate or appropriate cause is not found.'[99] By contrast, writes Pawson, weeping is 'far more common', even if it should not be taken as a manifestation of the Spirit *per se*, but rather as a possible 'response of the human spirit to his work'.[100] Meanwhile, animal noises are noted as occurring in Scripture, 'but only in judgement, never in blessing'. Besides, animal behaviour is generally 'far more likely to be of demonic than of divine origin, as everyone involved in exorcism knows'.[101] As for 'drunkenness in the Spirit', Pawson advises that 'in view of the fact that loss of self-control is the prime result of drunkenness, it would be astonishing if the Spirit were to lead us into a simulation of this'.[102]

Moving on to the practical matter of ministering in the midst of manifestations, Pawson emphasises that they should not be seen in any way as the focus of corporate Christian experience. Defining guidelines for leaders, he urges in regard to physical phenomena that they should not be forbidden, highlighted, encouraged, publicised, exclusivised, misinterpreted, homogenised or sought.[103]

Unusually among those who have written on TTB so far, Pawson questions the implied eschatology of TTB – that is, whether the association of 'times of refreshing' or 'revival' with the end-times is actually a valid understanding of Scripture. Rejecting such a view as prone to postmillennial triumphalism, Pawson maintains instead that the Last Days will find the Church 'in Big Trouble' because of the Great Tribulation. He explains: 'Far from enjoying enormous growth, much less taking over the world, the Church is more likely to be reduced as 'many will turn away from the faith and ... the love of many will grow cold' (Matthew 24:10-12). The call is for endurance, to be faithful even to the point of death.' Like Stanley Porter (17th July 1995), Pawson argues that the 'times of refreshing' cited in Acts 3:19 have nothing to do with this future period, but apply instead to the impact of the incarnate Messiah, Jesus, upon the Jews of his own time.

In conclusion, Pawson gives a 'yellow' light to TTB rather than an unequivocal red for 'stop' or a green for 'go'. Toronto, he suggests, has thus far represented a 'mixed blessing'. It is necessary to proceed with caution, avoiding 'uncritical enthusiasm' on the one hand and undifferentiated 'negative criticism' on the other. As an avowed charismatic who has long sought to urge a biblical balance of Word and Spirit, his deepest fear, he writes, is that tension over TTB may inflict 'great damage ... to the unity of the body of Christ'. It would be a 'tragedy', he suggests, 'if division took place over something with debatable, if not questionable, basis in Scripture.'[104]

Friday 3rd November 1995

Hendrickson, the Massachusetts-based publisher, launch a detailed assessment of TTB in general, and holy laughter in particular, by W.J. Oropeza. Currently working at Durham University, Oropeza presents a careful examination of the roots of the Blessing in Latter Rain Pentecostalism, the Kansas City Prophets, the Argentinian Revival and the Wimberite Third Wave. He also devotes a chapter to Rodney Howard-Browne, which charts his development within Pentecostalism, traces his links to Word of Faith teaching, and demonstrates the impact he has had on the Vineyard through Randy Clark and others. Oropeza then moves on to assess the Blessing in relation to Scripture, and concludes by comparing and contrasting it with past evangelical revivals.[105] Although the TAV connection to Howard-Browne is clearly demonstrated by Oropeza, he is less convinced by those who have tried to tar the South African evangelist wholly with the WordFaith brush. Through careful scrutiny of Howard-Browne's own books and public statements, Oropeza concedes that the self-styled 'Holy Ghost Bartender' has latterly 'distanced himself from Word Faith teachers, and even pokes fun at the 'Word of Faith or Teaching movement' that refuses to make negative confessions'.[106]

Rather than attacking TTB as a mesmeric, shamanistic or Gnostic cult, Oropeza is far more concerned that it has succumbed to the introspection, individualism and superficiality of the postmodern West. It is primarily on this basis that he dismisses claims that it can be defined as revival:

> Revival? Until the church once again takes the driver's seat and makes the social-political impacts it did through people like Edwards and Finney – until the church once again produces evangelists like Wesley, reformers like Luther, artists like Bach, scientists like Mendel, inventors like Bell, thinkers like Pascal, and writers like Bunyan – don't make me laugh![107]

Saturday 11th November 1995

The Universities and Colleges Christian Fellowship (UCCF) hosts a day conference on TTB at London University's Institute of Historical Research. The title is 'The Toronto Blessing in Historical Perspective'. Speakers include Drs Nelson Kraybill, Bruce Hindmarsh and Richard Massey, each of whom assesses the current movement in the light of past Christian revivals.

Thursday 16th November 1995

Hodder publish Ken and Lois Gott's *The Sunderland Refreshing*. As with Andy and Jane Fitz-Gibbon's recently-launched *Something Extraordinary is Happening* (2nd October 1995), the book traces links between the Pentecostal-Anglican interactions at Alexander Boddy's All Saints Parish Church in 1907, and the TTB-inspired cross-fertilisation between Holy Trinity, Brompton and the Gotts' Assemblies of God congregation (Late July 1994). The Gotts also recall the earlier impact on their ministry of Benny Hinn (Summer 1987), and write enthusiastically of their ongoing relationship with John Arnott and TAV. 'Toronto Airport Vineyard', they declare, 'have a unique task and calling to cause fire to be ignited in hearts and spread throughout the world. That fire once received is imbibed into the genetics of our own churches.' They continue: 'In simple terms, all of us in our individual situations, having received the blessing, work out the fruit with a unique flavour of our own. As all the different streams and denominations have come together, we have not lost the glorious individuality of the local church.' For Sunderland Christian Centre, the 'working out of the fruit' has, say the Gotts, come about in the planting of two churches, and in plans to move the original congregation into a larger, warehouse-style building which will accommodate its fast-swelling numbers.[108]

Friday 17th November 1995

Eagle Press publishes *Blessing the Church?* – a sharp critique of TTB by Clifford Hill, Peter Fenwick, David Forbes and David Noakes. Hill's and Forbes' articles for *Prophecy Today* over the past fifteen months have consistently questioned the Blessing. Fenwick attacked it at the Bawtry Hall conferences held earlier this year, and at the subsequent Diakrisis consultation at High Leigh (16th-19th January, 15th April, 30th May-1st June 1995). Noakes spoke against it at the Evangelical Alliance forum on 2nd June. This new analysis shows that they have clearly not toned down their views of the movement.

Hill's contribution asserts that the charismatic movement was adversely affected by the fact that it arose in the permissive era of the 1960s and thereby imbibed an unhelpful spirit of individualism. This individualism, he adds, has lately been intensified under the influence of 1990s' 'rave' culture. As they have sought to deepen their experience of God against this backdrop, charismatics have, argues Hill, been prone to excessive sensualism, which has, in turn, eroded their commitment to the centrality of Scripture. Unafraid to name names, Hill accuses Gerald Coates, Graham Cray, Sandy Millar and David Pytches of contributing to this drift, and wonders whether they and others have mistaken genuine renewal and revival for human frustration at the failure and lethargy of the British church. He also sounds severe warnings about the influence of the Kansas City Prophets on such leaders, on the Vineyard, and on TAV in particular.[109]

Noakes underlines the importance of discernment and reminds readers that even highly regarded Christian leaders can be wrong. In particular, he begs to differ with those who have presented 'drunkenness in the Spirit' as an acceptable idea: 'Everywhere in Scripture drunkenness is condemned as ungodly', he writes, 'So how can we accept that the Spirit of God would deliberately bring about in the believer the evidence of drunken behaviour as if he were intoxicated with alcohol?' As he has done before, Fenwick rails against what he believes to be faulty exegesis and doctrinal misconception within the Toronto movement. Forbes construes the provenance of TTB through Latter Rain Pentecostalism, the Kansas City Prophets and Word of Faith teaching, implying a heretical dimension of which Christians should beware.[110]

Reviewing the book some weeks hence, Andrew Barton will complain that its oppositional tenor often detracts from its claims to sober assessment. In particular, he suggests that the other side of the argument has been inadequately represented. As an alternative, he suggests that 'perhaps a volume like the excellent series *When Christians Disagree* would have been better, and allowed a clearer discernment for all'.[111] The IVP venture to which Barton refers has brought together authors with competing perspectives to debate issues of evangelical concern. Although now discontinued, David Hilborn, Evangelical Alliance Theological Adviser, will cite its format as a model for Part I of this book (see *Introduction*).

Wednesday 22nd November 1995
The charismatic leaders' network Beulah convenes a day conference on TTB at Regent Hall in central London. The speakers are Clifford Hill, David Pawson and Rob Warner. Consistent with their previous pronouncements on the Blessing, they show themselves to be, respectively, concerned, open but cautious, and convinced.

Friday 24th November 1995
The *Christian Irishman* publishes 'Practical Guidelines' on TTB. These have been approved by the General Board of the Presbyterian Church of Ireland at its October meeting, and constitute the first official statement on the Blessing from a mainline denomination in the British Isles (the Full text of the P.C.I Statement appears in Part III).

A preamble to the Guidelines acknowledges the 'considerable publicity' which TTB has attracted, and the divisions which are opening up between Christians on the subject. Underlining that its advice is 'provisional', it trusts that it will be 'helpful in the present situation'.

First, the General Board's text encourages ministers to ensure that 'sufficient attention' is given to the Holy Spirit in their regular teaching and preaching. The conduct of public worship is their responsibility, it goes on, but 'any radical innovations should only be introduced after due consultation and preparation'. Furthermore, it states, 'sensational phenomena are to be strongly discouraged when they are the product of false emotionalism and any hint of audience manipulation'. Rather, spiritual movements are to be tested according to their fruit, as defined by Galatians 5:22,23. Special care is urged when dealing with young people and 'other vulnerable groups'; if tensions emerge within a congregation, ministers and elders are advised to approach the Presbytery at an early stage.

Monday 27th November 1995
Writing on the Ecunet 'New Wine' Bulletin Board, University of Akron sociologist Margaret Poloma responds to John Wimber's recent questioning of certain TAV ministry models. In an open letter to Wimber, she explains that she is conducting research on the Blessing with the consent of John Arnott. She is also, she writes, 'a born-again, Spirit-filled believer', who as best as she can discern, was 'led by the Spirit to TAV.' She continues: 'After reviewing scores of conference tapes, interviewing with staff at TAV, and participating in the renewal services and conferences, I judge the renewal to be in its "charismatic moment". More importantly, I found few examples of the cautionary concerns that you have raised in your articles. There are always going to be weeds mixed with the wheat, but I have been very impressed with the leadership's ability to allow the wheat to grow undisturbed without nurturing the weeds.'[112] Poloma goes to publish the first fruits of her research. Her findings and analysis will be expanded and refined through a number of articles over the next five years, up to and including the paper published in Part I of this book.

Monday 4th – Thursday 7th December 1995

Rodney Howard-Browne leads five days of meetings at Earls Court, London. Publicity for the meeting carries endorsements from Colin Dye, Terry Virgo, Gerald Coates, Wynne Lewis (General Superintendent of Elim), Bryn Jones, R.T. Kendall and Lyndon Bowring (Executive Chairman of Christian Action, Research and Education (CARE)). R.T. Kendall appears on stage with his wife, and tells the 1500 crowd, 'I unashamedly endorse the ministry this man.' Having related how she has been healed through Howard-Browne, Kendall brings his wife forward to speak, but after a few sentences she is struck dumb and returns to her seat.[113]

The meetings also attract a picket from a group of 20 led by Mark Haville, a former Word of Faith teacher and 'signs and wonders' minister who now spends time opposing such things. The group, which also includes Rev Philip Foster of Cambridge and former Queen's Road Baptist Church staff member Chris Hand, distributes a pamphlet entitled *Think Before You Drink* – a reference to Howard-Browne's characteristic injunction to get 'drunk in the Spirit'.[114]

Subsequent reports of the Earls Court meetings in *The Church of England Newspaper*, *Evangelical Times* and *Evangelicals Now* quote Howard-Browne as having stated that in the current movement God was emphasising his desire to save people through displays of power, rather than through reason and preaching: 'It's not great preaching or teaching that's going to bring revival. God has revealed to me that he is going to save every man, woman and child with his power.'[115]

Andrew Brown, Religious Affairs Correspondent of The *Independent*, subsequently reviews one of Howard-Browne's meetings. Brown concentrates sardonically on the South African's fund-raising techniques: 'Wastepaper baskets were passed around the crowd as he told stories of his poverty-stricken time in South Africa, when he could only afford a broken-down Mercedes ... "My God will liberally supply your every need. It worked for me, it can work for you".'[116]

Tuesday 5th December 1995

This is a critical day in the short history of TTB. John Wimber joins with AVC Board members Todd Hunter, Bob Fulton and Gary Best, to inform John Arnott and senior TAV staff that the Vineyard Association can no longer endorse the Toronto Airport Church and its ministry. The meeting lasts nearly three hours and ends with a request that the Airport Vineyard leaders review the Association's decision, meet with Best in his capacity as Canadian Vineyard Co-ordinator, and respond to the Board representatives the next day. Arnott and his colleagues are deeply shocked, but after two further hours, Arnott writes a brief letter confirming that TAV have agreed to accept the Board's decision.[117]

Arnott's letter is later published on the TAV web site. It expresses thanks to Wimber 'for taking so much 'heat' and criticism' on behalf of the Toronto congregation. Arnott then apologises to him 'for the stress and hurt we have caused you'. Furthermore, Arnott accepts on behalf of TAV that 'some of what is happening in Toronto is outside the Vineyard model.' He also agrees that Wimber and the Vineyard movement 'should not have to continue answering for the move of God's Spirit in Toronto'. Arnott assures Wimber, 'We are doing our best to be faithful stewards of what God has entrusted to us, as are you.' He ends by asking Wimber to let TAV leave AVC with his blessing, in order 'to minimize serious hurtful repercussions in the body of Christ.'[118]

Wednesday 6th December 1995

John Arnott e-mails news of the split from AVC to four key supporters, saying that the previous day's meeting 'was conducted very well, no anger or tension'. He adds, 'All our senior staff pastors were present. We parted on reasonably good terms and are at present sensing a great peace from God.' One of the recipients of Arnott's message is St Louis Vineyard pastor and early TB advocate Randy Clark; another is Drew University church historian Richard Riss, who has devoted a good deal of his career to chronicling the Third Wave.[119] Riss openly forwards the TAV leader's note to others and adds his own personal commentary on what has occurred. In this commentary, Riss criticises John Wimber for a 'precipitous separation of the sheep from the goats' and warns that he is 'putting himself in the position of Saul' over against TAV's 'David'. Looking to the future, he also remarks: 'I see this as a good thing in which there will be greater liberty for the Spirit of God to move unhindered.'[120]

Tuesday 12th December 1995

An open letter from John Arnott is posted on the Ecunet 'New Wine' bulletin board. It reports the 5th December meeting with the AVC Board and explains the subsequent disengagement of TAV from AVC. Arnott states that despite the Board's past endorsement of TTB as a move of the Holy Spirit (14th September 1994), John Wimber and his colleagues no longer felt that Airport Vineyard services were 'mirroring the Vineyard model', and saw themselves unable to shepherd something which fell outside that model.

Arnott confirms that TAV staff were 'surprised at the finality of [the Board's] decision'. He adds:

> We had hoped to have some input into the process. We thought the Board was not getting an accurate picture of what was taking place at the renewal meetings and that any issues could be explained and resolved. The Board, we were told, thought otherwise and we were offered no opportunity for discussion. We were removed without due process.

Confirming that the AVC Board have accepted the apology he conveyed to them in his letter of 5th December, Arnott adds, 'We will be parting on friendly terms. We still have the same Saviour and the same enemy. We realize that God is Sovereign over everything, including any mistakes his children might make.' He then expresses his thanks to Wimber and the Vineyard for their 'love, faith, courage and patience'. He continues:

This current move of God's Spirit would not have achieved its worldwide reach and impact without them. They have modelled Christ to us; they have been ministers of healing to us – we cannot thank them enough. We are not saying goodbye. We simply recognise that the sovereign Lord is moving this stream of the Holy Spirit along a new tributary.

Arnott also announces that TAV has asked 'several senior leaders from around the world' to form a new 'International Renewal Network', through which TAV will chart a more independent course while remaining on good terms with AVC. This will, he says, 'act as a temporary leadership covering for our church until such time as new alliances are formed'. In addition, he confirms that TAV will officially break with AVC on 20th January, when it will also announce its new name. He notes that this will mark 'the second anniversary celebration of the outpouring of God's Spirit at the Toronto Airport Vineyard' (cf. 20th January 1994).[121]

Also today, news of the AVC-TAV split reaches the British press. Fred Langan in the *Daily Telegraph* reports that 'the Association of Vineyard Fellowships in Anaheim, California, which has two hundred thousand members in six hundred congregations worldwide, said it would give a full statement later in the week on why it asked the Airport Vineyard Fellowship to leave.'[122]

Wednesday 13th December 1995

Taking their cue from Anaheim, the UK Association of Vineyard Churches, now numbering some 23 congregations, issues a press statement on the expulsion of TAV. The statement acknowledges that TTB 'has reintroduced a vitality into many churches and has been a blessing to those who have received it'. Even so, it goes on to state that over the past year, 'the Association has expressed concern to the leadership of the Toronto church that it cannot endorse, encourage, offer theological justification or biblical proof-texting for practices or manifestations which are not to be found in the Bible'. Furthermore,

> The Association does not accept that such practices can be presented as criteria for true spirituality or a mark of true renewal. Although appreciating that the power of God may cause unusual phenomena it is the Association's conviction that these manifestations should be neither promoted, placed on stage, nor used as a basis for theologising that leads to new teaching.

> In light of the Association's position and the fact that the leadership of the Toronto church had chosen not to minister within the framework of values and ministry style of the Association and considered themselves no longer representative of, accountable to, or under the authority of the Association the Board resolved to withdraw its endorsement from the leadership of the Toronto church.

Recounting the events of the AVC Board meeting on 5th December, the statement reports that on that occasion 'the [Toronto] leadership apologised for misreading the Board's concerns and that apology was accepted. The leadership accepted that they should be released from oversight by the Association to pursue the ministry that God has called them to at this time.' It adds: 'The decision to release the Toronto church was an amicable one.'

The press release then quotes John Arnott's message of thanks to John Wimber and the Vineyard from the open letter he published yesterday on the TAV web site.

John Wimber is also quoted:

> We love [the leaders of the Toronto Airport Vineyard] and desire only the best for them as they pursue what they believe to be God's intent for their lives. We simply have recognised during the last two years that we are not their leaders and that the stream called the Toronto Blessing is moving along a tributary different than ours.[123]

Thursday 14th December 1995

Victoria Coombe writes in *The Times* of the fissure between AVC and TAV. She says that as a consequence of what has happened, church leaders are urging 'caution' in regard to TTB. She then quotes Evangelical Alliance UK Director Joel Edwards as calling on churches to maintain perspective while they seek to 're-evaluate' the movement in the light of recent events. 'The pursuit of manifestations as an end in themselves', says Edwards, 'is wrong.' He adds that Christians should balance concern for supernatural experience with work in the community among the poor and the old.

Coombe also quotes Holy Trinity Brompton's Press Officer, Mark Elsdon-Dew: 'I want to stress we have always said what happens here is not a Toronto blessing but a blessing of the Holy Spirit. What has happened in Toronto this week will make no difference to the way we conduct our services.'[124] In a similar statement given to Cole Moreton of the *Church Times*, Elsdon-Dew concedes that although the Toronto split will not radically alter HTB's approach, 'it is yet another warning that we must continue to take care about what we do.'[125]

Friday 15th December 1995

The *Church of England Newspaper* recounts the detachment of TAV from AVC on 5th December.[126] Its report includes news of the e-mail sent by John Arnott to four colleagues on 6th December and 'leaked' by Richard Riss. It transpires that the TAV staff have now forced Riss to make an apology for the leak, and for his accompanying 'pejorative' remarks about AVC. In pressuring Riss to do this, the TAV leadership have warned him that he and they must 'give an account for every word spoken'.[127]

In addition to the official reasons already given for the split by John Wimber (13th December), *CEN* suggests that he and the AVC have expelled TAV because of 'his illness and exhaustion, leading him to the point that he felt "unable to field questions about the Toronto Blessing"'. The 'illness' to which the report refers here is a legacy of the cancer from which Wimber recovered in 1993, and a stroke he has suffered earlier this year, in September–October.[128]

The *CEN* report goes on to suggest that key British church leaders have known 'for some time' of tensions between Wimber's approach and TAV's emphasis on 'interpreting the "manifestations"', singling out people at the front for prayer to encourage manifestations, and John Arnott's more 'hands-on style of ministry'. One such unnamed leader tells *CEN*: 'The Toronto church would never have become as well-known if it didn't have the Vineyard stamp of authority', and in the light of this, *CEN* wonders what effect the break might have 'on the many thousands of Christians who have visited Toronto and have great loyalty to it'.[129]

Saturday 16th December 1995

Christian Herald garners reaction from British church leaders to the parting between the Vineyard Association and the Toronto Airport church. Gerald Coates tells the paper: 'John Wimber has been under constant pressure from a minority of the Vineyard churches regarding Toronto. Given the manifestation and response to the Spirit's presence in his conferences, this is an astonishing decision.' On a more phlegmatic note, Roger Forster of Ichthus says, 'Diverse ministries are essential for true Christian unity. It is not only not surprising but necessary that two streams of blessing should pursue their own channels in love.' Peter Fenwick, the Sheffield House Church leader who has been at the forefront of opposition to TTB, takes a predictably sharper view: 'Things wouldn't have come to this without a serious difference of opinion. They would naturally do all in their power to bridge the gulf, so the rift must be very big.' *Christian Herald* itself reports some commentators as also having suggested that 'John Wimber was playing safe, reserving a future position for himself in case the Toronto movement were to founder.'[130]

Sunday 17th December 1995

The *Sunday Telegraph* reports that 'recriminations are already beginning to fly' about what it calls the 'excommunication' of TAV from AVC. Gerald Coates tells Religious Correspondent Jonathan Petre: 'Some are saying that John Wimber's real motives are jealousy or competitiveness. It is difficult to see into someone's heart, but I am very disappointed by the lack of discussion about his differences with John Arnott.' Mark Elsdon-Dew of Holy Trinity, Brompton, however, maintains the caution of his earlier remarks on the split: 'We are not taking sides. Something happened and continues to happen. We are not looking for the Spirit of Toronto or of any other place.' Petre also reports that Arnott will be travelling to the UK in February to lead meetings in Telford and Bournemouth.[131]

In the same newspaper, Fred Langan reports from Toronto that despite their disengagement, it is 'business as usual' at TAV, with the congregation 'still rolling around in a state of holy laughter'. He has also spoken with John Arnott about the split: 'It has opened up a whole new horizon,' says the TAV leader. 'Now we can give renewal to churches around the world.' Clearly, however, Arnott is still very upset with the AVC: 'They've done a very foolish thing. We pleaded with them to give us time. We had already implemented changes they asked for.' He adds that they have made 'a mountain out of a molehill'. In response, Todd Hunter of the AVC Board tells Langan why the expulsion has occurred: 'Crowds can be manipulated by suggestions and emotions. Examples are used of tape on the floor and assigning of catchers to each person being prayed for.'[132]

Thursday 21st December 1995

The Evangelical Alliance hosts a third consultation on TTB, following up the previous forums which it convened at the Ibis Hotel, Euston on 19th-20th December 1994, and at its own offices in Whitefield House, Kennington earlier this year, on 2nd June. Today's meeting also takes place at Whitefield House and is addressed by Rob Warner of Queen's Road Baptist Church, Brian Edwards, Chairman of the Fellowship of Independent Evangelical Churches' Theological Commission, the leading Anglican evangelical Philip Hacking, and ACUTE Convenor Dave Cave.

Warner begins by evaluating the various roots and strands of TTB. In Argentina, he reports, many of those who have been involved in the 'eruptions' of the Spirit which first influenced the Arnotts and other Vineyard leaders in October-November 1993 have come to regard what is happening at Toronto and elsewhere as 'a prelude to revival', which must be further developed through prayer and evangelism in order to avoid a lapse into introspection and self-indulgence.

Turning to Rodney Howard-Browne, Warner acknowledges that the South African has adopted the style of a 'North American blue-collar itinerant evangelist, with all the vigour and excess of that culture; for example, an excitable rhetorical style, a tendency to caricature opponents [and] up-front appeals for money'. While some British Christians have been greatly blessed by Howard-Browne's ministry, says Warner, others have been unable to commend his meetings.

While conceding that some elements within the 'Toronto' movement have been influenced by Word of Faith teaching and approaches, Warner contends that these have had a negligible effect on British expressions of the Blessing. Furthermore, although some opponents of TTB have 'been tempted to suggest that everyone involved has surreptitiously embraced prosperity teaching', Warner insists that 'there is no evidence to justify such assertions' and adds that 'the present move of the Spirit has not changed the general repudiation in Britain of prosperity teaching.'

Where the Toronto Airport church itself is concerned, Warner does not mention the recent split from the Vineyard, but instead stresses that the staff and members of John Arnott's congregation have shown a 'remarkable generosity of spirit, being eager to serve and give away all that they have'. Moreover, the church, according to Warner, 'offers no package deal and imposes no theological, methodological or pastoral framework on its members or visitors'.

Shifting attention to the UK, Warner points out that TTB cannot fairly be characterised as a homogeneous movement. Rather, he argues, it has often been successfully assimilated with existing denominational emphases, whether with classical Pentecostal approaches at Sunderland Christian Centre, or with the distinctive liturgy of Anglicanism in parishes up and down the country.

Warner also traces several different strands of reaction to the Blessing. Some non-charismatics have, he says, been 'judicious, measured and constructive', while others have been more 'intemperate'. Ex-charismatics have, he adds, often made assessments which have been 'more symptomatic of their own self-reappraisal, often revealing more about their own journey than appraising others objectively'. Then again, there have been those who 'can be relied upon to speak against any tide or consensus', and whose very contrariness is thus 'reliable'. Among all these brands of commentator, however, Warner reserves a particular scorn for those who, in criticising the Blessing, have claimed that it offers 'no Christ, no cross, no Bible, no repentance, no call to submission and service, no preaching, no evangelism [and] no social action'. To such detractors he replies:

> ...please hear me. Such is not the blessing I preach and encounter week after week. A movement of God cannot be properly evaluated by caricature. A work of God cannot be undone by such caricature. Smears, distortion and guilt by association are not devices of good evangelical theology. Are you opposed to emotionalism and manipulation? So am I. Are you equally opposed to what Paul described as 'holding to the form of religion while denying its power?' So am I.

Urging that the evangelical community needs to show mutual generosity and humility in this context if it is to maintain its precious but vulnerable unity, Warner suggests that there are dangers and excesses which must be avoided by proponents and sceptics alike. Advocates and supporters of TTB should be on their guard, he says, against pride, manipulation, illuminism and over-interpretation; critics, however, should to be aware that they can perpetuate the same kinds of errors, with pride driving their possible rejection of any new move of God, manipulation lying behind their potential 'quenching' of the Spirit, illuminism motivating them to announce, from personal conviction, that the entire movement is demonic, and over-interpretation mistaking certain more dubious roots for universally rotten fruit.

Warner concludes by underling that while evangelicals will always disagree to some extent because of their 'high regard for truth', this can be no excuse for their tendency at times to 'disagree badly' and so perpetrate internal division which harms the cause of the gospel. It would, he adds, be a 'tragedy' if TTB were to become the focus of such division. Despite undoubted distortions and excesses, it is, he reiterates, an essentially orthodox and godly movement:

> What I commend is not the 'Toronto Blessing', a misnomer coined by a *Daily Telegraph* journalist [sic], but rather the 'Jesus Blessing'. We wish to receive and live in submission to nothing less and nothing more than the fullness of biblical blessing and empowerment that Jesus desires for his Church and for the world through his Church.

Brian Edwards is considerably less sanguine about TTB, depicting it as symptomatic of the drift of many evangelicals away from commitment to the inerrancy and sufficiency of Scripture, towards a more 'inductive' hermeneutic which begins with personal experience and immediate local concerns rather than with objective propositional revelation. Thus, he asserts:

> From whatever perspective you begin, an honest biblical exegete will admit that any attempt to justify from the Bible such phenomena as 'slaying in the Spirit', what has flippantly been referred to as 'carpet time', uncontrolled hysterical laughter and various animal noises, reveals either an ignorance of or a disregard for sound principles of hermeneutics.

Animal noises in particular, declares Edwards, have been defended on grounds which distort and traduce the plain, deductively-derived meaning of the Biblical text: 'we all know that while in Scripture there are two occasions when animals spoke like people (Gen. 3 and Num. 22), there is not one instance of people speaking like animals; the nearest is the behaviour of Nebuchadnezzar under severe judgment of God!' Hence, according to Edwards, 'The conclusion [should] be that for the redeemed to behave like animals can give pleasure only to the Prince of Darkness and certainly not to the King of Light.' This would be the classic evangelical deduction of the matter. By contrast, however, Edwards holds that in many 'Toronto' contexts, and not least in respect of animal noises, 'it is confidently asserted that when the Spirit is powerfully at work many strange things happen that are beyond the test of Scripture. Therefore the Scriptures are no longer sufficient. Apparently, there is a realm in which the Spirit operates outside his own word and for which his word can therefore offer us no help.'

Against this model, Edwards calls for a reaffirmation of traditional doctrines of Scripture and the historic evangelical approach to hermeneutics.

In a somewhat briefer contribution based on Philippians 1:15-18 and Galatians 1:7-9, Philip Hacking echoes Brian Edwards' basic concerns about the place of the Bible. He states that 'Toronto' is 'only the tip of an iceberg' which conceals a greater underlying threat to evangelical integrity – namely, a relinquishing of the 'final authority of Scripture'. Some of the 'Toronto' manifestations are, he says, 'so far removed from Scripture that I find it very difficult to accept the movement as being divinely inspired'. Furthermore, he comments,

> My greatest problem is that some 'Toronto' enthusiasts do not even wish to make Scripture the yardstick. They believe that God can do anything at any time and that the only means we have of discovering that something is of God is by a gut reaction and by judging whether or not some people seem to benefit spiritually from it.

In specific relation to his chosen texts, Hacking suggests that they together provide a helpful guide to the balance needed in regard to TTB. On one hand, he says, it is important to be generous towards those who approach ministry differently from ourselves, just so long as the gospel is genuinely proclaimed. On the other hand, it is crucial to maintain the clarity of that gospel.

Hacking concludes by surmising that 'in many ways the "Toronto" issue itself is fading'. Even so, he adds, 'I have no doubt that there will come something equally challenging and probably more frightening in the future.' In such circumstances, he declares, it is 'urgent that as evangelicals across the denominations we come together on the authority of Scripture. If we compromise that, even in the name of some clever teaching about hermeneutics and culture, we are in danger.'

In his summing up, Dave Cave details the work done by himself, ACUTE and the Alliance on TTB since it arose in the UK in the summer of 1994. He confirms that the Commission has sent representatives to a number of major consultations on the issue, and has gathered and absorbed an extensive archive related to it. It has also maintained close contact and correspondence on TTB with a circle of some 55 theologians representing a range of viewpoints. Furthermore, many have written to the Alliance expressing their opinions. These letters, together with the consultations and published materials, have led Cave to identify six major categories of respondent on TTB up to this point:

1. Those who feel that their walk with God has dramatically improved as a result of their encounter with TTB, sometimes testifying to dramatic healing.
2. Those who have been badly hurt and sometimes rejected by their congregation because they have not welcomed 'Toronto' as a move of God.
3. Those who have left churches which reject the experience for others where it has been welcomed.
4. Those who feel it is their duty to speak out against the movement, using publications and tapes to raise their concerns.
5. Those who have been concerned to examine the biblical and/or theological implications in some depth, through writing books.
6. Denominational or church networks who have published collaborative reports on the Blessing.

Cave presents examples of positive feedback on TTB; he draws particular attention to the increasing success of the Alpha course, which, he says, is now operating in around two thousand UK churches. Even so, he also highlights the difficulties that the Blessing has caused, both within and beyond the Alliance:

> There [have been] more books and articles written on this subject in the Christian community in the UK than on any other issue since the charismatic renewal movement of the 1960s to early 1970s, but in a much shorter time-span. It has resulted in significant tensions between evangelicals, not only between charismatic/Pentecostal and non-charismatic, but [also between] Pentecostals and charismatics [themselves] … The time and energy which have been expended on the 'Toronto Blessing' appear not only to have put evangelical against evangelical, but also to have diverted us from

our two main tasks – to glorify God and to go out into all the world and preach the good news.

Cave concludes with a passionate call to emphasise the essentials of evangelical faith over and above the often less crucial disputes which have characterised debate on TTB:

> Is the 'Toronto' issue sufficiently important to divide evangelicals? It is my belief that
> it is not. There are clearly some aspects of this current movement which give rise to
> disquiet, and not without cause. There has been some immaturity and inexperience,
> but very little which is unquestionably demonic … It is transparently obvious that
> there is no heresy here and, if there is, then many leading and respected Bible-
> believing scholars will agree to differ on the subject as a secondary rather than a
> primary issue, as they have in the past over baptism, predestination, millennialism,
> Pentecostalism and charismatic gifts, while still working together in essentials for the
> sake of the Good News in unity and truth.

Today also sees John Capon report on the TAV-AVC split in the *Baptist Times*; he notes that a Southern Baptist missionary couple in Singapore have had their service terminated for advocating TTB. On appeal to the Southern Baptist denomination's Foreign Missions Board in Memphis, Tennessee, Charles and Sharon Carroll have apparently been told that they have moved 'outside of generally accepted practices for Southern Baptists'.[133]

Friday 22nd December 1995

In the *Church of England Newspaper*, Andrew Carey reviews recent events at Toronto. He also quotes from an additional letter written by John Wimber, which has been distributed to Vineyard pastors and posted on the internet. Wimber writes in more detail about the reasons why TAV has been disengaged from AVC. 'The AVC Board has taken a stand that these manifestations are not to be encouraged, spotlighted, explained, defended or prayed for. We do not believe that they are an essential part of renewal or of the work of the Holy Spirit,' he says. Despite this, Wimber argues that Arnott and TAV have con-tinued to 'encourage, spotlight and defend these manifestations', and have 'attempted to give [them] prophetic and eschatological meanings, which we also do not accept as valid'. Furthermore, he stresses, they have failed 'publicly and pastorally [to] test the spirits or manifestations or to sort out the good from the bad'. He goes on to decry as manipulative TAV's featuring of manifestations in testimonies, their use of tape on the floor to mark areas for falling, and their deployment of 'catchers' for individual people.

Andrew Carey comments that Wimber's 'unprecedented action in cutting off the most successful of his churches … is either authoritarian audacity or an expression of amazing courage – depending on your viewpoint'. He suggests that 'it is bizarre to an Anglican that churches can split so freely and yet still throw around words like "the body of Christ"'. Moreover, 'It may prove to have been a fundamental ecclesiological mistake, by Wimber, to refer to his group of churches as an "association" rather than a "union".' Nonetheless, concludes Carey, 'if there are indeed major problems with manipulation and crowd control then church leaders need to sit up and take notice. They may need to reject the Toronto practices completely in order to have more healthy, spirit-filled worship'.[134]

In a similar review to Carey's, the *Church Times'* Cole Moreton produces an extra quote, this time from Bob Fulton of the AVC Board: 'Catchers, lines of tape on the floor and endless prayer for someone until they fall down put the idea into people's minds that falling down is the issue.'[135]

Saturday 30th December 1995

The Toronto split is reported in the January editions of *Evangelicals Now*,[136] *Evangelism Today*,[137] and *Evangelical Times*.[138] Characteristically, the *Evangelical Times* comments that now 'the whole issue of the validity of the Toronto Blessing experience must be called into question'. Also characteristically, they call upon Alan Morrison of Diakrisis Ministries for an opinion. Morrison has apparently been 'aware that the regional Vineyard leaders were becoming increasingly unhappy about the Rodney Howard-Browne and Benny Hinn dimension within the organisation'.

Also on the Toronto controversy, *Pioneer Update*, the newsletter of Gerald Coates' New Church network, carries a short account of developments. Coates himself is quoted: 'We are obviously very saddened that John Wimber does not feel that what is happening can come under his mandate,' he says. 'But I respect the pressures he has been under, particularly from those within the Vineyard Network of churches who are most unhappy with what is happening in Toronto. We are in full support of John and Carol Arnott and I am looking forward to having them with us in March at our 'After the Rain' conference.'

Meanwhile, the January issue of *Renewal* magazine reprints an article by Sandy Millar, originally published in *HTB in Focus*. The article appears to have been written prior to the TAV-AVC breach, since Millar does not even allude to this. He does, however, address the question of TTB's roots, and their much-debated effect on the TAV approach to ministry. He admits,

> Certainly some of the models are different from ours. But I think we ought to be very careful indeed before we suggest that some of those named, like Rodney Howard-Browne and Randy Clark (whom I haven't met but whom a number of people whose views I greatly respect value among their close friends) are other than servants of God trying to be obedient to the call of God on their lives.

Also, despite their disavowal by John Wimber in 1991, Millar defends the Kansas City Prophets: 'We watched them at close quarters when they were here and saw them demonstrating a degree of prophetic anointing that in my view we have yet to see in this country, even – or should I say especially? – among some who might criticise them.' In any event, he adds,

This current move of the Holy Spirit is now totally remote from its origins... We ask the *Holy* Spirit to come – not the Spirit of *x* or *y*. We have been asking the Spirit to come for the past nearly twenty years to my certain knowledge – and he comes. He was there before, of course, but he comes with different manifestations and in a different sense – to those who are hungry for him.

As for the fruit of the Blessing, Millar is upbeat:

There is a new love for Jesus, the Bible and fellow Christians. There is new hope and boldness, fresh faith and a new desire for freedom in prayer. We are hearing testimony after testimony of this and of many new Christians coming to faith through the Alpha courses and elsewhere too.[139]

In relation to the Rodney Howard-Browne meetings held at Olympia on 4th-7th December, and to the criticism they have received, *Evangelicals Now* print a letter by R.T. Kendall of Westminster Chapel. Acknowledging that 'there are godly people who read *EN* who are baffled by our acceptance of people like Rodney and Paul Cain', he writes as follows:

Rodney is a rough diamond. His Pentecostal and cultural trappings put many off. I understand this. His 40-minute sermon at Westminster Chapel was flawless, but I died a thousand deaths at Olympia. It taught me to be patient and not judgmental toward those who can't abide his style. But this one thing I know: when he prayed for my wife, Louise, she was instantly healed; her life was further transformed by his ministry in Florida one year ago. She had been seriously depressed and homesick for over five years. She has often said that, had she not been so desperate, she would have walked out in ten minutes. There is nothing wrong with being desperate; but it was God's way of getting our attention. Also, our son came back to Christ under Rodney's ministry. Rodney is only 34. God isn't finished with him yet. And he is beginning to listen to me, showing far more openness than some of us who are Reformed. What if, as I believe, we are on the brink of a great awakening this century – and that God sovereignly chose his ministry as the embryonic phase of it? I had to climb down (I didn't like it because it didn't start with me) after speaking against it. I chose to make this statement through *Evangelicals Now*. You are my 'stable'. I have not deserted you, and I never meant to let you down.[140]

At this time also, John Arnott tells the religion writer of the *Los Angeles Times*, Larry B. Stammer, that on 5th December, AVC declared TAV to have gone 'over the edge' by encouraging manifestations as part of testimony and worship. 'We weren't asked to leave,' he adds. 'We were told we were out.'[141]

In the midst of all the controversy, the January-February edition of *Ministries Today* prints an extract from John Arnott's newly published book, *The Father's Blessing*.[142] 'At times', writes Arnott, 'the intensity of the manifestations of the Holy Spirit in our meetings has been shocking. Occasionally we have found ourselves having to speak over the noise of people laughing and groaning or crying out, though things usually are quieter during the preaching of the Word. When all of this started happening in our church, we were greatly tempted to try to keep things tidy. I wondered how the shaking, collapsing, laughing and other things fit in with 1 Corinthians 14:40, which says that things should be done decently and in order.' Through his contemplation of this 'decency and order' issue, however, Arnott has concluded that Paul's phrase must finally be interpreted from God's point of view, rather than from any culturally-conditioned human perspective: 'The Holy Spirit reserves the right to do things none of us have ever seen before, such as falling upon people during the preaching of the Word in Cornelius' house (Acts 10:44) … [T]he question is, Whose understanding of 'decently and in order' should we use – yours, ours or God's?' In seeking to address this question, Arnott deals with four 'false assumptions' in respect of the Spirit's work.

First, Arnott argues, it is erroneous to presume that all acts of God have to be understandable in order to be valid. God's command to Abraham to sacrifice Isaac (Gen. 22) and Jesus' use of spittle and mud to heal the man born blind (John 9) are cited as apparently 'bewildering' incidents which have nonetheless been accepted in retrospect. Likewise, he avers, 'this new move of God is in line with the Word and with church history. It produces good fruit, and Jesus is glorified. Given all that, it seems less important that our minds can't grasp all the ways God chooses to move by His Spirit.'

Secondly, Arnott suggests that we are mistaken if we think that 'the Holy Spirit will never do anything against my will'. This, he contends, is to deny God's sovereignty. As well as maintaining that God may well cause people to shake or fall involuntarily if that is his purpose, he refers in particular to the slaying of Ananias and Sapphira in Acts 5:11: 'Was this move of the Spirit against their wills? Yes. But was it God? Indeed, it was.'

Thirdly, Arnott criticises the notion that if something is from God, it cannot possibly evoke fear in those who experience it. Instancing Daniel 10 and Exodus 20:19, he comments that 'feeling afraid might actually be a sign that you are in God's presence'. He also advises: 'Recognize that God is awesome. Don't be surprised if his power overwhelms you.'

Finally, Arnott dissents from the view that God must always be 'tidy and proper'. Jesus' ministry, he notes, was often marked by conflict, noise and apparent chaos, e.g. in the deliverance of the Gerasene demoniac in Mark 5 and Luke 8. He suggests:

Suppose such a thing happened at your church? You would need to have a country church with some pigs nearby. How would your parishioners and the neighbours react to a naked, screaming demoniac and thousands of suddenly insane pigs? People would wonder: *How could this be God? It's so loud and perplexing*…Yet if you asked the mother or father of that man if they thought this was God's work, what do you think they would have said? And if you asked the man himself if he was blessed in spite of the disorderly scene, what do you think he would have said? Would he have questioned whether it was all done 'decently and in order'? No, he was simply grateful and wanted to follow Jesus.[143]

Also in the same issue of *Ministries Today*, Arnott reflects on the recent split from AVC. He tells the magazine: 'We have a lot of very satisfied people who have come and been refreshed ... Our heart is to work it out and be friends.'[144]

Although he does not mention the immediate crisis in Toronto, David Forbes reflects in the January–February edition of *Prophecy Today* on the apparent line of continuity from the Latter Rain movement, through the 'elect seed' teaching of Kansas City Prophets, to TAV (cf. 3rd December 1988, 1st October, 24th October 1994, 3rd May, 17th May 1995). The article is adapted from his contribution to *Blessing the Church?*, which has been co-written with Clifford Hill, Peter Fenwick and David Noakes (17th November). Forbes submits that TB proponent Randy Clark has confirmed that the 'prophetic foundation for what is happening [was] clearly prophesied over ten years ago by Paul Cain and the Kansas City prophets'. Moreover, he writes, 'Rodney Howard-Browne, another of the leading exponents of the "blessing", has given Latter Rain-style prophecies and Mark Dupont, who has a prophetic ministry in the Toronto Vineyard church, has written that 'this move of the Spirit in 1994 is not just a charismatic and Pentecostal experience, concerning power of gifting. It is one thing to be clothed with power; it is another thing to be indwelt with the person of God.' Comparing the rise of such teachings with the historic propensity of heresies to 'sprout out by huddles and clusters', Forbes concludes that 'the charismatic movement might do well to pay heed'.[145]

Notes to Chapter 10

[1] 'D, Coffey, 'When the Spirit Comes', *Baptist Times*, 5th January 1995, pp.5,14.

[2] T. Higton, 'Opinion: Toronto Revisited', *Christian Herald*, 14th January 1994, p.3.

[3] Centre for Contemporary Ministry, *Charismatic Crossroads*.

[4] Ibid., pp. 7-8.

[5] R. Warner, *Prepare for Revival*.

[6] D. Roberts, 'Victory on Our Knees', *Alpha*, June 1995, pp.4-6.

[7] A. Brown, 'Church at Odds Over "Waves of Faith"', *Independent*, 28th January 1995, p.2. The story is picked up by The *Church of England Newspaper* on February 3rd: '"Toronto" is Only Hysteria, says Dean', p.3.

[8] *Evangelical Times*, February 1995, p.3.

[9] M. Taylor, 'What Happened Next?', *Evangelicals Now*, February 1995, pp.1-2.

[10] T. Thornborough, 'An Evening at the Airport', *Evangelicals Now*, February 1995, pp.6-7.

[11] G. Coates, 'On the Crest of the Spirit's Wave', *Renewal*, February 1995, pp.18-20.

[12] A. Galbraith, '"Soaking" in the Spirit in Scotland', *Renewal*, February, 1995, pp.28-30.

[13] O. Boycott, '"Toronto Blessing" Has Believers Fainting in the Aisles', *Guardian*, Monday 30th January 1995.

[14] T. Smail, 'Why my Middle Name is Certainly Not Gamaliel', *Church of England Newspaper*, 3rd February 1995, p.8.

[15] D. Atkinson, 'Why my Middle Name is Certainly Not Gamaliel', *Church of England Newspaper*, 3rd February 1995, p.17.

[16] M. Thomas, 'Signs Mike Wonders About', *Reachout*, Spring 1995, p.3-5.

[17] T. Sargent, 'Physical Phenomena and Revival', *Evangelism Today*, March 1995.

[18] 'Lloyd-Jones. Edwards and Toronto', *Renewal*, April 1995, pp.28-31.

[19] D. Roberts, 'Victory on Our Knees', *Alpha*, June 1995, p.4.

[20] S. Kellough, 'If You Missed "Toronto" You Could Now Be "Wheatoned"', *Church of England Newspaper*, 7th April 1995, p.7.

[21] 'Blessed or Not Blessed?' *Idea*, April-May 1995, pp.12-3.

[22] W. Davies, 'John Wesley: Healing and the Toronto Blessing', *Healing and Wholeness*, April 1995, pp.16-9.

[23] C. Gardner, 'Catching a Glimpse of God's Glory', *Joy*, March 1995, pp.17-8.

[24] S. Kellough, 'If You Missed "Toronto" You Could Now Be "Wheatoned"', *Church of England Newspaper*, 7th April 1995, p.7.

[25] 'Fresh Encouragements at This Year's Spring Harvest', *Renewal*, July 1995, p.5.

[26] 'Wheaton Awakening Brings Hundreds of Students to their Knees', *Baptist Times*, 20th April 1995, p.4.

[27] Gott, *Sunderland Refreshing*.

[28] C. Price, 'Surfing the Toronto Wave', *Alpha*, May 1995, pp.6-9.

[29] W. Boulton, 'Preface', in W. Boulton (ed.), *The Impact of Toronto*, pp.9-10.

[30] 'Thousands More Undergo "Revival"', *Christian Herald*, 6th May 1995.

[31] A. Morrison *A Different Gospel: The Origin and Purpose of the Toronto Blessing* (Video).

[32] *Evangelism Today*, August 1995, p.8.

[33] M. Stibbe, 'Revival Phenomena: Beware of Pitfalls', *Renewal*, June 1995, pp.33-4.

[34] R. Clements, 'Toronto: A Personal Appraisal', *Evangelicals Now*, June 1995, pp.16-7.

[35] 'Toronto Blessing: "A Great Deception"', 15th June, 1995, p.4.

[36] 'Toronto "Defaces the Image of God"', *Christian Herald*, 17th June, 1995, p.20.

[37] 'Strange Fire', *Evangelicals Now*, July 1995, p.24.

[38] 'The Toronto Blessing: The Serious Debate Begins', *Evangelism Today*, July, 1995, p.8.

[39] 'Toronto Gets "Rigorous Assessment" at Conference', *Evangelical Times*, July 1995.

[40] Quotations from the consultation are taken from transcripts of the talks given. These transcripts have been published on the Evangelical Alliance web site: www.eauk.org

[41] C. Hails, 'Do the Experience and the Biblical Theology Match Up?' *Church of England Newspaper*, Friday 2nd June 1995, p.9.

[42] J. Richardson, 'Stand Up, Stand Up for Jesus', *Church of England Newspaper*, Friday 2nd June 1995, p.8.

[43] 'Call for More Theological Research on the Toronto Blessing', *Baptist Times*, 8th June 1995, p.3; 'Toronto Splits Evangelicals', *Church of England Newspaper*, 9th June 1995; 'EA Toronto Consultation "A Confusion"', *Evangelical Times*, July 1995.

[44] H. Kamsteeg, 'Toronto Blessing Pro and Contra', *Challenge Weekly*, 7th June 1995, p.1.

[45] Interview with evangelist Steve Hill in Pensacola: 'They've Seen the Power of Satan, Now They See the Power of God', *Challenge Weekly*, 29th January 1997, pp.1, 3.

[46] I. McFarlane, 'Is This Revival?', *Baptist Times*, 26th November 1996, p.5; B. Davies, 'Pensacola: "A Command to Repent"', *Renewal*, February 1997, pp.19-20; 'Pensacola Outpouring Keeps Gushing', *Christianity Today*, 3rd March 1997, pp.54-6.

[47] M. Green, 'The Blessing? It's All in the Bible!', *Church of England Newspaper*, 23rd June 1995, p.9.

[48] 'EA Toronto Consultation "A Confusion"', *Evangelical Times*, July 1995, p.10.

[49] 'EA Toronto Consultation "A Confusion"', *Evangelical Times*, July 1995, p.10.

[50] C. Dye, 'Ready to Face the Giants', *Joy*, July 1995.

[51] D. Butler, 'Training the Toronto Team (Interview with Mary Audrey Raycroft)', *Joy*, July 1995.

[52] L. Belcham, *Toronto: The Baby or the Bathwater*; S. Jebb, *No Laughing Matter: The 'Toronto' Phenomenon and its Implications*.

[53] 'Toronto "Blessing"', *Methodist Recorder*, 6th July 1995, p.16.

[54] Stibbe, *Times of Refreshing*.

[55] 'New Call for True Holiness', *Christian Herald*, 15th July 1995. p.20.

[56] S.E. Porter & P.J. Richter (eds.), *The Toronto Blessing – Or Is It?*

[57] P.J. Richter, 'God Is Not a Gentleman!', in Porter & Richter (eds.), *Toronto Blessing*, p.34.

[58] S.E. Porter, 'Shaking the Biblical Foundations', in Porter & Richter (eds.), *Toronto Blessing*, pp.38-65.

[59] R. Murphy, 'Risen with Healing in His Wings: An Exploration of the Psychology of the Toronto Blessing', in Porter & Richter (eds.), *Toronto Blessing*, pp.66-85.

[60] J. Kent, 'Have We Been Here Before: A Historian Looks at the "Toronto Blessing"', in Porter & Richter (eds.), *The Toronto Blessing*, pp. 86-103.

[61] W. Porter, 'The Worship of the Toronto Blessing?', in Porter & Richter (eds.), *The Toronto Blessing*, pp.104-30.

[62] M. Stibbe, 'A Question Left Hanging', *Renewal*, December 1995, p.46.

[63] 'Major Figure Climbs Down over Toronto', *Joy*, August 1995, p.9.

[64] R. Elkins, 'Renewal Movement Unites Florida Churches', *Charisma*, August 1995, pp.18-9.

[65] P. Higton, 'Toronto Truths', *Woman Alive*, August 1995, pp.6-7.

[66] S. Watterson, 'I Went with an Open Mind', *Woman Alive*, August 1995, pp.7-8.

[67] Theological Educator, '"Blessed" and Broken', *Woman Alive*, August 1995, p.8.

[68] J. Edwards and Dave Cave, 'Toronto Surprise', *Evangelical Times*, August 1995, p.19.

[69] J. Wimber, 'For the Sake of the Lost', *Alpha*, August 1995, pp.4-7.

[70] A. & J. Fitz-Gibbon, 'God, Do What You Want to Do!', *Renewal*, August 1995, pp.14-16.

[71] 'What on Earth is Going On?', *Challenge Weekly*, 23rd August 1995, pp.8-9.

[72] *Rumours of Revival* (Video), Milton Keynes: Nelson Word, 1995.

[73] T. Higton, 'Affirming Toronto', *Christian Herald*, 26th August, 1995, p.3.

[74] C. Gardner, 'Evangelist Under Fire for Bringing Joy to the Church', *Joy*, September 1995.

[75] A. Morrison, 'No Great Surprise', *Evangelical Times* (Letters), September 1995, p.18.

[76] 'Comment', *Evangelical Times*, September 1995, p.2.

[77] Clifford Hill, 'Editorial: Love and Unity', *Prophecy Today*, Vol. 11, No. 5 (September-October 1995), pp.4-5.

[78] C. Hill, 'Assessing Toronto', *Prophecy Today*, Vol. 11, No.5 (September-October 1995), pp.14-15.

[79] P. Fenwick, 'The Case is Not Made', *Christian Herald*, 9th September 1995.

[80] J.A. Beverley, 'Toronto's Mixed Blessing', *Christianity Today*, 11th September 1995, pp.23-6.

[81] M. Percy, *Words, Wonders and Power: Understanding Contemporary Christian Fundamentalism and Revivalism*.

[82] *Spread the Fire*, October 1995, p.10.

[83] T. Payne, 'Toronto at a Tangent', *Evangelicals Now*, October 1995, p.16.

[84] R. McCloughry, 'High Profile: Interview with John Stott', *Third Way*, October 1995, pp.21-23.

[85] A. & J. Fitz-Gibbon, *Something Extraordinary is Happening*.

[86] 'Commitment to Evangelical Unity Affirmed Despite Differences', *Challenge Weekly*, 25th October 1995, p.9.

[87] 'Get It to Give It', *Charisma* (*Eurocharisma* Insert), November 1995, p.1.

[88] J. Lee Grady, 'Classical Pentecostals Wary of the 'Toronto Blessing', *Charisma*, November 1995, pp.41-2.

[89] D. Doucet, 'The "Blessing" Sweeps the Globe', *Charisma*, November 1995, p.63.

[90] C. Price, 'A Revival Without Walls', *Charisma*, November 1995, pp.55-8.

[91] C. Hand, 'Examining the fruit', *Prophecy Today*, Vol. 11, No. 6 (November-December 1995), pp.13-4.

[92] J. Prasch, 'Is the "Toronto Blessing" a Hands-On Experience?', *Prophecy Today*, Vol. 11 No. 6, pp.27-9.

[93] Pawson, *Is the Blessing Biblical?*

[94] Ibid., p.99.

[95] Pawson is referring here to his earlier study *The Road to Hell*.

[96] Pawson, *Is the Blessing Biblical?*, p.12.

[97] Ibid., p.27.

[98] Ibid., pp.34-6.

[99] Ibid., p.37.

[100] Ibid., p.38.

[101] Ibid., p.39.

[102] Ibid., p.49.

[103] Ibid., pp.89-93.

[104] Ibid., p.97.

[105] Oropeza, *A Time to Laugh*

[106] Ibid., p.38.

[107] Ibid., p.190.

[108] Gott, *Sunderland Refreshing*.

[109] C. Hill, in Hill et al, *Blessing the Church?*, p.204ff.

[110] Hill et al, *Blessing the Church?*. See also the adaptation by Forbes of his own chapter in the January-February issue of *Prophecy Today*: 'From North Battleford to Toronto', pp.14-7 (30th December 1995).

[111] A. Barton, 'Warnings on Renewal', *Church of England Newspaper*, 1st March 1996, p.14.

[112] 'Letter of Margaret Poloma to John Wimber', Ecunet 'New Wine' bulletin board, 27th November 1995. Also, 'Comments on "Vineyard Reflections: The Toronto Blessing"' on the same site. Poloma's published work on the Blessing prior to the paper which appears here is as follows: *The Toronto Report*. Bradford-upon-Avon: Terra Nova, 1996; 'The Toronto Blessing: Charisma, Institutionalization and Revival', 257-71; 'The "Toronto Blessing" in Postmodern Society', in Dempster et al (eds.), *Globalization*, pp.363-85.

[113] 'Toronto Meeting is Picketed By Evangelicals', *Church of England Newspaper*, 15th December 1995, p.3; P. Glover, 'Signs and Wonders Meeting Picketed', *Evangelical Times*, January 1996, p.9; P. Glover, 'Not By Preaching – But By "Power"', *Evangelicals Now*, January 1996, p.24.

[114] 'Toronto Meeting is Picketed by Evangelicals', *Church of England Newspaper*, 15th December 1995, p.3.

[115] Toronto Meeting is Picketed by Evangelicals', *Church of England Newspaper*, 15th December 1995, p.3; Peter Glover, 'Signs and Wonders Meeting Picketed', *Evangelical Times*, January 1996, p. 9; Peter Glover, 'Not by Preaching and Teaching – but by 'Power', *Evangelicals Now*, January 1996, p.24.

[116] A. Brown, 'Praying All the Way to the Bank', *Independent*, 9th December 1995.

[117] J.A. Beverley, 'Vineyard Severs Ties with "Toronto Blessing" Church', *Christianity Today*, 8th January 1996, p.66; Wright, *Strange Fire?*, p.29.

[118] J. Arnott, 'Letter to John Wimber', 5th December 1995, published on TAV web site, 12th December 1995.

[119] 'Vineyard Excommunicates Toronto Christians', *Church of England Newspaper*, 15th December 1995, p.3; James A. Beverley, 'Vineyard Severs Ties with "Toronto Blessing" Church', *Christianity Today*, 8th January 1996, p.66.

[120] 'Toronto Vineyard Exclusion: Leaders React', *Christian Herald*, 16th December 1995.

[121] Wright, *Strange Fire?*, p.29.

[122] F. Langan, 'Evangelicals Expelled By Their Church', *Daily Telegraph*, 12th December 1995.

[123] Association of Vineyard Churches (UK), 'Press Statement', 13th December 1995.

[124] V. Coombe, '"Toronto Blessing" Warning to Church', *Daily Telegraph*, 14th December 1995.

[125] C. Moreton, 'Toronto Cut from Vineyard', *Church Times*, 15th December 1995.

[126] 'Vineyard Excommunicates Toronto Christians', *Church of England Newspaper*, 15th December 1995, p.3.

[127] Ibid.

[128] These illnesses are mentioned in Wimber's obituary when he dies of a brain haemorrhage in November 1997 – 'Vineyard Founder Wimber Dies', *Christianity Today*, November 1997.

[129] 'Vineyard Excommunicates Toronto Christians', *Church of England Newspaper,* 15th December 1995, p.3.

[130] 'Toronto Vineyard Exclusion: Leaders React', *Christian Herald*, 16th December 1995.

[131] J. Petre, 'Religious Roadshow Set to Roll in Britain', *Sunday Telegraph*, 17th December 1995. p.9.

[132] F. Langan, 'Rebel Pastor Defies Ban on Church', *Sunday Telegraph*, 17th December 1995, p.9.

[133] J. Capon, 'Toronto Blessing: Parting of the Ways?', *Baptist Times*, 21st/28th December 1995, p.4.

[134] A. Carey, 'Why Wimber Excommunicated Toronto', *Church of England Newspaper*, December 22nd 1995, p.7.

[135] C. Moreton, 'Toronto Fell Down Over Hype', *Church Times*, 22nd December 1995.

[136] 'Toronto Airport Vineyard Flies the Coop', *Evangelicals Now*, January 1996; 'John Wimber Carpets "Toronto Blessing" Church', *Evangelism Today*, January 1996.

[137] 'John Wimber Carpets "Toronto Blessing" Church', *Evangelism Today*, January 1996.

[138] 'Toronto Withers on the Vine', *Evangelical Times*, January 1996, pp.1, 24.

[139] S. Millar, 'We ask the Holy Spirit to Come – and He Does', *Renewal*, January 1996, pp.14-5.

[140] Kendall, R.T., 'R.T. responds', *Evangelicals Now*, January 1996, p.24.

[141] D. Wooding, 'Toronto Group Ousted in "Spiritual Split"', *Challenge Weekly*, 3rd January 1996.

[142] Arnott, *Father's Blessing*, 1995.

[143] J. Arnott, 'Why Renewal Isn't Tidy', *Ministries Today*, January/February 1996, pp.45-8.

[144] 'Toronto Update', *Ministries Today*, January/February 1996, p.47.

[145] D. Forbes,, 'From North Battleford to Toronto', *Prophecy Today*, January-February 1996, pp.14-7

11

1996-2000: The Decline and Transmutation of the Blessing

Monday 8th January 1996
Reporting on the recent split between AVC and TAV for *Christianity Today*, James Beverley quotes Tom Stipe, a former Vineyard pastor from Denver: 'John Wimber has helped true biblical renewal by this decision. It's unfortunate that the airport Vineyard leaders didn't really hear his concerns.'

Saturday 13th January 1996
In its last issue before re-launching as *New Christian Herald*, *Christian Herald* reports that Mark Haville, who led the protests against Rodney Howard-Browne at Olympia on 4th-7th December, has challenged leading Toronto advocates Gerald Coates, R.T. Kendall and Nicky Gumbel of Holy Trinity, Brompton, to take part in a public debate on the Blessing with their detractors. He suggests a date of 3rd February at a London venue capable of holding five hundred, and says that the event would be recorded on video so as to reach a wider audience. It is subsequently reported that some of those challenged have declined Haville's invitation on the grounds that the Evangelical Alliance is conducting ongoing research and consultation on the matter.[1]

Saturday 20th January 1996
John Arnott and the Toronto Airport church celebrate the second anniversary of TTB. They also formally disengage from AVC and re-name themselves the Toronto Airport Christian Fellowship (TACF).

In the week of celebrations that follows, former Kansas City Prophet Paul Cain is invited to preach. TACF leader Guy Chevreau will later write: 'Paul can be considered one of this generation's prophetic grandfathers. He is a senior statesman for the Body of Christ; it was a high privilege to have him take part.'[2]

Saturday 27th January 1996
The February edition of *Alpha* magazine lends extensive coverage to the disengagement of the Toronto church from the Vineyard network. As well as the

information cited above, the magazine's record of what has happened includes comment from TACF pastor Marc Dupont, who urges the church's supporters 'not to get hurt [and] not to get embittered' about what has happened. From the Vineyard side, Todd Hunter reiterates the objections made by the AVC Board on 5th December, but adds, 'Our action does not mean that we have rejected the current renewal. Many of our churches have benefited greatly … and have incorporated it into their church life, within the healthy and biblical guidelines published over the last two years.'[3]

Elsewhere in the magazine, editor Dave Roberts scrutinises negative reaction to TTB. While accepting the need for doctrinal discernment, Roberts suggests that some criticism of the movement over the past year and a half has been 'tainted by generalisations, misrepresentations, faulty logic and a confrontational attitude'. For illustration, he singles out comments published by Wendy Porter, Alan Morrison and Clifford Hill.

Porter's attack on the lack of Christology exhibited by Toronto-style hymns and songs in her chapter for *The Toronto Blessing – Or Is It?*[4] is, says Roberts, both subjective and ignorant of evidence from recent recordings made by pro-Blessing musicians. Indeed, Roberts argues that lyrics written in the past year or so by Paul Oakley, Martin Smith and Matt Redman 'suggest just the opposite'.

As for Morrison's charge, made in his *A Different Gospel* video and elsewhere,[5] that TTB attempts 'to destroy the work of biblical evangelism', Roberts insists that 'the facts are quite clear'. Rodney Howard-Browne, he states, 'has seen thousands make a profession of faith since 1993'. Moreover, 'The Toronto Vineyard record between five and thirty conversions nightly', and 'The Sunderland Christian Centre, who meet nightly, have seen high profile local criminals and their families coming to Christ in renewal meetings.' If the point is definition of the word 'biblical', suggests Roberts, then Morrison and his supporters should heed John Arnott's response to the AVC Board on 5th December 1995, when he wrote: 'We too want to focus on preaching the Cross of Christ to all who come for refreshing.' Likewise, Roberts cites an Airport Vineyard leaflet on discernment which underlines the need to 'test all prophecies by the Spirit and the Word, since "we prophesy in part" (1 Cor. 13:9)'. In addition, Roberts points to the growing success of Holy Trinity, Brompton's Alpha course. This, he says, 'combines C.S. Lewis-style apologetics, resolute evangelical orthodoxy and charismatic spirituality', and 'is currently in use in as many as 2,000 churches.' Furthermore, 'It places a strong premium on friendship evangelism, a process of evangelism and the involvement of the whole person, including the mind, in the salvation process.' Morrison's allegation, writes Roberts, 'is all the more damaging because it is wrong.'

Whereas Clifford Hill has described TTB as 'a floodtide of deception'[6], Roberts argues that this in itself is a 'subjective perception', with little clear warrant in the 'plain and main' witness of Scripture.[7]

Also around this time, *Direction* magazine reports that two other Vineyard churches, in Pasadena and Missouri, have asked to leave the Vineyard network because of AVC's treatment of the Toronto Airport church.[8]

Saturday 3rd February 1996

Victoria Coombe reports in the *Daily Telegraph* on John Arnott's recent arrival in Britain, and on the 'Catch the Fire' Conference he has been leading in Telford. She comments that the Blessing has here 'apparently started to take on a new shape'. Instead of erupting in 'holy laughter', she writes, 'two thirds of the congregation simultaneously burst into tears and fell to their knees.' According to Gerald Coates, who has been touring with Arnott, this indicates that the Blessing has now changed its 'genetic code'.[9]

Today also, *New Christian Herald* reports that celebrations in Wales and Scotland to mark the 150th anniversary of the Evangelical Alliance have sought to strike a note of reconciliation in respect of TTB. In South Wales, Toronto supporter R.T. Kendall has preached from Matthew 22:29 on the need to maintain unity between those concerned to uphold biblical authority and those seeking to emphasise the power of God. He has added that he longs to see the day when 'those who come to church to see will hear, and those who come to hear will see!' Striking a similar note, Alliance Director General Clive Calver has told audiences in Llandudno and Glasgow that Christ is coming back to marry his bride, the Church, as a whole – 'not an arm, a leg, then a torso'.[10]

Thursday 8th February 1996

From the Bournemouth International Centre, *London Evening Standard* reporter Tom Hayes describes the latest leg of John Arnott's British tour. The Bournemouth meetings are being conducted under the title 'Waves of the Spirit', and as well as Arnott, are being addressed by David and Mary Pytches, Terry Virgo, Gerald Coates, Wes Campbell and Rob Warner. Between two and three thousand have paid £60 a head to attend.[11] Hayes recounts that he has fallen to the floor after being prayed for by Arnott and his wife Carol:

> Inexplicably, while under the influence of [Arnott's] insistent words, my resolve melted. I could feel my legs slowly weakening under me. Five times they wobbled and five times I resisted until eventually I couldn't be bothered to hold out any more and collapsed gratefully into the arms of a helper … Frankly, it was pretty disturbing but my legs were completely immobile so I lay back and thought of England. In truth, I had little choice. A strange sensation had filled my legs which rendered them completely useless. Mentally, I was alert but no matter how hard I told myself to move my legs, it didn't happen. Approximately half-an-hour later I stumbled to my feet, feeling no better and no worse than I had done earlier.

Despite all this, Hayes calls TTB 'an extreme branch of the charismatic movement' and writes that it reduces 'seemingly sensible people' to 'gibbering wrecks'. In conclusion, however, he resumes a more equivocal tone: 'apart from being a little worrying, it was actually quite pleasurable', he writes.[12]

Friday 9th February 1996

Also reporting from Bournemouth, Cole Moreton tells readers of the *Church Times* that one of the organisers of the 'Waves of the Spirit' conference, Rev Peter Lawrence of Canford Magna in Dorset, has issued a statement defending Arnott's presence in the wake of his recent split from AVC. The statement says that John Arnott has left the Vineyard not 'because of immorality, or because the Vineyard leaders feel the present move is not of God, but [because of] a difference of opinion in administering the renewal and handling its consequences'.

By contrast, Moreton confirms that Holy Trinity, Brompton has 'taken pains to stress its closeness to John Wimber and the Vineyard Association, and to distance itself from Toronto'. A spokesman for the London church is quoted as emphasising that while John Arnott 'as a man' would be 'enormously welcome', he is unlikely to be invited to speak because so many other people wish to do so.

Moreton also reports that the controversial former Bishop of Durham, Rt Rev David Jenkins, has denounced TTB as 'pure psychological violence'. Recording the first of a new BBC Radio 5 Live series called *For God's Sake*, Jenkins has told presenter Ted Harrison that the Blessing is 'a form of manipulation … which reinforces the superstitious side of religion.' He has added that it is 'increasingly clear this cannot be the work of the Holy Spirit, who is the vehicle of God in Jesus who loves us and treats us with respect'.[13]

Also today, the *Church of England Newspaper* claims that attendances at the recent ten-day tour of Britain by John Arnott have not been as high as expected. In a review of the two conferences which have comprised the tour – the 'Catch the Fire' event in Telford and the 'Waves of the Spirit' gathering in Bournemouth – *CEN* states that 'despite numbers that most church groups would be more than happy with, organisers still said they believed the split with Vineyard had affected numbers'. Arnott himself is quoted on the divide: 'It was a real blow to what we were about,' he reflects. 'The whole thrust of Vineyard was about grace and mercy, yet here we are with this split in our own backyard.' Whereas disagreement on the manifestations had been 'one on the scale' for TAV, he suggests, it had turned out to be '10 on the scale' as far as Wimber and the AVC Board were concerned: 'We did everything to try to negotiate, but it went nowhere.'

Saturday 17th February 1996

Andrew Boyd reports for *New Christian Herald* on the recent 'Waves of the Spirit' conference in Bournemouth. John Arnott is quoted as having told the two thousand or so delegates present: 'I believe that we are heading for the greatest harvest the world has ever seen … This is not manipulation. Manipulation and hysteria have never yet changed a life.' Echoing the title of his new book (30th December 1995), Arnott has insisted that 'it isn't the Toronto Blessing; it's the Father's Blessing'. Conference host Peter Lawrence has added: 'I would love to see this as a beginning of turning our godless country around. I believe it will lead to something if Christians receive it. If they don't, it will fade and go away.'

The fading of the Blessing is something which leading Toronto critic Clifford Hill now perceives as *already* in process. He tells Boyd that he thinks 'the phenomena is dying out [sic]'. Even so, Hill here strikes a somewhat more conciliatory tone than in his previous pronouncements on TTB: 'We are all brothers and sisters who love the Lord. We have to stop judging one another. Because both sides are sincere the Lord will find a way of bringing us back together.'

Also apparently softening his tone on Toronto is Tony Higton. Boyd confirms that despite his previously-expressed reservations, the Hawkwell vicar attended the Bournemouth gathering and has, by his own admission, since undergone 'a major change of understanding' which has led him to realise that he has had ' a lot of wrong attitudes'. Higton adds:

> After listening to John Arnott, who has been greatly maligned, focusing for an hour on the cross – unless the devil's got converted that can't be anything other than a man of God inspired by the Holy Spirit. What we are seeing is primarily of God. I would like to think that the divisions are going to be healed. I don't want any fewer brothers or sisters in Christ than God has children.

Higton will expand on his shift of perspective in an interview for The *Church of England Newspaper* on 22nd March.

Seemingly aware of the cooling of hostility evident in Hill and Higton, Gerald Coates tells Boyd: 'We have had many helpful discussions under the auspices of the Evangelical Alliance. And while I don't think we are going to change one another's minds, there is more of a softness of heart as we listen to one another.'[14]

Sunday 18th February 1996

David Jenkins' denunciation of TTB as 'pure psychological violence' (recorded on 9th February), is broadcast at 8pm on the BBC Radio 5 Live programme *For God's Sake*.

Saturday 24th February 1996

Dave Roberts summarises the key theological issues which have arisen so far in relation to TTB. The main sources for his two-page review, all discussed above, are Bill Jackson's Champaign Vineyard paper 'What in the World is Happening to Us?', Mark Stibbe's *Times of Refreshing*, David Pawson's *Is the Blessing Biblical?* and Clifford Hill et al's *Blessing the Church?*[15] He also quotes from a recently published pamphlet written by Metro Vineyard Kansas leaders Mike Bickle and Michael Sullivant, explaining the Vineyard doctrine of the 'manifest presence of God'.[16] Additional comments are quoted from magazine articles penned by Terry Virgo, David Pytches and others. In essence, writes Roberts, four main questions have dominated the debate:

- How should the Bible be interpreted in the wake of the Blessing?
- What is the role of the Holy Spirit in the physical manifestations?
- Is there a danger that the person of the Holy Spirit is being depersonalised in some pro-Blessing circles?
- What is the nature of revival anyway?

Roberts does not seek to take sides in his review, but instead simply presents the arguments one way and the other on each of these four points.[17]

The close of February also sees *Prophecy Today*'s Clifford Hill issue an Editorial Statement on TTB in the wake of the split between AVC and the Toronto Airport church. The Statement is written on behalf of the whole *Prophecy Today* Board and begins by expressing concern about 'the use of inappropriate proof-texting to justify the Toronto phenomena on biblical grounds', particularly in relation to animal behaviour and 'drunkenness'. Asserting that TTB is 'clearly associated' with 'Latter Rain belief and an end-time revival based on signs and wonders', Hill goes on to deny that these can be supported from the Bible. He also highlights a problem of 'basic principle' with respect to hermeneutics, stating, 'we regard the attempt to formulate doctrine on the basis of experience as highly dangerous'. Indeed, Hill avers, 'We have been increasingly concerned at what appears to be a general drift away from biblical standards in the church and we believe that the preoccupation with experience among charismatics has weakened evangelical witness in the nation at the very time when biblical truth is being rejected by an increasingly secularised nation.'

Specifically in relation to the role played by the Evangelical Alliance in the Blessing debate, Hill is noticeably unimpressed:

> We have been disappointed that the Evangelical Alliance has not taken a firm stand on the centrality of scripture in all matters of faith and practice as applied to the Toronto Blessing. We understand their desire for unity, especially in this 150th anniversary. But unless unity is based upon truth, it will be built upon a foundation that cannot last. Both privately and publicly we have urged the EA to affirm that the Bible is the final authority in judging the validity of the Toronto experience yet as far as we are aware this has not been made unequivocally clear.

Despite these comments, the Editorial proceeds to suggest that the 'Toronto wave is ebbing'. People, it observes, 'no longer flock to "receiving" meetings', and 'the prophecies of a great revival remain unfulfilled'. Furthermore, the *Prophecy Today* Board commends John Wimber for his expulsion of the Toronto Airport fellowship, stating that he has 'opted for biblical truth above unity at any price'.[18]

At this juncture, too, the Assemblies of God magazine *Joy* prints an article by Steve Bell which aims to bring readers up to date with developments at TACF. He records that some 700,000 visitors have attended the church over the last 23 months, '400,000 of whom' have not been Canadians. Contrary to some reports, he also notes a distinct 'lack of hype' with 'no flashy preaching, no dominant personality, nothing at all cultic or weird'. In fact, he adds, 'there is a clearly stated policy not to "own", "manipulate" or "shape" the renewal in any way.' Regretting the controversy which has arisen following the parting of TACF from AVC, he reflects that 'the anointing has been on me ever since my visit as a galvaniser in my full-time Christian work.'[19]

Sunday 3rd March 1996

In a three-page photo-feature for *The Observer's* Life Magazine, John Sweeney reports on last month's 'Catch the Fire' conference in Telford (3rd February 1996). Essaying a mordant wit, Sweeny remarks that John Arnott has 'become a wow with Christian fundamentalist evangelicals who want to feel the Good Lord inside them personally'. Adopting present-tense description for effect, he adds: 'The punters are mainly ordinary people, though there are a number of misfits and 'headbangers' – believers who display their absorption by the Holy Spirit by shaking their heads in the air.' As some begin to laugh and fall to the floor, Sweeny comments that 'this is how the anabaptist heretics used to behave before the Inquisition sorted them out'. Clearly uncomfortable with proceedings, he describes 'a huge, silent pressure to conform, to go with the wave, to swim with the mood'. This feeling is exacerbated, he says, when a woman volunteers that her stepfather abused her emotionally and sexually. 'There are hundreds of children around', writes Sweeny; 'It strikes me that this, if true, is not the best possible arena to talk through a private agony. But such priggish sensibility is out of place in the Toronto Blessing, where anything Godly goes.'

Unmoved by John Arnott's sermon on Matthew 13:33, Sweeny and his photographer retire to the bar. Sweeny reflects: 'I felt a prickly unease at the vulnerability of the believers, especially the young. As soon as they collapsed, they seemed entirely at the mercy of their strokers [Sweeny's term for members of the prayer team], despite the reassuring words offered by those at the top of the Blessing organisation.' In closing, Sweeny turns for guidance to those who have established themselves as Toronto critics. He quotes Hank Hanegraff's warning that TTB could be 'a road to the occult' (11th September 1995), and cites Clifford Hill as having dubbed Toronto-style services 'voodoo worship'. He claims that despite such brickbats, 'the Toronto Blessing [presumably TACF] now has a staff of 80, a $6 million budget and 45 missionaries around the world to spread the gospel of renewal'. His own final reaction remains hostile: 'I felt I had wandered inside a bizarre mass psychosis', he recalls, 'which to resist required an astonishing degree of emotional energy.'[20]

Friday 22nd March 1996

Explaining the 'change of heart' on Toronto that he announced following the Bournemouth 'Waves of the Spirit' conference (17th February 1996), Tony Higton tells The *Church of England Newspaper* that TTB has 'precipitated a theological rethink'. He continues: 'It was disturbing. I found myself asking had I got it wrong?' In fact, Higton reveals that this 'paradigm shift' has evolved over the past nine months, and has extended well beyond his position on the Blessing. He has gone so far as to apologise to the Archbishop of Canterbury for the way he has campaigned on various issues in the past, admitting that he has been too legalistic and judgemental. While upholding the content of his high-profile defences of traditional morality and Anglican doctrine, Higton now admits that his combative style has become counterproductive. 'I have transferred the aggressive communication of the first century, which was effective in a biblical culture, into a twentieth-century Anglican setting ... I wasn't negative in my heart [but] the negativism and judgmentalism of my public utterances was undermining the effect I had on the Church.'[21]

Saturday 30th March 1996

Recounting last month's 'Catch the Fire' conference in Bournemouth, *Alpha* feature writer Clive Price reports John Arnott as having told delegates, 'God works through authority, and he also works through power ... I believe there is tremendous power about to be released ... If we're faithful with a little, he's bound to give us more!' In an apparent reference to the rift with AVC, Arnott also told delegates that Christian 'Lone Rangers' were unhelpful, and that he himself was determined to stay 'teachable and accountable' in ministry. Even so, writes Price, the TACF leader was still ready to challenge the more vitriolic of his detractors: 'You need to know what the greatest deception is', he said, 'and that's failing to recognise a move of God when it comes through.' [22]

In the same feature, Price interviews John Arnott face-to-face. Arnott brings him up to date on relations with AVC. He says that he has had 'an apology of sorts' from John Wimber, and that 'there is a bit of dialogue going on'. Still, he adds, 'It wasn't something that the Vineyard movement wanted. I think there were a few leaders at the top that said, "We're much more conservative than they are, and we think we'll feel better if they were out". It's too bad it wasn't handled a lot more congenially and mercifully.' Going on to explain how TACF is implementing 'an independent church model that has outside senior leaders having input and counsel into what we're doing', Arnott adds, 'We have many, many friends in the Body of Christ who have offered to [help] ... We are continuing to interact with the Vineyard. We want to bring the thing to closure so there aren't any loose ends and suspicions.' Eschewing the idea that he might become a 'loose cannon', Arnott tells Price that he hopes TACF might be accorded 'friend of the Vineyard' status in due course.[23]

Returning to TTB itself, Arnott comments on the controversy surrounding animal behaviour. 'There isn't a problem with animal noises,' he insists; 'I've seen two people that I could honestly say have barked, and I've seen maybe three or four more that I could honestly say were roaring like a lion. So anything that could honestly, objectively be called an animal noise is like one in 100,000.' Despite this, Arnott affirms that such activities, while enjoying no direct endorsement from Scripture, are at least 'hinted at', and are certainly not forbidden. Far more common, in his perception, however, are the expression of 'birth pains': 'We have seen that several times', he says, 'and I think you're getting into travailing in prayer – with groanings that cannot be uttered, as the Bible says' [Rom. 8:26].

Meanwhile, Price reports that one of Arnott's team, Stacey Campbell, gave the Bournemouth delegates a prophecy that urged the UK church to recover the power of the blood of Christ, as it reaches out to those in 'the darkest part' of society. 'His arm is not so short that it cannot save England,' she said.[24]

Price also confirms that Arnott has written a new book, barely four months after his last, *The Father's Blessing*. Entitled *Keep the Fire*, it has just been published by HarperCollins.[25] The book recounts the development of TTB, from Arnott's early friendship with Benny Hinn, through his contact with leaders of the 'Argentinian revival' and Randy Clark's visit in January 1994, up to the end of 1995. Arnott devotes a whole chapter to 'animal behaviour', and examines other contentious aspects of the Blessing. He also reports that TACF has now planted three new churches and has established a Ministry Training School to 'spread the fire'.[26]

Around this time also, Hodder & Stoughton publish *Together We Stand* – a study of evangelical convictions, unity and vision jointly authored by Evangelical Alliance Director General Clive Calver and prominent TB proponent Rob Warner. The book does not discuss TTB in any depth, but in a chapter entitled 'Together for Truth', Calver writes that divisions over the Blessing 'have only highlighted what many have suspected for a long time, that evangelicals would concentrate on unity while they were declining, [but] when growth came it would be accompanied by the danger of fragmentation.'[27] The book does include, as an Appendix, the Alliance's Euston Statement of December 1994 (the full text of the Euston Statement is given in Part III).[28]

Tuesday 7th May 1996

The Darlington-based Evangelical Press publish an extensive critique of TTB by the Canadian Grace Baptist Eric E. Wright. Entitled *Strange Fire?*, Wright's book can claim to be the lengthiest and most thoroughly documented study of the movement published so far. For all its detail, however, its analysis is unashamedly driven by Wright's cessationism, which predisposes him to a decidedly unsympathetic view, not only of TTB as such, but of the charismatic movement in general.

Although Wright makes his own position clear from the outset, he points out that even within the Vineyard network, there have been divergent interpretations of TTB.[29] These observations have by now, of course, been borne out by the disengagement of the Toronto Airport church from AVC. Wright's publication schedule has just about allowed him to report this,[30] but a good deal of his critique is focused on the 'signs and wonders' movement in general, with Toronto functioning as a paradigm case.

Although he rejects the accusation that the Vineyard is heretical or a cult, Wright suggests that it is 'eroding biblical authority and sufficiency' through its emphasis on 'pragmatic experience, physical manifestations, inner impressions of guidance, testimonies [and] words of revelation'. He also criticises TTB especially, for reducing Christ to a 'background ... ethereal, undescribed figure', who is accorded significantly less attention than the Holy Spirit. On 'power healing', Wright disputes that the 'miracles' claimed by Wimber and others have a substantial empirical basis, assigning most of them to 'psychological suggestion'. On the now familiar precedents claimed from Jonathan Edwards, he points out that, like himself, the great revivalist actually believed in the cessation of supernatural gifts with the apostles. Nor is Wright enamoured of the 'tempestuous' worship style he has encountered at TACF and other 'Third Wave' churches, seeing it as in contravention of Paul's injunction to peace and order (1 Cor. 14:33). As for Vineyard ecclesiology, Wright detects elements of sectarianism and elitism:

> No matter how hard leaders of 'Third Wave Churches' try to declare their love for the whole body of Christ, it is clear that those of us who are not on their wavelength represent an inferior brand of the Christian faith. They imply that we have a defective relationship with the Spirit. We don't have 'the anointing'. We don't have 'power'. We cripple evangelism by failing to promote 'signs and wonders'. This movement fosters the classic charismatic caste system.[31]

Later in the book, Wright investigates alleged parallels with hypnotism; he concludes that the physical phenomena foregrounded in TTB 'correspond almost exactly with the results of hypnotism'. The Holy Spirit, he contends, is being reduced to a commodity in a manner that justifies parallels with occult, new age and psychologically suggestional techniques.[32] By contrast, says Wright, renewal and revival should now be focused on Christ-centred preaching, repentance, holiness, genuine unity in truth, sound doctrine and a proper conduct of the sacraments. Explaining the title of his book, he goes on to conclude in the following terms:

> Perhaps the Vineyard and the Toronto Blessing will be the burr under the saddle of evangelicalism that will provoke us to renewed passion for the things of God. Too many evangelicals are complacent, contented and lethargic. The salt is not very salty. The light is dim. But we must not let the Prince of Darkness persuade us that the pursuit of manifestations will cause the flame of witness to flare. All that will do is kindle strange fire [Num. 3:4] ...

> Would I encourage my friends to go to Toronto to seek the 'blessing'? Would I want my family or the church at large to drink at the Vineyard fountain? Is their vision of the evangelical landscape the vision I have for my grandchildren? Decidedly not! Instead, may the light of genuine revival illumine our benighted age, and may a passion for biblical holiness burn within.[33]

Saturday 11th May 1996

In *The Times* Ruth Gledhill reports Angie Golding's claim that she has been denied confirmation at St Mark's, Broadwater Down, Kent because she would not attend an Alpha course. The reason she gives for refusing to take part in the course is that she could not bring herself to 'snort like a pig and bark like a dog' on a programme which she feels is a 'brainwashing' exercise influenced by TTB. Fourteen members of the church have, writes Gledhill, left with Golding to form a new fellowship of their own. Rev Francis Cumberlege, the vicar, denies that the Alpha course has been compulsory for confirmands; he says that the problem has arisen from a 'misunderstanding'. Ruth Gledhill has also spoken to Holy Trinity Press Officer Mark Elsdon-Dew about the Toronto dimension of Alpha. He tells her that Alpha includes three lectures on the Holy Spirit, and that this section of the course 'affects different people in different ways'. He rejects the suggestion that people on the course are compelled to do anything 'weird or fanciful', and adds that some 250,000 will be doing the course this year, with 'overwhelming support' from church leaders and theologians.[34]

Saturday 22nd June 1996

Meeting in Blackpool, the Methodist Conference votes to receive and commend for study the report of its Faith and Order Committee on TTB (the Conclusions and Recommendations of the Methodist Report are printed in full in Part III). Commissioned at last year's conference, the text has been written by an 18-member working group assembled after Faith and Order Secretary Neil Dixon canvassed for participants and correspondents in the *Methodist Recorder* (cf. 29th June, 13th July 1995).

Having rehearsed the origins and development of TTB up to the breach between AVC and the Toronto Airport church, the working group's document recognises that complementary work is being undertaken on the movement by other Christian bodies, including the Evangelical Alliance. It then moves on to analyse the letters it has received in response to Neil Dixon's original request for comment. Over 26% of letters were from ministers, it states, '82% [of which] were broadly supportive of the "Blessing", and 18% non-supportive'. More than 73% of letters were from lay people, 'of whom approximately 65% were broadly supportive and 35% non-supportive'.[35] In both positive and negative submissions, however, the report notes substantial reference to 'the relationship of the manifestations to biblical teaching on the nature and work of the Holy Spirit' and to 'the link with the ministry of the Wesleys and the subsequent history of the Methodist Church'.[36]

After thorough sections on pneumatology, discernment and the theology of blessing, the report proceeds to offer biblical perspectives on the manifestations associated with TTB. These perspectives are informed, state the authors, by the so-called 'Wesleyan quadrilateral', i.e. by 'an appropriate relationship between Scripture, tradition, experience and reason'. On falling, the report suggests that although several characters fell in Scripture, they generally did so 'face down' in awe of God, whereas 'that is not always the case today'. In Scripture, it states, 'the falling was a spontaneous action', while 'today carpets and catchers are often provided in advance', although 'of course this need not deny the validity of the experience.' On laughter, the authors define the Bible as referring to both 'holy joy at the goodness of God' and also 'the laughter of scorn', but warn on the basis of James 4:9 that 'shallow or inappropriate laughter is not pleasing to God.'[37] Predictably, however, it is animal noises which are identified as 'the most controversial' of all the 'Toronto' phenomena. Noting that such expressions 'lack clear scriptural precedent', the report nonetheless allows that 'when such "growling" has a beneficial effect, such as "empowering", or "releasing", it might perhaps be justified'. Even so, it adds, 'serious questions remain about an experience which some may perceive as degrading or humiliating to God's people'.[38]

On historical precedents, the working group advises that 'it is always risky to draw historical parallels, because each age and generation has its own characteristics'. Still, it accepts, 'the kind of physical experiences associated with the 'Toronto Blessing' seem similar to numerous instances in the history of the Church, not least within Methodism'. Specifically, it acknowledges that together with George Whitefield, John Wesley certainly witnessed such phenomena in his meetings. Yet it recalls that 'the short-lived nature of the phenomena accompanying revival underlined for John Wesley the view that such movements would be a "rope of sand" unless people used the normal means of grace – the Bible, prayer, the Lord's Supper, 'Christian Conference' and fasting, and what he called 'prudential means of grace' [which] included preaching services, love feasts, watchnight, covenant, band meetings, class meetings.'[39]

Echoing the thesis originally proposed in July 1995 by one of its members, Philip Richter,[40] the working group considers the sociological context of TTB. It concludes:

> The form taken by the 'Blessing' … fits in with changing attitudes to bodily inhibi-
> tion in our late capitalist society where more ascetic 'work ethic' attitudes have been
> supplanted. The 'Blessing' also fits within the context of modern relativism in being
> a form of religious experience that needs little or no verbalization. This helps to over-
> come the difficulties faced by evangelicals (in common with all other Christians) in
> making their gospel intelligible to more than a minority in contemporary society, or
> even in finding it totally plausible themselves.[41]

Psychologically, they add that some have regarded it as an instance of 'dissociation', i.e. 'a process or reaction in which the different elements of the mind, normally experienced or expressed simultaneously, become split off and separated
from one another'. This, they note, is frequently seen in ecstatic religion and is
not unique to Christianity. In dissociative states, they point out, 'people can
think, feel or do certain things which seem "out of character" and can be experienced as "not me" (e.g. "this is of God"), when in fact they are generated
by a split-off part of the self'. As to whether such a process is good or bad, the
working group acknowledges that it can be prone to manipulation, but that it
is not intrinsically inimical to authentic Christian discipleship. 'If, as seems likely', the authors say, 'there has in some cases been genuine growth and a closer

walk with Christ as a result of the "Toronto Blessing", then we can all be thankful that God is able to bring good out of all situations, especially where the intention (as it undoubtedly mostly is) is sincere.'[42]

In its conclusions, the report recognises that TTB has 'enabled many people to feel a renewed sense of the love and presence of God' and notes that it has revealed a deep yearning among many Methodists for an integrated spirituality. Even so, the working group is clear that the Blessing must be biblically scrutinised in all its aspects, not least because it has been prone to pride, manipulation, insensitivity, self-righteousness and on occasion, 'possibly evil influences'.[43] Appealing to Wesley's reputation as a 'reasonable enthusiast', the report recommends TTB be taken seriously by Methodists as a whole, so that they might better be able to 'distinguish between external manifestations, which may indeed be disturbing, and the possibility that there is an inner catharsis whose lasting effects are beneficial and to be welcomed'. As part of this process, it urges 'a much more deliberate teaching and preaching programme on the doctrine and work of the Holy Spirit', so that 'charismatic and non-charismatic Christians [might] increasingly appreciate each other's strengths, as well as weaknesses'.[44]

Saturday 29th June 1996
The July issue of *Alpha* magazine reprints John Stott's comments on TTB, originally given as part of his interview with Roy McCloughry for the September 1995 edition of *Third Way* (30th September 1995).[45]

Sunday 30th June – Thursday 4th July 1996
King's Church, Slough, which has become a prominent focus for TTB, hosts a World Fire conference at the King's Centre. Speakers include King's Church team leader Wesley Richards, Ken Gott of Sunderland Christian Centre and David Holden of New Frontiers International. Leaders have also travelled to the event from Russia, Portugal, Spain, France and the USA. Richards announces, 'We are at a strategic phase in the current renewal. Either it now becomes institutionalised and self-indulgent, or it provides a major thrust of powerful Christian witness in Britain and beyond.'[46]

Friday 16th August 1996
Writing to the Birmingham area newspaper *Solihull News*, Alec Taylor, minister of Chelmsley Wood Reformed Baptist Church, compares the activities of the controversial Central Church of Christ to practices associated with TTB. He is also unhappy that the Evangelical Alliance has shown markedly more openness to the latter than the former:

> … many of those sheltering under the umbrella of the Evangelical Alliance … are no better than the Central Church of Christ. Some Anglican and Baptist churches have taken on extreme charismatic practices and the Evangelical Alliance has done nothing to discourage them. Many people have been left severely traumatised by the use

in these churches of occult techniques such as healing of the memories and the Toronto Blessing ... The so-called Toronto Blessing has nothing to do with Christianity. True Christianity does not cause us to behave or sound like animals! ... Paul specifically warns us that all things must be done decently and in order in our church services and that if his advice is ignored, unbelieving visitors to our churches would think we were out of our mind. All that glisters is not gold and all that calls itself evangelical is not evangelical.[47]

Saturday 26th October 1996

Rob Warner responds to John Stott's criticisms of TTB (cf. 30th September 1995, 29th June 1996). In the October issue of *Alpha* he answers Stott's three key reservations in turn.

On the charge that the Toronto movement is 'anti-intellectual', Warner complains that Stott has based this assertion on a single quote from one leader who apparently told people not to analyse what was happening. By contrast, writes Warner, TTB has in fact evolved from 'several parallel eruptions of the divine presence in the early months of 1994'. No individual or church served as the sole 'mediator' of the Blessing, contends Warner, and it is thus wrong to tar the whole with the blight of 'illuminism'. Warner himself, who has been a high-profile advocate and interpreter of TTB from early on, unequivocally rejects anti-intellectualism as 'a wretched distortion of the Christian gospel', but stresses that no sector of the evangelical world is immune from it, whether charismatic or non-charismatic, Calvinist, Arminian, Anglican or Free Church.

Despite all this, Warner adds that there is an 'equal and opposite excess' about which evangelicals should be wary. 'Just as some drift into the dream world of illuminism', he writes, 'others are confined within an anti-supernatural rationalism.' If anyone says 'Don't evaluate', Warner agrees, 'they're failing to be biblical'; yet 'the failure is just as great among those who cannot cope with the possibility of God moving in power today'.

On Stott's trenchant opposition to animal noises, Warner concedes that these can become chaotic and unedifying, but is not prepared to exclude them altogether. Pointing out that prophets like Isaiah and Ezekiel sometimes 'used their bodies as prophetic symbols, acting out the Word of the Lord', Warner suggests that 'we ... need to draw a distinction between behaving as no more than an animal – which can only be demeaning – and animal-like behaviour'. The Bible, he continues, 'is full of metaphors that derive from the animal world: we shall rise up on wings like eagles (Isa. 40:31), and Jesus likens his compassion for Jerusalem to a hen protecting her chicks (Mt. 23:37)'. And just as there are literary metaphors such as these, he argues, 'there are also visual and physical metaphors in the language of drama, mime and dance'. Warner also finds potential warrant for some such activity in Paul's reference to 'groans that words cannot express' in Romans 8:26.

Finally, where Stott has asserted that the Bible endorses only falling forwards rather than backwards, Warner suggests that this is a misleading polarisation. Many involved in TTB, he attests, have been prostrating themselves before God in reverence, even while others have been collapsing on their backs. Paul, he says, involuntarily crashed to the ground in Acts 9:3,4, and John fell as though dead on seeing the ascended Christ (Rev. 1:17). 'There's no suggestion that this ... kind of falling was composed, controlled and considered. We're not told whether Paul and John fell forwards, for the simple reason that it's irrelevant. If the acid test of an authentic falling were whether it was forwards or backwards, the Bible would expressly tell us so. The Bible's silence means that to propose such a test is unjustifiable for thinking evangelicals.'[48]

Friday 8th November 1996

New Frontiers leader Terry Virgo publishes *A People Prepared*, his reflection on TTB and its implications. Through 190 or so pages, Virgo seeks to apply the fruits of the Blessing to a broader agenda which takes in church growth strategy, prayer, worship, leadership and world mission. He is clear, though, that TTB has provided a new impetus for such things: 'I have never seen such radical changes in people who were previously formal and indifferent in their church-going. Now they are so thrilled with God, and particularly that he has come so near to them, that their personal communion with Christ has been transformed.'[49]

Virgo concludes by stating his belief that 'revival is coming to our land', but adds that 'revival is not as straightforward as people think'. It is often spoken against, he says, and will present tremendous challenges to the Church. 'Days of enormous upheaval lie ahead for the church,' he writes; 'I believe that much that has been traditionally part of church life will feel fresh shakings.'[50]

Monday 11th – Wednesday 13th November 1996

The Evangelical Alliance (UK) convenes an Assembly of Evangelicals at the Bournemouth International Centre to mark its 150th anniversary. Discussion of TTB runs through various sessions, but in his opening night address to delegates, Alliance Director General Clive Calver prefers to recall a recent trip he has made to Pensacola, Florida. Since 18th June last year, the Brownsville Assembly in the city has attracted hundreds of thousands of people to its meetings, which have featured a mix of traditional Pentecostal preaching and Toronto-style manifestations, and which have had a significant effect on the wider community. Calver says:

> I was in Brownsville, Florida and I was lost! I stopped at a Pensacola supermarket and asked a very ordinary man, 'Sorry to bother you, I'm looking for a church.' Back came the immediate reply, 'Ah, you'll mean the Assemblies of God. It's just five blocks down – just look for the cars.' I was to discover a queue of over a thousand people, both Christian and non-Christian, waiting to attend a service that would not begin for over two-and-a-half hours.
>
> It is hard to find words to describe the experience. Here was Pentecostal exuberance coupled with signs and wonders; 65,000 registered conversions in the space of 14

months; people running to the front, at 11.00pm after a four hour service, to give their lives to Christ; an uncompromising message stressing hell, the need for personal morality and the promise of forgiveness.

At Brownsville the County Sheriff visited a youth meeting to find a huge container stacked with illegal substances, weapons, pornographic magazines etc., which had been 'donated' by the audience that night! His comment was honest: 'Up till now I thought that the major impact of this on the community lay in the traffic jams – now I know different!'

Over the next weeks and months, Pensacola will attract many more British visitors, and will begin to attract the attention of the UK Christian press.

Thursday 28th November 1996

Ian McFarlane, the Minister of Bookham Baptist Church who was one of the first leaders in Britain to experience TTB (10th June 1994), reports for the *Baptist Times* on a visit made earlier this month to Pensacola (cf.18th June, 11th-13th November 1995). He first encountered the Pensacola phenomenon, he writes, through a video shown at Stoneleigh Bible Week in the past summer. One filmed testimony from the Assembly, says McFarlane, 'contained a deep heart cry to recognise the urgent need for evangelism and the anguish of those who were in darkness'. This cry, he says, 'swept through' Stoneleigh and deeply affected the leaders there: 'many of us spent a long time in tears and deep prayer for the lost'. Although McFarlane attests that he had never desired to go to TAV, 'this was different'. At Pensacola, he recalls, 'hundreds were coming to faith, not just being refreshed'.

McFarlane reflects that on arriving at the Brownsville Assembly, he encountered what was in many ways typical American Pentecostal preaching and worship. Still, he adds, 'we were led into the presence of God with sensitivity and care and there were many moments of breathtaking encounter with the awesome holiness of God'. Just as evangelist Steve Hill had helped to catalyse the Pensacola renewal after an encounter with TTB at Holy Trinity, Brompton, (18th June 1995), so McFarlane reports having been invited to 'get into the river' – an injunction based on a favourite Toronto metaphor from Ezekiel 47 (cf. 29th October 1994, 10th June 1995). Also echoing Toronto, McFarlane concludes:

> We shed many tears in confession and compassion for the lost; we laughed at times till it hurt; we rested in the presence of the glory of God. We certainly look to God to prepare us and our churches for a mighty work of revival that will be sustained by a call to holiness, purity and intercession.[51]

Saturday 25th January 1997

Ben Davies reports for the February edition of *Renewal* magazine on a six day visit he has recently paid to Pensacola. Despite having been to TAV twice, he notes 'some marked differences' between it the Brownsville Assemblies of God church. 'The preaching immediately struck me as very different. It changed me as I sat listening. The emphasis throughout was on the holiness of God, which made sin unbearable, and on the Cross and Jesus' shed blood. It took me back to the sermons I heard as a boy in Wales. The difference now was the anointing of he Holy Spirit. The difference too was that Steve Hill, the evangelist, was specific. He spoke in concrete terms, not conceptually. He named sins ... There was not so much an appeal to repent as a command.'[52]

Wednesday 29th January 1997

New Zealand Christian newspaper *Challenge Weekly* interviews Pensacola evangelist Steve Hill about physical manifestations at the Brownsville Assemblies of God. He comments:

> The Lord is welcome in this place to do anything he wants. But there is a balance here. They receive the gospel, they receive the cross, the blood. When the manifestations come, I welcome the manifestations, but I don't major on minors. This last days awakening, mark these words – I'm not a prophet, this is not a prophecy – but this is what is going to happen. This awakening is going to shake this country, the power is going to come down.

> I'm also a youth evangelist, and we are dealing with a culture that may not be demon-possessed, but they are possessed by demons. They are consumed with demonic warfare 24 hours a day. They have seen the power of Satan at work. You watch any rock concert, the frenzy, the fire, the pull, the enthusiasm that's there. We talk about the power of God. We sing, 'All Hail the Power of Jesus' Name', and they're going, 'Where is it?' They want to believe, but they see mum and dad are limp, weak and they respond, 'Where is the power? Mom, you're popping valium and prozac and everything else and you're talking about the power of God? Give me a break, Momma.' And so they come into this meeting, the punkers [sic] come in here, every age, every kind of person in the world comes into this meeting and they are hit by the power of God. Undeniably swept off their feet by the power of God and they basically by the hundreds say, 'What must I do to be saved?'[53]

Monday 3rd March 1997

MacMillan publish TAV pastor Guy Chevreau's sequel to his 1994 study *Catch the Fire*. Entitled *Share the Fire*, the new book seeks to define a model of 'grace-based evangelism' which is complementary to TTB. This involves relying on the Holy Spirit for guidance as to the appropriate approach for sharing the gospel with each individual. Also, however, it is placed within a broader eschatological schema:

> Obviously not all of us are called to the nations. But this present outpouring of God's Spirit *is* preparing his Church for the end-time harvest, whenever the Lord sovereignly calls it in. That *is* the eschatological horizon towards which we are moving ...

[It] doesn't mean that twos and threes will be added to our churches on a given Sunday. It doesn't mean that 20 or 30 new believers will be added in a single week. Like the early Church, we may well see 3,000 come to the Lord in a given day … This kind of growth will only be assimilated by a church that is completely dependent, completely yielded, completely attentive and completely abandoned to, and unashamed of, whatever the Spirit calls forth, wherever, and whenever the Lord calls.[54]

At this time also, the Eastbourne-based publisher Day One launch *The Signs and Wonders Movement – Exposed*. Edited by Peter Glover, this contains various essays by different contributors. The book as a whole stands as a wide-ranging attack on Third Wave and Word Faith-style ministries, but contains an article on TTB by former Queen's Road Baptist Church pastor Chris Hand.

In this article, Hand repeats and extends criticisms made in the piece he wrote for *Prophecy Today* in the autumn (28th October 1995). Recalling his experience as pastoral assistant at Queen's Road Baptist Church, Hand complains that the behaviour of the congregation there in mid-late 1994 was culpable of 'profaning the holiness of the Lord and the dignity of his Church'. After dealing with his own 'shocked state of mind', he says, 'it was time to part company'. Beyond this immediate crisis, however, Hand admits to having begun to question the Third Wave some time before the arrival of TTB: 'The accounts in Acts did not indicate widespread "signs and wonders" beyond the apostolic company. New Testament healings and works were vastly superior to those I had witnessed. I was also compelled to admit that there was no great change in my own spiritual life stemming from my various experiences. "Holy laughter", being "slain in the Spirit", and supposed deliverance, had not produced greater holiness or effectiveness.'[55]

Hand is now convinced, he writes, that TTB is 'non-evangelical' in practice, despite retaining evangelical terminology. Indeed, he contends that this disjunction between language and reality has become endemic within evangelicalism as a whole.[56] He goes on to question the 'fruit' which has been claimed, doubting figures on conversion and suggesting that the division which TTB has wrought may actually result in a net decline.[57]

Hand proceeds to liken the 'ambient culture' of Toronto-style meetings, with their 'loud music', public demonstrations of physical phenomena and stress on feeling rather than reason, to 'the methods of hypnotists'. Decrying the tendency of TTB to produce 'altered states of consciousness', Hand adds that 'these practices are not to be found in Scripture. The Lord Jesus never used them, neither did the apostles, neither any of the prophets of the Old Testament. They are not how the Lord reveals himself or requires people to worship him.'[58]

Hand concludes by confirming that he has now 'come home' to what he calls 'Reformed evangelical doctrine about the Church [and] about Scripture'. Applying such doctrine to TTB, he concludes:

No new teachings or revelations are needed as the Reformers and Puritans have been this way before. Our generation is privileged above any other in the opportunity it has to learn from their insights. Many churches need to recognise that they have been sold a pale imitation of evangelicalism. Their practice no longer matches up to their evangelical creed. Their quiet, subtle but wholesale 'paradigm shift' has been taking place and we need to return to the ancient paths.[59]

On this date too, *Christianity Today* compares and contrasts the respective outpourings in Toronto and Pensacola. Despite the fact that 'hundreds of people are at times sprawled seemingly unconscious on the church's carpeted floor', and notwithstanding the point that 'some of the [Pensacola] revival's principal players have passed through the Toronto Airport Christian Fellowship', *CT* emphasises that 'Pensacola is a much more sober affair.' It goes on:

Instead of Toronto's giddiness and proclivity for unusual signs, the mood at Brownsville Assembly is somber, even penitential. There is more emphasis on forgiveness than filling, more sermons on repentance than rejoicing. Brownsville worshippers are discouraged from being highly emotional or demonstrative. In some cases, [Pastor John Kilpatrick] pleads from the pulpit for worshippers to remain calm, as he did at a recent service, saying, 'No one draw attention to yourself. No one fracture this holy moment.' In other cases, ushers escort the overly exuberant from the sanctuary.[60]

In addition, the report now puts the number of converts and repentant backsliders produced from Brownsville since last June at 86,000, as compared with the 63,000 noted by Clive Calver in his Evangelical Alliance Assembly address on 11th November. This emphasis on soul-winning has been a key factor, says *CT*, in leading various commentators to place the Pensacola movement in the mainstream of American religious history. Vinson Synan of Regent University Divinity School is quoted: 'Brownsville', he says, 'with its emphasis on conversion and people weeping over conviction of sin, seems to be a revival in the long tradition of American native revivals dating back to the preaching of Jonathan Edwards. There's a lot of heavy preaching on sin, repentance, conversion, and holiness. And there's a lot more weeping and wailing over sin than there are so-called exotic manifestations.'

The report also notes that the Assemblies of God denomination has readily endorsed the new outpouring. 'We are very comfortable with what's happening here,' says AOG Assistant General Superintendent Charles Crabtree. 'They have maintained doctrinal purity throughout. They allow a freedom of the Spirit, but at the same time, there's a point where they deal with excesses.' This response contrasts with the somewhat lukewarm reaction to TTB that was evident at the 17th World Conference of Pentecostals in Jerusalem in October 1995 (cf. 29th October 1995).[61]

Friday 21st March 1997
The *Church Times* reports that a 12 year-old boy was so traumatised at a Toronto-style church weekend that he could not eat for 24 hours and spoke

only in monosyllables. The boy's mother, writing under an assumed name, says that he lost consciousness after two of the church's leaders laid hands on him and 'invoked the Toronto Blessing'. The mother goes on to describe TTB as 'spiritual and psychological abuse', and notes that the leaders responsible have agreed not to repeat their actions at future events.[62]

Friday 4th April 1997

The Church of Scotland's Panel on Doctrine publishes a 45-page report on TTB, for discussion at the Kirk's forthcoming General Assembly.[63] The report was commissioned by last year's Assembly, which asked the Panel 'to consider issues arising out of what has been called the Toronto Blessing'.

The report begins by identifying its approach to the subject with that adopted by Gamaliel in Acts 5:38-9: 'If it is of human origin, it will collapse; but if it is from God, you will never be able to put them down' (cf. 14th July, 29th July, 29th October 1994; 3rd February, 23rd June, 29th July 1995). 'Because we are dealing with that which is essentially fluid', it adds, 'we should resist the tendency to offer definitive conclusions at this stage.'

Moving on from such 'caveats and cautions', the Panel seek to define TTB by tracing its roots from the ministries of Benny Hinn and Rodney Howard-Browne, the Argentinian revival, John Wimber and Randy Clark. It then examines the 'remarkable transferability' of the Blessing from TAV to other places, focusing particularly on its impact in Scotland (cf. 7th-12th August 1994; 28th January 1995). Here, it says, the first significant event was a 'Time of Refreshing' conference held in St Andrew's and St George's Church, Edinburgh, in October 1994. This, the panel note, was followed by several other large gatherings in various places, but by now, they write, 'it would be fair to suggest that within Scotland there has been a levelling off of general interest, and that this is now focused more particularly in certain churches and fellowships'. Even so, the Panel do acknowledge that some are now claiming that TTB has led into a new 'wave' of God's work at Pensacola.[64]

The report then details the arguments and counter-arguments that have attended the disengagement of TACF from TAV.[65] It moves on from here to consider the historical precedents that have been adduced in respect of the Blessing. Such interrogation of history is seen as a 'healthy' process by the Panel: 'We may, or may not agree with the manner in which [Toronto advocates] receive and interpret ... tradition. However, insofar as their claims on tradition compel us to look at it once more, we may record our indebtedness to them.' As well as the widely discussed example of Jonathan Edwards, whom the Panel stress was a cessationist, the report suggests possible corollaries for what has been taking place in the Glasgow/Edinburgh 'Millennial Warning Mission' of 1710 and the Skye Revival of 1842-3. More extensively, however, they highlight the significance for the current debate of the London-based Church of Scotland minister and theologian Edward Irving (1792-1834).

Irving had organised meetings for prayer aimed at receiving a blessing from the Holy Spirit in 1830, the Panel point out. These meetings duly entertained

the exercise of tongues and prophecy from April 1831. It was when such charismata broke out in Irving's main Sunday services in October of the same year,
however, that controversy began to arise in earnest. In an apparent parallel to
the TAV-TACF split, Irving was ejected from his charge by the Kirk in May
1832 for condoning disorderly conduct in public worship. He left with several
of his congregation to form the Catholic Apostolic Church, but died shortly
afterwards, in December 1834. The report underlines that despite his ejection,
many now appreciate that Irving 'made the first authentic attempt … to interpret the charismatic phenomena in terms of Reformed theology'. Indeed, it
underlines that a major 1974 study by the Panel on Doctrine sided with Irving's
view that there was no biblical warrant for the long-standing Calvinistic teaching that the supernatural gifts died out with the apostles (cessationism).
Concluding their treatment of Irving and the Catholic Apostolic Church, the
Panel reiterate the comparison with TTB:

> If [our] discernment of these parallels is an accurate one, those who advocate the
> Blessing would do well to consider the outcome of this nineteenth-century move-
> ment. Further, they might question whether these parallels suggest the healthiness, or
> otherwise, of certain features of the movement originating in Toronto. On the other
> hand, those who do not advocate the Blessing would do well to consider whether
> the loss of Edward Irving to the Church of Scotland was not in fact the loss of a
> potentially healthy influence on the thought, life, liturgy and doctrine of our
> Church.[66]

The report moves on to assess TTB in relation to the Bible. It takes the now
familiar view that falling in Scripture seems mostly to be 'a natural process,
people prostrating themselves, rather than their collapsing because they are
no longer able to stand'. It further insists that 'nowhere is it suggested that
falling played a part in the worship of the New Testament Church, or was
the experience of the first Christians on receiving the Holy Spirit, or was
regarded by the early church as a normal response to being filled with the
Holy Spirit'. Laughter, the Panel add, is present in the Bible either as an
expression of divine derision (Ps. 2:4) or 'perfectly understandable human
rejoicing, as in Psalm 126:2'. For uncontrollable laughing, however, they
assert that 'there do not appear to be any biblical passages capable of providing a precedent.' Ezekiel 3:6 may be a proof-text for 'quasi-drunkenness',
they concede, but only of the 'weakest' kind. As for Acts 2:13-15, they
emphasise that 'Intelligibility, rather than incoherence, marks the event of
Pentecost.' The same criterion of intelligibility must apply, the Panel suggest,
to animal noises, which at the very least should be interpreted with as much
rigour as tongues.[67]

Beyond all this, the Panel express concern that TTB might have a tendency
to elitism and triumphalism. Although they accept that TACF has itself disavowed such things, they question 'whether this danger has been sufficiently
faced in circles influenced by the Toronto Blessing'.[68]

In conclusion, the Panel welcome 'the challenge to examine afresh our theology and understanding of the presence and renewing activity of the Holy Spirit', and invite the Church to 'consider ways in which the challenge to be "open to the Spirit" may be realised in our common life'. Even so, the report 'notes and endorses the pastoral concerns which have motivated those who have expressed reservations' about TTB, and about 'the scriptural precedents for the phenomena' associated with it. An Appendix on medical considerations then recognises that TTB may induce a sense of disinhibition which, 'in a society full of pressure and expectation, may be viewed as a highly desirable escape route and thus be genuinely beneficial psychologically'. It cautions, however, that 'If an individual returns time after time for the same ministry and release', there is a danger that this euphoric boost may become a substitute for 'actually working through problems'. [69]

Publication of the Church of Scotland document is reported by both *The Times* and The *Daily Telegraph*. In the former, Victoria Coombe focuses on the more critical passages and construes the text as a denial that TTB is a work of God. In the latter, Gillian Bowditch notes that the report 'does not condemn the Toronto Blessing outright', but that it perceives 'little scriptural backing' for it. She has also spoken to Rev John McPake, one of the authors, who has told her: 'The report articulates a range of serious concerns which advocates of the blessing would do well to ponder and reflect on.' [70]

Saturday 26th April 1997

May's *Christianity* magazine reports that Pensacola has become 'the hottest new destination for Christians bound for the blessing trail'. As a result, it continues, 'Refreshing is out [and] revival is in.' Pensacola is 'the new buzz word in the renewal movement that's been sweeping the nations since the so-called "Toronto Blessing" broke in 1994'. It is, says the report, 'another key element in a widespread revival culture'.

The article goes on to suggest the Brownsville Assembly shows 'differences from John Arnott's ministry approach'. In Toronto, it explains, 'there's time for stressed-out church leaders to "marinate in the Spirit"', whereas at Pensacola, 'inquirers are strongly urged to rush down to the front for prayer'. The traditional Pentecostal approach to evangelism, as modelled by Steve Hill, is also contrasted with the style of TACF. Indeed, the report points out that a number of churches who have been at the forefront of TTB in Britain have now begun to shift their focus on to soul-winning. Gerald Coates has, it records, 'warned leaders from his own stream recently that churches must start shifting resources and releasing evangelists in a bid to see revival start in their local communities'. Coates is also quoted as having said that Britain's spiritual landscape has 'totally changed' as 'joy and restoration' have swept across congregations in the wake of Toronto. Pioneer's own 'Event for Revival', Sunderland Christian Centre's recent recruitment of evangelist J. John to lead meetings, and TB-affected festivals such as Soul Survivor, New Wine, Stoneleigh Bible Week and Scotland's Soul Ablaze are cited as potential evidence of Coates' claim. The report ends by mentioning that the normally conservative evangelical theologian J.I. Packer has described the movement as 'an international phenomenon that is now too big to ignore'.[71]

Saturday 31st May 1997

Anti-TB campaigner Mark Haville alleges in *Evangelicals Now* that the physical and mental health of various people who have embraced the Blessing has subsequently deteriorated, with sometimes devastating consequences (cf. 4th-7th December 1995). Several of the cases he mentions pre-date the rise of the Blessing as such, but Haville links them to TTB through the Word Faith teaching which has influenced Rodney Howard-Browne. These instances include 'one lady' in Haville's former 'signs and wonders' fellowship 'who died of breast cancer after believing that the Lord had told her that she needed to laugh for 20 minutes a day for healing'; Jean Carr and Tom Montali, members of a Word-Faith church in North Wales who died tragically soon after being pronounced fully healed, and Ella Peppard, an 85 year-old who died after fracturing a hip when being 'slain in the Spirit' at a Benny Hinn rally.

The directly Toronto-related episodes are given by Haville as follows:

(a) One woman received a sprained ankle, broken glasses and a black eye while attending a Toronto-style meeting at which the Rt. Rev. David Pytches of Chorleywood prayed for her. Again, someone slain fell on top of her. A most worrying aspect was that later in testifying on video she appeared quite happy about what had happened and accepted these injuries as from the Lord.

(b) Kim Hemy ... had been regularly attending the Sunderland Christian Centre where she went for the 'Sunderland Refreshing' (a version of the Toronto phenomenon)... Kim had recently moved from Leicester, taking her young son with her after the break-up of a relationship. Because of eating disorders and a family history of schizophrenia she was under medical supervision and had undergone a psychiatric evaluation in May 1995 ... In October 1996 Durham Crown Court heard that she was suffering from congenital schizophrenia after stabbing her seven-month old son over 70 times! ... During the trial the court heard evidence of her loud sessions of 'self-deliverance' from demons, witnessed by her family who lived next door. She also spent long periods of religious chanting, often in her garden for all to hear. The Toronto-style phenomenon is an altered state of consciousness found in many religions which pursue meditation and hypnosis. Kim's background, before she moved to Tyne and Wear, was peppered with interest in Eastern meditative religions. But now it seems that altered states of consciousness are being espoused as orthodox Christian manifestations by church leaders.

Haville accepts that 'churches cannot be held responsible for the actions of everyone who walks through the doors' and concedes that 'individuals are responsible for their own actions'. Even so, he adds, 'we should surely be deeply concerned that whatever Kim received at the Sunderland Christian Centre could not prevent a tragedy occurring.' In conclusion, he writes of the apparent encouragement of 'altered states of consciousness' in TTB that 'this is a matter about which bodies like the Evangelical Alliance cannot afford to remain neutral'. He then expresses the hope 'that the sober members within the Alliance will take an honest look at these things. While wanting unity on the essentials this is a serious problem within the body of Christ.'[72]

Friday 27th June 1997

The Church Times reports publication of a special Church of England Board of Mission Paper on TTB. Prepared by Dr Anne Richards, Secretary to the Mission Theological Advisory Group, it tracks the development of TTB from Benny Hinn, through Rodney Howard-Browne and Randy Clark to John Arnott. It then notes the split between AVC and TACF in December 1995. [73]

Richards emphasises from the outset that TTB is not especially new. 'Ecstatic phenomena', she writes, 'are well known in many religions, in which dancing, whirling, singing, or meditating give rise to trance-like states in which a person or group is thought to be "possessed" by God or a spirit.' In this 'altered state of consciousness', she adds, 'people may fall down, jerk spasmodically, utter strange cries, and give oracles or prophecies.' While acknowledging that such phenomena have historically been associated with the two-thirds world, Richards suggests that the reason they have attracted so much attention now is 'because of the involvement of affluent, middle-class people in this kind of worship'. Indeed, she goes on to propose that TTB may be a means by which such people are 'catching up with what the Two-Thirds World has to teach us about holistic worship'.[74]

Next, Richards investigates the biblical material which has been cited in relation to TTB, and concentrates particularly on the category of 'ecstatic experience'. She accepts that such experience is an aspect of prophetic witness (cf. 1 Sam. 19; Ezek. 1; 3), but says that this is frequently in tension with so-called 'canonical' prophetic activity (e.g. 1 Kgs. 18:21-38; 22:1-8; 2 Kgs. 9:4-13). The same tension, she notes, occurs in 1 Corinthians 14. The point, she concludes, is that rational explanation or interpretation typically acts as a 'check' on more bizarre expressions of faith, and must be maintained in respect of TTB.[75]

After presenting various personal accounts of the Blessing by those who have claimed benefit from it, Richards proceeds to examine the debate about whether TTB is a form of hysteria (cf. 20th June, 16th July, 4th September, 11th November 1994; 19th January, 27th May, 7th August 1995; 17th February 1996). Ultimately, however, she appears to be more persuaded by Michael Lawson's notion that the Blessing may be akin to the controlled 'releasing therapies' sometimes used by psychiatrists to reduce stress in their clients:

In classic Pentecostalism, it is the poor who exhibit such phenomena, but the middle-class congregations in whom the Toronto Experience is now seen may also be subject to stresses, not of poverty, but of maintaining lives which are performance-related, and achievement-oriented. Combined with this is the sense of urgency and expectation of some kind of watershed or consummation engendered by the advent of the millennium, characterised by Dr Andrew Walker as Pre-Millennial Tension. In such an environment, the Church may provide a respectable outlet for disinhibited behaviour and release of tension in the laying aside of pressure.[76]

Richards' blunt inference from all this is that 'one person's hysteria is another person's time of refreshing'.[77] Still, however, she accepts that it is important to assess the potential abuses of ecstatic experiences under authoritarian leadership. She also cautions that a movement as physically focused as TTB might alienate the elderly, infirm and disabled.[78] In conclusion, she also worries that as yet, the Blessing has proved insufficiently soteriological and missiological, and urges those churches involved in it to 'look critically at their contribution to mission and evangelism in order to see whether they are visibly helping to build up the Body of Christ'.[79]

In an article accompanying a short review of Richards' report, the *Church Times* quotes various leading Anglican charismatics as suggesting that TTB is now 'quietening down'. Although Toronto-style conferences are still being organised and although St Andrew's, Chorleywood is still sending out teams of people to pray with other congregations, John Marsh of Anglican Renewal Ministries observes that the Blessing has 'died down a bit'. He adds: 'When some new feature of Christian truth or experience comes on stream, people tend to go over the top with it at first; then it begins to be integrated. Overexposure of certain phenomena is perhaps passing, but these have never been at the heart of it.' A spokesman from Holy Trinity, Brompton takes a similar view: 'I guess that there was a time when the manifestations might have been more noticeable', he says, 'but the Holy Spirit is working as much as ever.' Rev Peter Lawrence, Team Rector at Canford Magna, Dorset, adds that although unusual phenomena are still occurring, 'the voltage has been turned down'.[80]

Sunday 13th July 1997

John Wimber retires as Pastor of Anaheim Vineyard Christian Fellowship. He has been in ill health following triple-bypass heart surgery last year.[81]

To mark his retirement, Wimber gives a reflective interview to *Christianity Today*. During the interview, Tim Stafford and Jim Beverley ask him, 'What made you split with the Toronto Blessing?' Wimber replies:

Toronto was changing the definition of renewal in the Vineyard. I don't have any objection to the phenomenon at all. I think if it's fleshly and brought out by some sort of display, or promoted by somebody on stage, that's abysmal. But if God does something to somebody, that's between them and God.

When the Toronto thing first occurred, people were reciting 1 Corinthians 14 regarding orderliness in the service. I thought about it and wrote back saying, 'Whose orderliness?' Our current culture-adapted understanding of order, or the Holy Spirit's order?

When babies are born, is that orderly? It's as messy as anything. Blood all over the place. The child comes out all right, but it's not developed. It's not cultured. It's not brought into the world already mature. The norm for God moving among people is a pretty messy thing. If you go back to revival literature, you can say, Wow, that's messy.

Thursday 21st August 1997

Mowbray publish Roland Howard's *Charismania*, an exposé of the charismatic movement which includes a brief chapter on TTB. Howard authored the definitive study of the infamous 'Nine O'clock Service' scandal of August 1995,[82] and here attempts a similar kind of investigative religious journalism.

Essentially, Howard compiles quotations from various commentators whose views on TTB have already been well aired elsewhere, e.g. Mark Stibbe, Graham Cray, Philip Richter and Martyn Percy. His own reservations about the movement, however, are apparent in the fact that he leaves the last word to a new, highly critical voice – Lloyd Pietersen, a Sheffield doctoral student who will soon go on to edit a strong counterblast against TTB entitled *The Mark of the Spirit?* (16th January 1998). Pietersen suggests that the charismatics who have embraced the Blessing are exhibiting an increased 'cognitive dissonance'. This, he says, has been brought on by the failure of charismatic Christianity to deliver on its original promises of transforming the world and thereby preparing the way for Christ's return. TTB, for Pietersen, represents a retreat from these high ideals into a suggestive form of religious ecstasy that is 'isolated' from reality.[83]

Saturday 11th October 1997

The *New Christian Herald* reports that the Centre for Contemporary Ministry has integrated and summarised its previous declarations on TTB in a new Statement (the full text of the CCM Statement is given in Part III). This, the report continues, has been circulated among those who attended the CCM's two Bawtry Hall consultations in January and June 1995. It has also been 'discussed with the directors of the Evangelical Alliance before being sent for comment to a large number of leaders who had not attended the consultations'.

The new Statement urges charismatics to join with CCM 'in seeking the Lord afresh in humility and repentance'. In particular, it identifies 'neglect of Scripture' as a point for confession, and calls for a re-emphasis on the 'biblical doctrine of salvation' rather than 'a superficial message and methods which rob people of a true knowledge of salvation'. It goes on to bemoan the exalting of 'subjective experience' over doctrinal 'objectivity' and 'truth'. It adds that the charismatic movement has become 'too casual with God' and needs to restore 'a sense of [his] holiness' which is related to the imminence of Christ's return and an urgent commitment to mission.

Monday 17th November 1997

John Wimber dies, aged 63, from a brain haemorrhage following a fall.[84]

Friday 21st November 1997

The Anaheim Vineyard Christian Fellowship building overflows with worshippers at a memorial service for John Wimber. Forty-year-old Todd Hunter has assumed the role of Acting National Director of AVC, and is being widely tipped to succeed Wimber on a permanent basis.[85]

Saturday 29th November 1997

In a major feature for December's *Christianity* magazine, Baptist minister Gethin Russell-Jones seeks to answer the question, 'Whatever Happened to the Promised Revival?'[86] He writes:

> This was to be the year of blessing, of extravagant favour from on high. We drowned ourselves in extraordinary hyperbole; the waves got higher, the rivers deeper and the waterfalls louder. Someone announced May as the official revival month, a declaration accompanied by more fasting, praying and prophesying than has been seen for many a year. Well-known speakers cancelled existing engagements and sat tight waiting for something called revival to land in Britain. It didn't.[87]

Reflecting on the failure of TTB, Pensacola and various recent evangelistic initiatives to make a sustained impact on British society, Russell-Jones laments that evangelicals are 'suckers for a good story, however badly written'. He adds, 'Revival sickens me. It also constitutes my deepest longing. This contradiction has been chiselling away at my spiritual sanity for some years now, simultaneously enabling me to cry "more, Lord" and "oh God, this is dreadful" in the same breath.' He goes on,

> Revival is part of evangelicalism's doctrinal arsenal. It may not enjoy the same status as substitutionary atonement or scriptural inerrancy, but it's in there somewhere. And though it has, like the rest of modern Western evangelicalism, as many flavours and brands as a supermarket's shelf, its function is like everyone's favourite uncle. One day it will turn up and make everything happy once again. It symbolises the powerful desire in most Protestant Christians to see God work extravagantly in his church.[88]

Noting that contemporary evangelical revivalism owes more to the pragmatism of Charles Finney, the nineteenth-century American preacher, than to the Reformed theological heritage of Jonathan Edwards and George Whitefield, Russell-Jones finds support from Dr Andrew Walker, who tells him: 'The House churches need to keep at the radical cutting edge to keep in business. They have an inward necessity to demonstrate their radicality.' Even so, he avers, 'There's a lot of rhetoric, but no evidence of cultural change.' Walker then suggests that Holy Trinity, Brompton's Alpha course has 'replaced and conveniently eclipsed the Toronto phenomenon'.

As for Russell-Jones, he warns that although revival will continue to be promised and reported, it may prove 'so arcane and hidden that it requires a degree in mysticism to have any chance of locating it'.[89]

The end of November also sees Hank Hanegraff publish a new exposé of TTB and Pensacola as part of a wider assault on contemporary charismatic movements. Entitled *Counterfeit Revival*, the book pays particular attention to visions and prophecies associated with Toronto. Hanegraff takes exception to John Arnott's claim in his book, *The Father's Blessing*, to have heard Jesus say that he wanted to wash his (Arnott's) feet. Hanegraff also recoils from Arnott's reported vision of Jesus marrying his wife, Carol. Hanegraff goes on to accuse TACF-related 'prophets' such as Larry Randolph, James Ryle and Rick Joyner of encouraging division and spiritual elitism in the church.[90]

The preface to *Counterfeit Revival* is penned by a former associate of John Wimber, Tom Snipe. Against the background of TTB, Snipe writes: 'Most pastors I know have bouts of insecurity, performance anxiety and periods when they are unsure that they have made the right ministry decisions. The most effective entry point into the church for any 'new' teaching is through the pastor.'[91]

Hanegraff's text is assessed in the December edition of *Evangelicals Now* by R.T. Kendall. Although Kendall recognises that Hanegraff has done 'some good work in the past', he suggests that on this occasion he has 'been promoted to the level of his incompetence'. 'It seems to me', Kendall writes, 'that Hanegraff has managed to criticise nearly everything that is largely explained by the immediate power of the Holy Spirit. He may or may not be a cessationist ... but he might as well be. He seems threatened by nearly anything that is real or supernatural and needs to play into good people's fears to bolster his case.'[92]

Saturday 6th December 1997

New Christian Herald reports that the Brownsville Assembly of God in Pensacola has been investigated by the local *Pensacola News Journal*, which has alleged financial irregularities. The allegations include non-payment of tax on organisations set up by individual church leaders, and concealment of Pastor John Kilpatrick's salary. In response, Kilpatrick has assured members and visitors that any problems which have emerged have been due to ignorance of complex tax procedures rather than anything more sinister. 'Where we have been unwise', he says, 'we are very, very sorry'. He has also confirmed that his salary is $73,000 and that he would have been willing to provide further details of his personal finances had the *Journal* not shown such an 'accusatory attitude'.

For their part, the congregation at Brownsville have, says the report, given a 100% vote of confidence to their leaders. They have also issued a statement, which the *Journal* has now printed alongside a reiteration of its own charges. The statement says:

> Although we are grieved by the misinformation, poor reporting and scurrilous nature of the ... series on the Brownsville Revival, we nonetheless want to bless them, and we ask the Lord to pour out all his grace on all the correspondents who worked on these articles.[93]

Friday 16th January 1998

Paternoster Press publishes a self-styled 'charismatic critique' of TTB. Edited by Lloyd Pietersen under the title *Mark of the Spirit?*, this collects together essays by four scholars associated with the Department of Biblical Studies at Sheffield University. The specific concern of the contributors is the work on the Blessing, and on revival generally, published by their Sheffield colleague, Mark Stibbe, in his book *Times of Refreshing* (7th July 1995).

Pieterson notes in his Introduction that the volume is 'polemical', but that the authors 'do not write primarily as academics'. He stresses, 'We write as … charismatics who are concerned to see genuine evidence of life in the Spirit in the church and, as such, are critical of much of current charismatic praxis.' Underlining the validity of their enterprise in relation to the injunction of 1 Thessalonians 5:19-21 to 'test everything', Pietersen expresses the hope that the book will 'contribute to an open debate on the nature of the "Toronto Blessing"'.[94]

Pietersen's own essay is placed first, and addresses Stibbe's thesis that TTB represents a divine accommodation to the 'ecstatic' culture of the postmodern West. Firstly, Pietersen points out that while cultural engagement is certainly part of the Church's mission, it need not lead to cultural conformity. Ecstatic behaviour and ecstatic religion were part of first-century Graeco-Roman culture, writes Pietersen, and were in evidence at the church of Corinth (1 Cor. 14). And yet, Pietersen argues, Paul encouraged orderliness and self-control as a check against such things. Indeed, Pietersen describes his prescription in this case as 'charismatic but not ecstatic'.

Beyond all this, Pietersen writes that Stibbe's hypothesis overlooks the degree to which TTB confirms the growing secularisation of the church. The rise of the 'ecstatic culture', with its quest for psychological dissociation, its susceptibility to hype, its neophilia and its narcissism, has, according to Pietersen, been absorbed into the charismatic movement without due critique and discernment. Drawing on work in the sociology of religion, Pietersen concludes that rather than relating to contemporary culture in order to *transform* it, TTB has demonstrated the 'cultural captivity' of the charismatic church.[95]

In the second of the book's essays, Mark Smith examines Stibbe's apologetic for the inductive, experience-driven model of interpretation identified in *Times of Refreshing* as 'Pentecostal' or 'This-Is-That' hermeneutics. Against this model, Smith argues robustly for the priority of the 'original sense' and authorial intent of the text; he adds that in any case, 'most [Pentecostals] would ascribe greater importance to the original sense than [Stibbe] seems to allow'. Such historically informed exegesis provides a vital check on 'speculative' and 'fanciful' readings of Scripture, argues Smith, and Stibbe's apparent marginalisation of it makes him prone to the charge that he would happily allow us to 'read our own messages into [the text]'.[96]

The third contribution by Vivian Culver interrogates the issue of ecstatic laughter. Having dismissed Stibbe's appeal to Wesley and Edwards on this matter as a distortion of the great revivalists' mature position, Culver proceeds to offer a taxonomy of the relevant biblical vocabulary which varies sharply from that proposed by Stibbe. Culver notes that references to laughter in the Old Testament overwhelmingly denote mocking or derisive laughter, and that Luke 6:21 is 'the only verse in the Bible which positively and specifically predicates laughter of Christians'. Culver insists, however, that even this must be read as indicating the future laughter of those who inherit the kingdom of God, rather than any present, Torontoesque laughter – that is, laughter of an uncontrolled or prolonged sort.

Culver is aware that some, such as Gerald Coates, have argued that it is not necessary to find explicit warrant for every church activity from the Scriptures – that the Bible should be treated as a *test* book rather than a text book (cf. 24th October 1994). Culver is also familiar with Coates' point that there is no less biblical warrant for Sunday school than for TTB. In response, Culver writes:

> The claims made for the manifestations are pitched much higher than in the case of the Sunday school. The Sunday school makes no greater claim for itself than that it is an expedient method of performing certain God-given tasks. It is also provisional; we are free to abandon it if a better method occurs to us. In such a case, it is enough that we receive God's *nihil obstat*; that though there is nothing in the Bible to indicate that he approves of this particular method, there is nothing to indicate that he disapproves. But the claim in the case of the manifestations is different; here is no question of a provisional expedient but a response to the very presence of the Holy Spirit himself. Surely it is not unreasonable to demand that such large claims produce stronger credentials than are required in the case of a provisional expedient? The magnitude of the claim should be reflected in the strength of the evidence … The only sort of evidence which bears the weight of such claims is evidence which assures us that God wholly approves of these phenomena.[97]

The fourth and final essay in *Mark of the Spirit?* is written by John Lyons. Like Tom Smail (3rd February 1995), Lyons questions the relevance of the 'Gamaliel Principle' to assessment of TTB. Derived from Acts 5:39, Lyons shows how this pragmatic, 'wait and see' approach has come to be 'quoted incessantly' by Toronto proponents like Stibbe. Even so, he contends that it is 'untrue in its context in Acts … as Gamaliel uses it there'; it is 'in effect a distortion of a properly Christian view of divine providence'. Hence, he adds, in relation to TTB, it is 'not simply inadequate but rather useless and, possibly, contrary to God's will'.

Lyons proceeds to defend his position on the basis that key Jewish sources confirm Gamaliel to have been a 'paradigmatic Pharisee'; they would not have done so had he in fact meant his words to encourage Christians. Indeed, Lyons argues he was an inveterate opponent of the gospel, that it was the early church fathers who 'Christianised' him, and that there is nothing in the text itself to suggest that he was sympathetic to the church. Rather, writes Lyons, while Luke applies Gamaliel's words favourably to the apostolic cause, he does so 'on an ironic level':

Gamaliel himself is unaware of the significance of his own words and is himself thoroughly discredited by them. Luke's intended irony becomes clear when one recognizes the importance of Peter's statements in Acts 4:19-20 and 5:29, namely, that he and John must obey God rather than men, that is, Israel's discredited leaders.[98]

Even as used by Luke, however, Lyons disputes that Acts 5:39 means that every individual doing God's work or every individual movement of God will necessarily succeed. After all, he writes, 'Stephen is stoned to death (Acts 7:60). James, the brother of John, is killed by Herod (Acts 12:2). Paul and Barnabas flee from Iconium (Acts 14:6). Paul is stoned as Lystra, and thrown out of the city (Acts 14:19). Paul and Silas are beaten and jailed in Philippi, before leaving the city (Acts 16:22,23,40).' As a consequence of all this, Lyons proposes that Luke uses Gamaliel's words eschatologically, to confirm that the Christian movement *as a whole* will not *ultimately* be overthrown, rather than to declare that each godly endeavour must, *ipso facto* meet with obvious success. At a systematic theological level, Lyons relates this interpretation to G.C. Berkouwer's insistence that because we are fallen human beings, we cannot reliably discern what God is doing from the events of history apart from what a holistic reading of Scripture allows us to say. In relation to Gamaliel, this is construed as follows:

> Gamaliel's theological understanding is at fault because it does not take account of the 'fullness' revealed in the Hebrew Scriptures; it is based upon a false and partial theology of success which implicitly denies the Scripture's witness to the theology of suffering and, in the case of Christians, to the theology of the cross.[99]

Saturday 31st January 1998
Writing in the February edition of *Evangelicals Now*, Mark Haville highlights further press accusations against the Brownsville Assembly of God. These have been gleaned from the local *News-Journal*, and from the 20th December issue of *World* magazine. As well as claiming that services at the church play down the doctrine of salvation in favour of emotive techniques of persuasion, journalists have, says Haville, alleged that resident evangelist Steve Hill has bought a $390,000 farmhouse, that pastor John Kilpatrick has approved purchase of a $130,000 luxury coach for his travelling Feast of Fire ministry, and that only 2% of the church's significantly increased income is being given to missions. Moreover, contrary to claims of decreased crime in the Pensacola area since the new wave began, Haville reports local police complaining of an increase in offences. The *News-Journal* has also accused Kilpatrick of exaggerating aspects of his past in his recently published autobiography *Stone Cold Heart*.[100]

Saturday 30th May 1998
Renewal magazine reports that TACF and the Canadian Association of Vineyard Churches have joined in a public act of reconciliation. At a service attended by

one thousand five hundred people, leaders from both constituencies have affirmed one another and pledged to move ahead in mutual respect. TAV national director Gary Best described the two years since the separation as painful and difficult, but underlined that all present at the meeting, on both sides, have 'honoured the Lord'. He then read out to the TACF team four statements which had been agreed by the Vineyard leadership across Canada:

- It truly has been the Son of God who has raised you up and has produced that which others have called the Toronto Blessing but which is really the Lord's blessing.
- We have been wonderfully served by the blessing and your part in it. We appreciate your service to us and the body of Christ.
- Our prayers are for you, not against you. God has given you a difficult call, but we are praying that he will give you wisdom, protect you and allow you to see his blessing to the second, third and fourth generation.
- We covenant to speak well of you and assume the best of you.[101]

Responding on behalf of TACF, Marc Dupont said, 'We thank God for the whole Vineyard movement and what the Holy Spirit has birthed through John Wimber. "Lord, thank you that your cross is so much greater that our petty peripheral differences".' John Arnott then gave thanks for Gary Best's appearance, describing it as 'a precious moment to all of us'. He added: 'We want to join hands and hearts – let love strengthen the bonds we already have.' There then followed hugs and tears on the stage, as the congregation rose in a one minute ovation of shouts, cheers and applause. Gary Best then spoke on forgiveness and unity, stressing that forgiveness comes not so much from humans as from God. While theological agreement was important, unity was not solely dependent on it, he said. The key was learning to accept one another's differences within the body of Christ.[102]

Saturday 1st August 1998

In a major feature for the *Salvationist*, Salvation Army Divisional Director Alan Bateman, asks, 'Whatever Happened to the Toronto Blessing?' A Major responsible for the Army's Southern Division Field Programme, Bateman notes that it is now 'some time since we heard about the impact of the Toronto Blessing', but warns that 'if we try to forget the issue, or sweep it under the carpet in the hope that it will go away, we do so at our peril'.

Although he is very familiar with the negative reaction that the Blessing has received in some quarters, Bateman is still 'inclined to settle for a more positive frame of mind'. The Church, he writes, is in 'desperate need' of a 'breath of fresh air', and in many of the venues where TTB has been experienced there has, he believes, been 'an undoubted and overwhelming sense of the presence of God'. He accepts that at times the Blessing has served as a reminder not to seek signs as an end in themselves, but invokes the Gamaliel Principle as he urges Christians to judge the movement by its 'long-term fruit'. In conclusion, he writes:

We may not be seeing widespread signs of revival but there are plenty of signs around for those with eyes to see and ears to hear. With world revival gathering pace it can only be a matter of time. When countries like Brazil are planning to send several thousand missionaries to Europe it becomes obvious that even Europe itself will, one day, catch alight … For this we will need constant refreshing! Continual giving, without receiving, leads to exhaustion and burn-out … God wants us around for the long haul, not the short sprint.[103]

Wednesday 10th – Friday 12th March 1999

At a TACF Intercessors' Conference, John Arnott reports that on a recent trip to South Africa, he has seen people's teeth filled with gold as they have been prayed for. A video clip is shown of the trip and the apparent new miracle, and Arnott then asks anyone who wishes to receive it for themselves to stand, believe for it and touch their cheeks. Some ten people go forward, shouting with joy and declaring that they now have gold fillings, which they did not possess before. By the end of the conference, on Friday 12th, it is claimed on the Revival Net News web site that 198 people have left the conference with some sort of new gold in their mouths.[104]

Charismatic dentistry such as this was brought to the attention of British evangelicals in the early '90s by, among others, David Pytches. Having been a Bishop in Chile, Pytches reported in his account of the Kansas City Prophets, *Some Said It Thundered*, that he and his wife had encountered 'many strange things [in South America], such as people, even in our own churches, having their teeth miraculously filled *(creatio ex nihilo)*'.[105] Later, during the 'Argentinian Revival', which so influenced John Arnott and others from the Vineyard network, the same occurrence was also observed.[106]

Although no one mentions it in this context, Peter Partner's soon-to-be-published book on church history, *Two Thousand Years*, will point out that a similar 'gold tooth' claim was made on behalf of a Silesian child in 1599, later to be simultaneously highlighted and rubbished by the rationalist sceptic Bernard de Fontenelle (1657-1757).[107]

Saturday 15th May 1999

Writing in *Christian Herald*, Rob Warner addresses the 'gold fillings' issue. He recalls hearing reports of the phenomenon from South America some years previously, and asserts that now, as then, it is important to recognise that a sovereign God can do such things if he so wishes. Advising that the main focus for healing must remain on the seriously sick and distressed, Warner nevertheless suggests that this latest movement might be interpreted in terms of healing and grace:

Maybe God wants to make it clear that he has really intervened. Beautiful white enamel could make someone suppose that they had imagined any previous problem with their teeth. Maybe God is being practical. If someone has already neglected their teeth, only a gold filling will see them through their lifetime. Maybe in the developing world gold fillings can be interpreted as highly relevant expressions of divine mercy. Without access to professional dental care, the poor will often suffer agonising toothache and lose their teeth at an early age.

Beyond these possible explanations, however, Warner cautions against the extremes of anti-supernatural cynicism on the one hand and gullible excitability on the other. He rejects as spurious a claim that Psalm 81:10 ('Open wide your mouth and I will fill it') supports gold fillings, on the grounds that it speaks of God's desire to feed the poor with bread. He then goes on to urge thorough testing, responsible exegesis and a refusal to 'major on minors'. 'We don't want Christians obsessively looking into their own mouths for gold fillings', he writes. 'Instead, we need to search our hearts for the fruit of the Spirit, the true gold of inner growth towards the character of Christ.'[108]

Thursday 23rd December 1999
As part of his newly published textbook *Psychology and Religion*, Michael Argyle offers a 3-page account of TTB. He reports estimates that the first 23 months of the Blessing saw two hundred and thirty five thousand people visiting the Airport fellowship, 'most of them going several times'. Seeking to account for the manifestations, Argyle suggests that they engender a 'collective excitement', which in turn generates 'social cohesion'. He also submits that the loud, rhythmic music often played at Toronto-style meetings has the potential to produce 'over-arousal', uninhibited behaviour' and 'heightened suggestibility'. He adds that such stimuli may also prompt the production of endorphins, which can induce 'states of euphoria and eventually trance' akin to those seen in TTB.[109]

Friday 17th March 2000
Eagle issue an extensively revised edition of Nigel Scotland's authoritative study *Charismatics and the New Millennium*. The original version of the book, published in 1995 by Hodder & Stoughton, could not deal in depth with TTB. The intervening period has, however, afforded Scotland the opportunity to assess the new movement, and here he devotes some thirty pages to it.[110]

After surveying the roots and development of the Blessing from Rodney Howard-Browne through Randy Clark and the Vineyard to TAV/TACF, South West London Vineyard, Holy Trinity, Brompton and the British charismatic scene in general, Scotland recounts his own visit to the Toronto Airport church in August 1994. He recalls 'standard Vineyard worship' followed by the full range of manifestations, but stresses that what most impressed him and his wife was the fact that TAV 'ran on prayer'. This, he writes, meant that 'for most who went to Toronto between 1994 and 1997 the heart of the blessing was a much deeper consciousness and awareness of the presence of Jesus in their lives'. Where such people were concerned, Scotland adds, 'Their walk with [God] was no longer just a cerebral affair, there [was] a genuine experiential dimension. For many their level of expectancy and confidence in the ability of Jesus to help them in their situation was raised.'[111]

Despite this positive response, Scotland reviews the debate and controversy which TTB aroused, and draws comparisons and contrasts with earlier periods of evangelical renewal and revival. His conclusion is that 'the revivalism advocated with Toronto has had an impact that is both dysfunctional and positive'. He continues:

> On the downside there was and continues to be in some places an over-prizing of religious phenomena. Too many people were travelling from place to place to experience the next piece of powerful ministry. Indeed the feeling still persists that if people shake, cry or fall it's 'powerful'. It needs to be recognised that spirit phenomena are no necessary guarantee of genuine spirituality. In fact psychic or religious phenomena can readily occur without any prompting of the Spirit of God at all.[112]

Furthermore, Scotland notes that six years on, the Blessing 'does not appear to have significantly increased the membership of UK churches as a whole'. Indeed, he reports that it 'in fact had a divisive effect on the charismatic section of the church'. Since Toronto, he explains, 'two distinct strands of charismatic Christianity seem to have emerged'. He explains this bifurcation thus:

> One [strand] continues to have its roots in the earlier emphasis of the Fountain Trust and stands far aloof from Toronto. This group might be termed 'renewal charismatics'. The other, which embraces the Toronto Blessing and its associated phenomena and continues to talk up revival, might be categorised as 'revivalist charismatics'.[113]

More positively, Scotland accepts that TTB might best be described by the now familiar term 'times of refreshing', rather than by the designation 'revival'. Many people, he writes, did genuinely experience a 'heightened consciousness of the presence of Jesus in their lives', while some knew 'release from burdens, pains, sickness and emotional hurt'. What is more, he contends, some of the harsher criticisms made of the movement by detractors like Alan Morrison and Clifford Hill were unjustified. Thus, according to Scotland, definitions of 'orderliness' and 'rationality' can be culturally-conditioned rather than biblically absolute; accusations of hypnotism and hysteria may apply in isolated instances, but cannot satisfactorily explain the world-wide phenomenon of TTB, and the supposedly heterodox practice of calling down the Holy Spirit in fact goes back at least to the 'very early tradition' of *epiclesis* at the Lord's Supper and the 'ancient ... second century' hymn 'Come Holy Ghost, eternal God, proceeding from above'.[114]

For all this, Scotland concedes that TTB did not effect the wide-scale social transformation that had accompanied the ministry of the Wesleys or George Whitefield.[115] Furthermore, 'As things turned out the impetus of Toronto had begun to diminish by the end of 1996. The leaders were running out of steam and the rhetoric could no longer be sustained. In sociological terms the charisma was "evaporating".'[116]

Then again, he concludes, Toronto can be viewed as an authentic, if limited, season of new spiritual life. What is more, in its wake, 'the Alpha course took off in a way which has been beyond all expectation. Indeed at the beginning of the year 2000 the number of churches running Alpha courses was still rising.' (On Alpha and TTB cf. 24th May, 3rd, 19th June 1994, 28th January, 19th May, 30th December 1995, 27th January, 11th May 1996, 29th November 1997; 21st October 2000).

Friday 25th August 2000

The September/October edition of the Evangelical Alliance magazine *Idea* carries a feature reassessing TTB.[117] The context is the forthcoming publication of this book. *Idea* editor Phil Seager explains the Alliance's involvement in the Toronto issue, from the Euston and Whitefield House Consultations in 1994-95, through to Clive Calver and Rob Warner's 1996 book, *Together We Stand*. He then questions the editor of this book on why it has taken four years since the decline of the Blessing to produce it, when the Alliance had originally suggested that something would be published sooner. The editor responds by explaining that although Dave Cave, his predecessor, had collected material in 1994-95, he himself had only joined the Alliance in the later half of 1997, when the Blessing had largely dissipated. At this point, 'follow on' issues such as Pensacola and gold teeth had become relevant, and it seemed judicious to chart their development before moving to publication. The editor then adds:

> I accept that some people have expressed impatience with EA over this matter. It should not be forgotten that a 12-point, 1,000 word statement [the Euston Statement] was made freely available ... when the controversy was at its height. Nor should the efforts of the Alliance in brokering crucial dialogue and debate on this issue be overlooked. However, we have been aware of the need for more detailed reflection. Some may say that we have taken our time, but theology cannot be confined to a journalistic timescale. It would be strange if all doctrinal analysis had to be written in the heat of the moment. Phenomena such as the 'Toronto Blessing' need to be weighed up at a distance.[118]

Seager goes on to interview John Arnott at TACF about his reflections on the Blessing nearly seven years after it first emerged at the Airport church. Seager finds that meetings are still being held there six nights a week, that classrooms and a new café have been built, and that 50 leaders have arrived to attend an annual summer school. He also notes that 'the TACF congregation seems to have levelled off at around 2,000 regular attendees', but that 'thousands of pilgrims from around the world' are still turning up each week.

In conversation with Seager, Arnott reiterates the point made often in his earlier statements and books, that the Holy Spirit, while frequently gentle, is capable of overriding people's wills and faculties. He then adds:

> People think it's all about falling, roaring, shaking, etc. That's not what it's about. It's about a profound love affair that happens in the heart of the person that's a direct

result of the Holy Spirit. I've been a Christian for almost 40 years. I've seen a lot of things come and go in the Body of Christ, and in the charismatic movement. And I have never found anything as powerful and as wonderful as what we're involved in right now. We would die for this. I wouldn't die for a career in the ministry, but for this – this is it, for us.

Arnott brushes off his detractors as 'people who occupy such a small segment of my time', but does commend the empirical research that has been conducted by Margaret Poloma (cf. 27th November 1995). He also warns those who assign TTB to the Devil to heed Jesus' words on 'the unpardonable sin' in Luke 12:10. Moreover, he says, 'it's a tragedy that so many are frightened away because of (the critics). I weep over those who have been frightened away, because they could have had the intimacy with God that we're talking about.' To charges of emotionalism, he offers a robust response:

> My question is: however are you going to have a profound, intimate love relationship with God without any emotion? You have to experience the Holy Spirit. Experience is the best.

On the debate about whether TTB represents renewal, revival, refreshment or something else, Arnott asserts that 'after a while, it is just semantics'. Even so, he is happy enough with 'revival', and points to new ministries, vocations, church plants, conversions and healings, as well as reduced crime rates, to support the description. He also makes a general connection with the rapid spread of charismatic and Pentecostal churches world wide, although he concedes that the specific relationship between this and Toronto 'might be a bit harder to nail down'.

Seager proceeds to explain that TACF now has an established international network of churches under the headings Partners in Harvest and Friends in Harvest. Arnott tells him that the outpouring in Pensacola represents an extension of the work begun at Toronto. As for the future, Arnott is hopeful:

> All things being equal, we'll just keep on expanding like we're doing. We still want more. This is good, but it's not the Book of Acts. If you rated the Book of Acts and the ministry of Jesus as 'category five' type miracles (in the hurricane scale) we're probably operating at a one or two right now. Prior to '94 I'd say it was 0.5. Since '94, it has been progressively notching up. I have a feeling that God is increasing the anointing. I think that probably some unknown person in some unknown place will come up with another whole wave of this thing.

Friday 20th October 2000

In a feature for the *Church Times*, Bryony Martin takes stock of TTB. After rehearsing the main points in its development, she mentions the forthcoming publication of this book and quotes its editor. He tells her: 'In a way the Toronto Blessing was a litmus test because it clarified the distinctions between conservative and charismatic'. She also quotes Lloyd Pietersen, the editor of the critical 1998 volume *Mark of the Spirit?* (16th January 1998). He repeats the accusation, made in his book, that TTB represented an attempt by certain charismatics to address a 'cognitive dissonance' induced by the failure of past expectations. Again, however, he says that TTB exacerbated the problem rather than solving it.

Michael Mitton, Director of Anglican Renewal Ministries when the Blessing was at its height, offers more sanguine opinions. He tells Martin that TTB has borne lasting and worthwhile fruit in 'compassionate ministries focussed on social justice'. At his own church, St Alkmund's, Derby, Toronto-influenced renewal has, he says, resulted in the establishment of homelessness and food-distribution projects. 'The church wouldn't have done something like that a few years back', he adds; 'There is now a close connection between evangelism and social action.' Mitton also comments that the Blessing has encouraged several people to explore more deeply the mystical traditions of Christianity.

Martin also mentions Sandy Millar of Holy Trinity, Brompton; he acknowledges that not everyone found TTB helpful. Even so, he insists, 'It is impossible to deny that a lot of it was distinctively God.' After quoting from the recent article on Toronto in the Evangelical Alliance's *Idea* magazine, and acknowledging the continuing activity at TACF itself, Martin concludes:

> The rest of the church has moved on. Many are relieved that the embarrassing phenomena have passed; others are adamant that they have enriched their Christian lives and ministry. All are agreed on one thing: that, in the realm of charismatic experience, no categorical judgements can be made.[119]

Saturday 21st October 2000

In an extensive article on the Alpha course for the *Guardian Weekend* supplement, Jon Ronson interviews Holy Trinity, Brompton's Nicky Gumbel.[120] The feature focuses on the phenomenal success of Alpha itself, which Ronson reports has now spread to 112 countries. Still, Gumbel does offer one brief comment on TTB. He says:

> I don't talk about it now. It divides people. It splits churches. It is very controversial. But I'll tell you – I think the Toronto Blessing was a wonderful, wonderful thing.[121]

Ronson himself surmises that TTB was 'the kick-start Alpha needed', serving as a major factor in the 'explosion' of the course through the 1990s.[122]

Saturday 28th October 2000

Writing for the November issue of *Renewal* magazine, new church leader John Noble concedes that 'the controversies surrounding the 'Toronto Blessing' seem, for the most part, to have died down.' Even so, he says, 'I was extremely blessed and challenged and feel my understanding of how God works is revolutionised. I feel I'm more open to God than ever, less quick to pass judgment and more ready for whatever God wants me to do.'[123]

Recalling his part in the Evangelical Alliance's Whitefield House consultation in June 1995, Noble writes that after a period of heated debate on the manifestations, he was moved to suggest that 'If laughter, rolling on the floor and a few strange noises were the worst things that were happening in our congregations, we should be deliriously happy!' Biblically, he adds that Isaac was actually named after the laughter expressed by his mother, Sarah, when she heard that she had become pregnant. Moreover, while accepting that some laughter 'can be fleshly, even demonic', he stresses that 'it can also be a natural human reaction to a real work of the Holy Spirit in our lives'.[124]

As for animal noises, he writes that these have presented 'even less of a problem':

> Having experienced bereavement and extreme pain over the years, at various times, I've bawled like a banshee on numerous occasions. Furthermore, watching the results of so much ethnic strife on TV news, I observe that grieving mothers do not react with measured silence when their children or husbands are blown apart by shrapnel – they wail like dogs who have lost their puppies. It takes a special breed of stiff upper lip English evangelical to respond with a 'bit of a bad show chaps', when half the rest of the world caves in … No wonder some people groups find it hard to take the church seriously when we're apparently so unaffected by the cataclysmic events which take place around us.[125]

Noble concludes by offering Micah 1:8 as support for this view, and suggests that it is not good enough to dismiss the apparent 'excess' of Micah's howling like a jackal and moaning like an owl as a no longer applicable Old Testament detail.

Saturday 16th December 2000

Reflecting on its importance for his own charismatic development, Rob Warner pays tribute to *Renewal* magazine, and assesses the current state of the renewal movement. Part of his analysis focuses on TTB. Warner is markedly more downbeat than in his previous statements on the issue:

> Toronto came in with a bang but, frankly, seems to have ended with a whimper. For me, it was a time of deep spiritual enrichment and rekindled hope for revival. Yet it was also a time of being turned off by the threefold ministries of unreality – exaggeration, manipulation and hysteria. Not all crying out, falling down, or exalted emotions come from God – but some do. Perhaps Toronto is best seen as a parable of the mixed brew that is renewal. Paul put it so well: we need to test everything, hold onto the good and not extinguish the Spirit's fire.[126]

January 2001

The Evangelical Alliance makes selected sections of this book available on its web site, as a prelude to paperback publication of the full text by Paternoster Press in the autumn of 2001.

Notes to Chapter 11

[1] 'Evangelical Unity Urged', *New Christian Herald*, 3rd February 1996.

[2] G. Chevreau, *Share the Fire: The Toronto Blessing and Grace-Based Evangelism*, p.176.

[3] 'Toronto Airport Church No Longer a Vineyard', *Alpha*, February 1996, pp.4–8.

[4] W. Porter, 'The Worship of the Toronto Blessing?' in Porter & Richter (eds.) *The Toronto Blessing – Or Is It?*, pp.104-30.

[5] A. Morrison, *A Different Gospel: The Origin and Purpose of the Toronto Blessing*, (Video). See 17th May 1995 and Bibliography. A similar accusation is made in Morrison's pamphlet *Falling for the Lie*. See Friday 30th September 1994 and Bibliography.

[6] In C. Hill et al *Blessing the Church?* See 17th November 1995 and Bibliography.

[7] D. Roberts, 'The Toronto Divide', *Alpha*, February 1996, pp.4-6.

[8] '"Toronto Blessing" Group is Ousted', *Direction*, February 1996, pp.40-41.

[9] Victoria Coombe, 'Telford Blessing "Ends in Tears"', *Daily Telegraph*, 3rd February 1996.

[10] 'Evangelical Unity Urged', *New Christian Herald*, 3rd July 1995.

[11] 'Toronto Preacher Wins Widespread Support', *Church of England Newspaper*, 19th February 1996, p.2.

[12] T. Hayes, 'Legless for Jesus? Now I'm a Believer', *Evening Standard*, 8th February 1996.

[13] C. Moreton, 'Toronto Pastor is Still Laughing', *Church Times*, 9th February, 1996, p.5. The comments by David Jenkins were actually broadcast on BBC Radio at 8pm on 18th February.

[14] A. Boyd, 'Toronto: Calm After the Storm?', *New Christian Herald*, 17th February 1996.

[15] For details see Bibliography.

[16] M Bickle, & M. Sullivant, *God's Manifest Presence*.

[17] D. Roberts, 'A Blessing Beyond Belief?', *Alpha*, March 1996, pp.24-6.

[18] C. Hill, 'Editorial Statement on the Toronto Blessing', *Prophecy Today*, Vol. 12 No. 2, (March-April 1996), p.17.

[19] S. Bell, 'Toronto Prepares for A Niagara Falls of Holy Spirit Glory', *Joy*, March 1996, p.44-5.

[20] J. Sweeny, *Observer*, 3rd March 1996.

[21] 'T. Higton: My Spiritual Renaissance', *Church of England Newspaper*, 22nd March 1996.

[22] C. Price, 'Fire in the Gulf', *Alpha*, pp.28-31.

[23] Ibid., pp.30-31.

[24] C. Price, 'Taste for the Exotic', *Alpha*, p.29.

[25] J. Arnott, *Keep the Fire*.

[26] Ibid. See also C. Price, 'Fire in the Gulf', *Alpha*, April 1996, pp.28-31.

[27] C. Calver, 'Together for Truth', in C. Calver & R. Warner, *Together We Stand: Evangelical Convictions, Unity and Vision*, p.135.

[28] 'Appendix I: An Evangelical Consultation on "The Toronto Blessing"', in ibid., pp.162-5.

[29] Wright, *Strange Fire?*, pp.31-8.

[30] Ibid., pp.29-30.

[31] Ibid., pp. 65 [64-72].

[32] Ibid., pp.199-211.

[33] Ibid., pp.325-6.

[34] R. Gledhill, 'Woman Leads Church Boycott in Row Over Evangelical "Pig Snorting"', *The Times*, 11th May 1996.

[35] Methodist Faith and Order Committee: 'A) The Toronto Blessing', *Methodist Conference Agenda*, pp.161-79.

[36] Ibid., p.164.

[37] Ibid., p.169.

[38] Ibid., p.170.

[39] Ibid., p.172.

[40] See Richter's 'God is Not a Gentleman!', pp.5-37. Details at 17th July 1995.

[41] Methodist Faith and Order Committee: 'A) The Toronto Blessing', p.173.

[42] Ibid., p.174.

[43] Ibid., p.176.

[44] Ibid., p.178. For a summary of the report, see *Methodist Recorder*, 16th May 1996, pp.13-4.

[45] 'Stott on Toronto', *Alpha*, July 1996, p.35.

[46] 'Toronto Effect Must Lead to Mission', *New Christian Herald*, 22nd June 1996, p.5.

[47] A. Taylor, 'Church Choice' (Letter), *Solihull News*, 16th August 1996.

[48] R. Warner, 'The Stott Debate: Truth and Toronto', *Alpha*, October 1996, pp.4-7.

[49] Virgo, *A People Prepared*, p.19.

[50] Ibid., p.191.

[51] I. McFarlane, 'Is This Revival?', *Baptist Times*, 28th November 1996, p.5.

[52] B. Davies, 'Pensacola: "A Command to Repent"', *Renewal*, February 1997, pp.19-20.

[53] 'Interview with Evangelist Steve Hill in Pensacola: 'They've seen the Power of Satan, Now They See the Power of God', *Challenge Weekly*, 29th January 1997, pp.1, 5.

[54] Chevreau, *Share the Fire*, pp.174, 177, 178.

[55] Hand, 'Tasting the Fruit', p.40.

[56] Ibid., p.45.

[57] Ibid., p.47.

[58] Ibid., p.53.

[59] Ibid., p.59.

[60] 'Pentecostal Outpouring Keeps Gushing', *Christianity Today*, 3rd March 1997, pp. 54-6.

[61] Ibid.

[62] *Church Times*, Letters, 21st March 1997; 'Toronto Blessing "Traumatised Boy"', *The Times*, 21st March 1997.

[63] Church of Scotland Panel on Doctrine, *The Toronto Blessing*, Edinburgh: Church of Scotland, 1997.

[64] Ibid., pp.6-8.

[65] Ibid., pp.10-13.

[66] Ibid., pp.17-9.

[67] Ibid., pp.24-7.

[68] Ibid., p.36.

[69] Ibid., pp.38-41.

[70] V. Coombe, 'Toronto Blessing Attacked by Kirk', *The Times*, 4th April, 1994; G. Bowditch, 'Kirk Warning over Toronto Blessing', *Daily Telegraph*, 4th April 1994.

[71] 'Breeding a Culture of Revival', *Christianity*, May 1997, p.7.

[72] M. Haville, 'Giving Their Lives for "The Faith"', *Evangelicals Now*, June 1997, p.10.

[73] Richards, *Toronto Experience*, pp.1-2.

[74] Ibid., p.3.

[75] Ibid., pp.5-6.

[76] Ibid., p.13.

[77] Ibid., p.20

[78] Ibid., pp.23-4.

[79] Ibid., p.27.

[80] H. Pinnell, 'Blessing is "Still Going Strong"', *Church Times*, 27th June 1997, p.1.

[81] 'Vineyard Founder Wimber Dies', *Christianity Today*, November 1997.

[82] R. Howard, *The Rise and Fall of the Nine O'clock Service*, London: Mowbray, 1996.

[83] R. Howard, *Charismania: When Christian Fundamentalism Goes Wrong*, pp.109-17.

[84] 'Vineyard Founder Wimber Dies', *Christianity Today*, November 1997.

[85] Ibid.

[86] G. Russell-Jones, 'Whatever Happened to the Promised Revival?', *Christianity*, December 1997, pp.28-30.

[87] Ibid., p.29.

[88] Ibid., p.29.

[89] Ibid., p.30.

[90] H. Hanegraff, *Counterfeit Revival*.

[91] T. Stipe, 'Foreword', in Hanegraff, *Counterfeit Revival*.

[92] R.T. Kendall, 'A Response to Hank Hanegraff's Book', *Evangelicals Now*, December 1997, p.18.

[93] 'Pensacola: "Church Vote of Confidence"', *New Christian Herald*, 6th December 1997, p.3.

[94] L. Pieterson, 'Introduction', in Pietersen (ed.), *Mark of the Spirit?*, pp.1-5.

[95] L. Pietersen, 'Ecstatic Phenomena for an Ecstatic Culture?' in ibid., pp.7-32.

[96] M. Smith, '"This-Is-That" Hermeneutics', in ibid., pp.33-62.

[97] V. Culver, 'Ecstatic Laughter', in ibid., pp.63-86.

[98] J. Lyons, 'The Gamaliel Principle', in ibid., p.111.

[99] Ibid. p.117.

[100] M. Haville, 'USA: Pensacola Problems', *Evangelicals Now*, February 1998, p.24.

[101] 'Vineyard-Toronto Rift is Publicly Healed', *Renewal*, June 1998, p.7.

[102] Ibid.

[103] A. Bateman, 'Whatever Happened to the Toronto Blessing?', *Salvationist*, 1st August 1998, pp.12-13.

[104] K. Walters, 'TACF Experience Gold Teeth Miracle!', news@revival.net, Friday 12th March 1999.

[105] D. Pytches, *Some Said It Thundered*, p.138.

[106] R. Warner, 'God's Gold or Fool's Gold?', *Christian Herald*, 15th May 1999, p.9.

[107] P. Partner, *Two Thousand Years. The Second Millennium: From Medieval Christendom to Global Christianity*, p.131.

[108] R. Warner, 'God's Gold or Fool's Gold?', *Christian Herald*, 15th May 1999, p.9.

[109] M. Argyle, *Psychology and Religion*, pp.135-7.

[110] Scotland, pp.220-50.

[111] Ibid., p.224.

[112] Ibid., pp.246-7.

[113] Ibid., p.247.

[114] Ibid., pp.241, 247.

[115] Ibid., pp.247-8.

[116] Ibid., p.249.

[117] P. Seager, 'Back to the Blessing', *Idea*, September-October 2000, pp.30-32.

[118] Ibid., p.30.

[119] B. Martin, 'After the Animal Noises, Are People Feeling Sheepish?', *Church Times*, 20th October 2000, pp.16-7.

[120] J. Ronson, 'Catch Me if You Can', *Guardian Weekend*, 21st October 2000, pp.10-21

[121] Ibid., p.19.

[122] Ibid., p.19.

[123] J. Noble, 'A Very English Blessing?', *Renewal*, November 2000, pp.34-5.

[124] Ibid., p.35.

[125] Ibid., p.35.

[126] R. Warner, '21st Century Renewal: Only Just Begun', *Renewal*, January 2001, p.54

PART III

STATEMENTS ON THE TORONTO BLESSING

12

Champaign Vineyard Suggested Ministry Tips
May 1994

The following paper was published in May 1994 by Bill Jackson and the Champaign Vineyard Christian Fellowship (VCF), Urbana, Illinois. It soon became a major point of reference for Vineyard and other churches touched by the Toronto Blessing.1

Written to help teach the Champaign Vineyard church body wholesome techniques for enhancing times of ministry, this paper contains some helpful hints about four specific areas:

● Tips for facilitating ministry as a leader;
● Tips for praying for people;
● Tips for catching people;
● Tips for receiving ministry.

Written by the church staff, it is not intended to be considered an official 'position paper' about how the Champaign Vineyard, or any other church – Vineyard or otherwise - should handle times of ministry. These tips have been compiled based on the experience of the Champaign staff and the suggestions of others.

Tips for facilitating ministry as a leader
1. It is usually helpful to begin every time with worship followed by testimonies of people who have been touched. Immediately after the testimonies, invite the Holy Spirit to come upon these individuals again and do a further work. There seems to be a special grace for these people to receive another 'drink' of the new wine when they are up front giving testimonies. They often begin to experience the same outward manifestations again.
2. When ministry begins, look for those who are most obviously anointed. This can be done by looking for manifestations such as crying, shaking, laughing, etc.
3. If you don't notice any outward manifestations of the Holy Spirit, ask those who sense a strong anointing within them to come for ministry. This might manifest as a burning, tingling, 'knowing', etc.

4. Encourage people to freely receive ministry. It's OK to receive several times of prayer in the same meeting. It's also OK to receive prayer every time we gather. In fact, people seem to receive better and more fully each successive time. The more the 'soaking', the deeper the impact.

5. Keep reassuring people that it's OK if they do not manifest anything unusual when they receive prayer. God works differently in different people. Remember to encourage people that it's not manifestations we are after but changed hearts. The manifestations are simply a by-product.

6. Encourage people not to be fearful of what God is doing. This requires reassuring words from the leaders.

7. Be willing to be prayed for yourself. People always respond best when the leaders are also responding. It seems that the leaders are the gatekeepers and what they will allow, the people feel confident to allow.

8. Sometimes children are afraid to receive until they see their parents or other known adults receive. Some children have even been reported as being fearful of some of the manifestations they have experienced, such as being pinned to the floor.

9. Keep the 'environment' light and easy. This is not a season for heavy ministry, great deliverance, or deep inner healing. It seems the Holy Spirit is emphasising joy and release from heaviness.

10. Please refer to these manifestations as 'times of refreshing' (Acts 3:19) or renewal rather than revival. Revival has the connotation of touching the larger community. Use the phrase 'resting in the Spirit' rather than 'slain in the Spirit'.

11. When the number of people wanting prayer is large, it seems that the quality of prayer goes down and vice versa. We've found that the people who linger around the longest and get multiple times of prayer generally get the most. Meeting and prayer times seem to move from low anointing to higher as time goes on.

12. Current prayer methods do not contradict the Vineyard prayer model. Both are important and should be used as led by the Spirit.

13. The 'event flavour' of this season does not nullify the idea that some things happen as a process.

14. Let's be careful about pride and presumption.

Tips for praying for people

1. When praying for individuals, watch closely what the Spirit is doing (Jn. 5:19). If no manifestation of the Holy Spirit comes within a few minutes, it is often wise to simply allow that person to 'soak' and come back later. We've found it is even advisable to say something like this, 'I want you to soak a little while, and I will be back to you later.' Meanwhile, others will pray for them, or you can come back when you are done with the next individual.

2. When people fall in the Spirit (called 'resting in the Spirit'), keep praying for them. It seems that everyone wants to get up way too quickly. God

continues to do work even when we are down on the floor. Sometimes it will be noticeable and other times it might be quiet and inward. Allowing people to get up too quickly seems to work against what the Lord wants to do.

3. Generally, it is helpful to have people stand to receive ministry. This seems to allow the Holy Spirit more freedom to move. Be sure to put someone behind the person receiving ministry to catch them.

4. Be careful not to push people over. This is offensive and will backfire by causing people to grow resistant to the real thing.

5. Don't force ministry. If the Spirit is not doing something, relax and remember that there will always be another opportunity.

6. There is at times a 'backwash phenomenon'. This means that the anointing is not received by the individual you are praying for and can actually come back to you.

7. If the person is one of the 'hard ones', you might help them do the following. Help them to deal with a tendency to rationalise, with their fears, or with a loss of control. Calm their fear of loss of control by helping them know what to expect. For example, let them know that they will have a clear mind; that they can usually stop the process at any point if they want to, and that the Spirit comes in waves.

8. Pray biblical prayers such as some of the following. Come Holy Spirit. Let the Kingdom of God come on earth as it is in Heaven. Outpouring of the Father's love for them and for others. A deeper revelation of the Father's love in Christ. Anointing for service. Release of the gifts and callings. Bring the light and expel the darkness. Note: 'More Lord' is just a shortened form of blessing what the Father is doing, from John 5:19.

9. If you are getting 'words of knowledge', pray biblical prayers related to those words.

10. Some people have 'fear of falling' issues. Help them to sit down or to fall carefully, especially if they have back problems, pregnancy or fear of falling.

11. It's OK to talk to the person during the engagement process.

12. If your hand/body is shaking, pray with hands slightly away from the person so as not to distract them.

13. Don't project what God has been doing with you on to the person you are praying for. For example, if you've been laughing, don't pressure them to laugh. Find out what God is doing for them and bless it.

14. Encourage the people you pray for to put testimonies in written form immediately. Please use the forms 'New Wines at the Vineyard' for adults and children.

Tips for catching people

1. Please do not push or pull anyone over. This will ultimately backfire.

2. Do not hold anyone up by grabbing their shoulders or upper back.

3. When laying hands on people, do just that. Do not rub or do other things that might be annoying.

4. When catching someone, put your hands lightly in the small of their back. This gives people confidence that you are behind them and does not interfere with the prayer process.

Tips for receiving ministry

1. Come humble and hungry. Forget preconceived ideas and what has happened to others.
2. Experience it before trying to analyse it. It is something like worshipping God which has no rational explanation. Others have likened it to kissing, which is more emotional than analytical.
3. Face your fears. The fear of deception; the fear of being hurt again or not receiving at all; the fear of losing control. (This can often be seen when people try to step backward rather than fall.)
4. Focus on the Lord, not on falling. Give the Holy Spirit permission to do with you what he wants to do.

©1994. All rights reserved. Bill Jackson & The Champaign Vineyard Christian Fellowship (VCF), Urbana, Illinois.

---

1 Reprinted in Dixon, *Signs of Revival*, pp. 327-31. The text carries the following permission notice: 'This document is hereby made freely available for the edification, and exhortation, and comfort of any and all worldwide. Specifically, permission is granted to anyone to make or distribute verbatim copies of this document in any medium, provided that the copyright notice and permission notice are preserved, and that the distributor grants the recipient permission for further redistribution as permitted by this copyright. No charge for any redistribution may be assessed save those incurred during duplication (including, but not limited to, costs incurred through photocopying, laserprinting, and electronic media distribution). The Champaign Area Vineyard thanks you for your compliance.

13

Evangelical Alliance (UK) Preliminary Statement on the Toronto Blessing

July 1994

This, the first and briefer of two statements produced by the Alliance when the Blessing was on the increase, was drafted on 14th July by the then UK Director (later General Director) Joel Edwards, and approved by his fellow Senior Managers for distribution and public quotation. It would be superseded by the considerably more detailed 'Euston Statement' of December 1994 (see Section III 18, p353).

The current spiritual phenomenon described as the 'Toronto Blessing' has become a source of much attention within the evangelical church.

The Evangelical Alliance has attempted to keep abreast of the developments which have affected a wide cross-section of churches. From our observations, we would wish to offer the following points:

1. Evangelicals should make every effort to measure all spiritual phenomena by biblical criteria. In every case, the devotional hallmarks of holiness, prayer and witness provide reliable indicators of authentic moves of God.

2. We also acknowledge that the current phenomenon is not new. During the eighteenth, nineteenth and early twentieth centuries revivals associated with respected figures such as Jonathan Edwards, Wesley, Whitefield and the Jeffreys were also characterised by unusual events which attracted controversy and blessings.

3. We rejoice with those who testify to deeper level of commitment and joy as a result of their experience but would equally urge them to avoid excessive behaviour which may discredit the Gospel or distance those who genuinely seek an encounter with God.

4. Whilst we would caution against indiscriminate enthusiasm, we would equally urge Evangelicals to avoid preclusive or condemnatory behaviour which dismisses *all* unusual events out of hand.

5. Finally, we would advocate the Gamaliel principle; if the phenomenon is genuinely of God it will certainly bear lasting fruit.

Our hope and sincere prayer is that Evangelicals will not allow the issue to polarise and divide our witness at a time when it is most acutely needed.

14

Association of Vineyard Churches Board Report: Summary Report on the Current Renewal and the Phenomena Surrounding It

September/October 1994

By the autumn of 1994, the Blessing had affected a significant number of churches in the Vineyard network. As the Chronicle in Part II makes clear, Randy Clark of the St Louis Vineyard had played a key role in introducing it to other Vineyard pastors after his encounter with Rodney Howard-Browne in Tulsa in August 1993. He had then been invited by John Arnott to preach at a series of meetings at the Toronto Airport Vineyard in January 1994. These meetings are generally recognised to have initiated the Blessing proper. Bill Jackson of Champaign Vineyard had subsequently produced two influential position papers on the movement in May: a practical text on 'Ministry Tips' (see p333), and a much longer biblical and theological apologetic for the new movement entitled 'What in the World is Happening to Us?' (for details see entry for April-May 1994 in Part II). The following statement is an attempt to consider these developments within the existing framework of Vineyard / 'Third Wave' theology and practice. It was published on the ecunet bulletin board.

Introduction

The guidelines that follow represent the majority consensus of the board. It is not possible in a brief document to adequately express all the discussion or all of the minority positions that are held by various board members. It is, therefore, important to remember that this statement is subject to the autonomy of the local church and its pastor. All of this must be worked through in a way that does not violate one's faith or conscience.

The Pastoral Administration of Phenomena

1. We are willing to allow 'experiences' to happen without endorsing, encouraging or stimulating them; nor should we seek to 'explain' them by inappropriate 'proof-texting'. Biblical metaphors (similar to those concerning a lion or a dove, etc.) do not justify or provide a proof-text for animal behaviour.

   There are some manifestations, that while socially uncomfortable (i.e., they wouldn't seem 'decent and in order' in most church contexts today), have biblical precedent (cf. Dan. 8:16-18,27; 10:8-10; Mt: 17:6,7; Rev. 1:17, etc.). The absence of a proof-text, however, does not necessarily disallow an experience. If so, none of us could go to Disneyland, use computers to write messages, or have worship bands. The point is, don't try to defend unusual manifestations from biblical texts that obviously lack a one-to-one correspondence with a current experience.

We also need to be careful in our use of revival history and tradition to justify manifestations. People like Jonathan Edwards are helpful in that they give us examples of how godly men, who submitted themselves to the Scriptures as their final authority, sorted out similar issues. But in fairness to them, we don't know exactly what they would say about the current phenomena. What we do know is that men like Edwards are shining examples of how to responsibly use Scripture.

We do not necessarily equate an 'experience' as a manifestation of the Holy Spirit. For example, one person may have a genuine response to the presence of God which involves shaking and/or falling down. A person standing next to him or her, however, may do the exact same thing out of emotionalism or some other excess. While there has been some excess in our meetings, questionable manifestations have not been the major part of the renewal, but have attracted a disproportionate amount of attention.

2. Although there was some particular concern about animal noises (some would discourage them; others would rule them out completely), the board was not prepared to make a blanket statement rejecting or 'tarring' any particular manifestation unless it is prohibited by Scripture. Such extra-biblical manifestations must be discerned individually. The ultimate test of manifestations should be the long-term fruit produced in a person's life, and the edification of the body of Christ (i.e., through prophecy, etc. – see enclosed article by John Wimber [reprinted here in the next section]).

3. Rather than promoting, displaying or focusing on phenomena, we want to focus on the main/plain issues of Scripture. For instance, witnessing, healing, demon expulsion, ministering to the poor and widows, etc. This way, people will find their identity, in doing Scriptural work, not in experiencing phenomena. We would like people to be known as 'evangelists' or 'zealous Christian workers' rather than 'roarers' or 'shakers'. We do not want manifestations to be a mark of spirituality. Rather the fruit and the gifts of the Spirit and a godly character should attest to true spirituality.

4. When extra-biblical or exotic phenomena do occur, we want to avoid theologising from them. *No doctrine should be based on a prophetic interpretation of a particular manifestation.* Admitting 'I don't know' about an occurrence of a phenomenon will promote more balance in the ongoing development of this renewal than focusing people on it by endorsing everything as a work of God.

Tentative 'observations' can be made concerning patterns we witness in ministry; but they should never be cataloged as doctrine. For example, our

'Five-Step Healing Model' is a useful tool to initiate people into praying for the sick; but it is not doctrinal in nature. It is methodological.

It has also proven unhelpful to describe vocal sounds as 'animal noises' (lions, chickens, dogs, etc.). In most cases, the people making the sounds are, in fact, not intentionally imitating animals, and therefore, should not be labelled as such.

5. We want to avoid linking the present work of the Spirit to any precise eschatological scenario (e.g., Hal Lindsey or the Latter Rain Movement. etc.). It would probably be wiser to maintain the loose pre-millennial views held by the vast majority, but not all – namely, that we have been in 'the last days' since Pentecost and we don't know when the precise last moments of time are. Consequently, we don't know if this current renewal is 'the last big one' or not.

6. We want this renewal to motivate people to the obvious kingdom works of Scripture (cf. #3). People should go home from our meetings telling a well-rounded story: 'I've got it to give it away!' Those who are the most filled with the Spirit and a renewed love for Jesus naturally and easily express it by demonstrating His love for the lost, broken sick and demonised.

7. We want the ongoing lives of Vineyard churches to be governed by our previously stated values and priorities. Key values to remember in a re-newal context are; simplicity, do nothing for effects' sake (i.e., hype or manipulate), always equip the saints, respect the privacy and dignity of individuals, etc. (cf., the current AVC Statement of Faith) We do not want to establish a new pattern of church life that revolves only around re-newal meetings. We are encouraging pastors to maintain the basic infra-structure and program of their churches so as to meet all the needs of all the people.

8. While we will listen to our critics and learn from them, we do not want to be governed by them. If they can prove to us by sound exegesis and logic that we are wrong, we will change. By the nature of our movement (re-newal of the things of the Spirit) we have always had, and always will have, critics; let's interact with them as godly men and women without becom-ing reactionary, bitter, unteachable, or controlled by them.

9. We do not want to equate the experiencing of phenomena with instant healing unless there is clear evidence for such a claim. Because a person shakes or falls does not mean all his or her problems and temptations or testings are over.

Concerning the Application of 1 Corinthians 14

Some people have been concerned that a proper understanding and application of 1 Corinthians 14 would rule out much of the current phenomena. Below are the board's thoughts on the matter:

1. The nature and purpose of a meeting determines the context for its admin-istration. 1 Corinthians 14 is the main guideline we have in Scripture to govern Christian meetings. Because Paul was not writing with every imag-

inable modern context in view, we must seek to properly understand the principles he lays out and apply the same to our situation.

The main questions that arise out of the text are 'what should be limited?' (vv. 27-29) and 'what should be encouraged?' (v.39). Though some would see Paul's own application of his principles (vv.27-29) as completely ruling out extra-biblical phenomena (anything that could cause someone to say, 'you are out of your mind,' 1 Cor. 14:23 NIV), the majority of the board were content to judge each manifestation on its own merit.

2. The principles that emerge from 1 Corinthians 14 are:
(i) For an experience, manifestation, phenomenon, or gift to be 'decent and in order', it must edify the body of Christ. In order to edify, it must be intelligible. Therefore, someone in the group must make spiritual manifestations understandable to all (i.e., interpretation of tongues, etc.).

Gordon Fee's commentary on 1 Corinthians (NICNT) is helpful here. Fee says, 'the real issue is not tongues or prophecy per se, but the building up of the community, which can only be effected by understandable utterances, prophecy being the primary representative' (p. 652) … 'edification controls the thought of the entire chapter' (p. 657).

Edification in its verb and noun form is used seven times in this chapter along with related words which seem to describe what Paul means by 'edification'. They are:

- Encouragement/exhortation (v.3);
- Profit/benefit (v.6);
- Teach/instruct (v 19);
- Worship (v.25);
- Learn (v.31).

(ii) Manifestations should have:
- Christ-exalting content (1 Cor. 12:3; cf. Jn. 4:1-3; Rev. 19:10)
- Christ-resembling character (1 Cor. 13, esp. vv.4-7): 'only when charisma is manifested as the expression of grace (i.e., humble, selfless love) will it benefit either the individual or the community' (J. Dunn, *Jesus and the Spirit*, p.294).
- Community-building consequences – Paul's argument with the Corinthians was not so much whether their manifestations were from God or not (cf. 1:17), but whether they were building up or tearing down the unity and spiritual growth of the body of Christ.
- Paul's criteria for community-building are:
  (a) a sense of unity amidst the diversity of gifts,
  (b) intelligibility, and
  (c) order – meaning corporate etiquette (vv.26-27; 29-31) in consonance with God's character (v.33).

3. If an extra-biblical or exotic manifestation is thought to have some prophetic value to the group, and is helpful in the context of a meeting, it

is the responsibility of the leader to ensure that it is made intelligible to all (vv. 16, 17). If it is not prophetic or intelligible or is disrupting the preaching of the Word, it is to be controlled and kept from dominating the attention of the group.

4. There will always be an inherent tension as we seek to apply these principles to our meetings. The tension is between appropriately 'controlling' a meeting using the principles of 1 Corinthians 14, versus 'quenching' the Holy Spirit (cf. 1 Thess. 5:19-21). In 1 Corinthians 14 Paul is obviously not arguing that we should 'quench' the Spirit. Rather, his concern is that as leaders or participants we should 'control' ourselves so as to ensure our expressions of the Spirit build up the body of Christ.

The Messages and Themes of This Renewal

Some have asked, 'What does all this mean?' 'Where is it going?' 'Is there any central thrust?' etc. Below are the themes the board would like to see emphasized:

- Passion for Christ
- Intimacy with God expressed in fervent worship
- Compassion for others
- A new reality of the love of the Father
- Refreshing, emboldening; and impartation of power for kingdom service
- Isaiah 55: 'Come and drink!'
- Renewal of godly character
- Final result of effective discipleship

Conclusion

You may ask, 'in simple terms, what does all the above mean?' It means that it is our desire to embrace all that is good about this renewal while correcting that which is excessive, long-term hurtful or contrary to biblical mandates. We also want to interact with the renewal based on our historical and firmly held vision, mission and purpose. Namely, that we are committed to 'power evangelism', not just 'power'; we are committed to 'signs and wonders and church growth', not just 'signs and wonders'. The Lord has clearly instructed us to direct these current blessings into practical activities that will minister to and bless those outside of our churches. It is our hope that every Vineyard pastor will do so through the grace and power of God.

Todd Hunter, for the AVC Board
Anaheim, California
October 1994
© The Association of Vineyard Churches and Vineyard Ministries International. Used by permission.

15

John Wimber Responds to the Phenomena
September/October 1994

The following is an excerpt taken from a letter by Vineyard leader John Wimber, in which he responds to questions regarding some of the phenomena experienced in the Toronto Blessing. It was published, along with the AVC Board Report (see p339), on the ecunet bulletin board.

My views as to the issue of 'roaring' under the anointing

1. I would say that there is no biblical or theological framework for such phenomena. I don't see anywhere in the New Testament where Jesus and/or the apostles encouraged such phenomena or encountered such phenomena. Therefore, I think these kinds of things have to be put in a category of 'non-biblical' and 'exotic'.

2. However, there have been some revival reports in church tradition where people have made various and sundry 'animal noises' (or noise that could labelled as such, though I doubt making animal sounds was the intent of the people). For instance, at the Cane Ridge Revival in Kentucky during the Second Great Awakening, there were a number of people that did so.

   Furthermore, I understand that Charles Finney had some sort of experience where he made a kind of 'roaring noise', although I don't think he, in retrospect, equated it with a lion. He did equate it, however, with an anointing from God that transformed his life and ministry.

3. I've had, to date, seven or eight testimonies from people who have 'roared'. Here are the conclusions they drew from the experience:

   (i) There was a sense of God's indignation at the state of the church and the impact of the enemy's presence in the church. As a consequence, people responded with a 'prophetic roar' which was sort of an 'announcement' of God's intention to take back territory.

   (ii) Furthermore, it seemed to affirm the issue of the Lord's authority in their lives and ministries, and as a consequence they've been very excited about the potential for more powerful ministry in the future.

   (iii) It seems to me that nearly all of them have equated this with some sort of prophetic experience, either personal anointing for prophecy and/or prophetic in the sense that God is saying to the church, 'Rise up, and take back the land/people/things that the enemy has one way or another wrongfully usurped control of.'

(iv) However, having said that, I must point out that there is some disagreement in our circles here in the Vineyard.

- There are those that are very enthusiastic endorsers of the experience and I think are, as a consequence, even encouraging others in this kind of experience. I strongly feel that it is excessive to do so, in that again I know of no biblical mandate for encouraging anyone to 'roar'. However, based on the rubric of 'bless what the Father's doing', I suppose if I were in a ministry context and somebody started 'roaring', I would bless what I thought the Father was doing, regardless of the 'roaring' or any other manifestation. Keep in mind, however, we do not equate phenomena with God; we see these usually as human responses to God.

- On the other hand, there are people who sharply disagree with the notion that anything such as this kind of phenomena could be perceived to be something of God, and would quickly point out that there's no biblical support for equating the experience with God, and I would have to agree that this, indeed, has to be viewed as an exotic and non-biblically endorsed experience.

  Having said that, I do not, personally, hold the opinion that this is 'demonic' and/or necessarily 'divine'. I put this in the category of 'pondering'/'I don't know'. I am looking for, in the aftermath, the effects of the experience to see how it relates to the person's life. If we see fruit (i.e. Mt. 7: 15ff; 1 Cor. 14; Acts 5:33ff.; I Jn. 4:1-3), then I suppose I would accept the notion that, if the people who have had the experience are advancing, perhaps it was something from God.

In light of all the above, here my are my views on 'phenomena'

1. I cannot endorse or even encourage this experience in our movement and ministry, but at the same time I recognise that it is happening and I would just leave it in the same category as I have of people shaking, or falling or having other kinds of exotic phenomena that may have some limited biblical representation. Therefore, this is not necessarily anything that we ought to equate as 'always' something of God, or even 'sometimes' something of God, though it may be a reaction to the Spirit's activity. I think that we ought to endorse and encourage the 'main and the plain things' of Scripture: i.e. salvation, sanctification, justification by faith and the consequent experiences of such, where people would have testimonies of how they are advancing in their initial relationship with God and then moving on in progression with God.

2. I feel that it's very important that we direct this 'refreshing' and 'enabling' move of the Spirit to the New Testament works of the church, that is to say, having been refreshed, we now must channel these people into work that would express that refreshing in solid, biblical context. That is to say that

they should be encouraged to begin interceding, sharing their faith in an evangelistic context: they should be feeding the hungry, ministering to the poor, the widow, the divorcee, etc., etc. I believe that if we channel this energy away from a 'bless me' kind of focus to a 'bless them' kind of focus we will indeed be utilizing this fresh anointing in a biblically appropriate fashion.

Finally, I want to close by saying this. I feel that the exuberant and initial response of many in this area is well taken, and I'm happy for their testimonies. I just don't want to make our meetings a focus on 'phenomena'. I would like to make our meetings focused on the Word and works of the Spirit.

Now, having said all that, I recognize that there are certain manifestations of the Spirit that have gone on in our meetings for fifteen years that we supposed were demonic in origin. And there have been times in the past where we've attempted to cast demons out of people who made 'animal noises'. On some occasions demons manifested and we did cast them out and on other occasions we were puzzled by the lack of deliverance.

Therefore, I think in the past we've had a simplistic view of all of these kinds of things. These new phenomena and their apparent 'fruit' have been a circumstance that has caused me to stop and think and review again my presuppositions as they relate to this all.

16

'In the Light of Toronto': Gerald Coates, with help from Bryn Jones, Sandy Millar, David Pytches and Vineyard USA

October 1994

This collaborative statement first appeared in the October 1994 issue of Renewal *magazine. It was subsequently published in the February 1995 edition of* 'Aware'.[1]

What Should Leaders Do When the Spirit Comes?

1. *Make a swift response to the work of the Spirit.* We must be willing to embrace the work of God's Spirit even if it means changes to our structures, programmes and agendas. The main key is the entire leadership submitting themselves to the Holy Spirit and being willing to receive prayer.

2. *Repent with humility and faith.* Faith will overcome our fears, uncertainty and doubt. Humility will keep us from superiority and elitism. We have been praying for renewal and revival, we should not be surprised if God responds. 'Which of you if his son asked for bread would give him a stone? Or if he asked for a fish would give him a snake?' (Mt.7:9-10).

3. *Take responsibility for what is happening.* The elders in Corinth had a hands-off approach. It was a mixture of manifestations of the Spirit, the work of the flesh and even the devil. As leaders we have to give an account for what we allow and encourage in our churches. God puts no premium on ignorance. While it is a time of refreshing, it is also a time when we as leaders must help the church understand what is happening.

4. *Ensure that we are overseeing and administering what is going on.* We do not want things to simply become introspective. We want to see people ultimately look to those outside the Christian community. Otherwise self-indulgence will take root, and either we will be responding to people's needs and manifestations or, eventually we will dry up.

Practical Help

● Ensure that you do not seek personal gain, prominence or benefit from what is clearly a divine visitation.

- Do not develop a ministry of manifestations, when God is wanting to do something deeper.
- Do not hype meetings; be relaxed but full of expectancy.
- Maintain a focus on the source of the blessing, Christ himself, and do not transfer people's faith either to a person, a place or a method.
- Do not be afraid of praying with children as well as adults. Most children believe this to be a little like heaven and are much more responsive than some adults. When praying with children it is helpful to have parents or a parent present. If parents have been touched by God we should be looking out for their children.
- Explain any unusual activities. It may be of God or the devil but you will be responsible for determining which. Do not leave the church confused.
- Endeavour to understand that events like these place great demands on you as a leader emotionally and physically. Ensure you rest: do not stagger from meeting to meeting.
- Enjoy what is going on; do not become over heavy, serious and certainly not religious.
- Be prepared for criticism. Some will not understand what is going on, others will be fearful. This is a time for sensitive action not emotional reaction.
- While not discouraging people from visiting other churches to see what is happening, be wary of competitiveness and comparisons. Also of people simply running around to 'get blessed' without that blessing being allowed to bring about a radical change of life.
- Be careful about prolonged times of men praying for women or women men. It is preferable that prayer should be single sex or in groups.
- If there is a fleshly or demonic manifestation which you are unable to deal with make sure someone is drawn alongside you immediately. Such manifestations can be a distraction to the rest of the meeting.
- Encourage people when they feel that 'nothing has happened'. Some have sat under this sort of ministry for up to 12 hours with 'nothing happening' but now they are prominent channels of this blessing.

Facing Opposition

There has never been a move of God which hasn't faced serious opposition. We see this in Jesus' ministry and in the Acts of the Apostles from the religious as well as the godless.

So we need to minister to the Lord and his people with 'clean hands and a pure heart'. Therefore, let us ensure that our behaviour is in line with the biblical mandate, with as little physical contact as possible, never pushing people over, or saying things which amount to triumphalism or pure fantasy. Don't invite criticism and opposition.

When we are attacked by people in the church, or other churches, or in the Christian press, it is easy to be reactionary, cynical, dismissive or superior. This could be more a matter of attitude than word, and comes across with a 'What do they know?' attitude. Remain calm, rational and reasonable. Learn to disagree without being disagreeable.

- Endeavour to read Scripture into what is going on, without becoming preachy or sermonising. We must not be awash in a sea of subjectivity.
- Create a worshipping environment and give room for testimonies that speak of the fruit rather than the manifestations.
- Encourage people to 'drink' as Jesus promises to quench our thirst. Also encourage people to allow the rivers of living water to touch those outside the Christian community.
- Wait on God. Things cannot be rushed. Jesus told the early disciples to wait with expectancy in the upper room. It took days not moments.
- Encourage a continual response. C H Spurgeon, when asked why we need to be continually filled with the Spirit, responded 'Because I leak.' We should not be surprised when people keep responding: they are thirsty and needy.
- Encourage people to release their emotions. We are still a very controlled people. We are suspicious of anything emotional. Laughter, tears, shouting or physical jerks must be allowed to happen.
- Ensure that those leading meetings or who are praying with others, share the vision of the church, support the leadership and are open to the activity of the Holy Spirit.
- Do not become so taken up with the meeting that you fail to oversee the event. Ensure that you have a group of trusted senior people who can minister to those responding.

When You Pray for People
- When people's strength fails them, keep praying for them. Encourage them to stay down where they are and receive from the Lord. It is not unusual for people to stay down on the floor for significant periods.
- Do not be afraid of having people catching those falling down. It removes the unnecessary fear of falling, bumps or collision and while it is not vital it is helpful.
- Create floor space even if it means moving chairs. We are responsible for facilitating the work of the Holy Spirit.
- Do not in any way manipulate the activity of the Holy Spirit. People must not be allowed to believe that this is the work of human beings, but the work of God.
- Encourage people to remain open to God: not looking for manifestations but a work of the Spirit seen or unseen

The Pioneer People leadership team was recently given a vision of a heart, where the input valves were fine but the output valves were fractured. Barbed wire was also seen around the heart. To one side was a workman's bench and tools with nails.

I believe the interpretation was for our leadership team and may be appropriate for you. The heart is the heart of the church, which is the key leader, the leadership team and the committed members.

God is 'inputting' but when we get criticised, or there is a reactionary note to what is going on, we can react, get angry and generally marginalise those who do not understand what is going on or who are fearful.

The barbed wire speaks of defensiveness. Reacting can distract us from the work bench, where we are being asked to build rather that knock down, to put together rather than marginalise.

We must be prepared for opposition. We should expect it and count it all joy when we go through it and simply be willing to pray for people and bless them, treating them with courtesy.

Continually giving out, without receiving, can lead to exhaustion and burn out. Take time to receive, rest, read Scripture and do 'normal' things. God wants us around for the long haul not a short sprint.

---

1 *Renewal*, October 1994, pp.14–5

17

The Toronto Blessing – Practical Guideline

The General Board of the Presbyterian Church in Ireland
October 1995

Having been approved by the General Board of the P.C.I. in October 1995, the following text was published in the December 1995-January 1996 issue of The Christian Irishman.[1]

The experience known as the 'Toronto Blessing', and associated phenomena, have been given considerable publicity recently. Christians of many denominations are divided in their response. Some, who feel they have experienced spiritual benefit from 'the Blessing', are convinced it is a visitation of the Holy Spirit. Others dismiss it, and especially its more bizarre aspects such as uncontrollable laughter and animal-like noises, as unbiblical and possibly even satanic. Any evaluation we offer at present must be provisional and ongoing. However, we must recognise that within our church, while some claim to have been helped and blessed by the experience, others are disturbed and perplexed.

In some cases congregations are being divided, and the witness of the church discredited by acrimonious argument. We therefore offer the following practical guidelines which may be helpful in the present situation.

1. Ministers should ensure that in the regular preaching and teaching of the congregation, sufficient attention is given to the person and work of the Holy Spirit, without whom there can be no Christian life and worship. We recognise that there is a broad movement for renewal in the churches, which encourages new music and forms of worship, and emphasises the variety of the gifts within a congregation. However, all aspects of public worship should flow from an informed biblical and theological basis.
2. While the conduct of public worship is the responsibility of the minister, any radical innovations should only be introduced after due consultation and preparation.

3. Sensational phenomena are to be strongly discouraged when they are the product of false emotionalism or any hint of audience manipulation. Recognising the sovereign freedom of the Spirit, meetings should never be arranged, nor audiences invited, in an attempt to induce such phenomena.

4. The work of the Spirit in an individual or congregation is not to be judged by purely subjective claims or by extreme and unexplained behaviour, but by the fruit evidenced e.g. in Galatians 5:22,23 (love, joy, peace, patience, kindness, goodness, faithfulness, humility and self-control).

5. No experience, however vivid, can ever be a short-cut to spiritual maturity. Opportunities for corporate prayer and study, together with encouragement to private devotions, should be ongoing in the life of our congregations.

6. Special care should be taken in ministry to young people or other vulnerable groups. Experienced and responsible leadership should always be present.

7. Where situations of tension or difficulty are developing in a congregation, the Presbytery should be approached for pastoral advice at an early stage and before positions become entrenched.

---

[1] 'Church Gives Guidelines on The Toronto Blessing', *Christian Irishman*, December 1995/January 1996, p.5

18

Evangelical Alliance 'Euston' Statement

From a Consultation on the Toronto Blessing
December 1994

As part of its consultation of key evangelical leaders held at the Ibis Hotel, Euston on 19th-20th December, the Evangelical Alliance sponsored production of this text, which went on to serve as its fullest statement on the Blessing. The document was drafted by Stephen Sizer and Rob Warner on the night of 19th-20th and then signed by all but one of the attendees. The signatories were: Gordon Hills, Dave Cave, Alan Gibson, Gerald Coates, John Butcher, Robert Amess, Tony Baker, Rob Warner, Philip Mohabir, Faith Forster, Paul Perkin, Matthew Ashimolowo, Derek Tidball, Stephen Sizer, Clive Calver, Joel Edwards, Bryn Jones, Phil Hill, Philip Hacking, David Abernethie, Tudur Jones, R T Kendall and David Enoch. As well as being reprinted extensively in the Christian press at the time, it was sub-sequently made available as an appendix to Alliance General Director Clive Calver and Council member Rob Warner's 1996 book, Together We Stand: Evangelical Convictions, Unity and Vision.

In relation to what has come to be known as the 'Toronto Blessing', a consultation of some leading Evangelicals recognised the need not only to evaluate such experiences but also to make clear distinctions between primary and secondary convictions among us. We therefore reaffirm the overwhelming measure of agreement among us as Evangelicals, even though we differ in our initial interpretations of these experiences.

1. We affirm together the classic evangelical convictions. The Scriptures are the inspired Word of God; our faith is centred on the person and atoning work of Christ; we stress the vital need for personal conversion; we are committed to active witness and service in the world.
2. We affirm the centrality of the Great Commission to the task of the church. We also rejoice that in our history God has poured out his Spirit in revivals, and these are intrinsic to the evangelical heritage we share.

3. We affirm the indivisible unity of the Word and Spirit. The Scriptures are God-breathed and their authority cannot be diminished. The Holy Spirit who inspired the unchanging Scriptures applies them to our lives, to both our minds and our hearts. We seek to live under the authority of the Word and in the power of the Spirit. The essence of work of the Spirit according to the Scriptures includes the following:

- Christ is central and glorified.
- Hunger grows for the Word and for prayer.
- Awareness of the holiness of God leads to repentance and holiness of life.
- Spiritual gifts are distributed and exercised in the Church.
- Preaching becomes empowered.
- The love and joy of God are poured into our hearts.
- Greater passion arises for the lost, who are without God and without hope.
- Greater compassion, demonstrated in social action, arises for the disadvantaged.
- Where the Spirit's work is intensified, we would expect to see a heightened awareness of these distinctives.

4. The Spirit of God comes to clothe the church with power from on high, both in the ongoing processes of continuing church life and growth, and also in dramatic periods of revival.

5. Where we differ, we remain committed to evangelical unity, based on our common convictions and priorities under the Lordship of Christ. We confess that in the past this unity has sometimes been undermined by a failure to listen to one another, and by a readiness to caricature and denigrate those with whom we disagree. In this consultation we have sought to ask questions of ourselves and one another, without compromising the integrity of our conscientiously held differences.

6. Where there have been revivals, there has generally been an increase in the frequency of manifestations associated with repentance and conversion and also with the joy of new and abundant life in Christ. However, we are all clear that these manifestations are secondary. Physical and emotional manifestations cannot in themselves prove that a movement is or is not a work of God. The test is the lasting, biblical fruit. No one should seek manifestations as an end in themselves. Rather, we need to seek to grow in the knowledge of God and in his service.

7. At present we are inevitably seeing that experience is not yet integrated with theological reflection. We rejoice with those who have known genuine life-changing encounters with the holiness and majesty, power and love of the risen Christ. We reject any tendency to pursue manifestations as an end in themselves. We regret that some have neglected the discipline of biblical preaching in the face of current manifestations, but we rejoice with those who speak of a new empowering in preaching in recent months. Our common priority is the proclamation of the gospel on fire.

8. We recognise that historical, theological and cultural influences can unconsciously condition our Christian perspective. The existentialist spirit of our age emphasises subjective experiences and feelings over convictions and objective truth. We also recognise the equal and opposite danger of enlightenment rationalism, which has in the past resulted in dead orthodoxy which leaves no room for the direct intervention of the Spirit of God. We must guard and proclaim the absolute truth of the gospel without compromise.

9. We do not believe that the church in the United Kingdom is presently experiencing revival. However, many have testified to an increased sense of the manifest presence of God in recent months, and to empowered preaching and conversions. This enrichment has been observed in some measure across the evangelical spectrum. This encourages us to hope that we may be in a period of preparation for revival.

10. The evaluation of present phenomena can only be provisional: it is too early for definitive judgements. While no work of God takes place without a fleshly dimension, or even the possibility of demonic counterfeit, opinions differ markedly among Evangelicals at present over precisely what is happening. Some have grave reservations about the value and significance of recent events in many churches; others speak of 1994 as a year of remarkable spiritual refreshing. We therefore recognise the need for a group within the Evangelical Alliance to continue to provide evaluation and theological reflection on these developments in the church. We suggest that such a group should plan to review these questions in a year's time.

11. We readily endorse the classic tests of a genuine work of God, as expounded by Jonathan Edwards:

   - Does it raise people's estimation of Jesus Christ?
   - Does it operate against the interests of Satan?
   - Does it lead to a greater regard for Scripture and truth?
   - Does it result in a greater awareness of and seriousness about the things of God?
   - Does it lead to a greater love for God, for other Christians and for the wider world?

12. Our nations, and indeed our continent and world, are in desperate need of the gospel. We therefore commit ourselves afresh to obey the command to proclaim the Good News and make disciples, and call the church to pray for the outpouring of the Spirit of God in revival power upon our land.

19

Joint UK Charismatic Leaders' Statement
May 1995

The following text was produced in mid-May 1995 by representatives of 25 ministries within the British charismatic movement. Organisations lending their support included Pioneer, Salt and Light, Ichthus, Cornerstone and New Frontiers International. The statement was reported in the 15th July issue of Christian Herald, *and was printed in full in the August issue of* Evangelism Today.

For many years we, along with tens of thousands of other Christians, have prayed for deepening renewal, revival and a great awakening. This prayer has taken place in our personal devotions, church meetings, city wide events, Bible weeks and leadership conferences as well as the international March for Jesus.

In deep gratitude for the work of God's Spirit in several thousand churches across the UK at this time, we wish to express our profound thanks to God for answered prayer and for his mercies over the nation and people groups within it.

We recognise that we are a diverse group of ministries, but one of the marks of the Spirit's activity has been a growing appreciation, respect and generosity towards one another. Many others could have put their names to this statement, had they had the opportunity.

We wish to record:

1. Our deep appreciation to God for answering our prayers by sending His Spirit in a variety of powerful ways. Personal lives have been transformed and ministries empowered.

2. The beneficial changes that have taken place in entire families and churches. Some of us know of a few churches that have doubled or trebled in number in the last few months. Others who have had longstanding conflicts and difficulties have seen these resolved because of a greater desire for prayer and intercession, Scripture, personal holiness and corporate usefulness.

3. We are aware that the devil will do all he can to divide God's people, do a counterfeiting work and dishonour the name of our Lord Jesus Christ. But we have greater confidence in God's ability to bless us than Satan's ability

to deceive us. We lament certain extreme statements that have been made in books and articles about The Toronto Blessing and these Times of Refreshing. Most have been without any serious investigation and much has been based upon hearsay. We must challenge ourselves to be accurate in our reporting and fair in our assessments and judgements.

4. We continue to weigh and judge all manifestations and reactions to the Spirit's presence, by Scripture, discernment, reason and testing the fruit. We bow to biblical and historical data which reveals that God often does the unusual. Signs are there to make us wonder and turn to God and Scripture in humility and obedience.

5. It is our prayer that the current work of the Holy Spirit will be gratefully encouraged. We pray this will deepen personal and corporate holiness, effectiveness in sharing our faith, making Jesus attractive and intelligible. Several revivals were preceded for some two or three years by the personal dealings of God eventually leading to a great evangelistic harvest. With prayer, care and humility we are asking God to deepen His work in our lives and sphere of influence, so that the heart of the nation will be touched once more with the good news of Jesus Christ.

We applaud the work of the Evangelical Alliance, who have already gathered a group of charismatic Evangelicals and non-charismatic Evangelicals to debate the current activity of the Holy Spirit. We request further conferences for those who are having difficulty with what is taking place, as well as those who are at the centre of what they regard to be an outpouring of the Holy Spirit.

20

Statement by The Evangelical Fellowship of New Zealand

October 1995

The following text was printed in the New Zealand Christian weekly Challenge *on 25th October 1995. The Evangelical Fellowship of New Zealand (EFNZ) is a parallel body to the Evangelical Alliance in the UK, and this document is in fact a revised and expanded version of the EA (UK) 'Euston Statement' (see p353). It was prepared by the Executive of the EFNZ for a special forum on the Blessing held in Auckland on Saturday 28th October 1995.*

In relation to what has come to be known as the 'Toronto blessing', a consultation of some evangelical leaders in the UK, sponsored by the Evangelical Alliance there, recognised the need not only to evaluate such experiences but also to make clear distinctions between primary and secondary convictions among them.

Their statement reaffirmed the overwhelming measure of agreement among them as Evangelicals, even though they differed in their initial interpretations of these experiences. We in New Zealand have found that we identify closely with their convictions.

We have therefore circulated their declaration to a wide range of evangelical leaders here for comments and suggestions and have incorporated these refinements. Many of us have put our names to this document in confirmation of the extent of unity we have in this.

1. We affirm the classic evangelical convictions:
   God is revealed as Trinity.
   The Scriptures are the inspired Word of God.
   Our faith is centred on the person and atoning work of Jesus Christ.
   We stress the vital need for personal commitment to Christ, leading to active witness and service in the world.
   We believe in the personal return of Jesus Christ.
2. We affirm that the Great Commission of discipling the nations for Jesus is the central task of the church. We also believe that in the history of the church there have been sovereign moves of the Holy Spirit in periods of

revival resulting in wide-scale repentance, conversion and the joy of new and abundant life in Christ.

These revivals have also seen believers recommit themselves to the Lordship of Christ and the control of the Spirit resulting in a new awareness of and manifestation of the fruit of the Spirit.

3. We affirm the dynamic unity of the Word of God and the Holy Spirit of God. The Scriptures are the Word of God: they witness to Christ; they are God-breathed and their authority is absolute.

The Holy Spirit who inspired the unchanging Scriptures applies them to our lives, our minds and our hearts. We seek to live under the authority of the Word and in the power of the Spirit. The work of the Spirit according to the Scriptures includes the following:

- To glorify Christ;
- To increase hunger for the Word and for prayer;
- To bring awareness of the holiness of God;
- To lead us to repentance and holiness of life;
- To enable, equip and empower Christians to serve God;
- To distribute spiritual gifts;
- To promote the fruit of the Spirit in the life of the individual, pouring into our hearts the love of God and love for God;
- To inflame greater passion for the lost who are without God and without hope;
- To stir greater compassion for the disadvantaged, demonstrated in social action and social justice;
- Where the Spirit is at work we would expect to see a demonstrable awareness of these distinctives.

4. We recognise the sovereign freedom of the Spirit who works in a wide variety of ways of his choosing – though consistent with Holy Scripture.

5. Where we differ, we remain committed to evangelical unity, based on our shared allegiance to the Lordship of Christ and our adherence to our stated classic evangelical convictions (see paragraph 1). We confess that in the past this unity has sometimes been undermined by a failure to listen to one another and by a readiness to caricature and denigrate those with whom we disagree.

In our consultation we have sought to ask questions of ourselves, and one another, without compromising the integrity of our conscientiously held differences.

6. Where there have been revivals, there has often been an increase in the frequency of physical phenomena associated with repentance and conversion and also with the joy of new and abundant life in Christ. However, we are all clear that these phenomena are secondary.

There is considerable debate and controversy among Evangelicals about the meaning and validity of the phenomena associated with the 'Toronto blessing'. It is our belief that –

(a) Neither the absence nor the presence of physical and emotional phenomena prove of themselves that a movement is or is not of God.

(b) Any tendency to pursue phenomena is to be rejected. Rather, we need to seek to grow in the knowledge of God and his service.

(c) Many of the physical manifestations may be a person's response to the Spirit or even some other cause and should not be directly attributed in every case to the work of the Spirit.

(d) Theological debate and reflection on the nature of physical phenomena is to be encouraged but we strongly caution against polemical arguments that denigrate one another within the body of Christ.

7. At present we believe we are not seeing an adequate integration of experience with theological reflection. We view with concern any tendency to neglect the importance of biblical preaching by allowing preoccupation with experimental phenomena, but we rejoice with those who speak of a new commitment to and empowering in biblical preaching over recent months.

   Our common priority is the proclamation of the gospel – the cross of Christ at the centre.

8. We know that historical and cultural influences can unconsciously condition our theology.

   Modern subjectivity can compromise our understanding of the importance of objective truth, although the opposite danger of Enlightenment rationalism can easily dull our appreciation of any direct intervention by the Spirit of God. We must guard and proclaim the absolute truth of the gospel without compromise.

   We recognise that all experience of the Holy Spirit should lead us to uplift Christ crucified and risen by word and life, and to glorify God the Father.

9. While many testify to a growing sense of God's presence in recent months, and to empowered preaching and conversions, and while we rejoice with all who in whatever way have known genuine life-changing encounters with the risen Christ, we do not believe that the church in New Zealand is at present experiencing revival.

10. While no work of God takes place without a fleshly dimension, or even the possibility of demonic counterfeit, opinions differ among Evangelicals over precisely what is happening.

    Some have grave reservations about the value and significance of recent events in many churches: others speak of 1995 as a year of remarkable spiritual refreshing.

    (a) We therefore recognise the need for a group within the Evangelical Fellowship to continue to provide evaluation and theological reflection on these developments in the church. We suggest that such a group should plan to review these questions in a year's time.

(b) We also recognise that the power of God manifested is always ministered *for* people and never *over* them, so that none are to be abused,
coerced or dominated by any spiritual authority. Divine power
invites, human power pushes.

11. We believe that the tests of a genuine work of God as expounded by
Jonathan Edwards are helpful:

- Does it raise people's expectations of Jesus Christ?
- Does it operate against the interests of Satan?
- Does it lead to a greater regard for Scripture and truth?
- Does it result in a greater awareness of and seriousness about the
things of God?
- Does it lead to a greater love for God, for other Christians and for the
wider world?

12. Our nation, like the rest of the world, is in desperate need of the gospel.
Therefore we repent of our materialism, and our preoccupation with
sensation, and we renew our commitment to obey God's command to
proclaim the Good News that will make disciples of men, women and
children.

We call upon the church to pray that each of us will be open to the
enabling, empowering and equipping of the Spirit that we might fulfil
our Christ-given commission in our land.

21

Centre for Contemporary Ministry: Statement on The Charismatic Movement

October 1995

The Christian Herald *newspaper printed the following analysis of the Toronto Blessing on 11th October 1997. Ray Borlase, Andrew Edwards, Peter Fenwick, David Forbes, Philip Foster, Clifford Hill, Russell Howell, Ron Lycett and David Noakes prepared the statement in conjunction with all those who attended consultations on the Toronto Blessing convened by the Centre for Contemporary Ministry at Bawtry Hall, Yorkshire in January and April 1995. It reflects the content of a much longer booklet on the Blessing published by CCM in early 1995 under the title* Charismatic Crossroads.[1] *A draft version of the statement was prepared and circulated among those who attended the residential consultations, and subsequent drafts were discussed with the directors of the Evangelical Alliance before being sent for comment to a large number of leaders who had not attended the consultations.*

We see the need for a fresh examination of the beliefs and practices which have been adopted by many within the charismatic movement, giving concern regarding the direction in which the movement is heading.

We believe that because we have sought every experience and form of excitement, without taking heed of God's Word, his anger has fallen upon us. We are now experiencing a 'wasting disease' in terms of false experience and pseudo-Christian theology and practice.

We ask all our brothers and sisters in the charismatic movement to join with us in seeking the Lord afresh in humility and repentance. We need to recognise the pride and arrogance which have given entrance to the enemy and our neglect of Scripture which has left us prey to deception and error. We therefore call on our brethren to:

1. *Restore the primacy of God's Word.* We believe the Scriptures alone are the supreme source of authority on matters of faith and practice. We need to recognise that the failure of many leaders both to teach and to encourage the study of Scripture has caused the neglect of many important aspects of

biblical teaching, resulting in ignorance of biblical truth and leaving its members prone to deception.

2. *Restore a biblical doctrine of salvation.* The preaching of the Gospel must include a clear call to repentance and justification by faith alone, with a recognition that such salvation delivers sinners from eternal judgement. We are in danger of using a superficial message and methods which rob people of a true knowledge of salvation.

3. *Restore objectivity to our faith.* So much of what is encouraged today is subjective experience and practice which is not tested at the bar of Scripture.

4. *Restore truth instead of error.* Some of the teaching in charismatic churches has been based on so-called revelational teaching (extra biblical) or even on false prophecies. There needs to be a fresh emphasis on the truth contained within God's Word.

5. *Restore true unity.* There has been an overemphasis on unity to the detriment of truth. True unity can only be based on truth. Prior to Jesus praying that they might be one, he prayed: 'Sanctify them in the truth. Thy Word is truth'. This is the right order, for truth leads to true unity! In order to seek this true unity we recognise the need for greater openness between those holding different viewpoints. We need to seek every opportunity to express our differences and evaluate them in the light of scriptural truth.

6. *Restore a sense of the holiness of God.* Within the charismatic movement we have become too casual with God. Although he is our Father, he is a holy God. Jesus often addressed God as 'Holy Father'. Without a sense of the awesomeness of God, there is little development of true and mature Christian character.

7. *Restore a biblical understanding of the mission and purpose of the church.* We believe that the doctrine of the second coming of Christ has often been distorted or neglected by today's church, thus leaving her ill-prepared and equipped for the last days. The church needs to engage fully in her mission to give a clear proclamation of her eternal hope, and prepare herself to be the bride of Christ.

This call, therefore, is not a call to return to dead formalism, but to live and teach the Word of God in the power and understanding of the Holy Spirit. This call is not to censure God's people, but to encourage us all to a full-hearted love of the Lord in obedience to his commands and purposes.

This call is not to introspection, but to a vital outward expression and witness of the love and mercy of God. This call is not to invalidate any past move of God in the charismatic movement, but is a fresh call to all believers (in which we include ourselves) to be the 'church of the living god, the pillar and foundation of the truth' (1 Tim. 3:15).

The Lord Jesus sent a strong warning to the church in Sardis which we believe is also a message for us today: 'Wake up; Strengthen what remains, and is about to die, for I have not found your deeds complete in the sight of my God.' (Revelation 3:2).

---

[1] Available from The Centre for Contemporary Ministry, Bawtry Hall, Bawtry, South Yorkshire DN10 6JH

22

Conference Report of the Faith and Order Committee of the Methodist Church: The 'Toronto Blessing' (Conclusions & Recommendations)

June 1996

After a debate on the Blessing, the 1995 Methodist Conference mandated its Faith and Order Committee to produce a report on the matter, and to present this a year later. A special 18-member working group was convened by Faith and Order Secretary Neil Dixon, and duly presented its findings. As instructed, these incorporated the results of a survey of ministers and church members, as well as providing biblical, historical and doctrinal reflections on the movement. The following extracts are taken from the section on biblical material, and from the concluding section of the whole report. (For further background detail, and a summary of the overall document, see entries for 29th June, 6th July 1995 and 22nd June 1996 in Part II of this book).

Conclusions from the biblical material

1.5.1 It is important to be open-minded. Scripture bears witness time and again to a person's total reaction to God, who seeks a response from the heart as well as the mind, the body as well as the spirit. Such a response may have physical, as well as spiritual, moral and emotional effects. Scripture also shows that the Spirit does not always work in quiet, hidden or predictable ways, and often the human response to the Spirit's prompting is unusual. Whilst being wary of 'excess', we should not try to confine the activity of God within the socially, culturally and psychologically acceptable limits of our preferences. Every genuine response will be compatible with the character and activity of God as revealed in Christ.

1.5.2 The emphases of the New Testament should be noted. For example, visionary, ecstatic or mystical experiences may be experienced by most Christians at some time or other, but they usually come unexpectedly, and there is no suggestion that they should be actively sought. Paul was mightily indebted to the Damascus Road event, but is more reticent about later 'visions and revelations', as 2 Corinthians 12:1-5 shows. Amongst other New Testament writers, James, in his characteristically down-to-earth way, describes true religion in moral and practical terms (James 1:22-27). Others stress that the Christian life is mainly characterised by suffering (for example, Hebrews 12:3-12; 1 Peter 4:12-19), a suffering which, as usual in the New Testament, is accompanied by joy (1 Peter 1:8).

1.5.3 There is no basis in Scripture for Christians claiming to be, or feeling superior to, other Christians. They may differ in their views and convictions, they may feel it right sometimes to criticise each other, but 'spiritual one-upmanship' (1 Corinthians 12-14) has no scriptural foundation. Indeed, Paul's teaching indicates the opposite (Romans 12:10; Galatians 5:25; Philippians 2:3), and Jesus himself taught that self-righteousness – a very 'religious' sin – is one of the most terrible of all (Matthew 23; Luke 15:25-31, 18:9-14).

1.5.4 God always offers us the whole richness of the Spirit (hence Ephesians1:3-14), but individuals and groups have had unexpected and often dramatic times of conversion and spiritual renewal from Pentecost onwards. Through baptism by water and the Spirit (Acts 2:37-41; Romans 6:2-4; 1 Peter 3:18-22; etc.) we are all initiated into the life which experiences the fruit of the Spirit (as outlined, for example, in Galatians 5:22-26). Some Christians also receive specific callings needing to be exercised on behalf of the church (as listed in I Corinthians 12:27-30 or Ephesians 4:11-16) but the essence of all our development is growth in caring love (hence such crucial teaching as in Matthew 5:43-48, 25:31-46; Romans 13:8-10; 1 Corinthians 13; James 2:8; 1 John 2:7-11, 4:7-21) and complete willingness to be used in whatever way Christ wills and the Spirit leads (hence Mark 8:34-37; Luke 9:57-62; 2 Corinthians 11: 23-33 and 12:10; Philippians 3:7-11).

1.5.5 The 'truth' by which we must live is always seen as the practice of love (for example 1 John 3:18-24). Our tradition in particular has emphasised the New Testament teaching on love. John Wesley taught us to grow into 'Scriptural holiness', which above all means living in 'perfect love' towards all…

General Conclusions

6.1 There is a significant number of Ministers and lay people who testify to the benefits of the 'Toronto Blessing', although few Methodist congregations have wholeheartedly embraced it. Many Methodists who have experienced the 'Blessing' have done so outside our own churches, or in special meetings and services separate from the regular programme of worship. Where it has affected Methodism, the manifestations are usually more 'restrained' than in some other settings.

6.2 The feature of the 'Toronto Blessing' which distinguishes it from other pentecostal/charismatic/signs-and-wonders ministries is the nature, widespread occurrence, frequency, intensity and duration of such common visible and audible phenomena as laughing, shaking, jumping, jerking, falling to the floor, roaring and barking. Christian history has few instances of outbreaks of phenomena on such a scale. The nature of modern communications (especially electronic media), and the ease of international travel, have undoubtedly accelerated the spread of this phenomenon.

6.3 The 'Toronto Blessing' phenomenon has revealed a deep need for 'attentive listening' to the hurts and longings of many people. In an age of increasing alienation and disease, this experience has enabled many people to feel a renewed sense of the love and presence of God, and to receive relevant, personally-focussed prayer. These needs are a challenge to the spiritual and pastoral life of our churches.

6.4 We see a need for far more help in the areas of spirituality, doctrine and biblical interpretation and application than we are currently giving. The lack of these things leaves people ill-equipped to understand and make sense of intense real or alleged experiences of the Spirit.

6.5 Whilst wanting to rejoice in every genuine move of the Holy Spirit we must be sure to test every movement that makes such strong claims for itself. Among the tests to be applied is that of time. Whilst it is natural to ask whether or not this (or any other phenomenon) is 'of God', at this, still relatively early stage, any answer must be a matter of faith. It is more helpful to ask whether or not God uses experiences such as are found in the 'Toronto Blessing', and our Methodist tradition provides ample criteria by which the activity of God may be discerned through its fruit in human lives. We have indicated above (paragraph 4.2.1) the sort of checks and balances which all Church life needs. However, we have seen that the 'Toronto Blessing' is an experience in which many people's awareness of God, and of their relationship to God, is heightened, and through which God ministers to them. In that way it can be a 'blessing'.

6.6 Whilst some of the manifestations of the 'Toronto Blessing' and the practices associated with it are consistent with Scriptural teaching and practice, some are not. On the other hand, as we have already affirmed, God is present in the Holy Spirit in all that is, and may enrich every experience with blessing.

6.7 It is undeniable that some people have been deeply disturbed by their experiences of the 'Toronto Blessing', and this has in some cases been exacerbated by insensitive responses from enthusiasts. Others are disappointed that they have not, it seems, received gifts that they have earnestly sought. There is a vital pastoral work to be done in helping all people, whether their experience has been positive or otherwise, to be assured that their integrity and faith are not being questioned nor are they unwelcome in the Methodist Church.

6.8 The quality of leadership has had a great deal to do with the forming of opinions. God has taken the risk of choosing to work through fallible human beings, so inevitably there will be faults, flaws and abuses of power. Being realistic therefore, in any movement of God through people there will always be the risk of:

- Pride, manipulation, control, power-seeking, and exhibitionism.
- Seeking religious experiences/manifestations for a 'feel good factor'.
- The opinion that 'this' is 'the answer', or 'the way for all people'.
- Self-righteousness, or conversely feelings of spiritual inadequacy.
- A diverse range of interpretations in terms of the 'spiritual forces' at work, such as the Holy Spirit, the human spirit or possibly evil agencies.

6.9   Many people may feel drawn to travel to Toronto itself or other 'centres' of the 'Blessing'. Such pilgrimages may well be a source of inspiration that can be informative and helpful to individuals and their home church. In some ways Toronto may stand in the tradition of Christian pilgrimage to such places as Jerusalem, Lourdes, Taizé and Iona. However, it is essential to examine one's motives for such a journey very carefully, and to be prepared to apply the insights of our tradition … in careful appraisal of what one finds.

6.10   The 'Toronto Blessing' is frequently referred to by analogy with the 'times of refreshing' of Acts 3: 19f. Such a description draws attention to the fact that this is primarily a movement in which 'saints are blessed' rather than 'sinners converted'. There are numerous reports of individual and corporate growth in terms of Christian Spirituality and a greater overt expression of love between Christians (especially husbands and wives). Also on record is the increased involvement of laity in ministry; for example in prayer and counselling, a desire to forward evangelism and hints of developments in social outreach. Among the fruit of this phenomenon may thus be Christian renewal, but there is little evidence as yet that we are witnessing 'revival', although some would see it as a prelude to that. Certainly Methodists would not want to identify themselves with any of the millenarian movements that are particularly prevalent at this time, and which tend to seize on any alleged 'evidence' to support their expectations. Within the life of our churches there are many and various movements through which renewal is being found, whether individually or corporately. We may be enriched by them all, but a sense of proportion is essential. This accords with the approach of Wesley, the 'reasonable enthusiast'.

6.11   Where churches have lost a sense of purpose, where their worship is emotionally inhibited and over-cerebral, where 'tradition' is used to excuse unwillingness to change, where church life is tedious and attractive mostly to the elderly and very young, it is not surprising that features of charismatic experience such as are found in the 'Toronto Blessing' are highly attractive. Its holistic spirituality, the 'holy anarchy' of its less-inhibited worship, the sense of excitement, participation, novelty and unpredictability in its experience of God's activity all combine to attract large and relatively young congregations. Charismatic experience is, however, at its most healthy when it forms part of the life and witness of broad churches and where appropriate checks and balances exist. Just as the balance in the church can sometimes tip so much towards order and tradition that the Spirit is stifled and change becomes impossible, similarly, too much charismatic disinhibition and spontaneity can lead to spiritual anarchy and superficiality.

6.12   The Kingdom of God is an inclusive community, in which all people are called to share. The church, as the Body of Christ, is called to witness in its corporate life to the inclusiveness of that Kingdom, and individuals are invited to join with others of diverse backgrounds in mutual love, praise and service. Participating in the life of the Kingdom, as members of Christ's church, we have much to learn from God and from each other. The experience of the 'Toronto Blessing' is one of the ways in which we may together discover more of God. Taken as a whole, the 'Toronto Blessing Movement' has many lessons for the worship, mission and prayer life of the Church at the end of the twentieth century.

Recommendations

7.1   We invite the Methodist people to explore the issues outlined in this Report without fear, but with open and prayerful minds, sharing their experiences and perceptions in an atmosphere of honesty and Christian love.

7.2   We affirm and encourage those who have been blessed by their experience of the 'Toronto Blessing'; at the same time, we ask that special care be given to those for whom it has been a cause of distress, division or disappointment for whatever reason.

7.3   We urge all those with responsibility for pastoral care to take seriously the phenomenon of the 'Toronto Blessing', and to seek informed guidance on appropriate ways to handle people's experiences. In particular, care needs to be taken to distinguish between external manifestations, which may indeed be disturbing, and the possibility that there is an inner catharsis whose lasting effects are beneficial and to be welcomed.

7.4   There is urgent need for a much more deliberate teaching and preaching programme on the doctrine and work of the Holy Spirit.

7.5   The renewed emphasis on prayer ministry is to be welcomed. Opportunities should be provided in all our churches for attentive listening to the spiritual hunger felt by many people, supported by relevant, personally-focussed prayer and by intercession.

7.6   To encourage fruitful developments and minimise the potential hazards which result from human sinfulness the following checks and balances are important:

Balance in church life in terms of:

● Proclamation and preaching of the Word; celebration of the Sacraments; styles of worship; a recognition that Christians are Trinitarian in matters of faith and worship; allowing the Spirit of God to use all the above means and others to make God's will and purpose known.

- Accountability/Supervision/Submission: a godly use of authority and discernment in church leadership at all levels and a willingness to deal lovingly and firmly with what is deemed inappropriate.
- A willingness to: listen to different points of view and tradition; learn from each other; admit that none of us possesses the whole truth revealed in Christ Jesus.

7.7 We recommend further study of the following Conference Reports, which have already addressed many of the issues touched upon in this Report:

- The Charismatic Movement (1974)
- Christian Initiation (1987)
- 'Let the People Worship' (1988)
- 'Called to Love and Praise' (1995)

7.8 … It is vital that charismatic and non-charismatic Christians should increasingly appreciate each others' strengths, as well as weaknesses. They need to meet each other not as members of two opposing parties, but as fellow pilgrims who enrich each other. Non-charismatics, for instance, could do with understanding the attractions of charismatic worship. It would be helpful to observe or experience the 'Toronto Blessing' phenomena for oneself before passing judgement. Charismatics and non-charismatics need to 'speak the truth in love' to each other, as fellow pilgrims on fundamentally the same road.

23

The Church of Scotland Panel on Doctrine Report To General Assembly 1997: 'The Toronto Blessing' (Conclusions)

April 1997

The Kirk's 1996 General Assembly asked the Panel on Doctrine 'to consider issues arising out of what has been called the Toronto Blessing'. The result was a 45-page study, which is re-counted in detail in the Chronicle in Part II of this book (see entry for Friday 4th April 1997). What follows is the concluding section of the report.

In our consideration of the Toronto Blessing, the Panel has sought to offer a fair and sympathetic exposition of the growth and development of the move-ment, allied to an analysis of the biblical and historical precedents which have been (or could be) used to support the claim that the Blessing is a significant movement of God in our time. We have sought to guard against an undue scepticism, whilst seeking to be faithful to the Scripture's call upon us to 'test the spirits'.

Perhaps inevitably, the most difficult part of our task was the drawing of conclusions as to the significance of the Blessing. In the Introduction to the report we intimated our intention to resist the tendency to offer definitive con-clusions at this stage. In so doing, we invite the ire of many. On the one hand, we shall seem deficient in the eyes of those who might wish to see the Church of Scotland wholly endorse the Blessing. We may even seem to them to run the risk of quenching the Spirit. However, we have endeavoured with this report to offer a fair analysis which articulates a range of serious concerns and carries with it a series of warnings which the advocates of the Blessing would do well to ponder and reflect upon. On the other hand, we shall be judged delinquent by those who would seek to have the Blessing well nigh proscribed. We would remind them again of the counsel of Scripture, articulated by Gamaliel. There are indeed more things in heaven and earth than are dreamt of in our theology. We would be most unwise to imagine that our particular tradition had so encapsulated the work of God as to have left nothing beyond its boundaries. We would be most impoverished if we had missed, albeit that its garb may seem odd to us, the passing of the presence of God.

Therefore we offer the following as our conclusions:

1. The Panel has welcomed the challenge to examine afresh our theology and understanding of the presence and renewing activity of the Holy Spirit, and invites the church to consider ways in which the challenge to be 'open to the Spirit' may be realised in our common life.
2. The Panel has welcomed the opportunity to reflect upon the history of the work of renewal within the life of the church. It invites the church to look at movements for renewal which are evident across the face of the church catholic, in order that it may discern that which is of God.
3. The Panel notes and endorses the pastoral concerns which have motivated those who have expressed reservations about the Blessing.
4. The Panel notes and endorses the concerns which have been expressed as to the scriptural precedents for the phenomena associated with the Blessing.
5. The Panel acknowledges again its indebtedness to the wise guidance and counsel found in the 1974 report of the Panel on Doctrine, 'The Charismatic Movement within the Church of Scotland', and would invite renewed reflection upon it.

24

The Church of England Board of Mission Occasional Paper No. 7: 'The Toronto Experience' (Conclusion)

June 1997

The Board of Mission commissioned its Secretary, Dr Anne Richards, to write a 31-page monograph on the Blessing. Details of the text as a whole are given in Part II of this book, in the entry for Friday 27th June 1997. The following is taken from the concluding section of the report.

As the media interest in the 'Toronto Blessing' wanes and churches talk of involvement in the 'Toronto Experience' and 'moves of the Holy Spirit', we are left with the question of what it all means in the larger context of Christian history and in the process of becoming the church of tomorrow. First, we must conclude that these phenomena in themselves are not unusual or new and are not restricted to one set of reactions, but to a range of experiences. Second, we must separate the experiences into their component parts: the role of the minister, the experience of the individual, the effect on the congregational community and the attitude of the outside observer. In the light of our discussion, we can see that each of these can be assessed in different ways even within the context of a single experience. Consequently, any blanket conclusion of a particular kind is likely to fall short of what is required.

It might be perfectly possible to explain all that happens in the Toronto Experience as psychologically stimulated and realised. However, even if this were entirely true in 100 per cent of the cases, God may perfectly well be able to use these psychological manifestations to enrich and sustain the lives of Christians. Equally, we cannot rule out that for some people, especially the emotionally unstable, the blessing may cause feelings of emptiness, unworthiness and despair. In particular, the concentration on personal experience cannot remain in isolation; there has to be relation to the rest of people's lives and a sense-making mechanism for the irrational and sensational aspects of the blessing. Without this, the experience, however beneficial, remains in a vacuum.

In this respect, it must be the responsibility of the church to encourage Christians to use their experiences in the service of mission to others. This means that all those congregations involved in, or touched by the Toronto Experience must themselves look critically at their contribution to mission and evangelism in order to see whether they are visibly helping to build up the Body of Christ: 'let all things be done for building up'. In cases where the witness of the Church is impaired by over-emphasis on the phenomena, it may be that a fresh appraisal of its place in the life of a congregation will be required, and where there has been distress or damage caused by using the phenomena to promote elitism, this must be seriously addressed. However, as the attention on 'Toronto' passes, there seem to be signs that churches are already realising this need for appraisal and are passing into a new phase of church life, alive to the reality of God's promises, and to the future which God has promised us. Consequently, whether or not those involved in manifesting the phenomena have indeed experienced a 'foretaste of heaven', there remains the potential to make the promise of God's new heaven and new earth a possibility for everyone.

Bibliography

This bibliography includes books, various articles and videos cited in the main text. More frequently cited works are marked ★.

The bibliography does not include newspaper and magazine articles, TV broadcasts and audiotapes; these are fully referenced in the notes. The Evangelical Alliance press archive on the Toronto Blessing, on which much of Part II of this book is based, is available at the Evangelical Alliance offices: for further details e-mail: *acute@eauk.org* or write to the Evangelical Alliance, Whitefield House, Kennington Park Road, London SE11 4BT.

Books and Articles
ACUTE, *Faith, Hope and Homosexuality* (Carlisle: Paternoster, 1998)
ACUTE, *The Nature of Hell* (Carlisle: Paternoster, 2000)
Aitchison, Jean, *Language Change: Progress or Decay?* (London: Fontana, 1981)
Anderson, Allan H. and W.J. Hollenweger (eds.), *Pentecostals after a Century: Global Perspectives on a Movement in Transition* (Sheffield: Sheffield Academic Press, 1999)
Argyle, Michael, *Psychology and Religion* (London: Routledge, 2000)
Arndt, Walter and F.W. Gingrich, *A Greek-English Lexicon of the New Testament and Other Early Christian Literature* (2nd edn; Chicago/London: University of Chicago Press, 1979)
Arnott, John, 'Letter to John Wimber', 5th December 1995, published on TAV web site, 12th December 1995
—, *The Father's Blessing* (Orlando: Creation House, 1995)
—, *Keep the Fire* (London: Harper Collins, 1996)
Association of Vineyard Churches, 'Board Report: Sept/Oct 1994': 'Summary Report on the Current Renewal and the Phenomena Surrounding It'. Published on TAV web site, 14th September 1994.
Aune, David E., *Prophecy in Early Christianity and the Ancient Mediterranean World* (Grand Rapids: Eerdmans, 1983)
Barber, Theodore X., *Hypnotism, Imagination and Human Potentialities* (New York: Pergamon Press, 1974)
Barr, James, *The Semantics of Biblical Language* (Oxford: Oxford University Press, 1961)
Barth, Karl, *Church Dogmatics II/I: The Doctrine of God* (tr. G.W. Bromilley & T.F. Torrance; Edinburgh: T&T Clark, 1957)
Bebbington, David, *Evangelicalism in Modern Britain* (London: Unwin &Hyman, 1989)

Belcham, Leigh, *Toronto: The Baby or the Bathwater* (Bromley: Day One, 1995)

Beougher, Timothy K., 'Revival, Revivals' in Scott Moreau, Harold Netland & Charles van Engen (eds.), *Evangelical Dictionary of World Missions* (Grand Rapids/Carlisle: Baker Books/Paternoster, 2000), pp.830-33

Beverley, James A., *Holy Laughter and the Toronto Blessing* (Grand Rapids: Zondervan, 1995)

Bickle, Mike & Michael Sullivant, *God's Manifest Presence* (Kansas: Metro Vineyard, 1995)

*Boulton, Wallace (ed.), *The Impact of Toronto* (Crowborough: Monarch, 1995)

Brandon, Andrew, *Health and Wealth* (Eastbourne: Kingsway, 1987)

Bray, Gerald, *Creeds, Councils and Christ* (Leicester: IVP, 1984)

Brierley, Peter, *The Tide is Running Out: What the English Church Census Reveals* (Eltham: Christian Research, 2000)

Brown, Stewart J., 'Revivals (British Isles)', in Donald K. McKim & David F. Wright (eds.), *Encyclopedia of the Reformed Faith* (Edinburgh: Saint Andrew Press, 1992), pp.325-7

*Burgess, Stanley M., Gary B. McGee & Patrick H. Alexander (eds.), *Dictionary of Pentecostal and Charismatic Movements* (Grand Rapids: Zondervan, 1988)

*Calver, Clive & Rob Warner, *Together We Stand: Evangelical Convictions, Unity and Vision* (London: Hodder & Stoughton, 1996)

Cartledge, Mark J., 'Interpreting Charismatic Experience: Hypnosis, Altered States of Consciousness and Holy Spirit?', *Journal of Pentecostal Theology* 13 (1998), pp.117-32

—, 'Prophecy in the Contemporary Church: A Theological Examination' (unpublished M.Phil. thesis; Council for National Academic Awards, Oak Hill College, London, 1989)

—, 'Tongues of the Spirit: An Empirical-Theological Study of Charismatic Glossolalia' (unpublished Ph.D. thesis; Trinity College, Carmarthen, University of Wales, 1999)

*Centre for Contemporary Ministry, *Charismatic Crossroads: The Report of a Leadership Consultation on the Current Situation in the Charismatic Churches* (London: PWM Team Ministries, 1995)

*Chevreau, Guy, *Catch the Fire: The Toronto Blessing – An Experience of Renewal and Revival* (London: Marshall Pickering, 1994)

*—, *Share the Fire: The Toronto Blessing and Grace-Based Evangelism* (London: Marshall Pickering, 1997)

*Church of Scotland Panel on Doctrine, *The Toronto Blessing: Report to the General Assembly* (Edinburgh: Church of Scotland, 1997)

Coates, Gerald, '"Toronto" and Scripture', in Wallace Boulton (ed.), *The Impact of Toronto* (Eastbourne: Monarch, 1995), pp.47-52

Cockroft, Robert & Susan M. Cockroft, *Persuading People: An Introduction to Rhetoric* (Basingstoke: Macmillan, 1992)

Cotton, Ian, *The Hallelujah Revolution: The Rise of the New Christians* (London: Warner Books, 1995)

Cox, Harvey, *Fire from Heaven: The Rise of Pentecostal Spirituality and the Reshaping of Religion in the Twenty-First Century* (London: Cassell, 1996)

Culver, Vivian, 'Ecstatic Laughter', in Lloyd Pietersen (ed.), *The Mark of the Spirit? A Charismatic Critique of the Toronto Blessing* (Carlisle: Paternoster, 1998), pp.63-86

Davis, R.E., *I Will Pour Out My Spirit: A History and Theology of Revivals and Evangelical Awakenings* (Tonbridge Wells: Monarch, 1992)

Deere, Jack, *Surprised by the Power of the Spirit* (Grand Rapids: Zondervan, 1993)

Dempster, Murray W., Byron D. Klaus & Douglas Petersen (eds.), *The Globalization of Pentecostalism: A Religion Made to Travel* (Carlisle: Regnum, 1999)

Duewel, Wesley, *Revival Fire* (Grand Rapids: Zondervan, 1995)

*Dixon, Patrick, *Signs of Revival: Detailed Historical Research Throws Light on Today's Move of God's Spirit* (Eastbourne: Kingsway, 1994)

Duffield, Guy P. & Nathaniel M. Van Cleave, *Foundations of Pentecostal Theology* (Los Angeles:L.I.F.E Bible College, 1987)

Dunn, James D.G., *The Acts of the Apostles* (Peterborough: Epworth, 1996)

Edwards, Jonathan, *The Religious Affections* (Edinburgh: Banner of Truth Trust, 1961 [1746])

—, *Jonathan Edwards on Revival: A Narrative of Surprising Conversions; The Distinguishing Marks of a Work of The Spirit of God; An Account of the Revival of Religion in Northampton 1740-1742* (Edinburgh: Banner of Truth Trust, 1965)

—, *The Works of Jonathan Edwards* Vols. 1 & 2 (Edinburgh: Banner of Truth Trust, 1974 [1834])

*Fearon, Mike, *A Breath of Fresh Air: A Balanced and Informed Perspective on the Unusual Phenomena Sweeping the Worldwide Church* (Guildford: Eagle, 1994)

Fee, Gordon D, *God's Empowering Presence: The Holy Spirit in the Letters of Paul* (Peabody, Mass.: Hendrickson, 1994)

Fitz-Gibbon, Andy & Jane, *Something Extraordinary is Happening* (Crowborough: Monarch, 1995)

Foster, Philip, *Suggestibilty, Hysteria and Hypnosis* (Cambridge: St Matthew Publications, 1995)

Fyall, Robert S., *Charismatic and Reformed* (Edinburgh: Handsel Press/Rutherford House, 1992)

Glover, Peter (ed.), *The Signs and Wonders Movement: Exposed* (Epsom: Day One, 1997)

Gonzales, Mark, *Psalm Eighteen: The Warriors Psalm – A Word for Cleveland* (Cleveland: Metro Church South, 2000)

*Gott, Ken & Lois Gott, *The Sunderland Refreshing: How the Holy Spirit Invaded One British Town* (London: Hodder & Stoughton, 1995)

Guinness, Os, *Fit Bodies, Fat Minds: Why Evangelicals Don't Think and What to Do About It* (London: Hodder & Stoughton, 1995)

*Hand, Chris, 'Tasting the Fruit of the Toronto Blessing', in Peter Glover (ed.). *The Signs and Wonders Movement : Exposed* (Eastbourne: Day One, 1997), pp.38-60

—, *Falling Short? The Alpha Course Examined* (Epsom: Day One, 1998)

★Hanegraff, Hank, *Christianity in Crisis* (Eugene: Harvest House, 1993)

—, *Counterfeit Revival* (Waco: Word, 1997)

Haville, Mark, 'An Illusion of Power', in Peter Glover (ed.), *The Signs and Wonders Movement: Exposed* (Epsom: Day One, 1997)

★Hill, Clifford, Peter Fenwick, David Forbes & David Noakes, *Blessing the Church?* (Guildford: Eagle, 1995)

★Hinn, Benny, *The Anointing*, (7th edn; Nashville: Thomas Nelson, 1993)

Hocken, Peter, *The Glory and the Shame: Reflections on the 20th Century Outpouring of the Holy Spirit* (Guildford: Eagle, 1994)

—, 'Theological Reflections on the "Toronto Blessing", 25th Annual Meeting of the Society for Pentecostal Studies (Wycliffe College: Toronto, 1996)

—, *Streams of Renewal: The Origins and Early Development of the Charismatic Movement in Great Britain* (Carlisle: Paternoster Press, 1997 [1986])

Hollenweger, Walter, *The Pentecostals* (London: SCM, 1972)

—, *Pentecostalism: Origins and Developments Worldwide* (Peabody: Hendrickson, 1997)

Howard, Roland, *The Rise and Fall of the Nine O'clock Service* (London: Mowbray, 1996)

—, *Charismania: When Christian Fundamentalism Goes Wrong* (London: Mowbray, 1997)

Howard-Browne, Rodney, *Manifesting the Holy Ghost* (Louisville: R.H.B.E.A, 1992)

—, *The Anointing* (Louisville: R.H.B.E.A, 1992)

—, *The Touch of God: A Practical Workbook* (nd)

Hunt, Stephen, 'The "Toronto Blessing": A Rumour of Angels?', *Journal of Contemporary Religion* 10.3 (1995), pp.257-71

Hunter, Charles & Frances Hunter, *Since Jesus Passed By* (Van Nuys: Time-Light Books, 1973)

Hylson-Smith, Ken, 'Roots of Pan-Evangelicalism 1735-1835', in Steve Brady & Harold Rowdon (eds.), *For Such a Time as This: Perspectives on Evangelicalism, Past, Present and Future* (London: Milton Keynes: Evangelical Alliance/Scripture Union, 1996)

Irish, Charles, *Back to the Upper Room* (Nashville: Thomas Nelson, 1993)

Jackson, Bill, 'What in the World is Happening to Us?', Vineyard Champaign, Urbana, Ill., May 1994, in Patrick Dixon, *Signs of Revival* (rev'd edn; Eastbourne: Kingsway, 1995 [1994]), pp.303-26

Jackson, Robert, 'Prosperity Theology and the Faith Movement', *Themelios*, Vol. 1, October (1989), pp.16-23

★Jebb, Stanley, *No Laughing Matter: The "Toronto" Phenomenon and Its Implications* (Bromley: Day One, 1995)

Kay, William K., *Pentecostals in Britain* (Carlisle: Paternoster, 2000)

Kent, John, 'Have We Been Here Before: A Historian Looks at the "Toronto Blessing"', in Stanley E. Porter & Philip J. Richter (eds.), *The Toronto Blessing – Or Is It?* (London: Darton, Longman & Todd, 1995), pp.86-103

Kruschel, K.J., *Laughter: A Theological Reflection* (London: SCM, 1994 (Trans. John Bowden)

Kydd, R., *Charismatic Gifts in the Early Church* (Peabody: Hendrickson, 1984)

Land, S., *Pentecostal Spirituality: A Passion for the Kingdom* (Sheffield: Sheffield Academic Press, 1993)

Larkin, Ernest E., 'Discernment of Spirits', in Gordon S. Wakefield (ed.), *A Dictionary of Christian Spirituality* (London: SCM, 1983)

Lewis, Peter, 'Renewal, Recovery and Growth: 1966 Onwards', in Steve Brady & Harold Rowdon (eds.), *For Such a Time as This: Perspectives on Evangelicalism, Past, Present and Future* (London/Milton Keynes: Evangelical Alliance/Scripture Union, 1996)

Lindsey, Hal, *The Late Great Planet Earth* (New York: Harper, 1970)

Lyons, John, *Semantics* Vol. 1 (2 Vols, Cambridge: Cambridge University Press, 1977)

Lyons, John, 'The Gamaliel Principle', in Lloyd Pietersen, (ed.), *The Mark of the Spirit? A Charismatic Critique of the Toronto Blessing* (Carlisle: Paternoster, 1998), pp.92-121

MacArthur, John F., *The Charismatics* (Grand Rapids: Zondervan, 1978)

—, *Reckless Faith* (Wheaton: Crossway Books, 1994)

*MacNutt, Francis, *Overcome by the Spirit*, (Grand Rapids: Baker Book House, 1984; UK edn: Guildford: Eagle, 1994)

McBain, Douglas, *Charismatic Christianity* (Basingstoke: Macmillan, 1997)

McConnell, Dan R., *The Promise of Health and Wealth: a Historical and Biblical Analysis of the Modern Faith Movement* (London: Hodder & Stoughton, 1990)

McGrath, Alister, *Evangelicalism and the Future of Christianity* (London: Hodder & Stoughton, 1994)

McHale, Gary W. with Michael A.G. Haykin, *The 'Toronto' Blessing: A Renewal from God?* (Ontario: Canadian Christian Publications) (nd)

*Methodist Church Faith and Order Committee, 'The 'Toronto Blessing'', in *Methodist Conference Agenda* (London: Methodist Publishing House, 1996), pp.161-78

Middlemiss, David, *Interpreting Charismatic Experience* (London: SCM, 1996)

Mitton, Michael, *The Heart of Toronto* (Cambridge: Grove Books, Sprituality Series No. 55, 1995)

Moriarty, Michael, *The New Charismatics* (Grand Rapids: Zondervan, 1992)

Morrison, Alan, *The Serpent and the Cross* (Rhyl: K&M Books, 1994)

*—, *We All Fall Down* (Crich: Diakrisis Publications, 1994)

*—, *Falling for the Lie* (Crich: Diakrisis Publications, 1994)

Mühlen, Heribert, *A Charismatic Theology: Initiation into the Spirit* (London: Burns & Oates, 1978)

Mundle, W., 'Ecstasy', in Colin Brown (ed.), *Dictionary of New Testament Theology* (Exeter: Paternoster, 1986), pp.527-30

Mumford, Eleanor, 'Spreading Like Wildfire', in Wallace Boulton (ed.), *The Impact of Toronto* (Crowborough: Monarch, 1995), pp.17-9.

Murphy, Royse, 'Risen with Healing in His Wings: An Exploration of the Psychology of the Toronto Blessing', in Stanley E. Porter & Philip J. Richter (eds.), *The Toronto Blessing – Or Is It?* (London: Darton, Longman & Todd, 1995), pp.66-85

Murray, Iain H., *David Martyn Lloyd-Jones: The Fight of Faith, 1939-1981* (Edinburgh: Banner of Truth, 1990)

—, *Revival and Revivalism: The Making and Marring of American Evangelicalism, 1750-1858* (Edinburgh: Banner of Truth, 1994)

Naish, Peter L.N., *What is Hypnosis?* (Philadelphia: Open University Press, 1986)

Nee, Watchman, *The Latent Power of the Soul* (New York: Christian Fellowship Publishers, 1972)

Newport, John P., *The New Age and the Biblical Worldview: Conflict and Dialogue* (Grand Rapids: Eerdmans, 1998)

Nodding, Peter, 'The Holy Spirit in Our Midst' (Interview), in Wallace Boulton (ed.), *The Impact of Toronto* (Crowborough: Monarch, 1995), pp.32-7

Noll, Mark A., *The Scandal of the Evangelical Mind* (Grand Rapids: Eerdmans, 1994)

★Oropeza, W.J., *A Time To Laugh: The Holy Laughter Phenomenon Examined – Guidelines for Distinguishing Genuine Renewal from Human-Induced Phenomena* (Peabody: Hendrickson, 1995)

Packer, J.I., *Hot Tub Religion* (London: Hodder & Stoughton, 1989)

Partner, Peter, *Two Thousand Years. The Second Millennium: From Medieval Christendom to Global Christianity* (London: Granada, 1999)

Pawson, David, *The Road to Hell* (London: Hodder & Stoughton, 1992)

★—, *Is the Blessing Biblical? Thinking Through the Toronto Phenomenon* (London: Hodder & Stoughton, 1995)

★Percy, Martyn, *Words, Wonders and Power: Understanding Contemporary Christian Fundamentalism and Revivalism* (London: SPCK, 1996)

—, *The Toronto Blessing* (Oxford: Latimer House, 1996)

—, 'Making Waves: a Perspective on Ministry and Revivalism', *Ministry Today* (RBIM) 8 (1996), pp. 27-37

—, 'Sweet Rapture: Subliminal Eroticism in Contemporary Charismatic Worship', *Theology and Sexuality* 6 (1997), pp.71-106

—, *Power and the Church: Ecclesiology in an Age of Transition* (London: Cassell, 1998)

Petersen, Douglas, *Not by Might Nor by Power: A Pentecostal Theology of Social Concern in Latin America* (Oxford: Regnum, 1996)

★Pietersen, Lloyd (ed.), *The Mark of the Spirit? A Charismatic Critique of the Toronto Blessing* (Carlisle: Paternoster, 1998)

Pietersen, Lloyd, 'Ecstatic Phenomena for an Ecstatic Culture?' in Lloyd Pietersen (ed.), *The Mark of the Spirit? A Charismatic Critique of the Toronto Blessing* (Carlisle: Paternoster, 1998), pp.7-32

Pilch, John J., 'The Transfiguration of Jesus', in Philip F. Esler (ed.), *Modelling Early Christianity: Social-Scientific Studies of the New Testament in its Context* (London: Routledge, 1995), pp. 47-64

Poloma, Margaret M., *The Charismatic Movement* (Boston: G.K. Hall, 1982)

—, *The Assemblies of God at the Crossroads: Charisma and Institutional Dilemmas* (Knoxville: The University of Tennessee Press, 1993)

—, 'Letter of Margaret Poloma to John Wimber', Ecunet 'New Wine' Bulletin Board, 27th November 1995

—, 'Comments on "Vineyard Reflections: The Toronto Blessing"', Ecunet 'New Wine' Bulletin Board, 27th November 1995

—, *The Toronto Report: A Preliminary Sociological Assessment of the Toronto Blessing* (Bradford-upon-Avon: Terra Nova, 1996)

—, 'By their Fruit...: A Sociological Assessment of the Toronto Blessing', *25th Annual Meeting of the Society for Pentecostal Studies* (Wycliffe College, Toronto, On., 1996), pp.20-22

—, 'The Toronto Blessing: Charisma, Institutionalization and Revival', *Journal for the Scientific Study of Religion* 36 (1997), pp.257-71

—, 'Inspecting the Fruit of the "Toronto Blessing": A Sociological Perspective', *PNEUMA: The Journal of the Society for Pentecostal Studies* 20.1 (1998), pp.71-84

—, 'The Spirit Movement in North America at the Millennium: From Azusa Street to Toronto, Pensacola and Beyond', *Journal of Pentecostal Theology* 12 (1998), pp.83-107

—, 'The "Toronto Blessing" in Postmodern Society: Manifestations, Metaphor and Myth', in Murray W. Dempster, Byron D. Klaus and Douglas Petersen (eds.), *The Globalization of Pentecostalism: A Religion Made to Travel* (Carlisle: Regnum, 1999), pp.363-85

Poloma, Margaret M. and L.F. Hoelter, 'The "Toronto Blessing": A Holistic Model of Healing', *Journal for the Scientific Study of Religion* 37 (1998), pp.257-72

Porter, Stanley, 'Shaking the Biblical Foundations', in Stanley E. Porter & Philip J. Richter (eds.), *The Toronto Blessing – Or Is It?* (London: Darton, Longman & Todd, 1995), pp.38-65

★Porter, Stanley and Philip J. Richter, (eds.), *The Toronto Blessing – Or Is It?* (London: Darton, Longman & Todd, 1995)

Porter, Wendy, 'The Worship of the Toronto Blessing?', in Stanley E. Porter & Philip J. Richter (eds.), *The Toronto Blessing – Or Is It?* (London: Darton, Longman & Todd, 1995), pp.104-30.

★Pytches, David, *Some Said It Thundered: A Personal Encounter with the 'Kansas City' Prophets* (London: Hodder & Stoughton, 1990)

Randles, Bill, *Weighed and Found Wanting* (Cambridge: St. Matthew Publications, 1995)

★Richards, Anne, *The Toronto Experience: An Exploration of the Issues* (Board of Mission Occasional Paper; London: Church House Publishing, 1997)

Richter, Philip J., 'God Is Not a Gentleman!', in Stanley E. Porter & Philip J. Richter (eds.), *The Toronto Blessing – Or Is It?* (London: Darton, Longman & Todd, 1995), pp.5-37

—, 'The Toronto Blessing: Charismatic Evangelical Global Warming', in Stephen Hunt, Malcolm Hamilton & Tony Walter (eds.), *Charismatic Christianity: Sociological Perspectives*, (London: Macmillan, 1997), pp. 97-119

Riss, R.M., 'Latter Rain Movement', in Stanley M. Burgess, Gary B. McGee and Patrick H. Alexander (eds.), *Dictionary of Pentecostal and Charismatic Movements* (Grand Rapids: Zondervan, 1988), pp.532-4

★Roberts, Dave, *The 'Toronto' Blessing* (Eastbourne: Kingsway, 1994)

Robertson, Murray, 'A Power Encounter Worth Laughing About', in Kevin Springer (ed.), *Power Encounters Among Christians in the Western World* (San Fransisco: Harper & Row, 1988), pp.149-57

Sandidge, J.L., 'Kathryn Kuhlman' in Stanley M. Burgess, Gary B. McGee and Patrick H. Alexander (eds.), *Dictionary of Pentecostal and Charismatic Movements* (Grand Rapids: Zondervan, 1988), pp.529-30

Schaeffer, Francis, *The Great Evangelical Disaster* (reprinted in *The Complete Works of Francis Schaeffer: Volume Four: A Christian View of the Church*; Carlisle: Paternoster, 1982), pp.301-411

Schneider, K., 'Judgment' in Colin Brown (ed.), *Dictionary of New Testament Theology* Vol. 2 (4 Vols, Carlisle: Paternoster, 1986 [1971]), pp.362-7

Scotland, Nigel, *Charismatics and the New Millennium: The Impact of Charismatic Christianity from 1960 into the New Millennium* (2nd edn; Guildford: Eagle, 2000 [1995])

Sheehan, Peter W. and Campbell W. Perry, *Methodologies of Hypnosis* (New York: Lawrence Earlbaum, 1967)

Smail, Tom, Andrew Walker and Nigel Wright, *Charismatic Renewal: The Search for a Theology*, (London: SPCK, 1993)

—, 'From "The Toronto Blessing" to Trinitarian Renewal: A Theological Conversation', in *Charismatic Renewal* (2nd edn; London: SPCK, 1995), pp.152-66

Smith, Mark, 'This-Is-That' Hermeneutics', in Lloyd Pietersen (ed.), *The Mark of the Spirit? A Charismatic Critique of the Toronto Blessing* (Carlisle: Paternoster, 1998), pp.33-62

Springer, Kevin (ed.), *Power Encounters* (San Fransisco: Harper & Row, 1988)

Stibbe, Mark, 'The Theology of Renewal and the Renewal of Theology', *Journal of Pentecostal Theology* 3 (1993), pp.71-90

—, 'Putting it to the Test', in Wallace Boulton (ed.), *The Impact of Toronto* (Crowborough: Monarch, 1995), pp.58-60

—, *O Brave New Church: Rescuing an Addictive Culture* (London: Darton, Longman & Todd, 1995)

★—, *Times of Refreshing: A Practical Theology of Renewal for Today* (London: Marshall Pickering, 1995)

Suurmond, J.J., *Word and Spirit at Play: Towards a Charismatic Theology* (tr. John Bowden; London: SCM, 1994)

Tillin, Tricia, *Looking Beyond Toronto: The Source and Goal of Pentecost*, (Derby: Banner Ministries, 1994)

Turner, Max, *Power from on High: The Spirit in Israel's Restoration and Witness in Luke-Acts*, (JPTS 9; Sheffield: Sheffield Academic Press, 1996)

★Virgo, Terry, *A People Prepared* (Eastbourne: Kingsway, 1996)

Wagner, C. Peter, *Look Out! The Pentecostals are Coming!* (Carol Streams: Creation House, 1973)

—, 'A Third Wave?' *Pastoral Renewal* (July-August, 1983), pp.1-5

—, 'The Third Wave', *Christian Life* (September, 1984), p.90

—, *The Third Wave of the Holy Spirit* (Ann Arbor: Servant 1988)

—, 'The Third Wave', in Stanley M. Burgess, Gary B. McGee, Patrick H. Alexander (eds.), *Dictionary of Pentecostal and Charismatic Movements* (Grand Rapids: Zondervan, 1988), pp.843-4

—, *Churchquake* (Ventura: Regal Books, 1999)

Walker, Andrew, *Restoring the Kingdom: The Radical Christianity of the House Church Movement* (rev'd edn; Guildford: Eagle, 1998 [1985])

Wardhaugh, Ronald, *Sociolinguistics* (2nd edn; Oxford: Blackwell, 1992 [1986])

Ware, Kallistos, *The Orthodox Way* (London: Mowbray, 1979)

★Warner, Rob, *Prepare for Revival* (London: Hodder & Stoughton, 1995)

Wells, David, F., *God in the Wasteland* (Grand Rapids: Eerdmans, 1994)

Wesley, John, *The Journal of the Rev. John Wesley, A.M.*, (8 vols; ed. N. Curnock.; London: Robert Culley, 1909–16)

—, '21: The Nature of Enthusiasm', *Wesley's Standard Sermons* Vol II (2 vols.; ed. Edward H. Sugden; 4th edn; London: The Epworth Press, 1956), pp.95–6

White, John, *When the Spirit Comes with Power: Signs and Wonders among God's People* (2nd edn; London: Hodder & Stoughton, 1992 [1988])

Whitefield, George, *Select Sermons of George Whitefield* (London: Banner of Truth Trust, 1958)

—, *Journals* (London: Banner of Truth, 1960)

Wiles, Maurice F., *The Remaking of Christian Doctrine* (London: SCM 1974)

Williams, J. Rodman, *Renewal Theology: Systematic Theology from a Charismatic Perspective* (Grand Rapids: Zondervan, 1996)

Wilson, D.J., 'Branham, William Marrion', in Stanley M. Burgess, Gary B. McGee & Patrick H. Alexander (eds.), *Dictionary of Pentecostal and Charismatic Movements* (Grand Rapids: Zondervan, 1988), pp.95–7

Wimber, John, 'Refreshing, Renewal and Revival', in *Vineyard Reflections* (Leadership Letter; July/August 1994)

Wimber, John and Kevin Springer, *Power Evangelism* (London: Hodder & Stoughton, 1985)

—, *Power Healing* (London: Hodder & Stoughton, 1985)

★Wright, Eric E., *Strange Fire? Assessing the Vineyard Movement and the Toronto Blessing* (Darlington: Evangelical Press, 1996)

Wright, Nigel, 'Restoration and the House Church Movement', *Themelios* 16/2 (Jan./Feb. 1991), pp.4–8

Videos

Morrison, Alan, *A Different Gospel: The Origin and Purpose of the Toronto Blessing* (Diakrisis/Crich Baptist Church, 1995)

Rumours of Revival (Milton Keynes: Nelson Word, 1995)

Toronto Airport Christian Fellowship, *Decently and in Order* (Toronto: TACF, 1995)

—, *God's Love: Bottom Line* (Toronto: TACF, 1995)

Short Titles

Arnott, *Father's Blessing*
Bebbington, *Evangelicalism*
Beougher, 'Revival, Revivals'
Beverley, *Holy Laughter*
Brady & Rowdon (eds.), *For Such a Time as This*
Brierley, *Tide is Running Out*
Cartledge, 'Interpreting Charismatic Experience'
Centre for Contemporary Ministry, *Charismatic Crossroads*
Chevreau, *Catch the Fire*
Chevreau, *Share the Fire*
Dixon, *Signs of Revival*
Edwards, *Distinguishing Marks*
Fearon, *Fresh Air*
Fitz-Gibbon, *God, Do What You Want to Do*
Forbes, *From North Battleford to Toronto*
Gott, *Sunderland Refreshing*
Hand, 'Tasting the Fruit'
Hill, 'Toronto Blessing – True or False?'
Hinn, *Anointing*
Howard-Browne, *Manifesting*
Mumford,' Spreading Like Wildfire'
Murray, *Revival and Revivalism*
Oropeza, *A Time To Laugh*
Pawson, *Is the Blessing Biblical?*
Percy, *Toronto Blessing*
Pietersen (ed.), *Mark of the Spirit?*
Poloma, 'By Their Fruit'
Poloma, 'Inspecting the Fruit'
Poloma, 'The "Toronto Blessing": Charisma, Institutionalization, and Revival'
Poloma, 'The "Toronto Blessing" in Postmodern Society'
Poloma, *Toronto Report*
Porter & Richter (eds.), *Toronto Blessing*
Porter, 'Shaking the Biblical Foundations?'
Price, 'Fire in the Gulf'
Pytches, *Some Said It Thundered*

Richards, *'Toronto'*
Richter, 'God is not a Gentleman!'
Roberts, *'Toronto'*
Robertson, 'Power Encounter'
Schaeffer, *Great Evangelical Disaster*
Scotland, *Charismatics*
Stibbe, *Times of Refreshing*
Virgo, *A People Prepared*
Warner, *Prepare for Revival*
Wright, *Strange Fire?*